LETTERS TO
PRESIDENT
OBAMA

**Americans Share Their Hopes and Dreams
with the First African-American President**

LETTERS TO
PRESIDENT
OBAMA

Americans Share Their Hopes and Dreams with the First African-American President

Edited by

**Hanes Walton, Jr., Josephine A.V. Allen,
Sherman C. Puckett, and Donald R. Deskins, Jr.**

Skyhorse Publishing

Skyhorse Publishing books may be purchased in bulk at special discounts for sales promotion, corporate gifts, fund-raising, or educational purposes. Special editions can also be created to specifications. For details, contact the Special Sales Department, Skyhorse Publishing, 555 Eighth Avenue, Suite 903, New York, NY 10018 or info@skyhorsepublishing.com.

www.skyhorsepublishing.com

10 9 8 7 6 5 4 3 2 1

Library of Congress Cataloging-in-Publication Data

Letters to President Obama : Americans share our hopes and dreams / edited by Hanes Walton, Jr. ... [et al.].
p. cm.
Includes index.
ISBN 978-1-60239-714-9 (alk. paper)
1. Obama, Barack--Correspondence. 2. American letters. I. Walton, Hanes, 1941-
E908.A4 2009
973.932092--dc22
2009006054

Printed in the United States of America

DEDICATIONS

From Hanes
To Edna and Pope Lane for their
generosity of spirit and success

From Josephine
To Damani, Jasmine, Jenea, and Mariya,
the embodiment of hope and
visions of peace, prosperity, and happiness for us all

From Sherman
To his friend Cheryl for her wonder of
character, love, and support

From Donald
To Lois for her love and steadfastness

CONTENTS

PREFACE

This volume of letters is a pioneering eyewitness account of the nomination, election, and inauguration of the 44th president of the United States, Barack Hussein Obama, Jr. And it just so happens that he is the very first African-American to achieve this position despite the fact that several members of his race have been running for this office since the nation bestowed upon its citizens of color the right to vote in national elections on February 3, 1870, with the ratification of the 15th Amendment. This pioneering volume differs from all of the other books of letters to American presidents in that the other volumes harvested their letters from presidential libraries, the National Archives, the Library of Congress, the White House, and various state historical societies. Thus, all of the previous books of letters came out after these presidents had left office and most of the letters in these volumes were not eyewitness accounts. As many of these volumes focused on these presidents and their administrations through the prism of time, they lack the freshness, topicality, and insight that come with writing at this moment in history. More importantly, none of these volumes have this historical advantage, nor could they match the timeframe in which Obama was elected to office. It was a moment that had never happened in America's political experience and will not happen again until a woman or another person of color is elected. The eyewitness letters in this volume pioneer in that they capture a rare event in American political history.

In addition to the uniqueness and timelessness of the Obama event, the letters in this volume basically cover the period from late October 2008 when the Web site www. letterstopresidentobama.com went live, until the week after his inaugural address in January 2009—roughly a period of four months. This allowed letter writers to cover all of the key moments in the Obama event—the convention, nomination, election campaign, election, the transition and selection of his cabinet, and his taking the presidential oath of office, as well as the inaugural parade and balls on January 20, 2008. Some of the letter writers worked in the campaign, attended his victory speech in Chicago, and were present at the inauguration. In sum, many were participating observers with up close and personal eye-witness accounts, while others caught it on television and/or iPhones.

These letter writers were there one way or another, and they have recorded this historical political breakthrough for subsequent generations of Americans. And each of them can enjoy or despair depending on their partisanship at this unusual moment in time. From this volume, even the president himself can see his impact and influence on the American people just as he gets his new administration underway.

Like all works of scholarship and learning, we owe a debt of acknowledgment and gratitude to a host of people who made this journey possible. First and foremost, we would like to thanks the students in Professor Walton's four political science classes at the University of Michigan who became letter writers for this volume. Two of his classes were in the fall semester of 2008 and the other two were in the winter semester of 2009. We would like to also thank the other letter writers who found the Web site and posted letters as well as those who personally sent us letters via e-mail, fax, and regular snail mail. Each of us who edited this volume wants to thank and acknowledge colleagues, family, and friends who joined us and/or wished us well on the project. When our deadline came on January 31, 2009, we had well over 600 letters that formed the twenty-seven categories that organize the book without any prodding or direction from us. We appreciate and thank each and every one of the letter writers.

Next, we want to thank the two students in the Graduate School of Library and Information Science at the University of Illinois and one who graduated from the University of South Florida—they created, maintained, and serviced our Web site. Their skills, talents, inventiveness, and innovativeness made it possible for us to collect and harvest all of the letters for this book. They answered many questions and assisted us as first-class troubleshooters when problems arose and potential letter writers had difficulty navigating the Web site. To Brent M. Walton, Matt Townsend, and Adam Kehoe we want to express our continuing appreciation and heartfelt thanks for their wonderful cooperation and assistance. Their skills with the technology made this timely volume possible. This is the very first book of letters accomplished with Internet technology. The other books were archival works, books of the "old technology," if it can be called that. So, thanks guys.

Then, there is the matter of the origination of the idea to use a Web site. Bill Wolfsthal, associate publisher and director of sales and marketing at Skyhorse, pitched the idea for the volume to Walton and he, in turn, pitched it to us. We discussed the venture and all agreed that it would be a wonderful project to undertake. And each of us can say that it has been an extraordinary project to undertake and extremely rewarding to bring to fruition. Indeed, this was an intellectual journey worth traveling.

However, before we close, we want to acknowledge several of our former teachers and mentors who enabled us to make this one-of-a-kind intellectual journey. Walton wants to offer thanks to the late Professor Robert Brisbane and Professor Tobe Johnson at Morehouse College, who made him aware of the importance of eyewitness accounts in scholarly endeavors. Professor Samuel Dubois Cook at Atlanta University stressed the creative potential and endless need for these accounts in accurately capturing African-American political innovations and experiences in America. And the late Professors Emmett Dorsey, Bernard Fall, and Harold Gosnell at Howard University insisted upon the use of this technique as a viable political science methodology. Walton would also like to thank Professor Lester P. Monts, the University of Michigan's Senior Vice Provost for Academic Affairs for supporting several research projects over the years.

Puckett notes that he has had the priceless opportunity and intense experience of working with Walton, Allen, and Deskins. He wishes to thank his past professors Brice Carnahan, Gary Fowler, and John Nystuen of the University of Michigan, for preparation imparted in skills ever useful in computer programming, statistical analysis, and geography and to his project mates for their friendship and the venture of making use of this preparation once again. The tenacity of academic drive exemplified by Deskins, Walton, and Allen was always a source of competitive inspiration and belief that any project is doable. Puckett is very grateful for the confidence and encouragement given by family and friends, especially Cheryl Laster, Blake and Che'Rai Laster, Solomon and Inicha Sparks, Veronica and Tyrone Rogers, his mother Rosetta, his sisters Ann and Wanda, and the loving memory of his sister Darlene. In addition, Puckett is grateful and very proud of the historic success of President Obama, without whom, of course, this project would not have been possible.

Donald R. Deskins wishes to thank his friends and especially his family for their patience and loving support. His wife Lois, daughters Sharon, Sheila, and Sharlene, and grandchildren James, Ryan, Celia, Jason, and Justin all share in the inspiration and joy that they have provided for this achievement. Deskins is also forever indebted to his mentor and friend John Nystuen, and the past academic and scholarly influences of Charles Davis, Sam Warner, and John Kolars.

Allen acknowledges with appreciation her mentors in the School of Social Work and in the Department of Political Science at the University of Michigan: Professors Roger Lind, Rosemary Sarri, Lawrence Gary, Harold Johnson, Cedric Robinson, and the late Archie Singham. She is eternally grateful for her parents, the late James and Gwendella Allen whose love and encouragement are largely responsible for her vision of a future that defined the journey that has become her life, professionally, socially, and spiritually. Her life is filled with inspiration and both loving and intellectual exchanges with her dear son, Damani Partridge. The days ahead promise continuing joyful and loving connections with Damani, with his dear wife, Sunita, and with their daughter, Jasmine Josephine. The future also belongs to the three most talented, curious, and lovely granddaughters on the planet, Jasmine, Jenea, and Mariya. Other family members and friends who have also contributed to her life and accomplishments through their positive support and care include Gerald and Michael Crowder, Vynita Thomas, Tyreon and Rashad Robertson, Valeria Wilson, Richard and Lola Garland, Travis Tatum, Amelia and Shawn Warren, Pamela and Douglas Porter, Eunice Rodriguez, and John Ford. The contributions to this volume of students in Julie Muzzy's third grade class at Beverly J. Martin Elementary School in Ithaca, New York are greatly appreciated.

In closing, Walton would like to thank his sons, Brandon and Brent, brother and sister-in-law Thomas and Gean Walton, and some of his relatives, Edna and Pope Lane, Maxie Foster, Katie Hampton, Geneva Foster, Judge Barbara Mobley, and Tanya, Mark, and Eric Smith for all of their generous personal encouragement during this intellectual journey.

Hanes Walton, Jr.
University of Michigan

Josephine A. Allen
Cornell University and Binghamton University

Sherman C. Puckett
Wayne County, Michigan

Donald R. Deskins, Jr.
University of Michigan

Introduction:

Letters to President

Barack Obama

President Barack Obama's historic and path-breaking campaign for the White House shattered immeasurable barriers and remade a long-sturdy tradition: Letters to Mr. President. This tradition was born on April 6, 1789, when the president of the U.S. Senate, John Langdon, penned the first letter to George Washington, notifying him that he had been elected the first president of the United States.[1] Once launched, this American tradition of citizens and undocumented immigrants alike writing letters to the highest-ranking elected official in the nation has unabatedly continued.

One of the archivists of the nation, Allen Weinstein, tells us that "these letters may be mundane, or memorable personal accounts of our lives at a moment in time."[2] Another scholar of this long tradition says that these letters came from "many . . . wholly unknown and undistinguished citizens,"[3] or from other presidents, as well as from foreign dignitaries, celebrities, prominent citizens and politicians, including famous and notable members of society. There are also letters from enemies, kooks, job-seekers, madmen, would-be assassins, as well as personal and perpetual writers. In a word, letters have emanated from both the elites and the masses. And the volume of this mail has been, for the most part, constantly increasing in quantity.

Inherent in this long-running tradition is the belief in the political culture that "the right to be heard, even at the highest levels, is something Americans take for granted."[4] On this same matter, another belief says that writing to the president of the United States of America means that citizens "have something important to say, and we expect the most powerful person on earth to pay attention to our concerns."[5] Remarking further on this belief in American political culture, the first head of the White House mailroom and eventually the chief of mails, wrote: "I guess that it is a natural result of our system of government that every citizen—as well as quite a few who weren't citizens—feel perfectly free to write to the president about his troubles or about his ideas of how the administration ought to be run."[6] Thus, a main motivation in this endless tradition in American presidential politics is the belief that a "right" exists for every American citizen and non-citizen to inform and discuss matters of great and small importance with the highest-elected official in the land and to expect some sort of reply—even if it is only an acknowledgment—that their letters have been received and noticed. From 1789 to 2004, a pattern and trend has been discerned that shows that the greatest number of letters tends to arrive shortly after the party nomination and the day after the presidential inauguration. Here is how one scholar noted it:

> For Lincoln the "flood" began after his nomination to the Presidency. Just prior to election he was receiving some 50 letters a day. When he became President-elect, the number increased to over 100 . . . [and] . . . after his inauguration, Lincoln continued to receive large quantities of mail.[7]

Later, this same scholar indicated that "when [Woodrow] Wilson took office, he received 'thousands' of congratulatory messages."[8] And "during Franklin D. Roosevelt's first week in office, letter-writing to the White House leaped suddenly to new heights. Roosevelt received 450,000 communications from the public during the first seven days as president."[9]

Looking specifically at the Lincoln case during his nomination and inauguration, historian and Lincoln scholar Harold Holzer found that:

> Lincoln's mailbag swelled to nearly unmanageable proportions almost as soon as the final votes were counted in the presidential election of 1860.

> A full three months before he formerly took office as president, he would invariably return from even a brief trip away from his Springfield base to encounter a huge stack of "accumulated correspondence."[10]

With every newly elected president and his inaugural came an abundance of letters expressing hopes, fears, and concerns with this new beginning in the office of the chief executive. And it is on this moment that the book is now focused. However, this moment in a long tradition is unlike any other moment and/or time in American history.

The election of Obama as the 44th president of the United States offers for the first time in American history, correspondence with a president who is not a white male.[11] This is the unique and rare occasion that our most recent election provides. It gives an unprecedented opportunity to racial and ethnic minorities to write letters to a president with whom they have much in common. In other words, for the first time in American history, letters were written from not only the majority groups in American society, but also from the minority groups in society to reflect and reminisce on the progress that America has made toward its great ideals and promise. Clearly, here is a great breakthrough that letter writers will have at this most historic moment. This is a breakthrough moment because in the past, letters from African-Americans and other minority groups never really landed on the president's desk, as we shall later see.[12]

The Literature on Letters to the President

Early books and monographs that make up the literature on letters written to American presidents are organized and structured in Table 1.1.

This table reveals that there are eight different categories of books and monographs in this ever-emerging literature that at the moment, are comprised of twenty-eight books and monographs.

The largest of these eight categories are the books and monographs of letters written to individual presidents. Such works began with president Franklin Pierce then continued with presidents James Buchanan, Abraham Lincoln, Andrew Johnson, Rutherford Hayes, Woodrow Wilson, George W. Bush, and William J. Clinton. Although each of these individual presidents has at least one book/monograph addressed to them, President Lincoln has three such works containing letters written to him.

In terms of the political party affiliation of these eight presidents, four are Democrats (Pierce, Buchanan, Wilson, and Clinton), while four are Republicans (Lincoln, Johnson, Hayes, and Bush). Thus, the volumes of letters to individual presidents are, at this writing, perfectly balanced between Republican and Democratic presidents. However, the number of volumes of letters to Lincoln totals three, which is nearly as many as the total associated with each political party.

Finally, in this large category, one can look at the publication dates in the table and discern that the clear majority of books/monographs were written in the eighteenth century, while only three were written to presidents in the nineteenth century (Woodrow Wilson, William J. Clinton, and George W. Bush).

In Table 1.1, the second-largest category is "Kids' Letters to Individual Presidents," with seven books. Six of these books are part of a series single-handedly edited by Bill Adler. He launched the series in 1963 with *Kids' Letters to President Kennedy* and followed it up with Kids' Letters to Presidents Johnson, Carter, Bush, Reagan, and Vice President Spiro Agnew. The latter book is the only one dealing with letters to a Vice President. The last volume in this category tends to adhere to the pattern and organizational schema set forth in the Adler series; it was written to President Clinton by two *Washington Post* journalists.[13] Although written only by kids, this category of books has proven to be much more popular than those books/monographs written by academics, scholars, laymen, and other political notables. In this category, there are four Democratic, and three Republican presidents.

The third-largest category of books in this Table, "Novelized Letters to Individual Presidents" contains five books: two written by one author and the other three written by single authors, each book in the series published in 2001 by the same press. In keeping with the "novelized letter," each author researched the era in which the presidents lived, drafted a fictional letter from a non-existent individual who lived in this era, and "sent it to the president." A fictional response letter was "sent from the president" to this individual. The "presidential recipients" included in this five-book series were Democratic-Republican Presidents Jefferson and John Quincy Adams; Republicans Lincoln and Theodore Roosevelt; and one Democrat, Franklin D. Roosevelt. There was the promise of more fictionalized accounts in the offing. But, in the final analysis, this category is unlike any of the other seven categories because these letters were never real and never written to these presidents. The books in all the other categories are real and were written.

Table 1.1 The Book/Monograph Literature on Letters to American Presidents

President	Party	Authors and Books	Publication Date
		Letters to Individual Presidents	
Franklin Pierce	Democrat	Jesse Chickering, *Letter Addressed to President of the United States on Slavery*	1855
James Buchanan	Democrat	Amos Kendall, *Secession: Letters of Amos Kendall; also, his letters to Colonel Orr and President James Buchanan*	1861
Abraham Lincoln	Republican	Robert Owen, *The Policy of Emancipation in Three Letters to the Secretary of War, the President of the United States, and the Secretary of the Treasury*	1863
Andrew Johnson	Republican	Agenor Gaspain, *Reconstruction: A Letter to President Johnson*	1865
Rutherford Hayes	Republican	William E. Chandler, *Letters of Mr. Chandler Relative to the So-called Southern Policy of President Hayes*	1878
Woodrow Wilson	Democrat	Robert Wallace, *Letters to President Wilson*	1930
William Clinton	Democrat	Stuart Hample, *Dear Mr. President*	1993
Abraham Lincoln	Republican	Harold Holzer, *Dear Mr. Lincoln*	1993
Abraham Lincoln	Republican	Harold Holzer, *The Lincoln Mailbag*	1998
William Clinton	Democrat	David Kavanagh, *Letters to a U.S. President*	2002
George W. Bush	Republican	Jim Carfagna, *Letters to the President: A Look Inside an Administration*	2007

President	Party	Authors and Books	Publication Date
		Kids' Letters to Individual Presidents	
John Kennedy	Democrat	Bill Adler, *Kids' Letters to President Kennedy*	1963
Lyndon Johnson	Democrat	Bill Adler, *Dear President Johnson*	1964
Spiro Agnew*	Republican	Bill Adler, *Kids' Letters to Spiro Agnew*	1971
James Carter	Democrat	Bill Adler, *Kids' Letters to President Carter*	1978
Ronald Reagan	Republican	Bill Adler, *Kids' Letters to President Reagan*	1982
William Clinton	Democrat	Peggy Hackman & Don Oldenburg, *Dear Mr. President*	1993
George W. Bush	Republican	Bill Adler, *Kids' Letters to President Bush*	2005
		Novelized Letters to Individual Presidents	
Thomas Jefferson	Democratic Republican	Jennifer Armstrong, *Thomas Jefferson: Letters from a Philadelphia Bookworm*	2001
John Quincy Adam	Democratic Republican	Steven Kroll, *John Quincy Adams: Letters from a Southern Planter's Son*	2001
Abraham Lincoln	Republican	Andrew Pinkney, *Abraham Lincoln: Letters from a Slave Girl*	2001
Theodore Roosevelt	Republican	Jennifer Armstrong, *Theodore Roosevelt: Letters from a Young Coal Miner*	2001

* Spiro Agnew was vice-president to Richard Nixon, the 37th president of the United States

Source: Various Bibliographies

President	Party	Authors and Books	Publication Date
Franklin Roosevelt	Democrat	Elizabeth Winthrop, *Franklin Delano Roosevelt: Letters from Town Girl a Mill*	2001
Scholarly Analysis of Letters to Presidents			
McKinley to Truman		Ira Smith, *Dear. Mr. President: The Story of Fifty Years in the House Mail Room White*	1949
Franklin Roosevelt	Democrat	Leila Sussmann, *Dear FDR: A Study of Political Letter-Writing*	1963
Truman to Johnson		Taeku Lee, *Mobilizing Public Opinion: Black Insurgency and Racial Attitudes in the Civil Rights Era*	2002
Senatorial Letters to the Next President			
Unknown	Unknown	Senator Richard Lugar, *Letters to the Next President*	1988 and 2004
Unknown	Unknown	Senator Robert Byrd, *Letters to A New President*	2008
Letters to Several Presidents: A Compilation			
22 Presidents and 2 First Ladies		Dwight Young, *Dear Mr. President: Letters to the Oval Office From the Files of the National Archives*	2006
Letters to the Next President			
Unknown	Unknown	Carl Glickman, *Letters to the Next President: What We Can Do About the Real Crisis in Public Education*	2007
Comedic Letters to an Individual President			
Calvin Coolidge	Republican	Will Rogers, *Letters of a Self-Made Diplomat to His President*	1926

The fourth category contains three books that deal with scholarly and lay analyses of letters to several individuals and presidents. The first book in this category, *Dear Mr. President: The Story of Fifty Years in the White House Mail Room*, was written by Ira Smith. Initially, Smith headed up the White House mailroom, and by the time of his retirement fifty years later, he was chief of mails for the White House. He saw the operation evolve from a single individual to a major postal institution in the White House "from the days of President McKinley to the fourth year of President Truman's administration."[14] This participant/observer position allowed him to analyze the letters to presidents from 1897 to 1948, including some five decades and eight administrations.

The second book in this category, *Dear FDR: A Study of Political Letter-Writing*, is a pioneering work on political letters written to Franklin Delano Roosevelt. It began as a doctoral dissertation that became a full-fledged book by sociologist Leila Sussmann. The book places the letters written to Roosevelt in historical context by comparing his letters to those of previous presidents and a few of the presidents that came after him. Then it compares letters written to American presidents to those written to heads of state in Germany, and those letters written to Soviet and Chinese Heads of State that appeared in the Soviet and Chinese Communist presses. Finally, it compares findings from the letters written to President Roosevelt with those letters written to members of the House of Representatives and the U.S. Senate. This pioneering work reveals how unique this letter-writing institution is in American political culture and in the democratic system of government.

Using this case study and data from other studies, Sussmann sought to develop a theory about mass political letter writing in America and especially about how different stimuli could cause this political institution to rise and decline across time.[15] Her work is the first systematic and comprehensive effort to understand this political institution and process in scientific terms.

The final book in this category is by political scientist, Taeku Lee. Professor Lee took 6,765 letters written to presidents from 1948 to 1965 on race and civil rights and created a database to study public opinion and the roles played by elites and by the masses. In a creative way, he developed the study to understand the leadership of public opinion issues and its influence by the masses vis-à-vis the elites. He demonstrated that in terms of the civil rights issue, the masses, particularly the African-American masses, played a dominant leadership role.[16] This is the most sophisticated use of letters to presidents.[17] And this groundbreaking study of letters to presidents set the standard for further exploration with a potential for unique findings.

Next in Table 1.1 is "Senatorial Letters to the Next President." United States senator, Republican Richard Lugar of Indiana, who was chairman of the U.S. Senate Committee on Foreign Relations under Republican president Ronald Reagan, penned a book before the 1988 presidential election to inform the incoming president of ideas, suggestions, and positions that he had drawn from participant observation and his own foreign trips abroad. He wrote:

Each chapter was conceived as a distinct letter offering advice and observations on the conduct of U.S. foreign policy to the winner of the presidential contest. I did not seek to create a presidential briefing manual, with coverage of every known or potential policy issue. Rather, I endeavored to draw upon my personal experiences as an active participant in the foreign policy process and to distill some judgment and findings as a working member of the United States Senate.[18]

Little did Senator Lugar know at his writing that the next president would be a Republican one—President Reagan's vice president, George H. W. Bush. Although the Senate stayed in Democratic hands, in 1988, Senator Lugar's book of letters "emphasized that at the heart of U.S. foreign policy must be a vigorous advocacy of democracy backed up by presidential credibility and truth telling."[19] And this book, according to Lugar, signaled to the incoming Republican President Bush that he had support from Lugar and other liberal-minded Republicans in Congress. The book gave to the Bush administration "twelve 'rules' that could guide presidential conduct of foreign policy."

Therefore, it should come as no surprise that Lugar revised and re-released the book for the incoming president in 2004. In that election, 43rd president George W. Bush—the son of president George H. W. Bush—won reelection and committed himself to the foreign policy problems created by the 9/11 terrorist attack. Again, Lugar worked from the vantage point of becoming chairman of the Senate Committee on Foreign Relations in 2003 and his own run in the 1996 Republican presidential primaries for the party nomination that was won by Senator Robert Dole. By this time, there was the Nunn-Lugar (a.k.a. Cooperative Threat Reduction Program) which addressed terrorists with nuclear weapons. This time, the matter of "controlling and safeguarding weapons of mass destruction" was front and center, and it led to the presumptive strike against Iraq and its leader, Saddam Hussein. What aspects of the reissued book Bush drew upon are not clear at this point, but it is clear that some of his ideas did influence the then Senator, Barack Obama.[20] Lugar and Obama worked together to pass their own legislation. And their bipartisan approach to foreign policy did not stop when the Republicans lost control of the Senate in 2006.[21] There is the possibility that this alliance might continue as Obama won the presidency in 2008.

The other United States senator to pen a book of letters to the "next" president is the democratic Senator of West Virginia, Robert Byrd who was elected in 1958. Formerly, he was chair of the powerful Senate Committee on Appropriations but also served as Senate majority and minority leader, majority and minority whip, and president pro tempore.

Writing from his long service in the U.S. Senate and his personal knowledge of "eleven presidents," Byrd started his book with the line: "To be read on Tuesday, January 20, 2009."[22] Senator Byrd's "Letters to the Next President" advised the new president to use "commonsense values" to lead the nation. He urged the new president to tell the truth, be accountable, assist the media in doing their job, stop photo-op diplomacy, gain influence with nation-states and their leaders, have real debate about policy and action, and most of all, have great patience.

Of this last bit of advice in his letters, Byrd called attention to it in the following manner:

> Take time in office to reflect, new President. Try to discern if you are following your vision for the future or if you are first casting about from crisis to crisis . . . budget the time to make sense of it all and to be sure you are steering the ship of state as you intended.[23]

Next, Byrd asked the new incoming president to have a sense of humility and morality. He writes:

> In *Dead Certain* . . . President Bush confessed to author Robert Draper, that it 'may be true' when people accuse him of 'unilateral arrogance', a stunning admission. I truly do not know how to reconcile boasting about 'unilateral arrogance' with President Bush's frequent mention of religion, which urges one to void unchecked arrogance for the evil it can unleash.[24]

Finally, Byrd concluded with the comment that "only through a combination of thoughtful and serious words, on the one hand, and a respect for the quiet need for deliberation and dialogue with the other are we ever going to get ourselves back on track as a land truly governed by the people."[25] One of the shortcomings of the Byrd volume is the omission of key democratic leaders.

Overall, these two books of letters (one by a Republican and one by a Democrat) advised the next president—who in each instance was a man from their own political party—and offered domestic and foreign policy advice as to how the president should formulate and implement the nation's foreign affairs and international relationships. But it is the Republican senator, Lugar, who forged a bipartisan legislative alliance with democratic president, Barack Obama.

Before we leave this category of senate letters, a word must be said about members in the House of Representatives. No such work has been penned by a representative. No comparable works exist, although in some of the books written by representatives, one will find advice to the president, but such books are not written in letter format. However, there are single and multiple letters written by presidents to other presidents.[26]

Finally, there are three different categories where we have only one book. They are: (1) "Letters to Several Presidents: A Compilation;" (2) "Letters to the Next President;" and (3) "Comedic Letters to an Individual President." The first category, which is a compilation of letters written to twenty-two different presidents and two first ladies, consists of letters selected from the National Archives. Of this volume, the archivist of the United States says:

"The 87 letters contained in this wonderful volume are but a few examples of the ten of thousands of such letters that have crossed [the] Presidents' desk since 1789."[27]

The archivist adds: "In this book you will find letters of grave importance such as the personal appeal of Albert Einstein to President Roosevelt urging him to take action on the construction of an atomic bomb . . . other letters were matters of conscience. In May, 1958, baseball great Jackie Robinson wrote to President Eisenhower chastising him for the slow pace of progress on civil rights."[28]

The editor of this volume, Dwight Young, added to the insights and comments of the archivist by noting that Jackie Robinson "since his retirement from baseball, had become an outspoken champion of civil rights, and it was in this role that he wrote to the White House the day after the May 12 (1958) meeting of . . . (African-American) leaders" sponsored by the National Newspaper Public Association (NNPA). This African-American organization invited President Eisenhower to speak. In his address to the group, he urged patience and going slow. Robinson responded to President Eisenhower's African-American leaders by saying, "I respectfully remind you sir, that we have been the most patient of all people. When you said we must have self-respect, I wondered how we could have self-respect and remain patient considering the treatment accorded us through the years. Seventeen million Negroes cannot do as you suggest and wait for the heads of men to change."[29]

Besides, there are other types of letters in this unique and usual compilation. "Some letters provided comfort to the President," along with other letters from other presidents that offer advice and understanding. Archivist, Weinstein, said, "Finally, no volume of Presidential letters would be complete without letters from children."[30] Thus, beyond the letters to presidents in the National Archives, there are many more such letters in the eleven presidential libraries. The addresses of these libraries are listed in the appendix of this one-of-a-kind volume. In this systematic and comprehensive volume, there are fifty-one different categories of letters to the twenty-two presidents and two first ladies, Lady Bird Johnson and Betty Ford.[31]

Although it is not listed in Table 1.1, there is another book written by Dwight Young and Margaret Johnson titled *Dear First Lady: Letters to the White House from the Collections of the Library of Congress and National Archives*. This book covers letters to thirty of the "39 women who were married to Presidents between 1789 and 2007."[32]

After this single book category comes another: "Letters to the Next President." This book, while very similar to the category of works written by U.S. Senators, is different in that it is edited by an educator, Professor Carl Glickman in the Educational Administration and Policy program at the University of Georgia in Athens, Georgia.[33] There are forty-two contributors to this edited volume of letters and they have produced thirty-four articles that tell the incoming president what is wrong with the education system and how the president ought to fix the system.

Among the forty-two contributors of *Letters to the Next President* are two United States senators, Democrat John Glenn and former Republican James "Jim" Jeffords.[34] The other high-profile contributor to this volume is William (Bill) Cosby, Jr., who wrote the foreword. Although the volume initially came out in 2007, an updated edition was release during the 2008 election year.[35] This new release emerged while Obama was winning the democratic presidential primaries and both he and his major competitor, Senator Hillary Clinton had proposals to fix the American education system. This book addresses the strengths and weaknesses of Bush's No Child Left Behind Act (NCLB), which evolved from the federal Elementary and Secondary Education Act (ESEA).[36] The NCLB "was quickly planned and passed shortly after September 11, 2001, at the height of America's concern with terrorism" and many critics and supporters, including Obama, Clinton, and McCain felt at least during the primaries and general election, that the nation's system of education needs reforming.

The last and final one of the eight categories in Table 1.1 that has only one book is "Comedic Letters to an Individual President." The nationally known comedian of the 1920s and 30s, Will Rogers, took a trip to Europe during 1926 and wrote a series of letters to President Coolidge about his trip and the different conversations he had with foreign leaders, the U.S. diplomatic corp., and other individuals he met during this trip.[37] To undertake this task, Rogers called himself an "ambassador without portfolio" and gave himself a code name—WillRog—like other U.S. Ambassadors had. The letters to President Coolidge expressed, in very comedic terms, Rogers's musings about his trip, European leaders, various foreign policies, and American involvement during the trip.[38] Listed below is one of the many letters in the volume.

White House, Washington, D.C.
Mr. Calvin Coolidge:

Certain news is so urgent that it is necessary for me to cable you, so from time to time you may get something "Collect." I hope there is an appropriation to cover this, look under the heading "Ways and Means."
WillRog (Diplomatic code name).[39]

Radiogram.

SOMEWHERE IN THE
MIDDLE OF ENGLAND'S OCEAN.
Date_____ What's time to a guy in the
Middle of an ocean.

My Dear President: Will you kindly find out for me through our intelligence Department who is the fellow that said a big Boat dident rock? Hold him till I return.
Yours feeble but still devotedly,
WillRog.
That's code name for Will Rogers.[40]

Special Cable

CALCOOL, *Washhousewhite*:

LONDON, Sept. I.—Former Secretary of State Hughes had an interview with former Premier Briand of France, but nothing official transpired, as neither carried an employee's card.

Russia wants to discuss debt payments with us. If you promise to pay America, it will loan you twice as much as you promise to pay. Wise guys, those Russians.

I see Newt is entered for the 1928 Democratic Follies.

Yours in exile,

WillRog.

Special Cable

CALCOOL, *Whitewashhouse*:

LONDON, Sept. 3.—The League of Nations to perpetuate peace is in session. On account of Spain not being in the last war, they won't let her in. If you want to help make peace you have to fight for it.

Yours for peace without politics,

WillRog.[41]

Overall, Rogers used those fictionalized letters of a so-called self-made diplomat to his president just to write another book. From beginning to end, this book simply pokes fun at domestic and foreign leaders as well as the American Foreign Service Association and its diplomatic corp. It also makes fun of the League of Nations and its peacekeeping activities that were supposed to make the world safe for democracy. Sadly it never did.

Taken collectively, these eight categories of books/monographs of "Letters to American Presidents" provide a grand tour of this literature and the nature and scope of the coverage and analysis of this literature. With this assessment of this body of literature, we now have a systematic and comprehensive background as well as the context of the letters to American presidents. We know that such letters started with George Washington and has continued up through the two terms of George W. Bush. Letter-writing to American presidents is now an American institution and a major factor in political culture.

However, technology has changed this institution. Today, "the modern-day White House receives faxes, cables, and e-mails in addition to traditional letters. All are read, though not necessarily by the occupant of the Oval Office. While the President may or may not have a personal e-mail account, many electronic missives sent to the White House bear the salutation, 'Dear Mr. President.'"[42] The Presidential Records Act (PRA) of 1978 changed the legal ownership of the president's official records—from private papers of the president to public ownership under the stewardship of the Archivist of the Untied States once an administration ends.[43] In order to protect his father's papers, George W. Bush issued an executive order extending the period that certain papers of a president can be sealed from the public if they deal with matters of national security.* Numerous scholars and academics sued President Bush, but the court upheld his time extension.[44]

African-American and Ethnic Minorities' Letters to Presidents

Mass political letter writing to American presidents has been impacted and influenced by the question of race and its numerous manifestations in America's long history. It is not a question of whether African-Americans and other ethnic groups wrote letters to different presidents throughout American history (because they did). Rather, their letters were more likely not to end up on the president's desk. One of the first scholars to acknowledge and write publicly about this problem was the historian and eminent Lincoln scholar, Harold Holzer.[45]

Upon writing his first book on correspondence with Lincoln, Holzer noticed that letters from African-Americans were systematically excluded from Lincoln's readings of citizen letters. This suggests that few letters from African-Americans ever crossed his desk. All of his secretaries never allowed such mail to be reviewed and read by this chief executive.[46] Nor did the historical record reveal that Lincoln had any interest in "letters from African-Americans and/or other ethnic groups and/or Native Americans." Seemingly from the historical record, he never requested that his secretaries provide him with letters from members of these groups.[47]

Of this matter, Holzer tells us, "Nearly every letter written to President Lincoln during the Civil War by an African-American was routinely, often mindlessly, sent on to the War Department's Bureau of Colored Troops. In many instances such was their fate, even if the letters had nothing at all to do with military affairs."[48]

In fact, Holzer expands further by saying:

> For example, there are hardly any letters from black people in the archive of Lincoln's correspondence. The ex-slave and abolitionist leader Frederick Douglass wrote but once, and his was an extraordinary, leader-to-leader communication on a matter of crucial national policy.
>
> Of course, blacks were largely illiterate in Lincoln's America, which accounts in great measure for the scarcity of letters from their pens. Yet even among the exceptionally rare letters sent to Lincoln by freed blacks, there is evidence of reluctance and distance not similarly expressed by white correspondence.[49]

---

* One of the first executive orders of President Obama was to undo the secrecy instituted by Bush. Eventually, however, all of the papers and letters and documents must be opened to the public.

Nevertheless, the direct approach of Douglass and other free blacks was not the only technique used by African-Americans in writing letters to Lincoln. Holzer again:

> One freedman writing from South Carolina used a White acquaintance to take down his words. And even a soldier from the fabled 54 for Massachusetts—the best-known "colored" regiment of the Civil War—thought it proper to send his letter to Lincoln via White intermediaries rather than posting it to the President directly, perhaps concluding that with this information, it would stand a better chance of reaching the President. Even so, his well-written entreaty was promptly forwarded to a government department and not retained for Lincoln's files; perhaps Lincoln never ever saw it. The fact is, in Lincoln's America, the White House was an aptly named destination for mail. It was for Whites only.[50]

Armed with this knowledge, Holzer was concerned about "whether the White House Clerks' refusal to lay them [African-American letters] before the president diminished the sincerity of the sentiments they expressed or the importance of those sentiments in illuminating black citizen concerns during the Civil War."[51] His answer was "no" and he immediately went back to the Lincoln mailbag in search of African-American, women, and other ethnic minority leaders.

According to him, since these letters had been "purged once from the White House mailbag, I had unwittingly purged them again a century and a quarter later in assembling *Dear Mr. Lincoln.* I now had the precious opportunity to correct any mistake."[52] At this writing, no other scholar has been as forthright as Holzer.

In searching through Lincoln's mailbag, Holzer describes what he found. "Here were letters from black soldiers and their families seeking justice and recognition. . . . [53] Here finally, are the voices of African-Americans who had been denied their hearing before Lincoln by an office routine that effectively barred them from inclusion in the screened mail set before the president day."[54]

If one moves from the evidence provided by Holzer's case study of the correspondence to Lincoln and begins an analysis of other books/monographs dealing with letters to presidents, one finds very little. The *lone* and major exception is the compilation by Dwight Young, *Letters to the Oval Office.* Looking at the fifty-one categories in this book, eight of these categories (15.7 percent) are devoted to letters from African-Americans. And of these eight categories, there are thirteen letters from African-Americans. In fact, these thirteen letters out of the eighty-seven in this volume amounts to 9.2 percent of the total number of letters. Clearly, this is nearly representative of the African-American population percentage in the nation. These eight letters were sent to Presidents Lincoln, McKinley, Harding, Hoover, Taft, Wilson, Truman, Eisenhower, Kennedy, and Johnson.

These letters were sent by slaves; a Civil War soldier; former congressman, George Murray; baseball great, Jackie Robinson; and Civil Rights leaders, Martin Luther King, Jr., and Roy Wilkins. Also in this volume are letters from Native Americans, Jewish Americans, Ku Klux Klan women, Japanese Americans, and Mother Teresa of India. No other volume comes as close as this one to including the voices of the racial and ethnic groups in America as expressed in various presidential mailbags. Still, there is a long way to go.

Besides the Lincoln and compilation volumes, the only other places African-Americans may find letters to presidents from African-Americans are in documentary histories about African-American experiences—written by historians. One of the very first of these documentary histories is one by Herbert Aphtheker.[55] In this volume, one will uncover one of the earliest letters written by an African-American named Benjamin Banneker, to future president, Thomas Jefferson in 1791—eight years before he assumed the presidency. Jefferson replied, recommended his publication, and urged him to "contact the Secretary of the Academy of Sciences in Paris."[56] It was Jefferson who recommended Banneker to Washington for a place on the commission to lay out the boundaries of the District of Columbia.

In the most recent documentary history, *Let Nobody Turn Us Around: Voices of Resistance, Reform, and Renewal: An African-American Anthology*, there is not *one* letter to any president among the ninety-nine documents.[57] It is as if none of the resisters, reformers, and protesters in the African-American experiences ever thought of mass-letter writing to an American president. This is simply not true because many individuals did, including Booker T. Washington, William Monroe Trotter, and Martin Luther King, Jr. Yet, this form of African-American protest politics simply did not end up in this documentary history. African-American letters to presidents simply do not appear in any consistent and systematic way in the letter volumes and/or in these documentary histories. Yet they exist.

This omission is also to be found in the leading reader-text for black Studies, *A Turbulent Voyage*. Seemingly, students in these courses need not know about how African-Americans used mass-political letter-writing to American presidents to state their problems and suffering in this American democracy and seek a redress of their grievances.[58] Despite the legitimacy of this political institution and African-Americans' massive use of it, it is treated as if it is somehow a worthless and inadequate one despite the fact that it has proven a fairly successful one. Nothing could be further from the truth.[59]

In closing, it is essential that any book of letters to an African-American president include from African-Americans from all walks of life—kids as well as adults—if some historical balance and correction of this earlier reality is to take place. It is also important to bring to the readers' attention the aforementioned pioneering work by Professor Taeku Lee, who tried to use these African-American letters to presidents to explain the nature, scope, and emergence of African-American public opinion in the Civil Rights Era.[60] This book, in no uncertain terms, demonstrates how important such letters are.

Letters to President Barack Obama

At this moment in time, there is not any book/monograph of racial, ethnic, minority groups', or foreigners' letters to any American president. Although several works may be in the offing, there is a book of letters to the first African-American first lady, Michelle Obama titled: *Go, Tell Michelle; African-American Women Write to the New First Lady*.[61] Despite the innovative nature of this recent volume, there is still not one to an American president.

Moreover, there is not a combined or integrated volume where one can read and hear a wide diversity of attitudes, opinions, comments, reflections, and sentiments. In fact, not a single volume in Table 1.1 provides a full demographic representation of the multiracial nature of America citizenry and those non-citizens who visit this country from various foreign nations. Yet, this nation has long revered and prized different visions and reflections about itself when it was written by outsiders. There is Alex de Toqueville's *Democracy in America*, Gunnar Myrdal's *An American Dilemma: The Negro Problem and Modern Democracy*; as well as the lesser known work by James Bryce, *The American Commonwealth*, which analyzes American political parties. These portraits of American political institutions are now considered classics. Yet none of the books of letters in Table 1.1 offer the views and remarks of outsiders along with that of American citizens.

More importantly, no books until today could have addressed an African-American presidential candidate, noted his successful and victorious campaign to secure a major party nomination, and congratulated him on his win of the nation's 56th presidential election as the first of his race to become president of the United States.[62] Truly, others of his race have tried, but their journey did not impact or influence the genre of "letters to the president" books. This is the first—and a historic moment in this nation.

Mindful of these lacunae in the genre, this volume launched the Web site, www. letterstopresidentobama.com in late October 2008 to collect letters voluntarily submitted by those site visitors of the nation's citizens and non-citizens of every conceivable demographic group, ideology, culture, partisanship, religious persuasion, and age. After the inauguration of Obama on January 20, 2009, we harvested some 600 letters for consideration and possible inclusion in this unique volume. Collecting these letters from this nearly four-month period meant that we would be covering every major aspect of this historic election. There were the primary and convention elements of the election, the general election campaign and its major event, and the Wall Street financial meltdown, together with the election itself. And finally, there was the historic inauguration with almost two million people from all over the nation and the world in attendance, followed by more than ten inaugural balls to celebrate this impressive first-time reality. The four-month timeframe for the letter writing offered the type of panorama not possible in the books in Table 1.1. All of these books of letters to presidents are letters that were collected after these presidents left office. And while they try to cover an entire presidency of four to eight years, this volume looks at how individual citizens and foreigners got caught up in the moment of change and the many different ways they reacted to this watershed change in American politics. These letters were written at the very moment of this signal breakthrough, and they record the feelings and responses as the Obama events were actually happening—not through hindsight or the prisms of a one- or two-term president.

This volume of letters from an eyewitness approach was helped by the fact that students from four of Professor Walton's political science classes at the University of Michigan, and students in two of Professor Allen's social welfare classes at Binghamton University were asked to participate in this historic project The majority of the letters to the Web site came from these students. One undergraduate class and four upper-level and graduate seminars give the volume a mix of beginning students, continuing, and mature students. Thus, some of the letters are written by first-time voters who recount how Obama shaped their initial foray into the politics of democratic America. Continuing and more advanced students included in their letters their stories of both realigning and dealigning in their political affiliations. Students at this level revealed much about issues and concerns such as their employment situation as well as those of their parents. Thus, the student base of this project offers the reader a chance to see a dynamic in not only political socialization to politics but also in political partisanship as and prospects for the future of our democratic political system. From these students one sees glimpses of the future.

This student base also allowed visiting students from other nations to remark on this historic transfer of power in the democracy that they have heard and read so much about. They too observed first hand democracy at work and in practice. The very rich diversity of these students from numerous countries and different cultures and all walks of life makes these letters sparkle with interesting revelations and great amazement. As the reader will find, most students were simply thrilled at what they saw. Their descriptions of what they heard, felt, and participated in cannot be recaptured except by others who shared the moment.

But the letters didn't just come from college students; they came from kids and high school students, from academics, elected officials, ministers, and ordinary citizens who were swept up in this historical moment. Many tell us in their letters that they saw a new America, a new nation, a new beginning, even while understanding that the nation is in the midst of a very real crisis. For many of them, Obama is truly an inspiration and beacon of hope and a leader with a path to an even greater future for America. True to the letter writers of yesteryear, these too have endless suggestions of help and direction for their new president because so many want him to succeed and achieve great things for the nation and himself.

But as the readers move through the volume, they will soon discover that not all of the letter writers supported Obama and other are quite apprehensive about his ability to turn the nation around and secure a great future for it. They worry, and some even urge the new president not to head down a road toward socialism. Others want affordable health care, video games, peace, gay marriage rights, a college football play-off system, greater spending for science, a greener planet, and sundry other public policies, both foreign and domestic. The list is long and nearly endless. Yet, this is democracy in action, people talking to their incoming governmental leader.

Overall, here is nearly a holistic portrait of eye-witnessing citizens and non-citizens who have recorded in words their opinions, attitudes, and sentiments and/or their deeds during the election of the nation's first African-American president. Such an event will not again happen until the nation elects its first woman, Hispanic, or other ethnic individual. These eyewitnesses were here at the initial breakthrough and have left a record of this historic moment.

In making our call for letters for this volume, we avoided surveys and polls with predetermined categories and questions. We left it up to the letter writers to decide what they wanted to discuss about this historic Obama event. Nothing was preconceived, nor did we give directions or hint toward areas of concern. This unique approach allowed writers not only a maximum amount of freedom of expression but also a similar amount of choice in selecting their topics. When we harvested the letters, we categorized and grouped them according to the self-selected topics determined by the letter writers.

As shown in the table of contents, chapters 2 through 28 represent twenty-seven topics that cover literally every detail of the historic Obama event. Although some of the categories are quite broad like "Presidential Character," many of the writers in this group go well beyond mere congratulations to the new president and get into careful and interesting discussion about how inspirational Obama is to them, the younger generation, and to those that have turned cynical after several previous presidential contenders and winners. Such is also true for nearly every one of the other twenty-six categories in the volume.

The "Public Policy" category had to be divided into several others because some of the letters addressed very topical and current event issues. These public policy areas simply needed to stand on their own. Even with this subdivision of four additional domestic public policy matters, there are still numerous subsections inside the larger area of public policy (e.g., gay marriage, which would have also been placed in a separate subdivision).

This same reality is true when one comes to the category of "Foreign Policy," which has one subdivision. There could have been more, but the cutoff had to be fixed somewhere, and it was more of the decision of the editors than the visions of the letter writers that determined twenty-seven categories as diverse enough to give the readers a broad overview of coverage inherent in this volume of letters. These letters from Americans caught up in this historic timeframe, through their eyewitness accounts, will provide readers of this volume from this time and times to come a wonderful opportunity to live and relive a transformative event in this nation's ever evolving political experience and the further maturation of its democratic electoral system.

Endnotes

1 Dwight Young (ed), *Dear Mr. President: Letters to the Oval Office from the Files of the National Archives* (Washington, D.C.: National Geographic Society, 2006), p. 19.

2 Alan Weinstein, "Foreword", Ibid. p. 12.

3 Leila Sussmann, *Dear FDR: A Study of Political Letter-Writing* (Totowa, New Jersey: Bedminster Press, 1973), p. 6.

4 Young, p. 194.

5 Weinstein, p. 12.

6 Ira Smith, *Dear Mr. President: The Story of Fifty Years in the White House Mail Room* (New York: Julian Messner, 1949), p. 2.

7 Sussmann, pp. 2–3.

8 Ibid. p. 6.

9 Ibid., p. 9.

10 Harold Holzer, (compiled), *Dear Mr. Lincoln: Letters to the President* (Massachusetts: Addison-Wesley, 1993), p. 5.

11 Donald Deskins, Jr., Hanes Walton, Jr., and Sherman C. Puckett, *Presidential Elections, 1789–2008: County, State, and National Mapping of Election Data* (Ann Arbor: University of Michigan Press, 2010).

12 Harold Holzer (ed), *The Lincoln Mail Boy: America Writers to the President 1861–1865* (Southern Illinois University Press, 1998), p. xvii.

13 For more on President Clinton, see Hanes Walton, Jr., *Reelection: William J. Clinton as a Native-Son Presidential Candidate* (New York: Columbia University Press, 2002).

14 Ira Smith, *Dear Mr. President: The Story of Fifty Years in the White House Mail Room* (New York: Julian Messner, 1949), pp. 1–2.

15 This theory began in an article and was then expanded later into a book. See Leila Sussmann, "Mass Political Letter Writing in America: The Growth of an Institution," *Public Opinion Quarterly*, Vol. 23 (Summer, 1949), pp. 203–212. The book, *Dear FDR: A Study of Political Letter-Writing* (Totowa, New Jersey: Bedminster Press, 1963).

16 Taeku Lee, *Mobilizing Public Opinion: Black Insurgency and Racial Attitudes in the Civil Rights Era* (Chicago: University of Chicago Press, 2002), pp. 104–105.

17 See the review of this book in Hanes Walton, Jr., "African-American Public Opinion, White Scholars and a Neo-Conservative Political Context," *DuBois Review*, Vol. 1 (Fall, 2004), pp. 393–397.

18 Senator Richard Lugar, *Letters to the Next President* (Bloomington: Author House, 1988), p. ix.

19 Ibid., p. 2.

20 David Mendell, *Obama: From Promise to Power* (New York: Amistad, 2007), p. 313.

21 Barack Obama, *The Audacity of Hope: Thoughts on Reclaiming the American dream* (New York: Crown Publishers, 2006), pp. 170–71; 311–14, and 326.

22 Senator Robert Byrd, *Letters to a New President: Commonsense Lessons for Our Next Leader* (New York: Thomas Dunne, 2008), p. 1.

23 Ibid., p. 167.

24 Ibid., p. 8.

25 Ibid., p. 173.

26 Dwight Young (ed.), *Dear Mr. President: Letters to the Oval Office from the Files of the National Archives* (Washington, D.C.: National Geographic Society, 2006), pp. 136–141.

27 Ibid., p. 13.

28 Ibid., p. 12.

29 Young, p. 109.

30 Ibid., p. 13.

31 Ibid., p. 8.

32 Dwight Young and Margaret Johnson, *Dear First Lady: Letters to the White House from the Collections of the Library of Congress & National Archives* (Washington, D.C. : National Geographic Society, 2008), p. 18.

33 Carl Glickman, *Letters to the Next President: What We Can Do About the Real Crisis in Public Education* (New York: Teachers College of Columbia University Press, 2008), p. 270.

34 Senator James M. Jeffords, *My Declaration of Independence* (New York: Simon and Schuster, 2001) and Senator James M. Jeffords, Yvonne Daley, and Howard Coffin, *An Independent Man: Adventures of a Public Servant* (New York: Simon and Schuster, 2003).

35 Glickman, pp. 1–5.

36 Ibid., p. 3.

37 Will Rogers, *Letters of a Self-Made Diplomat to His President* (New York: Albert & Charles Boni, 1926), pp. ix–xv.

38 Ibid., pp. 17–25.

39 Ibid., p. 36.

40 Ibid., p. 37.

41 Ibid., p. 259.

42 Young, p. 8.

43 Ibid., p. 176.

44 Jonathan Alter, "The Steep Price of Secrecy," *Newsweek Magazine*, www.newsweek.com/id/181278 (accessed January 28, 2009) and President Barack Obama, "Presidential Records: Executive Order 13489 of January 21, 2009" *Federal Register,* vol. 74 (January 26, 2009) pp. 4669–4671.

45 See his Harold Holzer (ed.), *Dear Mr. Lincoln: Letters to the President* (Massachusetts: Addison-Wesley, 1993), pp. 5–31.

46 Ibid., pp. 31–33.

[47] Ibid., pp. 5–29.

[48] Harold Holzer (ed.), *The Lincoln Mailbag: America Writes to the President*, 1861–1865 (Carbondale: Southern Illinois University Press, 1998), p. xv.

[49] Holzer, *Dear Mr. Lincoln*, pp. 31–32.

[50] Ibid., p. 32.

[51] Holzer, *The Lincoln Mailbag*, p. xv.

[52] Ibid.

[53] Ibid.

[54] Ibid., p. xvii.

[55] Herbert Aphtheker, *A Documentary History of the Negro People in the United States* (New York: Citadel Press, 1969).

[56] John Hope Franklin and Alfred Moss, Jr., *From Slavery to Freedom* 7th edition (New York: McGraw-Hill, 1994), p. 96.

[57] Manning Marable and Leith Mullings (eds.), *Let Nobody Turn Us Around: Voices of Resistance, Reform, and Renewal: An African-American Anthology* (Lanham, Maryland: Rowman & Littlefield, 2000), pp. v–xii.

[58] Floyd Hayes, III, *A Turbulent Voyage: Readings in African-American Studies* (California: Collegiate Press, 1997), pp. vii-x.

[59] For an early analysis of this political institution and its usage within the African-American community even with its own cultural institution, see Hanes Walton, Jr., *Invisible Politics: Black Political Behavior* (Albany: State University Press of New York, 1985), pp. 36–39.

[60] Lee, pp. 104–105.

[61] A. Seals Barbara Nevergold and Peggy Brooks-Bertram, (eds.) *Go, Tell Michelle: African-American Women Write to the New First Lady* (Albany: State University of New York Press, 2009).

[62] Hanes Walton, Jr., Josephine A.V. Allen, Sherman Puckett, Donald R. Deskins, Jr., and Billie Dee Tate, "The Literature on African-American Presidential Candidates," *Journal of Race & Policy* (Spring/Summer, 2008), pp. 103–124.
This article provides the first initial assessment and evaluation of books by and on all of the previous African-Americans who ran for president before Barack Obama. However, this is not a comprehensive list of these candidates, only those that have books on them.

CHAPTER 1

The Historical

Moment

O n November 4, 2008, the nation, in its 56th presidential election, chose an African-American as the 44th president of the United States. This was a first for our country, and it was both a political breakthrough and a precedent-setting moment in America's political history. Several of the contributors to this volume of letters noted, emphasized, and celebrated this unique turning point in America. They also set the stage for what is to come.

January 30, 2009
The Honorable President Barack H. Obama, Jr.
The White House
1600 Pennsylvania Avenue
Washington, D.C.

Dear President Obama:

Please let me make mention to you of the fact that your historic moment in the nation's 56th presidential election creates as you well understand other historic possibilities. Among them is a unique and rare historical epistemological reality. Immediately upon the media announcement that you had defeated your rival Republican Senator John McCain, a number of commercial, scholarly, and popular publishers began the search for all of those African-Americans who have run for the presidency. No such list of individuals existed prior to your victory. Despite the voluminous studies and compendiums on the history of presidential elections and presidential candidates, none offered any type of systematic and comprehensive coverage of such candidates in the past. Even studies of third- and minor-party presidential candidates bothered to provide coverage of the African-American candidates on these presidential ballots.

To be sure, there is some discussion of the presidential candidacies of Reverend Jesse Jackson, and to a lesser extend those of the pioneering Congresswoman Shirley Chisholm, former Senator Carol Moseley-Braun, Reverend Al Sharpton, and maybe, depending on the work, the sixties radicals like Eldridge Cleaver and Dick Gregory, to say nothing of the likes of Angela Davis and Cynthia McKinney. Other presidential candidates, have either fallen through the crack in history or simply have been omitted because of the lack of knowledge or space. The policy of some publishers of reference books is that if the candidate did not get ten percent of the vote in either the presidential primaries or the general election could not be listed in the volume. Such a shortsighted publishing policy affected these African-American presidential candidates because most did not reach this threshold level. Even Congresswoman Chisholm failed such a cut-off.

Now as a consequence of your victory, all of these minor and major candidates will be resurrected from the fringes and obscure pages, papers and publications in the historical past, and they will be recorded. Not only will they be recovered but will be treated seriously and given their proper place alongside those whose "protest" and reform presidential candidates has marked key and major moments in the nations past, and point ever so dimly to your political breakthrough. They too had a better vision for America.

Many thanks to you for giving the nation's forgotten political past a chance to link-up with its present and promising future.

Sincerely
Hanes Walton, Jr.

Dear President Obama,

Your election into the Presidency, the most powerful position our government has, was certainly no small feat. It was historic, and will be remembered for scores of generations to come. There are those who thought such an occurrence inconceivable, but the fact that it's happened just shows how far America has come as a nation, and the potential for what else can come to pass in the future. I look forward to the next four years with great anticipation.

J.B.

Mr. President,

Your leadership has rallied such energy, such focus, and such heightened knowledge of democratic values. Our country breathes life again. You have defined democracy as a form of decision-making that provides our society with a basic sense of fairness and equality. Democracy is unique and cherished in America, but does not always guide the decisions that citizens make in their daily lives.

To unite our states again, one of your greatest challenges is to lead through democracy; to encourage Americans to use this decision-making tool and to believe in its peace-making abilities. A precursor to democratic decision-making is debate. Please remind our citizens that a debate is not a venue for talking points (many times used as methods of persuasion to force a pre-determined outcome). Instead, please embolden debate as an informative dialogue that provides answers about policies or decisions that many Americans may not fully agree with or understand.

Democratic decision-making encourages unity. Please continue to rally our citizens to organize, collaborate, and seek agreement. Dissenters may remain, but in a state of unity our society will become more ethical in business and among the accords of coalitions and individuals. In the change process you have inspired, the daily lives of Americans will transform in some way, and our adaptive instinct will be activated. What will be will become what is and in the life of our country, we will mature; developing from the fledgling democracy, est. 1776.

Warmest Regards,
Dr. David G. Gliddon

Dear President Obama,

I can't even begin to tell you how excited I am that you are our 44th president. I believe that you will be able to lead our nation in a new and exciting direction, and that your fresh perspective is precisely what America needs at this point in our nation's history. I am excited to tell my children that I helped elect the first African-American president with my very first vote. I am so inspired by the ideas that you have for our country.

I sincerely wish that, as you take office, you realize that America does not need any more partisan politics. You have promised before to work closely with both parties, and I hope that you will keep this promise throughout your term. I want an America that is not divided so sharply by political beliefs, and one that is more accepting of working together. I know that you can make that happen.

Also, I would ask you to please keep in mind what the American public wants. You have appealed to so many because you are someone that people relate to. Don't lose sight of what we want as Americans. Some ideas which you have advocated, such as nationalized health care, may not necessarily rest in the majority opinion. So don't be afraid to adapt your campaign promises if it will benefit America as a whole.

I have no doubt that you will be just what this country needs. Above all, I ask you not to get discouraged if change comes slow or things don't work out the way you would like them to. It's difficult to predict what challenges will arise before you come to them, and times will be tough, especially when pressure is on you to fix things. I chose you as my president because I know that you can handle this job, and I truly admire your vision for America. If, at any time, you feel discouraged, please remember what you have inspired. Your ability to reach people is unparalleled, and many answered your call for change.

Congratulations President Obama:

I am super elated that my almighty God has allowed me to be a "living witness" to "living history". As a sixty-three-year-old African-American male born in Jackson, Mississippi, grew up in St. Louis, Missouri, and Pasadena, California, I never thought that I would see the quest for universal freedom for the highest office in the United States being occupied by a person of color. It is mind blowing for me to conceive that a person's ancestors (slaves) who came to the U.S. by force, which is different than any other immigrant group, is now the President of the U.S. I am sure that our ancestors "a great cloud of witnesses" are shouting in heaven for this most monumental task being accomplished in such a short period of time since African-Americans have only had one generation since the passage of the Voting Rights Act of 1965 to accomplish this feat. I need not go into all of the legal and non-legal means of keeping blacks from the polls and voting the history and political science texts document those facts. President Obama, I know that your decisive victory and campaign strategy is one that will make many political scientists rewrite the textbooks on political campaigning. In addition, you and I and many others realize that the "quest for universal freedom" through political challenges and the civil rights activist laid the foundation for breaking through this "political glass ceiling." I am sure that the six black men from Frederick Douglas in 1888 who received one vote from the Kentucky delegation at the Republican convention in Chicago made him effectively the "first" black candidate nominated for president.

Julian Bond in 1976, Jesse Jackson in 1984 and 1986, Douglas Wilder, the first African-American Virginia Senator since Reconstruction in 1992, Alan Keys in 1996, 2000, and 2008; and Al Sharpton in 2004 are praising your success. The four African-American women include Shirley Chisholm in 1972, who was the first African-American female candidate in 1972; Lenora Fulani in 1985, who became the first African-American candidate to be listed on the ballots in all fifty states; Carol Mosley Braun in 2004, the only African-American woman to be elected to the Senate to date; and Cynthia Ann McKinney in 2008, the first African-American woman to represent Georgia in Congress. We are praying that this social and political change will foster in a new era of African-American Politics with our first African-American being sworn in on January 20, 2009. My kudos as well as my prayers is with you, your family and your cabinet for great success. My prayer is that God give you favor in everything that you do and that you go down in history as one of the greatest president of these *United* States. God Bless You and Keep You.

Dr. Willie E. Johnson, Professor
Department of Political Science
Savannah State University

CHAPTER 2

Presidential Character

Letters in this category discuss, describe, and explain the different personality traits and characteristics that citizens admire and are attracted to in this new president at first a candidate and then President-elect. In offering these insights, the writers emphasize the importance and necessity of strong leadership qualities, especially for a nation in crisis.

President-elect Barack Obama:

Congratulations on your tremendous election and thanks for volunteering to be our leader. I have never experienced a day like November 4th.

Though I am greatly concerned about our role in international affairs and our current economy, I voted for you utmost because I feel that you will be a role model, a leader whom we can look up to with respect and honor. I have never supported a candidate as strongly and with as much confidence as I have in you. (And I am almost 70.) The people, on the streets Tuesday evening, with joy in their faces and tears in their eyes, were not there because of the economy; they were there because they too look forward to a new kind of leadership. We look forward to your leadership and your ability to gather the advice of those who are experts in their fields.

Good luck. The congratulations are ours, the people of the United States who elected you, and the people around the globe.

I did not vote for President Obama because of his race, any more than I would have voted against him for that reason alone.

I voted for Obama because I thought and still think that he is an intelligent, thoughtful, and decent man who agrees with me on the issues I think are most important—and also because he and his platform were so far superior to anything the Republicans put up.

I am impressed by his careful preparation for the period following his inauguration. Although it may set a bad precedent for future presidents-elect, in this case it is plainly necessary. I join with almost all Americans in praying for his success.

Sincerely yours,
Peter R. Limburg

Dear President Obama,

Today I was brought to tears, again, as I sat in my car listening to an excerpt on the news from your rainy day speech, given without a hat, one week before election day 2008. My tears came because I felt your words so deeply, they resonated with my own not yet articulated hopes and concerns. Mr. Obama, I have been a fan of yours for four years. When you spoke at the Democratic Convention in 2004, I spontaneously stood up in my family room and proclaimed to the TV set, "I will vote for him for president!" Next week I have the privilege to do just that. You have consistently expressed what is in my heart and in my head. You make me proud to be an American.

My dreams for our country are to continue to find creative solutions to our challenges and problems; to think outside the box on improving education and making college affordable, ending this war, understanding and repairing the economy, saving the environment, protecting women's rights and human rights. I hope that as an American culture we can rebuild our image in the world and be seen as a country striving to release the past and becoming who we really are—an enlightened nation of intelligent, compassionate, articulate citizens. With you leading our country we can do just that. Thank you.

Dear Mr. President:

Congratulations. You have succeeded in running one of the best-managed, most disciplined, and yet most inspiring campaigns in history and you've reached your goal. Now: to govern.

I wanted to share with you one simple suggestion that might help you in the coming years. If you thought you'd been attacked or criticized unfairly during the campaign, I've got news for you: you ain't seen nothing yet. If you've grown tired of the scrutiny of the press and the public over the past two years, well, guess what: it's only going to be worse, and more constant, and more draining, and it's not going to end for another four (or, hopefully, eight) years. If you thought that being the most powerful person on the planet meant that you could do whatever you wanted, then think again; being president often requires that you relinquish large parts of yourself, your time, attention to your own wants and needs, in service to the rest of us.

After a while, all this relentless criticism, scrutiny, and lack of time for yourself will begin to wear on you and your family. You may wonder if the whole world is against you, or if anyone is really with you. It will become easy to adopt a bunker mentality, to begin to believe that it's "us versus them," and to see phantom foes everywhere.

Keeping your equilibrium is going to be really, really hard to do. Every president in the past fifty years has, for long stretches, experienced disappointment and disillusionment, and a sense of not being in control. And the forces that have caused these feelings grow stronger.

The best way I can think of for you to avoid falling into this trap is this: find ways to get outside the bubble. By bubble, I mean the bubble of the White House and your staff and your schedule and the media and the problems of the moment. I hope you'll be able to see past the constant barrage of voices and images that will soon envelope you, and take the time to clear your head and think about the really big things (and also the really small things). I don't mean, go on vacation more often; heaven knows over the past eight years we had quite enough of a president who escaped from one bubble only to place himself in another one. I'm talking about wandering intellectually; about staying emotionally agile; about removing yourself from the bunker in any way you can, and listening to different voices and ideas, and allowing yourself to explore new perspectives; about lifting up your head and looking around every once in a while, so that when you put your nose back to the grindstone it's with renewed purpose; and about surrounding yourself with advisors who are similarly emotionally mature enough to recognize the bunker mentality and help you eradicate it before it infects your administration. Find ways to penetrate the bubble, and you'll find yourself much better able to maintain your sense of self and trust your instincts.

Mr. President, so many of us are already so proud of you, and admire you so much. I wish you all the strength, energy and luck possible in the coming years.

Sincerely,
Tim Brandhorst

Dear President Obama,

Saying "President Obama" seems very natural to me, as I have been referring to you with that title for weeks prior to the election. I pray for you every day. As a peace-loving Buddhist, I am hopeful that you will utilize diplomacy rather than militarism, thoughtful, informed decisions rather than knee-jerk responses, equitable positions rather than favoritism of the powerful privileged. I believe that you understand the inter-dependent nature of our relationship with our fellow humans around the world and will act accordingly. In spite of the mammoth challenges that lay ahead of us, I feel in my heart than you are the dedicated statesman to lead and reunite our nation toward a healthier future and restore America to the gold standard of democracy, diversity, and opportunity that it once was. Yes we can together! A grateful "thank you" to you and your family for your willingness to make this personal sacrifice by taking on an enormous responsibility for the sake of your countrymen and women.

Constance A. Barr
Mother of 3 and Grandmother of 6
Small-business owner
Proud and optimistic American

President Obama:

This is a Nelson Mandela era for the US of A! When South Africa was so devastated from apartheid and AIDS and the ruling powers decided to call an end to their evil ways President Mandela became their first black president.

The new tomorrow that we have been given with you, President Obama—even though the past administration has annihilated our economy, sent our young to their deaths in an unnecessary war, been silent as homes have been taken from the poor and the elderly through numerous foreclosures (you get the picture)—the Bush group just doesn't comprehend how WE in these trenches are resilient, creative, and networked throughout the world in a nurturing, economical, visionary community! WE stand strong with our first black elected President in the United States of America!!!! We believe in your leadership and your vision! We are ONE!

Dear President Obama:

Your 2008 election to the presidency of the most powerful nation in the world is a testimony to your undaunted courage, calm tenacity, deep understanding of history and your place in it and your keen sense of America's need for unity to address its many problems. The core values that undergirded your meteoric rise to the White House are the mark of a moral person.

People the world over applaud your success. Americans are optimistic again. You have been proclaimed as the embodiment of the dreams of so many whose lives in America were marked by great struggles. You serve as a symbol for youth everywhere. Yet, as heady as this is, you have demonstrated time and time again that you are well grounded and will serve all Americans in this great nation to the best of your ability.

My husband Otis and I congratulate you, your wonderful wife Michelle, and your two beautiful little girls, who are such dignified little ladies. We are impressed with the dignity and class you take to the Office and the White House. Our prayer for you is that you will always seek to do good, stay principled, remain steadfast, even if success is slow or in some cases elusive, keep a sense of humor, trust God, and always, always enjoy the love of your family.

Mr. President, we salute you!

Sincerely,
Annette K. Brock

Dear President Obama,

Congratulations on the win. I voted for you and hope you do a great job as president. Most people who become president want to be remembered as a great president and remembered like Washington, Lincoln, and FDR, but often most don't become great. Most presidents become great because they are handed a crisis and it's how they react and solve that crisis that is remembered. Like FDR, you have been handed not one but two crises. One on the home front with the economy and a second on the international front with two wars going on and respect for us around the world at an all-time low. You have a great opportunity to be remembered for more than just being the first black or biracial president, so I hope when you start dealing and solving these crises you take a similar approach that both Roosevelts took, that is, they didn't care about what party they are from and took ideas from all sides of the political spectrum to move America forward and solve problems.

I hope and believe that you have a great opportunity to turn America around and set us once again on the path of greatness and restore America back to the country we all know it can be. We all know you can't solve everything, but if you show us that you are trying and restore our confidence and faith back into government, that's all most of us ask. Most Americans for the longest time have seemed to have little no faith or trust in government and do not feel inspired to serve it, but for the first time in a long time a President has, that is you. Use that gift wisely, by maybe doing your own version of FDR's "fireside chats" or something. Often history doesn't wait to see if you are ready; it comes when it comes and your time is now.

Thanks,
Patrick Demkowski

President Obama,

I am currently 18 years old and a freshman in college. Two years ago I was given an assignment in my English class to select a great orator, dead or living, and analyze a speech. While my classmates chose Martin Luther King, Jr., and John F. Kennedy, I struggled to find the perfect speech. My father suggested a speech given at the 2004 Democratic National Convention in support of John Kerry. I quickly the found the speech and watched it online. It did not take me long to decide this was the speech. The second part of the assignment was to create and deliver a speech to the class emulating the style and rhetorical devices in the speech we selected. We were given freedom to speak on any subject fictional or real. I decided to write a speech as if it was the year 2008, and I was endorsing you as the Democratic nominee. Truly inspired and excited, it was easy to speak from my heart about this make-believe event where I proudly spoke about the candidate I would vote for in my first election. I read my speech to everyone that I knew and anyone that would listen just so I could live in that dream. I never imagined that it would come true, especially in the 2008 election. I have watched your candidacy with great pride and I am delighted to say I voted for you in my first election. I know that if you continue to lead our country in a new direction my generation will support you. I am looking forward to your presidency.

Sincerely,
Meryl Hulteng

Dear President Obama:

We know that many young people helped you achieve victory in your dedication to become president of the United States of America. However, also many elders, like myself and my husband, were very happy to vote for you, and we are thrilled that you will be our president. As a semi-retired literary agent, I am also impressed with your writing ability as displayed in your two fine books. I am also impressed with the integrity you displayed in your campaign, and with the people of like integrity with whom you surrounded yourself during your travels across the United States.

The song lyrics that Frank Sinatra made popular many years ago, "The House I Live In," express my feeling about America and your willingness to serve your country:

"The house I live in, a plot of earth, a street; the grocer and the butcher and the people that I meet; the children in the playground, the faces that I see; all races and religions, that's America to me. The things I see about me, the big things and the small; the little corner newsstand and the house a mile tall; the wedding and the churchyard, the laughter and the tears, the dream that's been a-growing for a hundred fifty years. The town I live in, the street, the house, the room; the pavement of the city, or a garden all in bloom; the church, the school, the clubhouse, the million lights I see, but especially the people, that's America to me." (Words by Lewis Allan, music by Earl Robinson.)

When I sing this song at my piano, I think of how very lucky I am to be an American, and how lucky all Americans are that you will be our president.

With all good wishes to you and your family,
Rosalie Grace Thompson

Dear President-elect Obama,

Congratulations on your success and the progress of America. I was born an African-American male in 1939 into a South that many today have no real knowledge of: a South where African-Americans were required to step off of sidewalks to allow Caucasians to pass, a South where little emphasis was placed open educating non-Caucasians, a South where African-Americans were forced to relinquish their seats at the back of the bus for even the children of others, a South where laws seemed applicable only to non-Caucasians and we were terrorized by Caucasians and all seemed to conspire to demote us to the realm on inferiority and hopelessness.

At that time the constraints of segregation had the unintended consequence of forcing African-Americans to live together in the same communities where successful role models were easily available to serve as beacons of hope for eager youth. Many of us learned to negotiate within the despair and to utilize education as egress to something better and more positive. As a college student in the 1950s, I found myself rapt in the Zeitgeist that conscripted many African-American youth to rebel against the apartheid in America and to demand that she live up to her creed of justice for all.

My belief in education and being prepared led me to acquire a doctorate degree and to dedicate myself to assisting youth to aspire to something greater than the negative immediacy that surrounds them. Until now, optimistic or not, there has been a ceiling to any dreams that they might have. Unfortunately, the positive role models available during my youthful days are seldom seen by young African-Americans today. Hence many have fallen prey to influences that emphasize instant gratification at any price and promote negative and limited possibilities.

You, sir, are obvious and tangible proof that there is hope and dreams need not segue into a lower depth but are indeed free to soar. Moreover, you are the personification of what can occur when one is prepared to embrace opportunity when it comes.

Thank you for the inspiration that you are for our youth and for all of America. However, allow me to remind you that the weight of race must not be welded to that of the rest of the world and brought to rest upon your shoulders alone. While you must be conscious of the symbol that you have become, you must also realize that others demand GOD on a good day and that they cannot expect you to be HIM.

Good luck and God's speed.

Dear Mr. President,

The audacity of hope will never again be mistaken for an intangible dare. It is now real life. With your simple existence, you have proven to the world that any goal is attainable, any system is reformable, and no task is impossible. What the world needs beyond this is proof of change. It seems as though the population of the United States has turned invincible. No one seems to doubt their futures or your abilities. What I ask of you is to continue this hope. Even if nothing comes from your years in office, never let the people's faith in a better time falter. This would be your contribution to history. You are now president of the United States of America. And as silly as it may seem, this is your time to save the world.

Sincerely,
Me

Dear President Obama,

I wanted to write to you because I couldn't be happier that you've been elected as our next president. I think our country needs a change and a new direction, and I feel that you are the perfect match for the office in these desperate times.

The thing that has been most interesting to me about your campaign is that you have achieved a celebrity status that seems similar to the JFK election. I have never witnessed an election where a candidate has moved so many people and given citizens hope for the future. This is something that you should truly be proud of and something that I hope you use to your advantage during these next four years.

I'm anxious to see how these next four years turn out. I think that it's good that we have an extreme change in power because we need to adjust from the turmoil of the last eight years. I know that times can only get better, considering the state of recession that the U.S. is currently in. This is a truly scary time for our country, and I know I'm not alone in saying that. I have faith that you will bring up the morale of the U.S. and I wish you the best in these next four years.

Sincerely,
Kelsey Bishop

Dear President-elect Obama,

Your election to the presidency represents a defining moment in human history; at a time when we face almost insurmountable challenges, your historic campaign symbolizes the power of the individual to forge a new sense of purpose in the politics of our time. I believe that you emerged as a leader, because in a time of war, economic recession, and failed leadership both from the corporate sector and the White House, your message of change resonated with the American people. I also believe that your promise to instill hope and vitality to the American dream will involve first and foremost investing in human potential through the creation of jobs at home, investing in green technology, and making higher education more accessible and affordable to the average American. In order for the United States to continue to compete in the global economy we first need to direct our attention to the needs of the American people that have been neglected over the past eight years due to the war in Iraq, bailing out failed institutions, and exporting jobs overseas.

Much like John F. Kennedy's statement in his Inaugural Address (January 20, 1961), "So let us begin anew," I view your election as a fundamental opportunity for America to "begin anew" and to usher in a new era which departs from the cynicism, partisanship and apathy of the last eight years and towards a more bipartisan effort to solve the overwhelming issues that currently confront us. You appealed to the younger generation much like Kennedy did when on the night of your election you called upon the youth of America to adopt a "new spirit of service, a new spirit of sacrifice," which reminded me of one of President Kennedy's most famous quotations: "Ask not what your country can do for you—ask what you can do for your country." The notion of "self sacrifice" is a concept that has been woefully lacking in American culture, politics, and economics during the past decade. Your call to a renewed spirit of service rejuvenates within us the fundamental American ideal of individual sacrifice for the greater good of the nation.

Sincerely,
Jennifer Anne Brown

Dear Mr. President,

It is with great pride that I write to you, the first ever African-American president in the history of our country. Your achievements stand as a testament to the change this country has undergone from the frightening Civil Rights Movement, to today, in which the people of America chose to elect an African-American to lead them. I have tremendous faith in your ability to not only lead this country, but to take it in a direction that will ensure our prosperity and success in future generations. After all, when all is said and done, many people expect you to be on the same level as FDR, Lincoln, Teddy Roosevelt, and Jackson—America's finest presidents. Those are large shoes to fill, yet somehow the American people, including myself, remain optimistic about your presidency. Never before have I seen the American people so welcoming of a new president, even those who didn't vote for you seem to be open to see what changes you have in store for this country.

Dear President Obama,

I have been thinking a lot about your recent election and all the positive feelings it has brought with it. I was a supporter of you before the election and am now, but I realize you face many challenges once you actually take office. Also, from everything I have read you have almost no real political experience as far as making a difference in the Senate. Therefore, I am a little worried about what we can expect from you during your presidency. I also am currently reading a biography of Abraham Lincoln and you two have many commonalities. To name a few, you both are from Illinois, didn't have much political experience when elected president, are amazing orators, and faced numerous national issues upon taking office. Lincoln is looked upon as one of the greatest presidents of all time for his work dealing with an economic crisis (similar to the one we face now), but more importantly bringing the nation together during the Civil War. You are not faced with a Civil War, but there might as well be because of how separate this country has become over the years. Ultimately you are faced with an economic crisis, a war in Iraq, and running a government you don't have much experience with. Your presidency will be defined by the choices you make and their eventual outcome. In reading one of FDR's fireside chats I realized he had many plans to bring the country out of a depression and did this through many reforms. He, like Lincoln, also had many great advisors, but ultimately made his own decisions. Therefore, I just wanted to say I hope you realize how important your election and presidency is to everyone in the entire world, more so than any previous president. So, I hope that you surround yourself with adequate advisors, listen to their advice, but ultimately be strong and make your own decisions. I know you have the ability to change this country for the better or worse, and you will do everything in your power to not make it the latter. You have my fate and the country's in your hands; I hope you realize your power and the significance of your every move.

Sincerely,
Jake Zunamon

Dear President Obama,

First, I would just like to congratulate on making history by becoming the first African-American president. Secondly, I am very proud to be an American. You have changed the perspectives of millions and I am honored to call you my president. I am still eager to know how you are going to change our current economic situation. I mean I know your children and their children's children are going to be well taken care of, but what about mine? I am soooo scared yet excited about the changes that will be taken place under your administration. Hopefully, things will change for the better and I will see the effects of your policies during this lifetime. Thank you for being you and giving me hope to become something greater than I ever thought possible.

Honorable Barack Obama
President of the United States
Washington, D.C.

Dear Mr. President,

Firstly, I would like to congratulate you on becoming the nation's first African-American president. Your success has proven that race is not a deterring factor for an individual to pursue a successful career in politics in order to shape the nation and shape the minds of people.

In terms of foreign policy, I truly support your stand to withdraw American troops from Iraq. In my opinion, every country has its own sovereignty rights and this must be respected. It is not right for us to wage war against other nations. As a peace lover myself, I truly believe that the war in Iraq had devastated not only lives, but also the country's economy with the increasing spending on war efforts and military campaigns. Such atrocities must come to an end. Human lives, human rights, and human liberties must be respected at all costs.

In terms of economic policy, I believe that free market economy with no government intervention is just not feasible. Certain amount of government intervention must be present to steer the economy in the right direction and to prevent the economy from collapsing. Recently, the Congress had passed a legislation to allow a $700 billion bailout plan to rescue the economy. Although the bailout plan was a bit of a burden on taxpayer's money, I have to say that this had to be done to prevent further economic downturn.

You have all my support as the next president of the United States. Under your stewardship, I am sure that the U.S. will be able to reach greater heights.

Sincerely,
Ken Chong

Dear President Obama,

As I write, I am 9 months pregnant with my first child. I am so pleased that you will be shaping the course of our nation for the first years (hopefully 8) of his life. My husband and I can't agree on a name, so we've been calling the baby Bubba Chuck Norris, much to the dismay of my grandmother. Let's call him BCN for short. I am writing to encourage you to think of the baby. Think of little BCN. When you are making decisions that will affect the American people now and many years into the future, think of him. I know that as president, you must take many stakeholders into account when you make decisions. Giant multi-national corporations, small mom-and-pop businesses, nerdy Internet start-up companies, banks, stock exchanges, self-employed entrepreneurs, and many other participants in our economic system must have representation in the governmental decision-making process. In fact, the welfare of all Americans, BCN included, relies on a strong economic foundation. But I have felt in recent years that our leaders in Congress and in the White House, in the interest of fostering a strong economy, have been over-representing the interests of large corporations and under-representing the interests of the average American citizen.

My concept of the average American citizen is a complex one. I picture a worker who works hard to provide for his or her family but probably spends a little more each month than he brings in or finds him- or herself struggling to make mortgage, car, and credit card payments. I picture a parent who wants the best possible life for his or her child but struggles to provide a good education for that child. I picture a consumer who wants all of the comforts and luxuries of modern life in America, but cannot quite afford that plasma television. I picture a consumer who would prefer to buy goods manufactured in America under fair working conditions, but often is driven to choose items made in a third-world country under questionable working conditions because their price is so much lower. I picture a man or woman who sometimes gets sick and deserves the best medical care at an affordable price, but who often gets lost in the maze of the health care system or must go into debt to afford insurance or hospitalization. I picture a grocery shopper who wants to purchase the healthiest food possible for his or her family, but who is overwhelmed by the difficulty of determining what foods those might and who often cannot afford the time or money that it would take to prepare fresh, local, organic meals. I picture a human who must breathe, eat, live, and raise children in an environment that is permeated with substances that have known or suspected harmful effects on human health, but who lacks the power to fight the industries that produce these substances.

When I think of little BCN, this is how I must think of his life. This picture does not make me happy. When I imagine how my son will live his life, here is the United States; I would like to imagine a happier future for him. I want to help build a country where the interests of businesses and the interests of individuals are better balanced. I want to help build a country where excellent health care is available and affordable for every citizen. I want to help build a country where Americans can afford to eat fresh, local, organic meals. I want to help build a country where every citizen is entitled to a good education, so that each individual is equipped with the necessary knowledge to be an informed participant in our political system, in household economic decisions, in health care and dietary decisions, and in childrearing decisions. I want to help build a country where environmental regulations and consumer safeguards err on the side of caution, so our children have the best chance we can give them of living long, healthy, productive lives.

President Obama, when you are confronted with decisions that may steer the course of our country, I beg you to remember little BCN. You have the power to change the course of his life. You have the ability to build a better, healthier, more educated, more equitable country for our next generation. And if you have any suggestions for good boy names, please let me know, because I don't think Bubba Chuck Norris is going to stick.

Dear President-elect Obama,

While it's tempting to write to you about my favorite issues, I feel more drawn to speak to you now about deeper matters.

As I watched your acceptance speech last night on TV, I felt the same immense wonder and gratitude—tinged with slight disbelief—that so many others around the world were feeling. Can this be real? Is it a dream? If so, don't wake me up!

I sense something different in you, Mr. Obama: something that is rare and precious. It's the same quality that I recognize and feel and thrill to, when I watch video of Dr. Martin Luther King, Mahatma Gandhi, or John F. Kennedy, when I read the writings of Lincoln, or witness the work of Nelson Mandela. It ignites a fierce joy within me, a joy akin to ecstasy, because it is a powerful alignment with the highest good.

This morning, not even twelve hours after your confirmation as the President-elect, everyone is talking about how hard a task you have before you now. It's as though, having renewed our sense of hope as you led us to today, we're being cautioned to reduce our expectations.

I, for one, am unwilling to allow my jubilant hope to be dimmed. You gave me that gift, or helped me remember it and I will not lay it down now.

While I understand the thoughts of those who would warn us that there is much to fix, this campaign has reaffirmed my belief that it's only impossible if we allow it to be. We've proven that, by working together, we can affect miraculous things.

We CAN transform this situation. Yes, we can. In the process, we will change the whole world for the better. Yes, we can.

And you're the man to lead us there.

I see who you are, dear Mr. Obama, and I am profoundly grateful for you. I believe in you. I believe in your purpose and your dedication, and I believe in your ability to help us transform what is into what we want it to be. Yes, we can.

I have and will continue to support you with every means available to me. Thank you, for us and for our children, and for the seven generations beyond.

In love and light,
Eileen

Dear President Obama,

We were in a Hot Springs, Arkansas coffee shop last March when I saw you speaking on TV in Philadelphia. The screen was set up high with no sound but the words you were speaking were showing across the bottom of the TV. As I read the words you spoke, I felt quite moved. I told my husband you spoke like Abraham Lincoln. About eight or nine years ago, Desmond Tutu came to Cornell University to speak. As I listened to his words and the wisdom that unfolded from his thoughts, I wondered why we don't have a leader like Desmond Tutu.

I feel we now have an extraordinary leader in you. Capable of wisdom of understanding the many layers of leadership and the hard work of putting together a coalition of opposing parties and individuals while uniting the different groups that already back you. This is a time of patiently working through the enormous problems that have been presented to you. I think you have a rare and complex set of abilities, wisdom, and an instinct and skill of knowing how to work with both sides, fortitude, and faith in your fellow humans without being naive.

We are all blessed to have you appear at this time of great need. I wish you much success because our nation stands at a crossroads. We know you will lead us using the best skills you have during this difficult time of economic and armed-conflict crisis.

With great respect,
Susan Brown Eyster

CHAPTER 3

Michelle, Malia, Sasha, and the Puppy

Needless to say, there is great interest in the new African-American First Lady, Michelle Obama, who is also quite accomplished in her own right. This interest in the new first family, as this group of letters shows, is further extended to the children, Malia and Sasha, and their desire for a new pet: a puppy.

Dear Michelle,

January 20 was truly an extraordinary day and experience. I was very fortunate in getting tickets from my Congressman, airline tickets to Washington, D.C., and hotel accommodations in the area—all within three days prior to the Inauguration.

I would like to extend congratulations and my warmest wishes for a wonderful first term in the White House. You and your family are an inspiration to us all. The palpable love, respect, and admiration that you and your husband share are absolutely beautiful to behold. Your valuing of both you nuclear and extended family is in the rich tradition of African-American families. The daily presence of your mother and your children's grandmother will make such a difference in your daily lives and in this experience. The image of your family is one that will continue to be a wonderful beacon for families nationwide. Many relationships will model the form and the substance of your romance as well as that of your nourishing parenting. Thank you for keeping these images before us as you and we seek to sustain, repair, and in some cases, rebuild our communities, our families, and our lives.

Your grace and intellect together with your support and collaboration in the genuine partnership that you and Barack share will provide assurance and inspire our new president as well as citizens, women, men, youth, and families across our country and around the world. The commitment and passionate belief in the principles and values about which you spoke in South Carolina, at the Democratic convention, and during long campaign season are very important for all of us.

Continue to hold his hand and have him hold yours, share fist bumps, hugs, and kisses so that we can all be inspired to love and respect one another, to work with and appreciate our partners and family members while working to improve our communities and our world.

Education is such an important arena and gross disparities in that area are abundant in so many neighborhoods and communities in this country. Won't you consider championing this critical area of needed attention? Teacher professionalism, adequate resources, parental involvement, and genuine shifts in the culture of public education are all needed points of reinforcement, intervention, and restructuring.

The related need for creating opportunities and structures of hope for our youth generally and youth of color in particular as we envision the creation of sustainable and healthy social, economic, and political environments that support life in this and the next century must also become a priority. The commitment to serve is an awesome one. Call of us to empower ourselves as we make this world a better place for us all.

Hugs and warm wishes to you as you inspire the citizens of this country and the human family worldwide.

Josephine Aona Allen
Ithaca, New York

Breathing Life

Dear First Lady Michelle and President Barack Obama,

In the book, *Go, Tell Michelle: African-American Women Write to the New First Lady* (2009), I wrote about how I felt First Lady Michelle had and would continue to redefine black motherhood. When I had this opportunity to write this letter to you both, I thought about my own parents and their over fifty-year life together. They were my example.

In 2007, on December 21, my mother Mrs. Clemmie Lee Jackson Ward passed on. We found out shortly before Thanksgiving that she had stage-3 lung cancer. She was not a smoker. On the day she was to begin chemotherapy, she told the doctor, that, she was ready to go home to be with her Lord. I knew that statement affirmed her faith and belief in God, but it also was how she viewed my father, Mr. Emmett E. Ward, Jr., who had died in August of 2001, when I was completing my own chemotherapy treatment as a young African-American woman with breast cancer. I write this introduction because my mother was my father's rib. He would joke with people that he had to go home to be with "his rib." My mother knew she was my father's rib, and in that role she breathed life into her husband, just as you as a wife breathe life into your husband, President Obama. I would argue that you not only breathed life into him, but each other, and in your children.

In my mother's house, there was a porcelain wall hanging, which spoke to the idea that behind every strong man, there was an even stronger woman. I know as I have watched you support, introduce, and share the love of your husband with us, that you are the strength behind his movement forward. You are his rib. And even though he calls you his rock, he speaks to the long line of black women who have not only stood beside their man, but behind and if need be in front of him to provide protection, comfort, friendship, support and love. I have watched as you have done this, time, and time again, and I thank you for providing the U.S. with another image of black women: wife.

Yes, we have had the popular image of Claire Huxtable, but most believed she was a caricature an ectoplasm or worse, a "spoke that sate by the door." She was, after all, on television. They knew no one like her. But even as they attacked your patriotism, and your candor, and even your intelligence, they could not deny that you were intelligent, bright, loving, and caring. And you cared about the state of the U.S., as you traveled all over the U.S. including to my institution, Ohio University. Even though I did not get the opportunity to see you in public when you came to the University because of my teaching obligations, I did get to hear you the Sunday before election night when you introduced your husband to us at the State Capital in Columbus, Ohio. It was a touching moment.

I recognized that you supported your husband the way that many black women have for centuries supported their men. Like my mother supported my father. I think of Ida B. Wells, who strove to outlaw lynching while nursing her children, and how she had the support of her husband. I think of Mary Church Terrell as leader in the National Association of Colored Women, whose husband was a first as well. And yes, I remember when my husband, Dr. Lewis A. Randolph and I married, how our minister, Dr. Marcia Foster Boyd, spoke to us about the responsibility and example we would set as a two-Ph.D. family, even though I was still completing my degree. A couple, bound together by love, the hopes of our forefathers and mothers who gave their blessings that day, and our children who were and still are our future. But, we had no example. The only example I could think of was Ruby Dee and Ossie Davis, who shared a fierce love. Yet, we were not actors. We were academics. Still, I completed my Ph.D. with the support of my husband, and I looked forward to maintaining our blended family and to its growth.

As I look back now, I realize that I too was a first in many ways. I was the first person in my family to earn a Ph.D. I was the first African-American professor that many of my students had and would ever have. And I was the first person to earn tenure and promotion at Ohio University in the College of Education in its 100-year history in 2003. As I watch you time and time again take the hand of your husband, or give him the fist pump handshake, or hug and/or kiss, I recognize that you are the first African-American woman to hold your position, and I wish you well as you support not only your husbands' presidency, but also your children, and all of us as American citizens. Remember, however, you are his rock, and continue the historical linkage of many black women who we may never know were first, but also remember you are his rib—breath life into him, as he inspires us to our highest potential, challenges us to support each other regardless of race, class, or gender, and breaths life into the U.S. political, social, and economic systems.

Respectfully,
Adah Ward Randolph

Dear President Barack Obama,

I'm so excited for you to be our first black president. This is one of my most favorite times in the world. My honor goes straight to you. I am so thankful for you to be our first black president. I voted for you in my school. We had a mock election. Thank you so much for reading my letter. I will be praying for you.

Sincerely,
With Love
PS: I love your daughters' hair. I would like to have a play date with them.

Dear President-elect Barack Obama,

You are an inspiration to your country. We are trusting you to make our world a better place. Please take good care of our nation. Good luck!

Donna

P.S. If you haven't chosen what kind of dog to get, I would recommend a golden retriever. I've had one all my life and they are definitely the best, most friendly breed of dog around.

Dear President Obama,

First off, congratulations! It was pretty cool how you united the country, and energized the youth vote. I also need to give you props for your fundraising skills—using the Internet was clutch! You seem pretty innovative and I cannot wait to see all you have in store for the nation. I hope your ideals are realized quickly once you assume office, and that Congress doesn't give you too much trouble.

There is one issue that I would like to bring to your attention that is really important to me, along with 15,605 others at the time of writing this letter. Originally you had said that you would adopt a shelter dog for your girls if you won the presidency. Now, reports are surfacing that you're afraid your daughter, Malia, who is allergic to dogs, will have problems unless you get a hypoallergenic purebred. This is simply untrue. There are lots of measures you can take to lessen the effects of dog allergies, such as medication, shots, or rescuing non-shedding breeds. Many hypoallergenic dogs are in shelters across the country as I write this letter to you, Mr. President, who are just waiting for your love and attention.

I just hope this is not the first of many broken promises. I do not want to see you give up easily on this issue, and I think it would say a lot about your character and the next four years if you kept your word and did your best to rescue a dog that suits your family's needs.

Thank you,
Lisa Jacks

Hello President Obama and Family,

Congratulations and Welcome. Cocoa is my Chocolate Labrador . . . lol . . . that is like a child and protector in one package. I rescued her 10 years ago as a puppy. We watched all day . . . 1-20-2009! If you have not chosen a dog yet . . . please consider a Chocolate Labrador . . . from a puppy. You have to watch them for the first year and a half . . . but with LOVE they respond with devotion only God could teach me in life! Cocoa has a Christmas card for 2007 on YouTube if you care to see it. You can find it by going to YouTube's Web site and look for Cocoa's Christmas. Thank you for being my president . . . Cocoa and I have a lot of FAITH in you! May You, Mr. President, and your family be blessed.

Highest Regards,
Evelyn A. Hause

Dear President Obama,

I really like your campaign slogan: Yes We Can! You did an awesome job winning the election. Congratulations!

I hope your daughters, Sasha and Malia, have fun with the puppy. Enjoy the White House. Enjoy the adventure as our new President and First Lady, Barack and Michelle. I hope the whole Obama family has a great time as our First Family!

Yes We Can! (I Know We Can!) Yes We Can! (I Know We Can!) Yes We Can! (I Know We Can!)

I know we can,
Che'Rai Laster

CHAPTER 4

African-Americans

It should come as no surprise to the readers in that this is America's first African-American president that some of the letter writers would focus upon this aspect of the 56th presidential election and give it meaning from this particular perspective.

President Obama,

I am in my second term as vice chairman of the Savannah, Georgia City Council. I happened to be in China with a delegation to promote economic cooperation and tourism between China and the city of Savannah on the day you were elected. We were having lunch at noon on Wednesday, November 5, 2008 (13 hours ahead), when we learned that history had been made and that you were elected to be our nation's 44th President. While my political mind told me that, given the obstacles you faced, that your accomplishment was impossible; my spiritual mind told me that it was time.

As I am sure you know, the number forty represents a generation and it appears that God has an affinity for the number 40. For 40 years, the children of Israel wandered in the wilderness, it rained for 40 days and nights during Noah's flood, for 40 days for twelve spies explored the promised land, forty days was the period from Jesus' resurrection till his ascension into heaven—you get the point. More specifically, it was forty years since Dr. King was taken from us and Robert Kennedy predicted that a "negro" could become president in forty years. All that has occurred since has prepared us for this moment. You broke all of the political rules, you won without the blessing of some of the "civil rights elite," and you were the David slaying the Goliath. I believe that it was destiny.

I simply ask that you are responsible with your power. I ask that you remember the elderly ladies and gentlemen to whom you personify a dream. I ask that you remember those that are impoverished, those that are uneducated, unemployed, underemployed, locked down, locked up, and locked out of society. I ask that you remember those that are sick and just want to be well, but don't have health insurance. I ask that you remember those who paid the ultimate price to place timber upon the bridges that we both walked across. I ask that you remember those soldiers, sailors, and marines across the world who have accepted the challenge to protect us, but would love to be home with their parents, children, spouses, and loved ones. I ask that you not use your awesome power to put African-Americans in a place of advantage, but for you to use your power to ensure that "every mountain and hill shall be made low: and the crooked shall be made straight, and the rough places plain." I ask that you allow the United States to be the "city set on a hill," so that the world community may learn from our example, not from our military might. I ask that you leave our country much better than you found it.

As change has never been a singular or solo act, we, as citizens, also have to do our part. We have to change the way we do business. We have to parent our children, clean up our communities, spend our money prudently, protect our environment, treat each other with dignity and respect, and never allow anyone to be victimized. We have to act and live responsibly. I stand ready to do what is necessary to assist you.

I hope you continue to be a role model for elected officials such as myself—as a person of character, honor, dignity and service. You are the right man for this moment.

Thank you for stepping up to the challenge and accepting the most difficult (and lonely) position in the entire world.

God bless you, your family and God bless America.

Van R. Johnson, II
Vice Chairman
Savannah City Council
Savannah, GA

Hello President Obama,

I just want to say congratulations on being our 44th president. I am sure you will do well in the mission to save our Nation. Disregard all those negative and pessimistic views on your ability to change America's future because those people are just afraid of change. One of my concerns of America is the continue disenfranchisement of the black community, where many are located in impoverished areas with poor education and resources. Could you eliminate the effects of redlining and other techniques that were used to deny blacks' success, which still have effects even today?

Thank you President Obama and congratulations!

—Elizabeth L. Carter

President Obama,

I write this the very evening you, with the people's hearts firmly in your pocket and our private hopes on your shoulders, took the oath of office to become the 44th president of the United States. As I watched you today, I couldn't help but think of my own father, a member of your generation, and my grandfather, of the generation before. Both of these men grew up in the deep South at a time when the South was not a hospitable place for people of color, but despite this, both men where able to overcome the leftovers from a peculiar institution that was so uniquely American and keenly felt. My father's father left his family when he was twelve years old, and my mother's grandfather was absent for large parts of my grandfather's life. I know that it is because of these absences of men in my father and grandfather's lives, and not in spite of them, that I have had two invaluable male role models in my life. I do not have to spell out how the situations of my father and grandfather echo that of you and your father, for it is well known. Many more can relate with first-hand experiences of their own. For these individuals, the choice of what kind of man they will be—like their own fathers, or like otherwise—is a difficult one. People tend to stick to what they know and become those they know or knew. So if they know nothing, and know no one, that is what who and what they will be pulled to become. It is this tendency, this peculiar inertia, that shapes how men of color are seen in this country. To be the men that their fathers were not, or to improve on the flaws of their fathers they must struggle, they must grow, and they must push. I am fortunate to have had two wonderful examples of what a man is, and you will be one for many others, It is because of men like you, my father, and my grandfather, that I will only have to is point and say look here when it comes time for me to show my children what a man is. For that I thank you.

Desmond Davis

Dear Mr. President Barack Obama,

I am so proud of you for doing what was, to some, considered unrealistic. Despite the many trials, of which I am sure must have faced, you became the first African-American president of the United States. Your accomplishments have made me realize that my dream to become a Supreme Court Justice is not a dream that will be realized easily but, it is a dream that is attainable through hard work and perseverance.

Hard work and perseverance is exactly what many Americans expect of you during your presidency, and I know this must be a tremendous weight on your shoulders. I want you to know that I along with many others, especially those in the black community, you will be supported through all of your trials, your errors, and your successes.

As a financially burdened college student, during your presidency I would love to see you work hard to fix the horrible economy while working to make the costs of higher education less burdensome. For people like me who don't come from rich parents or have the financial abilities or capabilities to pay for their own education it's a struggle to afford to go to college, and to stay in college. Since I want to go to law school I will have plenty of loans to pay back in the future; so what I would like to see are policies that make it easier for college students to get loans, and also more government funds available for students who come from "middle-class families." I hope helping the future leaders of this nation will become one of your presidential agendas. I wish you luck Mr. President.

Sincerely,
Jamiela Sekou

Dear President-elect Obama,

When asked about affirmative action by moderator George Stephanopoulos in the closing minutes of the Democratic primary debate in Philadelphia, you stated, "I still believe in affirmative action as a means of overcoming both historic and potentially current discrimination, but I think that it can't be a quota system and it can't be something that is simply applied without looking at the whole person, whether that person is black, or white, or Hispanic, male or female. What we want to do is make sure that people who've been locked out of opportunity are going to be able to walk through those doors of opportunity in the future." This was the moment that I truly believed you were a post-racial candidate as many pundits and commentators contended. Your vision of providing educational opportunity for all underprivileged Americans, regardless of race, makes you a true progressive. My fear is that as you become comfortable in the White House, you will become susceptible to interests, both to the left and right. Please do not fall victim to the pleas from African-American interest groups to maintain race-based affirmative action. Or to conservatives, who may use your own successes to argue for an end to affirmative action all together. While you are clear proof that the racial boundaries that have defined American are dissipating, in no way does this mean that the American dream can be easily attained by those less fortunate than yourself. Only behind the weight of an African-American that has reached the pinnacle of political success can the still struggling minorities of this country understand and accept the fact that their own lack of economic and educational opportunity is shared by millions of Americans of all backgrounds and that all those that share their burdens deserve a chance. You have the chance to make this true, and I sincerely hope this goal is met.

Thank you,
Brendan Friedman

Dear friends, colleagues, and potential voters,

I decided to write and publish a letter of support for Barack Obama. If you find yourself still uninspired by the election, or undecided about a candidate, I hope my story interests you.

I have always felt that the history a person carries with them gives rise to how they look at the world and ultimately how they vote. I hope my story adds understanding of my reasons behind my decision to support Barack Obama enough to not just vote for him, but to ask you as my friend or colleague to make the effort to do the same. With all of the remaining members of my extended family having long since passed away, all I have from them is my memories of stories they would tell me . . . even those stories from my childhood are foggy. This has not only been a great reason to write some of them down, but through all of this, I get to fulfill a dream my family could only have wished for.

My mother met my father sometime in 1967. My father worked in Jersey City, his mother had come to the U.S. a teenage girl by herself on one of the now infamous boats that brought Italian immigrants to the U.S. My mother was the daughter of Ethel, the oldest of two brothers and two other sisters. The brothers had fallen victim to the mad rioting in Newark in the mid 60s. I'm uncertain of any details surrounding this. The whole family, having made the journey from Atlanta, GA, after WWI, settled first at Cutler Street in Newark, then on to Hinsdale Place, where I now live.

They fell in love at a time when racism was so rampant in the Jersey City and Newark vicinity; their situation was considered unacceptable through both families. My childhood stories of my parents' life together included the painful story of my mother not being allowed in the church with me and my father during my baptism. My father's mother lied that my mother was sick after giving birth to me and went to the church in place of my mother because she was white.

My father would tell me the stories of how racism played a part in their everyday lives in the areas of religion, politics, and even neighbors. Their plan was to move away from the Jersey City, Newark, and Passaic areas, and raise me in the countryside hills of northern New Jersey. Racism was still an enormous part of our everyday lives. I watched as a child called me 'nigger' at my bus stop where I was waiting in first grade. I had not yet heard the word spoken, and called the kid nigger back in a first-grade style of verbal self defense and ran back to the car where my father was waiting. Unknown to me, he waited for this day, knowing patiently what was coming. He made me watch my classmate at the bus stop as *his* father told him what a nigger was, why I was one, and how I was to be treated and why. My dad explained to me that someday he would like me to live in a world where this never happens.

As a country, we still have many miles to go on the road to end racism. Colin Powell and Condoleezza Rice, although they made it to great positions of power, didn't embody the need to embrace peace. In the great words of Keith Ellison, D-MN, in Congress, Martin Luther didn't die so you could own a Lexus and have a nice house . . . Our struggle continues—we must always embrace peace and justice in spite of oppression.

Barack Obama is not a perfect candidate, and there are some things that I wish he would stand stronger for, and I know that the political game must be played, but I must make the effort to follow my heart. Barack Obama has satisfied my voter's conscience intellectually, in spite of all of the issues I have learned about after five years engineering the greatest newscast in the U.S. I usually don't even have political discussions anymore, much less write open letters like this. I spent FAR too many years too close to the real stories; I've even lost a great friend to the throws of the post-NAFTA Mexico. I am too tired of others telling me that they know the issues. My daily life was spent feeling the hopelessness of the world each day with each 10-minute shock treatment of literally heart-wrenching headlines delivered by one of the most admirable journalists I know—Amy Goodman.

No one from either side of my parent's families could have imagined a world without racism. Their only moments of solace were talks of times where the oppressed went on to do great things. Both my mother and father would have truly enjoyed the day where the choice of president were between a woman and black man. I know for Obama, it is about change and coming together—great . . . For me and my life, and on behalf of my family, it is *ALSO* about race.

It is a privilege to know that I can fulfill their desires in a hopeful vote for Barack Obama, while satisfying my own criteria for a peaceful future and world.

I hope you join me with a vote for Barack Obama.

Dear President Obama,

Words cannot begin to express how elated I am over your recent accomplishment—becoming president-elect of the United States. Although I am 41-years old, I questioned whether I would see an African-American president in my lifetime. I was also impressed by your campaign. You exercised great judgment during your 2-year campaign. Further, you surrounded yourself with great advisors, strategists, and spokespersons.

Many have lamented the fact that you have inherited a terrible economy, two wars, etc. However, I strongly believe that these "issues" are "opportunities." I also believe that you and your administration will develop, present, and implement the necessary solutions to move our beloved country in the right direction.

While I could write volumes, I will end this letter by wishing you and yours well. God bless you, your family, and the United States of America!!

Respectfully,
Vince Truett
Ellicott City, Maryland

January 21, 2009
Dear President Obama,

Congratulations on your election as president of the United States of America. Yes, it has been a long time coming, but having arrived at last I sure hope you can make some sense of the situation America finds itself in today. Yes, this country is at risk. With two wars, an economic disaster emergency, and a host of defective policy measures facing your administration on day one. I just pray that you will put God first as you make the decisions you will now be responsible to make.

I was so proud and honored to be present for the inauguration. Although I did not have a ticket, it was inspiring to see what so many people like me had longed for and were present to see at this moment in history. The atmosphere was electrifying and unifying as we watched the event and all the well wishers who were there at the mall.

Change toward personal responsibility is such a needed element of this country. I sure trust that your efforts and ideas can change the course of so many high school drop outs, and help those who have to choose whether to buy medication or food. I realize you cannot single handedly make it all happen, however, I applaud your call to the country to make it happen. Electing you as president was such a change in itself, I just hope it began a unity of purpose long verbalized but not yet realized in the United States of America.

I feel that God has been in the move to place you where you are. I also pray that you will put him first in whatever you do and he will help you. He has brought you to it so let him take you through it. So you pray, and I shall be praying for you. May God be with you in every decision along the way.

Sincerely,
Lola Garland

Dear Mr. President:

I am the second African-American mayor of Savannah, Georgia. I was born in Savannah in 1942 and grew up in a segregated city. As a boy, I never dreamed that I would one day be mayor of the first city in the thirteenth British colony in North America. My generation was taught that education, good character, a strong work ethic, and being ambitious would bring success. But there was always the reality of the Jim Crow system in which we lived. Dr. Martin Luther King, Jr., and other freedom fighters before him, instilled in us a new vision of the possible as we were coming out of high school. The Civil Rights Movement made it possible for me and more than 600 other African-Americans to be mayors and provide leadership for our local communities. There are thousands of other African-Americans elected to local, state, and national positions as a result of the 1965 Voting Rights Act. Young African-Americans no longer doubt that they can become mayors, governors, representatives, and senators at the state and national levels. But, there was still doubt about making that final hurtle of electing an African-American President of the United States.

Your brilliant campaign and subsequent election on November 4, 2008 to become the 44th President of the United States has removed forever the doubt in my mind and millions of others, that an African-American could be elected president. You are the fulfillment of the message in Dr. King's famous "I Have A Dream" speech that one day in America we would judge people by the content of their character and not by the color of their skin. Tomorrow, I will witness you become the most powerful man in the world as you take the oath of office.

It is very significant that you will become president the day after the national celebration of the birth of Dr. King who was our modern day Moses, not just for African-Americans but also for all humanity. You can be our Joshua, not just for African-Americans, but for all humanity. Moses had the vision and Joshua made the vision a reality. You have been given a challenge like no other president since Franklin Delano Roosevelt. You are inheriting two wars and the worse economic conditions since the Great Depression. I, like many others, believe you were anointed to be our leader in this time of crisis to guide our country out of this wilderness. We will be there to help you fulfill your campaign pledge of bringing change to America with your slogan of "Yes We Can." We will be the soldiers in your army that will continue the march toward "The Promised Land" of full equality and opportunity for all Americans.

Tomorrow, as I brave the cold to see you sworn in, I will be thinking about how James Weldon Johnson summed up the aspirations of generations of African-Americans and other disadvantaged people in the words of his song "Lift Every Voice and Sing." Tomorrow, I will "sing a song full of the faith that the dark past has taught us." I will "sing a song full of the hope the resent has brought us." I will be on the Mall "facing the rising sun of our new day begun" with your inauguration and be ready to "march on till victory is won" in the struggle to make the American dream a reality for all Americans.

Sincerely,
Otis S. Johnson, Ph.D.
Mayor
Savannah, Georgia

CHAPTER 5

Campaign Workers

Quite a few of the letter writers acknowledged the fact that they are not only enthusiastic supporters of Obama but that they even joined his campaign and/or gave money to make his historic election possible. They write of this election from those experiences.

Come on Up for the Rising!

Linda C. Tillman, Ph.D.
University of North Carolina at Chapel Hill

This essay is dedicated to the descendants of Buck and Caroline Clark

Come on up for the rising
Come on up, lay your hands in mine
Come on up for the rising
Come on up for the rising tonight.

The words opening this essay are taken from Bruce Springsteen's 2002 recording titled "The Rising" written as a reflection on the September 11, 2001, attacks on America. While I had heard the song before, I had never really paid close attention to it until I heard it at the 2008 Democratic National Convention. It came blaring through the speakers when the Democratic nominee for president of the United States, Barack H. Obama, made a surprise visit to the Pepsi Center on Wednesday, August 27. I immediately started singing the chorus, over and over again—Come on up for the rising, come on up for the rising y'all! It's time to get ready for the fight of our lives. Come on up for the rising! The rising—a new movement, a forceful movement, a determined movement, a purposeful movement. A movement that could change America in positive ways? And for me a movement to elect the first African-American president of the United States of America. I began to claim his victory right then and there!

By the time I got to Invesco Field on August 28, 2008, the 45th anniversary of the March on Washington, I was singing many of the sacred songs of my Colored/Negro/black/African-American heritage and upbringing. "Amazing Grace," "We Shall Not Be Moved," "Ain't Gonna Let Nobody Turn Me Around." And when I listened to Bernice King and Martin Luther King, III, the children of Dr. Martin Luther King, Jr., I began to sing "We Shall Overcome." I could see Mahalia Jackson singing "I've Been Buked and I've Been Scorned" at that historic event so long ago. But by the end of the awesome experience at Invesco Field, I was singing "Come on up for the rising." It was more than appropriate—there was so much hope in the air!

As I worked in the Durham for Obama campaign, the chorus became my personal battle cry. I needed to get busy, get to work, help elect Barack H. Obama the 44th president of the United States of America. When I was in a great mood during the campaign, I always sang and danced to Stevie Wonder's "Signed, Sealed, Delivered, I'm Yours" and McFadden and Whitehead's "Ain't No Stopping Us Now!" But when I was really serious, when I was trying not to get too upset about the negative attacks on Mr. Obama, and thinking about the future, thinking about the possibility of Barack H. Obama being elected the first African-American president of the United States of America, I always sang "Come on up for the rising"! Even as I cried tears of joy and frustration, my mind would return to this song.

I was fortunate to be in Washington, D.C., for the 56th Inauguration celebration. On Sunday, January 19, 2009, I attended "We Are One: The Obama Inaugural Celebration at the Lincoln Memorial." It was a fabulous event—great music, great tributes, a great celebration!

Bruce Springsteen opened the concert with "The Rising". Even in the frigid temperature I became so energized and was really Baracking and rolling! The crowd was really into the song and it set the tone for the rest of the concert. I sang the chorus the rest of the day and constantly throughout all of the festivities.

I was blessed and highly favored to attend the Inauguration of Barack H. Obama as the 44th president of the United States of America on Tuesday, January 20, 2009. As I entered the Yellow Seating Area, I looked down the street to see the motorcade forming to bring President and Mrs. Obama and their daughters Malia and Sasha to the Capitol. Members of all of the branches of the military stood waiting for our next Commander in Chief. I stood there for several minutes trying to take it all in. It was awesome. I went to find a seat as I started to sing "Come on up for the rising."

I sat in Section 9, Yellow Seating Area, and was interviewed by Byron Pitts of CBS News. Through my tears I tried to put into words what "bearing witness" that day meant to me. Admittedly I did not do a very good job—I was so overcome with emotion. But what an awesome experience it was to see Mr. Obama take the oath! No words that I will ever write can express the profoundness of being a witness to history! I was there to see the first African-American sworn in as president of the United States and the first African-American female become our First Lady! My tears of joy were and are still endless.

Despite the election of Barack H. Obama as president of the United States, I do not believe that we now suddenly live in a "post-racial" America. To the contrary, I believe that racism remains perverse and pervasive in this country. But even with that in mind, I am hopeful that African-Americans will one day be treated as human beings, rather than "others" who are less than human beings. And as I continue to rejoice in President Obama's victory, I am also mindful of his words that there is much work to be done. So I must shake off any ambivalence toward participation in the political process, attempt to be a part of the solution rather than complaining about the problems, and replace pessimism with optimism.

Now with my dream and the dreams of my ancestors Buck and Caroline Clark realized, my hopes renewed, and with a grateful heart, I'm ready to "Come on up for the rising!"

President Obama,

I have been an avid and active supporter of the Obama campaign on my campus at the University of Michigan since the primaries began. As I watched the inauguration on January 20, 2009, I was overwhelmed with feelings of pride, hope, and patriotism that I have rarely experienced during my life. You truly are an inspiration to people of all races. I applaud your success and your policies, and wish you and your beautiful family the best over the next four years.

Sincerely,
Shawn Mach

Dear President Obama,

I am so excited to have you in the White House. I've been rooting for you since the beginning, since the first time I saw you in *Time* magazine working in Africa over two years ago. It has been amazing to watch your campaign and I can't wait to see what you do as president. I worked on the campaign, and it just seemed liked the people that supported you were doing it for a greater reason, not just because they believe in the party, but because we all believe that with you change can come to this country. It already feels like people are starting to have hope in their government again, and more people are actually interested in government than ever before.

I know you have a lot on your plate going into office, with the economy and the war. But I would really like to see you work beyond our borders; expand the Peace Corps, address the issues of genocide around the world, and support good leaders of other nations, not the dictators and oil barrens our country has been known to support.

I have faith in you, like so many others. And if you could do even a quarter of the things you have promised, I think this nation can be so much better.

Good luck in the next four years,
Kelsey

Dear President Obama,

Please don't underestimate us. It would be devastating and we don't deserve it. By us and by we I mean myself, a 19-year-old college student. The generation I am a part of has always been underestimated. We've been told that we are lazy, that we have no sense of our world today, that we are inconsequential. However, if these criticisms were true you would not be our president. We devoted our time and energy to you, registering our peers and campaigning for you on our campuses and in our communities. Our recognition of how America has been perceived in recent years helped bring us to the polls. Our numbers and commitment won you this election. So please stay connected to us. Our support requires it. We are the most interconnected generation that has ever been—from e-mail, to text messages, to Facebook—and we will not tolerate being ignored. We've happily bought into your ideology of hope and optimism, but don't underestimate our realism. We understand the scope of the task you face and we'll be patient, as long as you keep us in the loop. Just be real.

Dear President Obama,

I write this to you on Tuesday, January 20, 2009—inauguration day. Today was the culmination of not only your hard work and dedication, but the hope and inspiration you have instilled in others. Your election represents many firsts. But to me, you represented something much more personal; you were the first presidential candidate I ever voted for.

As someone who became involved with your election effort in the summer of 2008, I learned a lot about myself, this country, and my fellow citizens. Whether it was making a phone call to a stranger urging them to vote or arguing with my roommate, who is a staunch conservative, I had a lot of interesting and enlightening moments during the campaign. I was very receptive to your message of change and was determined to make it a reality. On election night, I was glad to see that my small efforts paid off. While others may have donated more money, put in more time, or organized more events than I did, your campaign was the first one I participated in, and I am proud of my work.

I believe you to be an honorable, decent man who will be receptive to the needs of our country. My only request is this: please follow through on your agenda you laid out during the campaign and keep your promises. The United States is under a lot of strain right now and I think drastic changes must be made in how our country is run. That is why you were elected; we believe in you and trust you to make the necessary changes to improve our country. You know firsthand how the United States is unique in its opportunity. You yourself were fortunate enough to live the American dream. I hope you can expand this dream for many more to come.

I wish you all the best Mr. President and I know you are the right choice for the United States. I hope God is with you as your presidency unfolds. Thank you for helping me and millions of others realize that we can make a difference.

Sincerely,
Blake Ivers

Dear President Obama,

After two years of writing for you . . . blogs, letters to editors, e-mails to volunteers, requests to donors . . . when asked to write to you, I found myself ironically without words. What can be said to a man who must have heard it all? What could I add that might convey what this movement has meant to me? What remains besides to join the chorus proclaiming "Thank you Barack Obama for the change you have brought to this world"? I don't imagine it is unique, but I have only my story to share.

Like many of your supporters, my introduction to you was the 2004 Democratic Convention. Your romantic view of the United States won my heart. Yet this was not what convinced me you should run for our highest office. It was your approach in Senate hearings and your lectures during book tours that illuminated you are a thoughtful pragmatist! While I suspected you were the one to address the confusion and division of our times, I was decisively convinced as I perused your Blueprint for Change. There I saw a vision of the country I love, only better, smarter, more caring, more productive, and more inclusive. Through intense primary battles, personal upheavals, and increasing chaos in our world, you maintained an air of steady calm . . . No Drama Obama. Because of that, over 2 years of campaigning for you, I never had a moment's doubt that you were the best person for the job. Despite never having worked for or donated to a candidate before, I only continued to up the ante of my involvement with your efforts until I was, to borrow a phrase, all in.

As much of a part of my life as you became, it eventually dawned on me that I no longer woke up each morning to ask, "What can I do for Barack today?" My concerns became more about the people I encountered along the way—your supporters, the people of my city, people who were hopeful and people who needed help. I did not want to let them down. I felt like I carried the weight of their hopes with me. And I couldn't imagine, then, what pressure you must be feeling. It was at once motivating and daunting. But there came a moment when I thought: We simply cannot afford to lose. For most people I met, this wasn't about a competition; it was about survival. My reaction on election night was relief. It was not so much a celebration as an exhalation. I could finally stop holding my breath.

I have discovered that in victory there is no rest. You have hit the ground running, taking no time to savor the campaign's end. The real work has just begun. Nowhere is this more evident than in my own New Orleans. We have been living for years in a paradoxical reality. Since the hurricanes of 2005 we have been living on hope. We would not have come home to rebuild our communities without it. At the same time, there has been a sense that we are helpless to change the things that do not work here. Since we live in a state that never had a chance of delivering electoral votes to you, we essentially self-managed the local campaign with our limited resources. Far from alienating voters, what occurred was a great emergence of involvement, quite out of character from the New Orleans cliché. This is the change you have already brought to our world. People everywhere, particularly in places where it is needed most, feel like they have been invited to participate in their government. This is a true gift for us, because we have seen the damage that can result when people are not heard or get left behind.

While your message of hope has inspired us, rebuilding our city will require hard work, money, integrity, cooperation, and clear-eyed pragmatism. We need our citizens to be engaged and to demand leadership from our politicians. These are the tasks that remain and I have not taken a break from organizing towards that end. What is perhaps most remarkable about this is that as of two years ago, I was convinced our government was broken. Yet today, in a time of financial, environmental and global political crisis, I see only the possibilities. My life has been enriched with a new extended family that includes people from all walks of life, faiths, and nationalities. I am grateful for having had a chance to be a part of this incredible moment and I look forward to participating in real solutions for my little corner of the universe. I now wake up everyday anticipating your inauguration, and reflecting back to the words of Maya Angelou from an earlier one:

Here on the pulse of this new day
You may have the grace to look up and out
And into your sister's eyes, into
Your brother's face, your country
And say simply
Very simply
With hope
Good morning.

It is an unexpected delight to find myself in this new day where we have the opportunity to renew America's promise. It all comes back to that simple idea: Thank you Barack Obama for the change you have brought to this world.

With endless gratitude,
Lynda

Dear President-elect Obama,

You are an inspiration to the world. I have never been interested in politics until last year when you were running in the primaries. I began volunteering around my community registering voters all because of you. You changed so many people's ideas and I have so much hope for the upcoming 8 years.

The best of luck,
Yael

Dear President Obama,

This was my first election and I can't tell you how proud I am to be a part of history. I think the first thing I heard about you was on some news station about two years ago when a news anchor was discussing the terms on which you decided to run for president. They discussed how you wanted to run a clean campaign—at first I was a bit skeptical because that seems near impossible nowadays. I remembered that news story as the campaign went on and I noticed that your ads always remained positive and hopeful. Having a politician that is able to keep a clean campaign sparked my interest in politics. I just wanted to let you know that your campaign has had a huge affect on this country as well as an inspiring affect on me!

Mackenzie Collins

Dear President-elect Obama,

Words cannot express my gratitude for all you have already done, and all you will do for our great nation. Nonetheless, I'll try. I gladly spent my summer working as an intern for you campaign headquarters in Jackson, Michigan (the birthplace of the Republican Party and as a matter of fact, the county went blue this year), and during that time I talked with hundreds of people here. I talked to people that had lost faith in the potential we have as the American people to do great things both here at home and abroad. My experience was incredibly eye-opening since I am only 19 and was blissfully ignorant to so many people's lack of faith in our leaders. I am proud to say, however, that so many of my neighbors that I talked to told me that for the first time in a while they were beginning to believe again. To believe in the American ideals that were instilled in our country so long ago and seemed to have been forgotten about—that is, until you came along.

You've given people hope again, including me. I had no idea how I was going to pay for college without my parent's help until you announced your groundbreaking education plan to give assistance to people willing to serve our country, not only through military service but through the Peace Corps and other service organizations. This idea is truly brilliant and I cannot tell you how excited I am to one day hopefully serve our country in the Peace Corps.

So thank you, Mr. President-elect, thank you. I sincerely hope that one day you will be able to know the scope of the difference you have made and will make in people's lives. You are truly an inspiration to me as well as to millions of others here in America and around the world. God bless.

Sincerely,
Brittany

Dear President-elect Obama (it's great to be able to say that!),

After pouring our souls into a cause greater than ourselves for the past year, I feel the need to continue to help you achieve your goals for America in some way.

The cause? In my mind, it is the united people of America. If anyone can bring us together, it's you; your speech at the Democratic Convention of 2004 convinced me. Observing your strengths during the seemingly endless presidential campaign has reinforced that belief.

When I look out my window, I see a life-sized HOPE poster of you on the door across the street. In my community, there are countless doors with Obama logos on them (largely due to my canvassing efforts), and when I go to work I see my Obama-supporter colleagues still euphoric since your election, their eyes filled with hope and smiles on their faces exuding impatient anticipation of January 20th.

But how do I make naysayers aware that in your heart you have a deep, abiding love for our country and that you are and throughout your adult life always have been working for the greater good? That you nobly sacrificed a life on Easy Street to work for the poor and downtrodden? How can I be a change agent to unite my community, including those who still believe the ridiculous tripe circulated on the Internet? I'm not angry with or resentful toward these people for many of whom I feel great affection but sad for them, as they have allowed themselves to be duped. In this election, some of us did the research required to learn the truth, while others myopically bought into the notion peddled by the Right that real Americans would find you unacceptable for a host of bogus reasons contrived to put not America but their quest for power first.

How do I help those in my community (who willingly almost eagerly buy into the fallacious rhetoric spewed forth by fear and hate mongers on the Right) to see they are being used by the derisive, divisive Limbaughs and FOX News pundits, and Right-Wing bloggers who unabashedly lie about your past and your intentions, and who, without any seeming semblance of conscience have embarked upon the blatant assassination of your character? How can I show them they're pawns in a game being played for fame, power, and ratings, and that the loser is America and her people?

After searching my soul and racking my brain, I've come to the realization that as much as I want to help lessen your immeasurable burden, you are the only one who can, through your acts and deeds as our president, open the eyes and hearts of those who doubt your sincerity and good will. May God keep you safe, protect you so you can bring your vision for our nation to fruition, and lead us into a time of American brotherhood and global peace. Travel safely on this path we have chosen for you. The world needs you.

Thank you for your past, present, and future service.

Dear President-elect Obama,

First I would like to say that I have never been more proud of my country as I was the day you were elected to be the 44th president of the US I never really envisioned anyone other than white men holding that office or the office of vice president.

I have been voting since 1974 and this year is the first time I have ever been anything more than what I call a "couch voter." I use this term to define that fact that I would talk to friends, usually on my couch, read the daily newspaper, on my couch, and watch the news to get information about candidates for all offices, on my couch. Initially I was also a couch voter in this election. I supported Hillary Clinton from my couch. Then you won the primary in June. I was still on my couch. That is until I received an e-mail about an "Obama meeting" to be held in Albuquerque, NM.

I live in Gallup, NM, and that's a total of 140 miles of driving to get to a meeting in Albuquerque. So, I responded to the e-mail by asking why there couldn't be a meeting in Gallup also. Later that night, I received an e-mail from someone else in Gallup asking the same question. That writer, Bryan, and I decided to send out a mini-notice in our local paper telling of our plans to have an "Obama meeting" right here in Gallup. A few people came to that meeting, including a few Obama supporters from the Democratic caucus held here in February.

That was the beginning of me becoming a campaign volunteer. Even though I am a mother of 2 differently abled children, a wife and, a full-time teacher I still made a point of volunteering at least 4 hours a week until the election was over. I was asked to be and accepted the position of Leadership of Women for Obama in my county. I had the opportunity to hear Michelle Obama and twice see and hear you. I learned more about you and your stand on many different issues then I ever thought I possibly could or would. When another volunteer would talk to an undecided voter, often I would be asked to help close the deal, especially with members of our Navajo community. While I am not Native American, I am married to a Native American and we adopted two Navajo children. So, American Indian or First Peoples Issues are extremely important to me as well as education, women's issues, and many other things.

Since that first Obama e-mail through today, I am passionate about you and Joe Biden. I know, or at least think I know, the realities of what is possible during the first 4 years and I want to help out when and where I can even more! A group of community people and I want to work on projects to help out our community and help you do more with you job.

That brings me to my hope for you and your first term as president. As I mentioned I am a member of a Native-American family. My husband is a member of the blackfeet tribe in north central Montana and my children, ages 9 and 10, are members of the Navajo or Dine tribe. Sir, you were the first person ever to run for president who visited a reservation. I was and still am impressed by that. However, much needs to be done to help Native Peoples. IHS (Indian Health Service) is unable to do an adequate job to help Native people. Often times IHS refuses to use Indian Preference. Native Americans understand other Native Americans and their culture much better than Anglo people. Native practitioners understand that traditional medicine alone does not always heal. Yet, too many Anglo practitioners refuse to see this or allow it.

I have driven too many roads on reservations that are impassible when the rains or snows come. People are isolated from food and help. Some of my students do not have running water or electricity even today. I have some students who only get new clothes once a year when the tribe gives them one set. The students wear these clothes for a full week until it's time to go to the Laundromat. It does not matter how dirty the clothes are or how much they smell.

The rate of suicide and substance abuse is extremely high. If the rates were this high in any Anglo community the community would raise tons of awareness and get lots of help via government funding of various sorts. That happens very rarely on reservations. Tribal people are treated like they are at the bottom of the totem pole, so to speak. Yet, this country was theirs first. My people invaded these lands, slaughtered the fish and wildlife native to this country without a care in the world.

Please sir, it is time for our country to stand up and put more time, effort, and funding into helping our reservations become self-sustaining. Most reservations do not have casinos to help them out. They are isolated from main roads and more urban areas needed to make casinos run.

My children and my grandchildren are depending on you and Congress to begin with the help they need. I will help out as much as possible but the funding needs to be their first.

Thanks.

President Obama,

I remember the first time I saw you, in your 2004 Democratic Convention keynote speech. When you finished that truly inspiration speech, I said, that guy is going to be our next president, and I went out and bought an Obama '08 T-shirt. Fortunately, I was right, and you will be inaugurated this January. With an almost unprecedented economic crisis, two wars, and a damaged American reputation abroad, you have inherited the country at a difficult time, but Americans are ready to try to set aside partisan differences and work together to overcome the numerous challenges that lie ahead. Remember, stay moderate, but don't be afraid to crush the Republicans if they try to get at you. You are a baller. Keep doing what you are doing.

Dan

Dear President-elect Obama,

Congratulations! Congratulations on winning the presidential election and congratulations for making history! No matter how much people would like to believe we are living in a colorblind society, our culture has yet to reach that state. I feel your dedication and consequential elections has put our society on a path to greater acceptance for all people.

I spent this summer interning for your tri-state financial office in New York City and could not have been happier. Every day I went to work I felt like I was actually helping this cause to change America, to influence, in some little way at least, what would happen on November 4, 2008. This great experience culminated with a frantic drive to Grant Park from the University of Michigan at 8 o'clock that night. Everything was worth it: spending my summer contributing to the campaign and a total of 7 hours driving to only be in Chicago for almost 2. These memories will be with me always and the personal experiences will forever tie me to this moment in history because that is what you did: made history. So thank you for myself, those who have always supported you, those whose lives you are about to change, and even those who have yet to see your greatness; you are about to amaze the world with your abilities and I am thankful to be a part of it.

Sincerely,
Becca Walis

Dear Barack Obama,

Recently I completed a project on the problem with the popular culture trend that was started with your campaign centered on change. I saw many of my friends vote for you because they believed in this supposed *change* that you seem to promise. Without knowing much about your specific policies or how you were going to *change* the nation, people attached themselves to this trendy slogan and this political trend really took off. It seemed as if it was cool to vote for you. While I am not here to say that this *change* you promised is unrealistic and misleading, I want to commend you on your political campaign efforts and really reaching out to those who weren't previously involved in politics. Although voter turnout wasn't the highest it could've been, it still was the highest voter turnout in the past thirty years, and I want to thank you for making this happen. Your knack for becoming the most popular person in the world and ability to relate to the American public is something that is unprecedented and should truly be cherished by you. I know that I am simply a white suburban kid whose letter will most likely have zero chance of being read by you, but please take a second to realize how big of an icon you have become for the American people. You have opened up dreams for the

American people, and I really would like to thank you for that. Use your ability as this popular iconic figure to continue your positive role as an American leader. Please bring peace to this world that is in desperate need of it. I really do believe in your promise to "change" America, and I hope you do everything it takes to make this place a better country. I have all the faith in you. Good luck, Barack.

Sincerely,
David Lakin

President Obama:

As a donor to your campaign I not only feel that I've watched you win a campaign, I feel victorious as well. You have revolutionized the way candidates utilize money in campaigns, as you urged your constituency not to donate a lump sum of money, but whatever they had. I am merely 18 years old. I never thought that, at such a young age and witnessing my first real presidential election where I knew exactly what was going on, that my lowly $25 contribution could go so far. You have direction, poise, and the leadership to take this country to the next level. Never before have I felt so honored to contribute to something.

Much Luck,
Benjamin Jacobs

Dear President-elect Obama,

Congratulations and thank you for leading us to a victory. I am a constituent, supporter, and member of the Internet media (host and executive producer of *The Ironic News Report* on FearlessRadio.com, a comedic news program).

Using a quote I often heard from my Italian Nonna, I'd just like to say, "It's been 3 days and you haven't called." During the campaign, my e-mail inbox was filled with messages from you, Michelle, "Joe the Vice President," and my phone rang off the hook. I know you are probably kind of busy right now, but, well, I miss hearing from you and the gang. I still want to help. I still want to be kept abreast of the latest developments as a supporter. I still want to be involved. And I believe there are a few million others out here that feel the same way.

I know, I know there is a "media" through which you will communicate and I'm sure you will get out your message though official press conferences. But this is ME. ME; the one that donated $25 to politics for the first time ever; the one that helped my husband correspond with his relatives in Pennsylvania who were on the fence; the one that volunteered, and made the calls, and kept up with the truth behind the smears, and risked my job as a stand-up comic by doing comedy that was supportive to you while staying positive and fair in very RED states. Its ME!! And there are a lot of "MEs" out here, waiting for you to call on us to support you. We hope you make use of this huge network of support you've built. We are tired of being told to "go shopping" and leave the governing up to the officials. We want in. We don't want to be taken care of, we want to participate. We want transparency. We want community. We want you to succeed. Most of all, we just want you to call.

Sincerely,
Julianna Forlano

I wrote this letter to Barack early in the election season to express my feeling on rumors going around.

Dear Senator Obama,

I recently received an e-mail speaking of many false things. It mentioned you being a "devout Muslim" and that you did not agree with the Pledge of Allegiance. Something inside me told me that this was not the case and these accusations were false. So in rebuttal I wrote an e-mail including facts that proved all these statements wrong. When reading the "slam" e-mail I was shocked and also offended that somebody would have the nerve to say such things about you, a person who has dedicated his life to make our country great. By you running for president you are truly giving America hope and I thank you for that. It is just unfortunate that all people cannot realize that. I guess there are always going to be those who oppose leadership, it just shocks me when they oppose a leader who can and will do so many amazing things for America.

Again, I thank you for bringing hope back to America after its seven-year absence. I watched one of your amazingly inspirational speeches and I heard something that I have never heard; you were speaking, and in between the "Yes we can!" cheers I heard a cheer for the USA. As Americans we hear many cheers at baseball games and other sporting events that put us in the mood and get us pumped up about the event, but never in my sixteen years of life have I ever heard a cheer like the one that night. People were proud to live in the USA and they knew that in a short period of time they would no longer have to worry about the war and all of the corrupt policies. People are looking forward to the years to come and I am looking forward to calling you my president. YES WE CAN!

Sincerely,
Sam Hickerson
Chicago, Illinois

Dear President-elect Obama,

When I was a sophomore in high school, I took a United States government class, which did not necessarily inspire me to major in political science as I am now, but it required that every student develop an amendment to alter the U.S. Constitution. During this time (2004), I was very much opposed to the war in Iraq, which I opposed from its inception. I never understood how America could take over a country that had not attacked us. I understood attacking Afghanistan, but never Iraq. Well, I am assuming you might know what part of the U.S. Constitution I changed in my project. I took away the wording that empowered the president to be the U.S. commander in chief of the armed forces, and I instead gave the power to Congress.

I was very naïve back then, I thought that taking away this power would prohibit the president from entering into future conflicts that were pointless. I am telling you this story because I know that you opposed the war since 2002, which is about the time I opposed the war. I know that you oppose the Iraq War since you gave a very famous speech about it. I know many people will be upset if you do not withdraw troops as soon as you are officially the president. However, while I opposed going into Iraq, I do not necessarily believe we need to withdraw all forces. I worry about the Iraqi people not having a stable Democratic government. My greatest worries are for our troops, and I pray about them every night; they are strong men and women who deserve our utmost respect. I pray for their families and ask God to save these valiant, conquering heroes.

Today, I am a sophomore at the University of Michigan, which has a critically acclaimed newspaper called the *Michigan Daily*. As I am sure many newspapers do, the *Michigan Daily* maintains data about the number of soldiers who have died in Iraq. The second semester of my freshmen year, the death toll in Iraq reached 4,000. I saved the *Michigan Daily* from that day. Too many lives have been killed over a war that has no point, not to mention the lives of the Iraqi people also lost. I thank God everyday that no one close to me has died in this conflict that seems utterly pointless and frivolous.

To be blunt Mr. Obama, I supported John Edwards in the presidential primaries. He had a better program for college education—college for everyone. I know I am considered a dreamer in this respect, but my dream for America is exactly that every person who aspires to receive a college diploma should be able to try to receive one. For the pundits who say that John Edwards cheated on his wife, I say look at John McCain who also had different extramarital affairs while he was working for the navy after being a prisoner of war. Regardless of this, I am asking you to redevelop your education plan. I know that the education plan is on the back burner because of this economic downturn, but please rethink your plans. You, sir, are living the dream. Why must other people who want to live their dreams not be able to? America needs better-funded education to support the growing technologies of the future.

Speaking of the economy, I blame president Ronald Reagan for the situation we are now experiencing. He was the president who invented deficit politics, which I think, is the worst plague of our nation. I am sure you know all of this, but 60 percent of our national debt is owned by China. Do you know what happens if China drops all of our debt on the world market? Our economy will collapse, as well as the global economy. So, I ask you as well to strengthen the value of the U.S. dollar, and to restore its strength as the world's reserve currency. I also encourage you to use whatever tools you have to fix this economy. The first bailout bill will not do enough, and I am sure you know this so I am not going to lecture you about it.

Well, the issues I mentioned above are always on my mind. Now that I have taken a few U of M political science classes, I no longer wish to take the power of the commander in chief away from the president, because it would not only be severely unsafe for a president who must respond to any attack as soon as possible, but Congress would not be able to decide what action to take in a short time period. I believe the power of commander in chief will be safe in your hands when you take office. Use the power well and of course all other powers well. I have faith in you—I have faith in this great American democracy, and I have faith in this remarkable country.

Sincerely,
Theresa Anne Bodwin
P.S. I hope to meet you if I become a United States senator.

Dear President Obama,

I, like thousands of your supporters, have knocked on countless doors and made innumerable telephone calls to strangers throughout this last year. My grand-daughter and my daddy accompanied me as well as I shared your thoughts on various issues. My husband, my hero, helped throughout the year and it was him who was at our polling location at 4:30 AM setting up a canopy. As the rain poured throughout the evening he was the one standing there handing out the sample ballots. But my letter isn't really about us—it's about Joanne R. and Patti Davis.

My dad was stationed at Pearl Harbor in the mid-1960s. I attended Aliumanu Elementary and I met a beautiful blond-haired girl named Joanne R. Two of Joanne's toes on both feet were still connected and I told her she had Siamese toes. She still wore flip flops like the rest of us and we giggled as only little girls do. Joanne was the prettiest girl in our class and we were best friends. On May Day when I met her parents I was wearing my new green pleated skirt with a white ruffled blouse. My mother had fixed my hair real special that day and I remember standing by Joanne and her parents but they didn't talk very much. When we returned to school the next day Joanne wouldn't talk to me. I didn't understand her silence and all throughout the day I tried to make her laugh but she just ignored me. Our friends tried to intercede but I couldn't understand why everyone was being so mean to me. I cried and the next day was a blur. Finally one of our friends told me Joanne wasn't allowed to play with me anymore because I was a n_____ and her dad beat her because she played with me. I was mortified. I'd never heard that word before much less understood the poison it represented. Whatever it was meant I understood that was bad not because of something I'd done but because of my skin. Finally, that afternoon, standing several yards away from me, Joanne yelled at me saying she couldn't play with me anymore. She conveyed my horror that I was bad. I don't know how I got through that day but someone told me the next day Joanne got another beating because she'd spoken to me again. We never spoke again and I don't know what happened to her. Her parents may have put her in a different class because she disappeared from my life.

Mercifully, God sent Patti Davis and her wonderful family into my life the following year. Patti had brown curly hair and we were best friends. While playing baseball during PE one day I slung the bat and it knocked her two front teeth out. Blood was everywhere and I was devastated. I thought I had killed my new best friend and no one would ever speak to me again. I became physically ill and stopped speaking. A few nights later my mother told me someone was on the telephone for me. I got on the telephone and it was Patti. In a very soft voice I could barely hear Patti said she wasn't mad with me and she would be back to school soon. I can't remember what else she said but before she called I felt as if I had died a thousand deaths. Patti had braces on her teeth when she returned to school and she still wanted to be my friend. The thoughtfulness of her parents was beyond belief as they invited me to my first ever sleepover at their home. Her daddy had a picture of a man in his living room and he told me that he and that man were best friends. I didn't understand at the time why he spent so much time talking about that man to me or why he was talking to me like that but I do now. The man in the picture was the same color as me.

President Obama, both of these stories comprise everything you represent. Our country has been hurt long enough by people like Joanne's parents. Patti Davis's parents understood what Dr. King meant when he said we shouldn't be judged by our skin color but rather by the "content of our character." That festering blight of a sore in our moral character can truly begin to heal now. We can finally "walk our talk" having acknowledged what our constitution proclaims, that "all men are created equal." God has called you to lead our country to the next level and my family is thrilled to welcome you to 1600 Pennsylvania Ave. You, your family, vice president Joe, and his family are in our prayers.

The Carolyn Jenkins Family

December 22, 2008

Dear President Obama,

I wanted you to know how much your campaign and win means to me as an African-American wife, mother, former labor organizer, and political science professor. Right now, I am so overcome with emotion—pride, joy, hope, inclusion, redemption—that I hope what I have to say to you just comes out right. I feel like I know you because through you there are the hopes of so many in the fabric of the patch work of what we call America. The Democratic Convention of 2004 was your introduction to the world, but for me it was a glimmer of hope. My son was four at the time and halfway into your speech he jumped up off of the couch and said, "Mommy, I want to be like him." He was glued to the TV and mesmerized, as were I and the friends and family watching. When you closed your speech a friend of mine and I both said at the same time, "There goes the first black vice president." We could not wrap our minds around the possibility of president, but maybe, just maybe, America would be willing to take baby-steps to elect a black vice president.

After Kerry's presidential defeat of 2004, I remember going to class the next day, partially in shock that Bush had won again and somewhat depressed about the future of America, but, the glimmer of hope was your victory and my graduate school colleagues and I felt that we had to hold tightly to that shred hope. I recall my professor, a child of the civil rights era still bearing scars of growing up in a segregated society as a second-class citizen, bitterly respond to a fellow classmate who said, "Well at least we have Obama," her reply, "And what's he going to do?" We all left class crushed and silenced.

When you announced in February of 2007 your candidacy for president of the United States I was elated. The dark cloud of the Bush years seemed to be clearing and for the first time, in a long time, I began to want to be involved. A political scientist who is disgusted with politics is an occupational nightmare that I had been sulking in since 2004. After your announcement, my son and I went to your Web site and printed out picture and we made homemade posters to hang in his room. I recall his babysitter saying to me, "Y'all voting him?" The next week I played your announcement speech for my American government classes and they also felt the same optimism I did. There were of course the skeptics that believed that America would never elect a black man to be president and I would respond, "We have to have faith. We have to have hope." The community college where I work is about

90 percent black so over the next several months heated debates dominated the hallways, offices, classrooms, and lunchrooms between the ones who hoped—the post–civil rights generations and the ones who just could not allow themselves to believe—the pre–civil rights generations. I found myself wondering why the older ones could not support our dreams, our expectation for what was possible, our aspirations to finally become part of the American dream. Maybe it was because of so many disappointments, maybe because of fear, maybe it was conditioning? Whatever it was, it was a painful reminder of the lingering shadow of our horrid past, like a wound that never fully heals and when you bend or stretch or it gets cold, it begins to ache.

The day after your Iowa win I remember driving to work with a smile and the feeling that all things were possible. In class I noticed that the students had a new-found pride, a sense of aspiration that I had never seen before in my seven years of teaching. All of the sudden politics was relevant and issues were discussed and debated without my prod. I encouraged the students to get involved, donate, make phone calls, canvass, and most importantly, vote. Every debate and primary became a feature of the week that we rushed home to watch with such anticipation. We all made donations—some as little as $5 and some much more but we all owned a piece of the campaign, we all had a stake in the outcome.

My good friend that I trained with as a labor organizer for SEIU over twelve years ago called me in July from Denver. She had been working on a voter registration campaign. I had no idea I was in for the shock of my life. "If you can get a way to Denver, I have a convention ticket with your name on it," she said. I think I stopped breathing for a minute. As we sat in the upper northwest section at Invesco Field, we talked about the nobility of being an organizer and reminiscing over campaigns we had worked on after college. I felt so encouraged that the Democratic nominee was a man who was truly a man of the people, who understood the struggles of everyday people and had served in the trenches. That day was so magical. There was a young black man that sat a few seat over from us with a UNITE/HERE T-Shirt and he was calling everyone in his family with such excitement. I finally said to him, "You are really excited," and he responded, "I could hardly sleep last night, I never thought I would be here, an eye-witness to history." I shared his emotion but the thing that touched me the most was when I looked around and I saw blacks, whites, Latinos, Asians, Native Americans, Arabs, and we were all waving American flags and we were all united as we watched your speech and for the first time in my life, I felt like I was really part of America. Not just an African-American, but an American. Period.

The days leading up to the general election I had so much anxiety. I wanted you to win so badly. I was so invested in your campaign—my time, my money, my hope. My son, my husband, and I prayed for your safety and victory for months and this was it. The weekend before the election I had made phone calls at your campaign office and was so inspired by the excitement and responses. Sunday, I remember watching Ballot Bowl on CNN and feeling how much of a loss it would be for America if we could not hear your voice everyday, if we allowed prejudice, bigotry, intolerance, and fear to override change, hope, and a new direction for the future. Tuesday, I worked the polls and so did my mother. I was encouraged at the long lines of young and old pulling into the polling place with Obama bumper stickers. Although we had a watch party on campus, I was too nervous and I did not want my students to see me on edge. So I went home and flipped the remote from CNN, to MSNBC, to ABC, from TV to TV all around the house. My husband and son had the DVRs on different time delays and I kept yelling, "I need real time." First Pennsylvania and Florida victories, then finally Ohio. At that moment I knew you were president. I did not have to wait for the West Coast. All the emotions rushed out of me through tears of joy. The phone rang off the hook as family and friends cried, yelled, jumped up and down—out of breath. It was like we had all given birth to a dream. I felt like America had said, "We accept you," "You too are American," "Let us show the world that we are ready to overcome our past and forge a new future." At that moment, my heart began to heal. So Mr. President, thank you for being a model husband, father, and leader. When my son was born, I wanted him to become president one day. Now I know that is really possible.

God Bless You and Keep You and Your Family,
Aisha Haynes-Belizaire
College Park, Georgia

CHAPTER 6

Election Night

These letters contain detailed descriptions and discussions of the euphoria, happiness, and sheer joy that swept over the University of Michigan college campus, and elsewhere, when Obama was declared the winner of the 2008 presidential election. These letters are full of emotion and capture the feelings and sentiments of Americans when our country turned another page in her political history.

Dear President-elect Obama,

This was the first election that I was able to vote in, and I must say that I am very pleased with its outcome.

Best Wishes,
Rebekah

Dear President Obama,

When I went to go vote for the first time in my life on November 4, 2008, I had no idea what an amazing experience it would be. I expected it to be like when I went with my parents when I was little, where there were no lines and you just walked in and voted. Instead, I voted in my dormitory at the University of Michigan, and the line was out the door all day. I waited two hours to vote, along with my peers. But everyone was devoted to voting; very few saw the long lines and turned around. Our generation finally had an impact on our government. We saw that change needed to happen and we took charge. Unlike our parents and grandparents, we aren't divided along racial or gender lines. We are sick of what our government has become; we wanted something different. And we achieved that through you. I want to thank you for inspiring this vigor within not only the youth of the nation but within so many people. On the night of the election, I watched hours of it on my little TV in my dorm room, along with many of my friends from my hall. When they announced that you had won, people went crazy. It was one of the greatest, most memorable experiences of my life. I will never, ever forget that. Everyone was hugging in our hall, and when we heard your speech, we started to cry. I finally had hope for our country and for the American people. I still remember the text message my mom sent me when you won. It said, "How does it feel to be an American?" I felt proud to be an American. I still do. So thank you, and I have great hopes for you. Also, being a native of Detroit, where everyone if affiliated with the Big Three in some way, I ask that you try your hardest to save them. I cannot even imagine what Detroit will be like without the auto industry, and, unfortunately, we are getting a glance of that right now. Times are tough right now, especially in Detroit. We cannot lose the Big Three, and we cannot lose any more jobs in this city. It is a great city, and I am proud to be a Detroiter, but we need help. I hope that you help the auto industry and hopefully Detroit will someday be a prosperous city again, because the people of Detroit are unlike any other in this country. Thank you for your courage and your inspiration, and thank you for not forgetting about the youth, as so many previous presidents have. Thank you for seeing us and for reaching out to us. It sure made a difference. Also, if you could find a way to help the Lions, that would be greatly appreciated. They definitely need more help than I can give them right now.

Sincerely,
Katie Rinkus

Dear President-elect Barack Obama,

My name is Caroline Humphrey, and I am a freshman at the University of Michigan. I am so honored to be writing to you, as your election was truly an inspiring experience for me. The 2008 election was the first election that I participated in, and I was so happy to believe that I helped make a change and a difference in this country. The University of Michigan truly erupted after CNN's confirmation you winning the election, and I joined probably 5,000 students who ran around Ann Arbor screaming, cheering, crying, singing, and simply celebrating the change and hope we all had so desperately desired. I didn't come back to my dorm from that night until 2:00 in the morning, but it was so worth it. I hope that in your travels you will be able to stop by the University of Michigan campus at some point, because the students here worked so hard for your campaign in order to secure your victory. I wish you the best of luck and am certainly looking forward to the next four years ahead, and I know that you can make this country a better place. I also hope to be a member of your 2012 campaign, which is the year I will be graduating from college, most likely with a political science major.

Congratulations, and thank you for being such an incredible man.

Sincerely,
Caroline E. Humphrey

Dear President Obama,

I would first like to congratulate you for your inspirational victory. I live in an extremely diverse college dormitory where we all shared in a spontaneous and emotional celebration as your victory was announced on election night. Since I just turned 18, this was the first election I could vote in. I am proud that I had the chance to participate in this historical election. The fact that your victory was based on your platforms rather than your race shows how far America has come in closing the gap of racial inequality. I had the privilege of meeting you two years ago as part of a group of Illinois high school students chosen to spend a week in Washington. Even then, before you ascended to the national stage, you inspired so many of us to pursue public service. I am currently studying political science at the University of

Michigan and hope to spend the coming summer working in Washington, D.C. I am excited for your upcoming inauguration and know that the next four years hold so much promise for all of us.

I wish you much success,
Alison Pollack

Dear President Obama,

I'm ecstatic to see all of the work that you have done in just forty-eight hours of occupying the White House. Your proactive attitude inspires us all and gives me faith in your ability to lead this nation. Since 9/11, the people of this country have become tired and weary of the War on Terror. Furthermore, the financial crisis has only worsened the situation for many at home. By taking office and immediately engaging the issues, which you have campaigned so long for, it shows the American people how much resolve you have to actually make a change and improve the lifestyle of every American.

While I voted for you because of your big plans, ideas, and the call to action for change, I also voted for you because of the way you have inspired the youth in this country. As a college student on the University of Michigan campus, I watched on November 4th as hundreds of students flooded the streets. The profound impact that this election had on thousands of students just like me brought me to the point of being at a loss for words. As I walked to the Michigan Union to get Pizza Hut after a fraternity meeting, I heard people running out buildings literally screaming with joy. Students ran down South University and filled the Diag, all the time chanting "USA, USA, USA," the Michigan fight song, the National Anthem, or "Yes We Did!" In my suit and tie I ran and joined the masses as we marched through the streets. At that moment, despite all of the critics that said you would not live up to your plans, I knew that you had already changed much more than just the party in government. Mr. Obama, you have inspired the next generation of politicians, leaders, and entrepreneurs. Citizens who voted just four years earlier were astounded at the sheer quantity of people at the polls to vote. Presidential nominee McCain did not have that impact. Not on us.

With my words of praise in mind, the only favor I can ask of you is that you continue to do what you have claimed: Change. Obviously, in the first week, two weeks, or even two months the press will have an eye on every bill you sign and every rule you change, and it will give the appearance that change is occurring. But don't let up. There are issues that cannot be changed in a day, and there are many who say that you will not change them. I pray to God that you do it. I want the optimistic phrase, "Yes We Can!" to become a part of every American's vernacular. I fear that right now our populace is negative with the financial crisis and our overseas conflicts. I wish that you will find solutions to these things, give our people jobs, and restore our confidence.

All the best,
Stephen

Dear President Obama,

CONGRATULATIONS!! I was so proud on November 4th to be able to say that I was a first-time voter and that I voted for you. I am a freshman at the University of Michigan, and when CNN announced that you were the projected winner, it was magical to hear all of the people in the dorms screaming out of joy. They were screams of hope.

I have faith in you, and know that you will do wonders for our country!

Good luck.
P.S. I hope your dog is cute!

President Obama:

Like so many other Americans, I decided for the first time in my life to financially support a candidate for president. My decision was not simply based on the fact that you were African-American because we have had other candidates. However, it was the first time that I felt an African-American was running for president who truly believed he could win. It was your confidence coupled with your credentials that led me to dig deep into my pocket and give.

As a small-business owner, many of my associates could not understand why I would support someone whose economic policies would be adversarial to me. I simply told them, "To whom much is given, much is required." Given the fact that the Republican Right claims to be so faith based you would think this would not be a foreign Principle to them. In truth, I think they selectively choose when to apply their faith (i.e., pro-life yet support capital punishment). These same associates of mine warned me in advance how badly they planned to ridicule me if Senator McCain were to win. I just heard their comments and rants for weeks and turned a deaf ear to them. At times, I engaged the more rational ones with thoughtful and sometimes prolonged dialogue.

So on the night of the election, my wife and I watched every single return come in. We prayed not just for you to be elected but rather we prayed "that if you were the Christian you claimed to be and were right for the country and world that God would give you victory—give us victory." At 11 PM my wife cried and I stood silent in disbelief. Overjoyed, we called our parents and siblings and shared our excitement with one another for hours upon hours. On my way to bed around 3 AM I went into the room of my 3-year-old daughter and I whispered in her ear, "Tonight history was made. Tonight America and the world has changed forever. Tonight you truly can be anything you want to be."

The next day my Republican associates and I were gathered at a meeting and many told me they were waiting on me to gloat and brag. I told them they had it all wrong. Gloating was not what I felt like doing. I just felt proud of America, and I just felt proud of you! Thank you for allowing my family and me to have these feelings. Thank God for you.

Dear President Obama,

Before election night, I was truly confused as to who I wanted to become our 44th president. When I went to vote, I literally had to pause, unsure what to do. While I ultimately voted for you, as I watched the election results come in, I was still uncertain of how I felt. If I had any doubts, they vanished the moment that I looked out my window at the University of Michigan and saw hundreds of my fellow classmates in tears of joy, running down the street. I followed a long stream of students to the center of our campus, where flags were waving, around a thousand students were chanting, and a percussion line was giving the event an energy that I simply cannot describe. I was officially won over when I looked around at my classmates who had campaigned so hard, and could not control their emotions, as everyone realized that we, the youth, had helped make history. As the mass group of students literally paraded through the streets, shutting them down, pausing to stop and sing that national anthem in front of the university president's house, I realized that what I was experiencing would probably be the one thing that I remember most about college. Someday when I am talking to my grandchildren, maybe I will have had time to find the words to describe to them the energy and rush of emotions that all of us felt as we celebrated your victory. Thank you for giving hope to so many people, and the unity that I felt that night is a feeling that can never be taken away from me. My support is yours.

Sincerely,
Samantha Cook
University of Michigan

President Obama,

The moment came. As CNN made its official prediction that Barack Obama would be the 44th president of the United States, my housemate and I embraced, tears forming in our eyes. We soon heard shouts and screams from our next door neighbors, so we ran outside to join in the celebration. The four consecutive houses down from ours each was celebrating in their own way. A group of guys hugged each other; a group of girls stood in front of the television with their front door open, transfixed; a lone celebrant ran into the intersection of State Street and Hoover in Ann Arbor, popped a champagne bottle, and did a victory dance. Soon, all the neighbors had converged in the middle of the street, myself and my roommate included. The group began to jump and shout as one. Soon we broke into groups and danced, tears of happiness resting in the corners of our eyes. Swing dance, hip-hop—cultures combined in a celebration of the progress that America had made, and in our collective ability to hope again.

It is because of you, President Obama. There is not a candidate from either party that could have inspired a nation in the way that you have. Your youth, your eloquence, your compassion, your vision—you have mobilized my generation in a way that forever indebts me to you, and I thank you.

Now, as you said in your acceptance speech, we must unite. Winning the election was only a small part of the battle. Major changes must be made, and in this letter I would like to ask for your help in successfully reforming policies relating to three issues that are of utmost importance to me: the wars in Iraq and Afghanistan; education; and health care. Please reform the two domestic issues of education and health care, and internationally, please try to rebuild America's soft power that we seem to have squandered away.

I have faith in you, President Obama.

Yours in service,
Katelyn

Dear President Obama:

On election night a television pundit asked what was going to happen to your amazing campaign organization. I knew immediately what I hoped.

Mr. President, please turn Obama.com into Obama.gov. Keep us informed, pick our brains, and call us to action. Let us know just what our country needs and what we can do to help.

You've revolutionized campaigning. Now revolutionize governance.

After years of exclusion, this change could not be more profound for our democracy.

All the best,
Chris

Dear President Obama,

It gives me chills just writing this. November 4 through 5, 2008, has been history-making. My hubby and I woke up and went to the polls. As I stood in the booth, it took me a second to realize that I was voting for a presidential candidate whose skin pigmentation was the same as my own. I had to pause and take in the moment. The whole day was "different." People seemed a lot happier. There was more camaraderie than usual. I don't really know how to explain it . . . I guess the word was "united." That night, I sat on the couch with my husband and my beagle watching the TV like I've never seen it before. And, when 11:00 (est) came around . . . it happened. We were in awe. It was almost blissful. All we could do is smile and hold each other as the tears fell. Never in our lifetime did we believe it could happen in this country. It made us realize that we had come a long way. We weren't alive during the civil rights movement, but we know the significance of it. Now, we have experienced our own history-making event. The night that President-elect Barack Obama was announced the future 44th-president of the United States.

The next day, I went to work and no one was really working. People were just talking, smiling, laughing, and crying. We all have been filled with so many emotions. I don't think I've ever experienced anything like it. People who are black, white, Indian, Hispanic, Asian, etc., were happy that you are the President-elect of the United States!

I know you understand the significance, but to us . . . it's MINDBLOWING. Not just because you are a man who has the same skin pigmentation as me and my hubby; but, because you are so much MORE than that. You are an educated man who proved that it really is about the content of your character and not the color of your skin. You proved that race does not have to matter in this country. You proved that running on a platform of the issues that impact our society, unity, and togetherness can win. You proved that my future children can one day strive to be POTUS and it would not be just a pipe dream. You give the country hope for a better tomorrow. You have changed many people's outlook on America and the World. No matter what happens in these next four years, you have changed all of our lives. All I can do is say, "Thank You!" and we'll do our part to make the change happen.

Sincerely,
Beverly J. Ampy

Dear President-elect Obama,

On the night of your election, I was working on a presentation for class until 2 AM that I had to give at 8 AM. I watched the results from my laptop while my group and I rehearsed and finalized our project. Every time I heard a scream from the dorm across the street, or cars honking, I shook my head, because I didn't vote for you.

Walking home, there were several people celebrating on the Diag, and cars driving around honking, late into the night. I felt left out. Why didn't I vote for you? I liked McCain's view of cutting government compared to your increasing government programs. From all I have witnessed, government is inept. The government can't improve just by increasing funding to broken programs. Hopefully that is not what you do.

I have hope you can improve this country. You already have given lots of hope. Although I didn't vote for you, I have faith that your intelligence can only move this country in the right direction.

I wish you luck.

Dear President Obama,

I want you to know that I have faith in you. I know the United States is not in a very good place right now and it's going to be very difficult to turn that around, but I believe that if there's anyone out there that can bring us back into the light, it's you. I have never seen something so inspiring as the pep rallies that took place the night of the election; it was an amazing feeling, to finally know that our country is headed in the right direction.

Dear President Obama,

I spent the night after your election became official at the University of Michigan's Diag, along with about 1,000 other students. We celebrated, cheered, played drums, marched down streets, all to celebrate the election of a candidate we believed finally deserved to enter the White House.

However, many people are still nervous in these days leading up to your inauguration. Many find it hard to believe that someone so well spoken, and especially someone appearing to be so moral, could actually enter the political scene. The general underlying feeling behind every voter's sense of triumph at your election is that twinge in the gut suggesting this may be too good to be true.

But we believe in you. And we have hopes for this country that we believe you can realize. This land has more unrealized potential than any of us can imagine.

Don't let us down.

Don't screw up.

Show us how great a place the world can truly be.

Dear President Obama,

On the night of the election, it was mayhem in Ann Arbor. Students were literally running through the streets with tears streaming down their cheeks. I was one of these students. For many of us it was our first election, and to have created history as we did is something that we will never forget. For many of us you are a beacon of hope, of change, of a new era. My dad tells me this joke about you, "Obama is on vacation, and do you know what he's doing there? Learning to walk on water." Many people are drawing comparisons between you and legends like JFK, Lincoln, and, although just a joke, Jesus. They are expecting you to turn America into what it used to be. Not a land of bailouts and foreclosed houses, but of hope and dreams. Good luck. My advice to you is don't get overwhelmed. You are just a man; you can't do everything in one day though it may seem like you need to. Keep in mind what and who your policies will affect and please work hard to further the best interests of the United States.

Thank you.

Dear President-elect Obama,

I am writing first of all to congratulate you on win. You ran one of the best campaigns and utilized all citizens. I believe that you have single-handedly changed American politics and I hope this is something you keep as a priority in your administration. Not in a long time have citizens of all ages and backgrounds been as motivated as this election to get involved. My generation especially has never participated as much as in this election. I have witnessed even in my sorority, a place where I did not believe people cared about politics at all. The majority of my sorority sat in our TV room, a place where people normally come together to watch movies or *Gossip Girl*, all night to watch the polls on election night. I believe your campaign motivated my friends, who normally might not even vote, to participate.

Having said that, I hope that you keep this positive energy and influence well into your tenure in office. I hope that you include citizens in the democratic process as much as you did during your campaign. Politics should not be reserved for the few people with enough money to win elected office. I hope that you listen to the people who helped on your campaign as much now when dealing with issues of foreign policy, like you listened to them when they were going door to door for you.

Lastly, I would like to thank you for appointing Hillary Clinton as secretary of state. This shows that you are willing to have diverse viewpoints in your cabinet considering there is nothing the two of you disagreed on more than foreign affairs. Considering there is a majority of Democrats in the Senate and House and Oval Office, I hope you continue to surround yourself with diverse thinkers to do what's best for this nation.

Thank you,
Sara Winik

Dear President Obama,

I'm so delighted that you will be our next president. Your victory was unbelievably amazing. I go to the University of Michigan and after you officially won, I ran down to the Diag to celebrate with fellow students. There must have been at least 300 students there, just smiling, laughing, dancing, and hugging about your triumphant victory. It was incredible.

It's time for a change in Washington, and I believe that you can help make that change. One thing you should particularly change is our current environmental policy. Our environmental policy is insufficient; it does not promote sustainability and is not proactive. We can't rely on technology alone to save us from the possibly disastrous changes that lay ahead. Our standards of living must be changed and that's where you come in: with effective policies, rules, and regulations, your administration can make it against the law to NOT be environmentally friendly. I know this is a daunting and general task, but it is not impossible. You should look to other countries, such as Switzerland and Germany, for guidance and ideas.

Good luck,
Molly Cohen

Dear Mr. President Barack Obama,

November 4, 2008, was the first time I ever voted in a presidential election. For that matter, I guess it was the first time I voted in any election, at least besides Homecoming Queen in high school (which I didn't win, by the way) and a near vote for "American Idol," so I guess you could call this my biggest election to date.

As a sophomore at the University of Michigan this election was the first for many of my fellow students as well, and I am proud to say that of my closest friends and I, four out of five cast our votes for you. The fifth doesn't have her citizenship yet, so don't let that get you down; she's from Chicago so I think we both know which way she would have voted had she been able to.

I wish I could give you some words of wisdom here, Mr. President, but you've done just fine so far without my advice, so somehow I think you'll be okay. What I would like to tell you, however, is that I live several blocks from the Diag in Ann Arbor, and that even from that distance I could still hear the crowd celebrating for more than an hour after your victory was announced. I'd like to tell you that as I walked around campus on November 4, 2008, I saw more students than not wearing "I Voted" stickers, and wearing them with pride. I'd like to tell you that no matter what happens during your presidency, what I will always remember is the feeling I had when I cast my vote for the first time, and the expression I saw on so many young faces after you won the election that night. What I would like to tell you is this: before your term has even begun, you have managed to make a positive difference in so many lives, and for what it's worth, I am already impressed.

Congratulations, Mr. President, and good luck. You certainly deserve them both.

Sincerely,
Anna Brown

President Obama,

First and foremost, I want to congratulate you on your well deserved and exciting victory as becoming our next president. Politics seems like a game sometimes because of all the dirty competitiveness of it but you stuck to the point through all of it. The country is in the dumps and you want to do your best to get us out of it. That's the point. Not what you wear or what your last name is. I was in my college dorm room when I heard that you won. I heard people screaming in joy for hours after, everybody gathering around a TV to watch your acceptance speech. I was very excited but I didn't cheer or scream; I just felt so much better. The worry that I could feel in my stomach was gone because I know that even though you will not be a miracle worker, the country will be in great hands in moving to repair the damage that has been made and left to rot. The main point of this letter was really to apologize. I am sorry that so many people had so much cynicism, even hate, towards you not because of your plans for the country, but because of your name, race, and even past associations that went wrong. I always sensed your sincere love for this country and am deeply sorry that others did not. Every time I saw you on television, whether it was for a debate or an interview, you looked exhausted but performed amazingly. I admire your perseverance and determination, it is truly inspiring. I wish you all the luck and want you to know that I, among millions, have faith in you President Obama.

Sincerely,
Lorin Shirwani

Dear President-elect Barack Obama,

It is with great honor to congratulate you on becoming the first African-American president of the United States of America. The people have spoken. You are the new leader, the new commander in chief, and the new person to lead the greatest country in the world. I congratulate you.

I come from a very Republican family but, I myself, am not Republican. I like to think of myself as a person open to everything and anything, a person with no party affiliation and no agenda.

But here I am not going to discuss anything party-related or anything about your campaign or the political process or anything like that. I want to tell you my story, the night you became president.

I attend the University of Michigan, in my biased opinion, the best school in America. On that Tuesday night, I was sitting in the Law Library on campus with a few friends, catching up on some much-needed studying. The time was about 11:45 PM and you had already been declared the winner. I didn't feel happy for you nor was I dismayed at the outcome. I was just happy it was over. I am one American, like many others, who wants to see the United States restored to its fullest potential: economically, politically, culturally, and socially.

That night, while sitting in that library, all four of us heard some noise outside. We thought that it would stop. It didn't. So we walked outside, out into the Law Quad and onto South University Street. What we witnessed was incredible. Students were marching: black, white, Asian, Mexican, of all races, ethnicities, and religious affiliations. They were marching for you.

You represent something the American people have longed for since the 1860s. You represent progress. You are a symbol for everyone in the United States. That night, students sang, cried, banged drums, honked car horns, and yelled your name all night.

You are the face of the American people and you are what so many people in this country are looking up to. Take this new opportunity and embrace it. Take this newfound position and lead this country. Everyone is expecting great things from you, President Obama.

As they say, "The ball's in your court."

You just need to take that ball and run with it.

NOTA BENE: This letter was composed as an e-mail to my Morehouse brothers, friends, and family on the afternoon of November 5, 2008, upon awakening from serving a 24-hour call shift the night before (Election Night 2008). I sincerely hope President Obama gets to read this . . . so, twenty years from now when someone asks me, "Where were you when Barack Hussein Obama was elected 44th president of the USA?" I will have a story unique to most Americans.

I did not have the benefit of being at a watch party, popping bottles, or clowning directly on unsupportive white folks I grew up around and that surround me daily. No, I was in the midst of supplying anesthesia to a middle-aged Caucasian gentleman with liver cancer, who came to my hospital to receive a liver transplant. Here I was, Okera sekou Hanshaw, a Mississippi native who graduated 5th in his class, top amongst blacks at his high school; a Morehouse College and University of Michigan Medical School graduate, and current trainee in the Henry Ford Anesthesiology Program, saving a previously unknown Caucasian man's life. I have no idea his political, personal, cultural, or social views, but being there, standing over him placing a large bore intravenous catheter into his neck, knowing that Barack Obama had just won Pennsylvania and the ramifications of such, I gained more perspective . . .

As the case wore on, which lasted from about 8:45 PM until 4 AM, I felt the constant buzzing of my Treo ringing on my hip as friends and family hit me up to celebrate, yell, scream, cry, and express emotion over this historic and meaningful event. I gained perspective on where I am and what I am doing here. Since I was young, I was taught to value my name and its meaning ("a likeness to God" and "fighter"), my ethnicity, my heritage, and all the fruits that were coming to harvest for me and mine because we EARNED it—no handouts, just hard work and togetherness of mind and people. As I looked around the OR and once again took personal note of the fact that I was once again the only African-American present, this great event of our lives started to mean more to me than the confirmation of "I told you this was gonna happen" lip service that I had been giving dissenting colleagues. I started to hear the reflections of the stories of the civil rights movement in which my parents and grandparents participated . . . I reflected on the stories of Emmitt Till, Medgar Evers, the Little Rock 9, Martin King and Malcolm X, even flashes of readings of the Middle Passages and slavery. . . . y'all I tell you I became so swept up, so enthralled in this new future for us all, it was very difficult to contain myself.

But I had to . . . and you know I was a bit bitter that I could not celebrate in Chicago or hug some friends and family . . . No, I celebrated silently in my call room, watching the McCain concession speech, which actually was a good one until people there started booing . . . that solidified it all for me . . . how bad off we would have been if he had stolen or pulled this election out . . . Notice which one I put first. But America finally got it right.

I know many of you have shared this unique moment with your family and friends, and I am happy and proud to have you to share it with, by text and e-mail. Just realizing how far we have come keeps ringing in my head everyday. I can only imagine just how our parents truly feel, who had to watch 2 if not 3 potential movers like Obama (MLK, JFK, and RFK) go down to senseless gunfire. Let's continue to pray that it doesn't come to that . . .

I went to bed after getting home around 9:30 AM, and I grabbed a shower, poured some Frosted Flakes, and lay in the bed, watching the different news stations for replays and what not. I finished my bowl, but thought that I had spilled milk on myself because my hands were wet. They were wet with tears—tears of feeling "freed," vindicated, RIGHT, justified, CERTIFIED, and BLESSED that this has happened, to me, to us, to the world. WE got to see this during our life time. This ranks very highly in the most important events in this my short life thus far on Earth. How many times have we seen an ENTIRE WORLD react to a presidential election? I don't recall people in Germany or Indonesia reacting to any of the last 12 years of elections, the way they showed it last night. And these were no small watch parties. Moreover, I have yet to return a phone call about this moment, as I am just waking up. But I needed to share this with you all because this person—Barack Obama—and this movement comes around once in a lifetime. . . . I'm expecting great things, and a lot of good that isn't monopolar.

Thanks for reading. We did it, and let's keep on doing it.
Okera

January 19, 2009

Dear President-elect Obama,

On November 4, 2008, I was one of many Chicagoans waiting with anticipation as you prepared to give your victory speech that night as it closed in on midnight—to honor our Nation in becoming our nation's 44th President-elect. As you delivered remarks to the hundreds of thousands who turned out to witness this historic event it seemed as if the entire population of the city had descended on Grant Park that night to hear your words of hope. One could not help but believe that we had finally come together as a people, confirming the promise of America as you said: "If there is anyone out there who still doubts that America is a place where all things are possible; who still wonders if the dream of our founders is alive in our time; who still questions the power of our democracy, tonight is your answer."

Your victory reminded all that witnessed history that night exactly what was the promise of America. Our founding fathers were willing to invest their hopes and dreams and indeed even sacrifice their lives and their honor—for a set of ideals that continues to be a beacon of hope to the world. In our society all men are created equal and our rights to life, liberty, and the pursuit of happiness are inalienable rights and the fundamental precepts of our democracy. Most of all your election to the presidency represents the power of the individual to instigate change and renew the promise of America.

As we witnessed the throngs that had assembled that victorious night in Grant Park, this scene brought to mind the words of President-elect John F. Kennedy in a speech delivered to a "Joint Convention of the General Court of the Commonwealth of Massachusetts" on January 9, 1961, as he spoke about the task of constructing an administration. He said that he had been guided by the standard John Winthrop set before his shipmates on the flagship Arbella 331 years ago, as they, too, faced the task of building a new government on a perilous frontier. "We must always consider," he said, "that we shall be as a city upon a hill . . ." the eyes of all people are upon us."

On November 4, 2008, Chicago became the metaphorical city upon a hill and the eyes of all people were upon our city as you and all who witnessed your historic election renewed the promise of America. Your election to the presidency represents a defining moment in human history; when our nation has responded to the call to reject partisanship and come together with a common purpose to conquer the challenges we now face as a nation that again threaten our democracy. Washington has become beset by partisan politics and has come to serve the interests of the few. I believe that you emerged as a leader because in these divisive times of war, economic recession, and failed leadership, both from the corporate sector and the White House, your message of bipartisanship, has united us. We can only meet these challenges if we come together as one people. The vitality of our democracy will involve first and foremost the hard work and dedication of all Americans to improving the lives of ordinary citizens affordable health care, rebuilding our cities infrastructure, investing in green technology, and making higher education more accessible and affordable to the average American. These things are all aspects of reclaiming our right to life, liberty, and the pursuit of happiness. In order for the United States to continue to compete in the global economy we first need to direct our attention to the needs of the American people that have been neglected over the past eight years due to the war in Iraq, bailing out failed institutions, and exporting jobs overseas.

Your election represents not only a renewal of the fundamental principles of our democracy, but a new era which departs from the cynicism, partisanship and apathy of the last eight years and towards a more bipartisan effort to solve the overwhelming issues that currently confront us. As President Kennedy stated in his inaugural address (January 20, 1961): "We dare not forget today that we are the heirs of that first revolution. Let the word go forth from this time and place, to friend and foe alike, that the torch has been passed to a new generation of Americans proud of our ancient heritage and unwilling to witness or permit the slow undoing of those human rights to which this nation has always been committed, and to which we are committed today at home and around the world."

Sincerely,
Jeffrey Brown

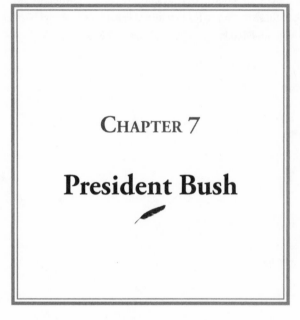

CHAPTER 7

President Bush

A few of the letter writers compare and contrast the hope that surrounds and finds root in the election of Obama to the gloom and disillusionment associated with the outgoing Bush administration. In their critiques, these letters provide a background and context for the role and function campaign slogans, such as change, hope and "Yes We Can," played in inspiring and motivating the electorate.

Mr. President,

I would first like to congratulate you on this extraordinary and historic victory. As a supporter and moreover as an American citizen this was the first election where I truly felt proud of my decision after leaving the voting booth. You have so much work ahead of you in the coming months and years. Everything from our national economy, and particularly our economy here in the rustbelt, to the international blight that is Guantanamo, to our misguided wars that are leaving our brothers and neighbors in harm's way, and finally to the restoration of our shredded Constitution, I hope and trust that you are up to this task.

Mr. President, I have but one request, and it is a substantial one; I ask that you seek criminal charges against your predecessor and his outgoing administration. In the past weeks our former president and vice president have issued statements admitting to their roles in the utilization of torture, under the guise of enhanced interrogation. I have been following the abuses at Gitmo and at Abu Ghraib for several years. I am aware that under U.S. law torture is illegal, that under International law torture is illegal, and that our treaties, despite the Bush administration's best efforts to dismiss them, are in fact binding. President Bush, Vice President Cheney, former Secretary of Defense Donald Rumsfeld, and a host of others are guilty not only of a perverse reading of our Constitution and the powers bestowed to the executive branch, they are guilty not only of going a little too far—no, Mr. President, they are guilty of war crimes. If in fact we are a nation of greater values and if in fact our laws exist as more than ink upon parchment then these men and others involved should and must be prosecuted to the full extent of the law. I speak not as an idealist but as one concerned with the potential reality given to my children and grandchildren if we fail to set this precedent, to stand collectively and say that we reject the inhumane treatment of any man, woman, or child be it in the name of security or justice, then we fail to secure the very values that you have promised to uphold and we open the door to tyranny.

The words of Charles de Montesquieu are poignant to this effect: "There is no crueler tyranny than that which is perpetuated under the shield of law and in the name of justice." I ask that instead of turning our backs on the past 8 years and forging ahead, we turn to face what our nation has become and in turning we cleanse it and restore it and ourselves to our once righteous place in this world.

With the Deepest Respect.

Dear President Obama,

I'm just an ordinary American, but I believe in representative democracy. And I believe that my government speaks, even if to a very small degree, in my name. I deserve to know what has been done in my name by the Bush administration to fight "terror."

We know some of the broad outlines. We know that too few questions were asked in the early days of the war about the depth and complexity of political alliances and rivalries in Afghanistan. We know that the war in Iraq was launched based on lies. We know about Iraqis tortured and humiliated in Abu Ghraib and suspected al Qaeda prisoners tortured and humiliated in Guantánamo Bay. We know the words "extraordinary rendition." We know that defense contractors have profited enormously from the misery of the Iraqi people. We know that security contractors have made murderous and tragic mistakes. We know that our soldiers have come home wounded in body and soul and broken in spirit from what they have witnessed and what they have been asked—and ordered—to do. And now we know that torture was authorized at the very highest levels of government.

Some of what has happened falls under international legal understandings of war crimes. Justice would demand that the law be applied. But I understand that the breadth and depth of responsibility is too great for the law to accommodate. Still, we need not stand silent and impotent in the face of these political realities. While what has happened has mostly not set American against American, South Africa's choice after the end of apartheid to seek out and hear the stories to preserve them provides a model that can work.

This is not a partisan issue. We must hear the truth from all who contributed to the wrongdoings and horrors of this war. The chain of responsibility reaches the mighty: those who facilitated the lies to the United Nations; those who voted to authorize the war in Iraq despite knowing that the justifications were shaky or false; those who wrote the memoranda authorizing torture; those who voted to take away the civil liberties of Americans and fundamental protections for human rights of non-Americans. It extends down to the nameless: the defense and security subcontractors who profited from pillaging and now stand beyond the law, the soldiers who unquestioningly accepted prisoners identified as Taliban by the Northern Alliance, the wire tappers, the pilots flying the planes to the black sites, the frightened young soldiers who opened fire on Afghanis and Iraqis who merely looked like threats.

In his second inaugural address, President Lincoln sought to bind up the wounds of the Civil War by calling for malice toward none and charity toward all. Your moderate inclinations may likewise lead you away from malice and toward charity. But I call on you to put the truth first, that we may know what we have done. And that it may not take us a hundred years this time to confront the wrongs that have been wrought in our names as Americans.

We must know the full stories. We must know how this has happened, from the top down to the bottom. This knowledge is more precious than any desire for vengeance, because only with this knowledge can we truly say, "Never again."

Sincerely,
Julie Novkov
Albany, NY

President Barack Obama,

First, like your millions of other supporters, I would like to commend you on your presidential victory. People have used many words to describe the journey from senator to president—historic, groundbreaking, and unprecedented, among many others—but I have just one word to sum up my reaction to your victory: "Finally!"

Your wife, Michelle, came under scrutiny during your campaign for saying "for the first time in my life, I am proud of my country." On November 4th, after watching Jon Stewart and Stephen Colbert announce that the Electoral College votes had conclusively tipped in your favor, and then watching your eloquent acceptance speech, tears came to my eyes and, quite different from my usual cynical view of politics, I felt proud to be an American.

Your acceptance speech truly touched me, because you and the majority of Americans agree: this time must be different. I am a 20-year-old student at the University of Michigan and I, along with an unprecedented amount of young voters, "rejected the myth of [our] generation's apathy." Indeed, this is no time for apathy when many of the consequences of past legislation will fall on us in the future. That is, if we let it. And if the political efficacy demonstrated in this election is any indication of the future, we will not, and we have you to thank for reminding us of the necessity for unity, partisanship, and hope.

Honesty is the highest virtue. With the past administration's blatant reluctance to be forthright and open with (the arguably self-induced) political messiness, America's confidence in its leaders was shaken. And this is a betrayal unlike any other, one difficult to disregard, though the Bush administration proved that popularity polls' correlation with political capital was a myth. After an era of divisiveness, a new beginning has been born. But, as I am sure you are aware, we will hold you to your promise to "always be honest with you about the challenges we face."

It is refreshing to be listened to, especially as a young voter that feels strongly of my political convictions but has been disillusioned by the seemingly ubiquitous corrupt nature of politics. It is refreshing to know that you will listen to the citizens you govern, "especially when we disagree." And it is refreshing to finally have a leader who will continue to strive to be better and offer a commitment toward unity: "And to those Americans whose support I have yet to earn—I may not have won your vote, but I hear your voices, I need your help, and I will be your president too."

It is imperative that we restore our international credibility and end our blatant disregard for foreign opinion. Fidel Castro has said that the Cuban government would meet with you; Iranian President Mahmoud Ahmadinejad offered his congratulations to you—the first time an Iranian leader has offered such wishes to a U.S. President-elect since the 1979 Islamic Revolution; and the majority of European leaders expressed their approval, stating that "today, we are all Americans."

The *San Francisco Chronicle* reported my favorite story of the election. Retirees Les Spencer and Tony Viessman are the sole members of the Missouri-based "Rednecks for Obama." You were the first presidential candidate to visit their hometown since Missouri-native Harry Truman, and I hope you saw the 3-by-7-foot sign welcoming you to town ("Cost me 25 bucks," Spencer said). "Sometimes change is hard for people," said Viessman. "But I don't care if you're black or Oriental or green, if you can do the job. And he can do the job. He's pretty near the smartest guy who's ever run for president."

A vindictive part of me wishes that you would prosecute all the many rule-breakers of the previous administration, but you have taught me that above all else, we must look forward to pragmatic solutions rather than dwelling on past injustices. The truth is, I am reluctant to trust a politician but you have earned my trust, my support, and my allegiance. This is a new era which separates the mockable political candidates that are easy targets for *Saturday Night Live*, but even *South Park* and the *Daily Show* find it hard to poke fun at your calm demeanor.

All I ask is this: Please don't disappoint us. I understand that things will get harder before they get better, but I am certain that for the first time in decades, we are on the right path. Americans deserve a president whose private life isn't riddled with scandal and whose public life isn't plagued with inconsistency and secrecy. We deserve you, and as of November 4th, America has decided that you deserve us. Though many have unrealistic expectations of you, all you need to do to retain my support is do what is best for our country. This will be an ongoing struggle, and I promise I will be patient if you promise your sincerity and honesty.

So now that you officially represent our country, all I can say is "Finally!"

Best wishes,
Natalie Pont

CHAPTER 8

Kids and High School Students

Caught up in this historic election were not only the voting electorate in America but also the next generation of voters: students from kindergarten up through high school. Quite moving, the letters from elementary and high school students are very poignant and offer a lesson in the political socialization process of American politics.

January 25, 2009
Dear President Obama,

I think you're one of the best presidents in the world. I want you to help the people by making sure they have enough food.

From
Jasmine Bose Partridge
Ann Arbor, Michigan
Age 5

December 8, 2008
Dear President Obama,

I love it that you won the election. Do you know why? Because you are extremely nice and brave. My grandma is collecting all of the letters to you!

Please make the war stop and send the soldiers home. Please stop global warming. Also, can you stop the cutting down of trees?

I am so glad that there is a black president. I am black too and some day I want to be president like you. I wish that I could meet you.

Your daughters are very pretty and black like the night sky.

Your daughters are like cherries and are so nice.

You are as shiny as a star. And your wife is as loveable as can be.

Michelle Obama, is really beautiful and wears wonderful clothes.

In the future, I would like for you to bring about peace and opportunities for everyone to have and poor people especially.

From
Mariya Allen Valez
Ithaca, New York
Age 8
P.S. WE LOVE YOU!!

January 22, 1009
Dear Mrs. Obama,

You always look pretty, just like your daughters. I know your daughters' names. I wish that I could see you some day. I wish that I could be president like your husband. I am seven years old and in second grade. I have a sister whose name is Mariya and she is eight years old. She wrote a letter to President Obama.

Last year I went to South Africa because my grandmother had a Fulbright. Have you ever visited South Africa? It was pretty fun there. If you haven't been there, this is to tell you that it is very beautiful. My friends there are Sibu, Alexandra, Tumi, Keke, and Sindy. My first grade teacher's name was Miss Kreel at St. Michael's School for Girls in Bloemfontein. We wore uniforms.

How is your life going? My life is going fine, if you wanted to know. In Ithaca where we live, I go to Beverly J. Martin Elementary school. My teacher's name is Miss Shank. We have academic classes and we go to art, gym, and music. After school, I go to Academic Plus where we do homework, play in the gym, and go to art. I like going to science.

On last Tuesday we watched the inauguration. You all looked so beautiful and handsome. I felt excited and happy because I am so glad that Obama is president and that you are the First Family. You, Michelle Obama, are the first black First Lady. You are so lucky.

What are you going to name your dog? How do you like living in the White House? Congratulations!

I live with my grandmother and my sister. I love them and I love your family too.

What is your grandmother's name?

Have a happy time living in the White House.

Bye bye,
Jenea Gwendella Allen
Second Grade
Ithaca, New York
Age 7

January 23, 2009
Dear President Barack Obama,

My name is Jacasta Manasseh-Lewis. I am six years of age.

On the day you were elected, I stayed awake until eleven o'clock. I was happy and excited. I could not sleep. I am excited about the history you are going to make as president.

I enjoy reading history and biographies. One of my first biographies was on Abraham Lincoln. I have read about other presidents, but Abraham Lincoln is my favorite because he tried to stop people from arguing over land and animals.

I want to help the environment. I try to get my parents to recycle bottles and cardboard boxes and switch off lights when they are not needed.

Please, Mr. President, make America a happier place for people, animals, and trees.

Jacasta Manasseh-Lewis
Ithaca, New York
Age 6

January 24, 2009
Dear President Obama,

I think you are going to be a good president for this country. My name is Irena. I am eight years old. I go to Beverly J. Martin Elementary School in Ithaca, New York. We had a Martin Luther King breakfast. After this breakfast I wrote a poem. Here it is:

Martin Luther King was a peace loving man. He knew that with the love of God he could do most anything. He wanted to change the law but not in war.

He walked for Jesus, and he had a dream. He stood for human rights and heled this country's fight for equal rights. He said we must be fair to all.

"We must let freedom ring." Jesus landed so Harriet Tubman could lead. Harriet Tubman led so Rosa Parks could sit. Rosa Parks sat so Martin could speak. Martin spoke so Obama could be elected. Martin Luther King was a brave, brave man. He stood up for himself. He thought that things were wrong so he tried to change them. I have a dream, Martin said, that black and white children would be holding hands together one day. We want freedom, we want freedom!!!!! They would say. We are proud of people who support our country. On Martin's gravestone it said, "Free at last, free at last, thank God oh mighty I am free at last". Martin Luther King was a brave peace loving man.

We saw you take the oath of office. Obama! Obama! Please say hello to your daughters for me.

Lots of love from Irena

December 8, 2008
Dear Obama,

My name is Christopher. I'm 8 years old and I go to school at BJM! What kind of dog will you get, because I'm getting one too? What are your daughters' names?

I voted for you! Do you have brother or a sister? Do you have any friends?

From
Christopher
Ithaca, New York, Grade 3

December 8, 2008
Dear President Obama,

Please can you come to our classroom? We are in room 311 at Beverly J. Martin Elementary School in Ithaca, New York. You can talk about whatever you want. Do you live in DC? Do you have a private jet or helicopter? If you do, please fly it here.

You're the best.
Sincerely,
Daquan
Ithaca, New York, Grade 3
P.S. will you write back?
P.P.S. Thank you

December 8, 2008
Dear President Obama,

I'm glad that you're the first black president. I wonder where you are right now. I' m at Beverly J. Martin Elementary School. Next week Tuesday is Nick's birthday. I'm going to be happy if you get a cute puppy. When in January are you going to be the president?

Love,
Tiarra V. Rosade
Ithaca, New York, Grade 3

December 8, 2008
Dear President Obama,

I think you should send all the troops home and stop the war and make gas prices low and stop global warming and give money to poor countries, because some countries are very poor and the kids are dying because they don't have enough food to eat.

About the global warming, the ice is melting where the penguins and polar bears live. They are dying because of global warming.

From
Zach
Ithaca, New York, Age 8
P.S. I think you should name your puppy Chocolate. It depends on the color.

Dear President Obama,

This is a letter I wrote on December 8, 2008 so by the time you get this, you might have already named your dog, but I still have a few suggestions for names. You could name your dog Sara or Awesome because he/she could probably blind people with too much exposure to awesomeness. (Sara is just a joke.) What is your favorite color?

Yours truly,
Noah
Ithaca, New York
Age 8

December 9, 2008
Dear President Obama,

I'm glad you are the president because when I have kids, I want to tell them that when I was a little kid, a person got elected who was the same color as me.

My mom is happy too.
From
Thulani

December 9, 2008
Dear President Obama,

You have wonderful kids. On YouTube you were singing "Live Your Life."
I am glad that you are the president. We love you. I like your dancing. It's good. We love you being the president because you care about the poor people and John McCain cares for the rich people.

From
Deja, age 8
Ithaca, New York

December 9, 2008

Dear President-elect Obama,

To make the world a better place, I would like you to please, please stop the war!

I hope you will send the troops home safely. Make the world stop cutting down the trees in the Amazon and please make the world stop polluting. Bring peace to the world.

Sincerely,

Aiden

P.S. Name your puppy Clover.

December 15, 2008

Dear President Obama,

I am happy that you are president. I'm happy that you're the first black President. I wonder where you are right now. I'm at Beverly J. Martin Elementary School. Next Tuesday is Nick's birthday. I wonder how much money you have. How many colors do you like? My favorite colors are blue and yellow. I love water. Do you like water?

Marcus

Ithaca, New York

Age 8

December 9, 2008

Dear President Obama,

I would like to suggest your dog's name. How about Sweetie Pie or Midnight or Lucy? I am happy about your going to become our president. Are you the President yet?

From

Nik

Ithaca, New York

Age 8

Dear President Obama,

I'm so glad you're the President. It's so cool because I voted for you at school. I'm 1 year older than your youngest daughter. I wish I lived in Washington, D.C. so I could meet you and your family, but I live in California. Maybe one day I'll get to meet you.

I hope you like your job and are the president for 8 years.

Your Friend,
Isabelle M. Hernandez Lizaola

Dear President Obama:

How are you doing? Do you have time to play with your kids? We heard your favorite food is chilli. Guess what, my dog's name is Chilli!

I love your speeches! I hope you will bring peace to the world! I think you will be the best president ever! How brave you must be! How do you comfort your daughters? Well, I give you 100% for being president! I am 6! You are a star*!

I will pray for you and your family.

Love,
Shannon

Dear President Obama,

I have some tips for you to help us and you. You should lower gas prices and taxes, take people out of the army, around Christmas make sure the prices are low, help endangered animals, and make it illegal to cut down trees, make schools not to have schools to let kids in if it is negative 10, help people that need money for food, drinks and their bills for their house or apartment. I would try to do that if I were president.

Our family was hoping you would make president. Also I hope you and your family have fun in the white house. Were you happy or excited you made president? Also do you think you will help us a lot and are you scared? Also I hope you will be happy in the white house! Congratulations!!!

Have fun,
Alex Fauxbel
Age 9
P.S. USA rocks like you!!!

Dear Obama,

Please give homeless people a safe home and some money. I wish you can give poor people medicines. Please give them food. Can you stop the pollution? Can you make everyone use electric cars? Can you make the people who are destroying the forests stop cutting trees and killing animals?

Have fun at the White House. I wish you good luck. I hope you will be the best President.

Sincerely Jeanne,
February 5, 2008

Dear Future President Obama:

I felt compelled to write this letter to you ever since I saw you speak at American University on January 28. I am an 11-year-old boy who began researching the presidential candidates when my mom made me do it for a home school project. At first, I thought politics was boring, but when I actually started learning about it, I got really into it!

I feel like I'm a lot like you, even down to pretty small details. The thing that is most similar, I think, is that I barely know my father. He came from Cameroon, Africa, to study at Howard University in Washington, D.C. He stayed in America for awhile, where he met my mother who is white. He went back to Cameroon when I was really little and I haven't seen him since I was a few months old. I've seen pictures of him and heard lots of stories about him from my mom and my uncle. I've always hoped he would come back. I guess God gave me my wish, because my dad is coming to visit me in March!

Since I'm around the same age you were when your father visited you, I want to ask what that felt like for you. I am feeling scared, worried, confident, happy, excited, and all of them at the same time. I also have fears that my father won't like me. Were you scared about that too? Did your father like you when he met you? I hope it's okay for me to ask you about this because I really need some advice.

I loved your speech at the American University and, I doubt you remember, but you shook my hand! That was really exciting for me because I really like you and to be able to shake your hand was really cool because I think you are going to be President. If that doesn't happen I want to move to Canada. I also watched your speech at Martin Luther King, Jr.'s church, your response to the State of the Union Address, and your debate with Senator Clinton. When I hear you speak I believe in you and then I reflect on our similarities and I believe in myself, too!

Thank you for reading my letter.

Sincerely,
Malik Geraci
P.S. Today is Super Tuesday so GOOD LUCK!

Dear President Obama:

Hi. My name is Melissa Valencia. I'm fourteen years old, and I am a ninth grader attending Hamilton High School in Milwaukee. I am very pleased to have you as our president. Not only are you the first African-American president, but you have also given back meaning to "The Land of Opportunity." I hope that you can cause change in our beloved country.

We have three major issues in this country that I hope you are more than willing to fix. The first issue is our economy. I believe we shouldn't be dependent on other countries for oil. I also believe taxpayers shouldn't have to bail out banks and the stock market when they worked hard for their money and they have problems of their own.

The second issue is immigration. People all over the world come to the United States not to be a nuisance, but because they believe they have a chance at having a better life. They just need a chance to prove it.

The last issues are health care and benefits. There are women, children, and men dying because they cannot afford health care, and that's a shame.

I congratulate you on your big win, and I hope you can fix the problems President Bush created. You are the future of our country.

Sincerely,
Melissa Valencia

Dear President Obama:

Hello. This is Danielle Tokarski writing to you. I am a freshman at Alexander Hamilton High School in Milwaukee. I am writing to you because I wanted to get in contact with the new president who wants to give America a change.

I wanted to tell you some things that would help America. If you would change them, it would be change for the better. One thing would be to try and help make buildings which would be shelters for the homeless. There are so many people who are homeless, it is sad. Also, with winter coming, more people will die from being homeless. Another good idea would be to lower prices on food, clothing, gas, etc. Those are other reasons why people are becoming homeless. It is really sad that, just because people don't have enough money, they have to live on the street. Lastly, could you actually be a president and not mess up America like George Bush did? Honestly, I think Bush didn't really care about America. It was all about himself. But I think you will be a great president. I really do believe in you.

Thank you for taking the time to read this letter. I look forward to hearing from you. Also, congratulations on becoming president. Know that you will be important in history.

Sincerely,
Danielle Tokarski

Dear President-elect Obama,

I think you, President Obama, will make a great new president because you promise to stop the terrible war, you're smart, and people are very fond of you. When you were giving your acceptance speech, my parents were telling my siblings and me to be very quiet and watch the television because we all knew history was being made. I will always remember the day you, Barack Obama, was elected forty-fourth president of the United States of America.

Sincerely,
Vienna Rynerson

Dear President Obama:

Hello. My name is Shekinah Hutchins. I am a fourteen-year-old ninth grader at Hamilton High School in Milwaukee who will be fifteen on February 14, 2009. I am writing this letter to let you know that I appreciate your being the president of the United States.

First off, let me say that I am truly sorry about the death of your grandmother, Toot. I hope you're okay.

Second, let me tell you about three things that I would like you to change about the U.S. The first is the number of racist people. I would also like you to change the way gas prices go up and down; I wish they could stay at $1 a gallon. I would also like you to change the amount people have to pay in order to get their prescribed medicine.

All these issues are important to me because I have experienced things related to them with my family. So, if you could, President Obama, please take what I'm saying into consideration.

Thank you for taking the time to read my letter. "Yes, we can!" and "Yes, we did!"

Sincerely,
Shekinah Hutchins

Dear President Obama:

My name is Monica Santos, and I am fourteen years old. I go to Hamilton High School in Milwaukee, Wisconsin. I wanted to say that I am extremely glad that you won the election. I was so happy that I almost cried! I always thought you were a very smart and great leader for the United States. Congratulations!

Although you might not want to hear advice from a fourteen-year-old, here are some of my opinions.

We all know you are going to become the busiest man on earth these next four years, but do not forget to spend some quality time with your beautiful daughters.

I mostly wanted to ask you to please, please not forget about immigrants. Everyone talks about how kids suffer because they get separated from their parents. Well, the truth is that teenagers do too! The feeling is horrible when you keep hearing, "We will have to go back to where we came from because they do not want us here." Many teenage immigrants actually want to stay here in the United States to have a better life, study here, and have a chance to be someone important like you. I have heard all of this personally through many years of living here. I hear all sorts of immigration problems from friends and family, and I just want it to stop once and for all. Do not forget what you mean to all of us—especially immigrants—right now.

I also want to ask you to end the war in Iraq as soon as possible. Even though I have no family in it, it feels really bad to think that there are many soldiers out there fighting for a war that should never have started. Many people are dying; please save them.

Sir, you are not alone. We are willing to follow your rules. We trust you, and we know you will change history forever. We are really counting on you; please do not let us down.

With much love,
Monica Santos

Dear President Obama:

My name is Diana Taylor. I am a fifteen-year-old high school student. I have a few concerns that I was hoping you could address.

I would like it if you raised the minimum wage from $5.90 to $7. I think you should also make more jobs available for teenagers starting at the age of fourteen. My biggest concern, however, is about foster care. I really think you should make a law that all foster homes and parents must actually spend the monthly check they get from the government on their foster child/children. Since everything is going up in cost, I would like it if you raised the minimum wage so we teens can actually have money in our pockets and get it in the right way. I find that there are very few jobs that hire teenagers because we have "no experience," but we have to start somewhere. It seems that most foster parents just do foster care for the checks; the kids hardly ever get any of the money. I think you should make the checks a little more and make a law that, if the child is a certain age, then he or she must get about 25% of each monthly check, and, if the foster parents refuse to give the child/children the money, they will get in trouble with the law. From personal experience, I know foster parents hardly give their foster child/children any money.

Thank you, President Obama, for taking your time and reading my letter. I'm looking forward to your reply.

Sincerely,
Diana Taylor

Dear President Obama:

My name is Ivonne Perez. I live in Milwaukee, Wisconsin. I am a freshman at Hamilton High School. I'm writing you this letter to tell you what I think you should do now that you are our new president.

My first piece of advice is to lower people's taxes because people work hard for their money and even work extra hours to earn more money, but the result is still the same. My second piece of advice is to get people to buy health insurance because some people are very sick but don't go to the doctor because they don't have it. My third piece of advice to you is not to fix other people's disasters. You did not create them. You have other things to worry about like the health and happiness of your own family. I also think that you should give immigrants papers because they came to the U.S. for a reason and that's to work. They work hard like other people, so why don't they have the right to stay?

Thanks, President Obama, for taking the time to read what I wrote. I'm looking forward to hearing from you.

Sincerely,
Ivonne Perez

Dear President Obama:

The first thing I would like to say is "CONGRATULATIONS!" How are you? My name is Elizabeth Wallich. I am a freshman at Hamilton High School. I am fourteen years old and will be fifteen on February 8, 2009. I want to write this letter to you because I am so proud that you are our president. It's not just because you're African-American either; it's because, for the longest, the United States of America has needed a big change, and, thanks to you, the big change has come.

Our economy is really bad, and, now that you are president, I hope you can change it. I know you can; I believe in everything you say and promise to do.

I don't want to ask you to change anything when you take office because that's what you're expecting because everyone is asking you to do what they want you to do. I'm not trying to say that the United States doesn't need a change because we do; I just know you can accomplish everything that will make the big change. In all your speeches I've heard, you've talked about the change we need.

I would like to thank you for taking the time to read this letter. I would also like to congratulate you again for being our president. I know you will take the right steps to change the United States of America. Remember: yes, we can.

Sincerely,
Elizabeth Wallich
P.S. YES WE CAN!

Dear President Obama:

My name is Deserae Brannin. I'm a ninth grader at Hamilton High School in Milwaukee, Wisconsin. My parents are divorced, and I live with my mom most of the time. I have a 21-year-old sister who has a two-year-old son named Cody Dean. I am going to tell you three things I would like you to try and change in our country.

First, I would like to ask you to make day cares safer. I honestly don't feel comfortable with my nephew being in day care with all the tragedies that keep happening like kids being left in day care vans in hot weather and dying as a result. Come on now! If you're going to work at a day care, then you need to be more responsible! Also, a lot of day cares don't have very good security alarms or locks.

Second, could you help fix the health care problems? Health care should be affordable to everyone, even poor families. It is not fair that people with no money should have to suffer! Everyone should be treated the same.

Third, I would like to ask you if you're going to stop the war. I may not have family in Iraq, but I feel like the ones who do who are sick of being terrified of losing their loved ones! It's not fair; hundreds and hundreds of people have lost their loved ones. They should not be scared about getting a phone call in the middle of the night telling them their son, daughter, wife, or husband is dead!

Fourth, as soon as I heard John McCain was against abortion, I was all for you. Women should have their own choice if they want to have children or not.

Last, I agree with you: homework should be done before TV or anything else.

I'm very happy that you're our president! Thank you for reading my letter. I hope you can make me feel happier and safer! Go Obama!

Sincerely,
Deserae Brannin

President Obama,

I would like to first thank you for your show of understanding and openness for other cultures. As a United States citizen of Indian descent it was disturbing to watch the ignorance that was prevalent in our former president's international policies. The attitudes that were displayed by our government were reminiscent of the former isolation policies. This blatant display of disregard for the numerous religious and cultural differences around the world increased the international animosity for our country and the animosity from minorities within our country.

I hope that you really are able to break away from these policies and attitudes and emphasize the fact that cultural understanding is a must. Religious understanding is a must. The past eight years were not just marred by cultural misunderstanding but by religious misunderstanding. Muslims, Hindus, and other minorities were ignored, misunderstood, and shunned. Please fulfill the promises made in you speeches. The first step to solving our international issues is to educate our government, armed forces and people. Please establish some sort of cultural sensitivity.

Open the minds of people to a world they otherwise would not know and ease the world's animosity. Everyone wants to be understood and for eight years our government never tried. Please continue to promote understanding it will benefit our country in both the short and the long run.

Sincerely,
Neha Paresh Khandhadia

Dear President Obama,

Well, first I would like to congratulate you on winning the 2008 election and for all of the hard work you put into your campaign. I am a young black teenager in high school and I have been thinking a lot about your plans for the country and I agree with them 100%. I like your plan to help the middle class with their financial debt because there are a lot of people in debt and in need of help. I think that the best part of your plans is to bring about affordable health care insurance for everyone.

Help is what we need right now, especially money wise. The economy needs change, especially in Michigan with the automobile crisis and with the recession, which isn't good right now. It's real sad from my point of view to see a lot of people struggling so hard to make ends meet or to have nice things. For instance, the gas prices go up and down and this is still the number one topic that people talk about right now. Then there are the many layoffs. The school systems are struggling and some are closing with teachers being laid off. There's even a new round happening with Blue Cross & Blue Shield. I could keep going on but you get the point.

There's hardly a better role model for me than you Mr. President. You've given me renewed courage to follow my dream to work someday as an engineer and I thank you for that. Even though black people aren't much respected, that doesn't really mean much at all. It's just like when others said that black people couldn't amount to much. But look who is laughing now because we have a smart black president in the White House.

All the Best,
Blake Laster

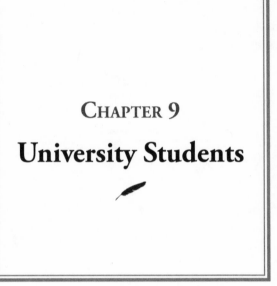

CHAPTER 9

University Students

Moving up the educational ladder, one finds letters from college students from all walks of life. Many are first-time voters, and they speak of the thrill and joy of this experience and provide great insight into how influential and important this election is to their lives and to our country as a whole. For many, this election removes the cynicism that they had acquired about politics from previous presidential elections and administrations.

Mr. Obama,

First off I want to congratulate you on your unbelievable campaign, which captivated the hearts and minds of millions of young people throughout the United States. I write to you as a college senior at the University of Michigan, and want to personally thank you for inspiring me to commit my life to politics and public service. In 2004, during the summer prior to my senior year of high school, I was working on John Kerry's presidential campaign as a press intern, where I heavily supported Senator Kerry and the Democratic Party. At the same time, however, I saw the same "politics as usual" rhetoric from both candidates and I did not think that either candidate was particularly appealing to the millions of first time voters. And then during the 2004 DNC, you delivered your now infamous Key Note Address, which has continued to have a meaningful impact on my life.

Only a week after your speech, I was preparing to write my college essay for the University of Michigan. One of the questions that I was asked what is one major problem you see that plagues youth today. In my essay, I spoke about political apathy and disillusionment in young voters, and told that the country needs to be united, and not divided, echoing your sentiments:

"Watching the Democratic National Convention at the end of July, I saw a man who inspired me. Barack Obama, the state senator of Illinois, who is running for United States Senate, gave a moving and powerful speech and focused on issues of concern to young people. Instead of hiding behind party lines and trying to appeal to PACs, Obama strives to unite the country."

I concluded my essay by asking, "If young people are not inspired to participate in politics today, then who is going to lead our country tomorrow?"

Now, nearly four years later, you have been elected to be the nation's president, and more young people than ever have been inspired by your campaign. I was fortunate enough to work at the convention this past August, and even more fortunate to get the opportunity to see you deliver your acceptance of the nomination. Looking back at the past four years of my life, and seeing you rise from state senator to United States president, all the while inspiring millions of young Americans, I truly believe that in the next four years of my life, anything is possible.

Best of luck, and I cannot wait to hear you speak on January 20, 2009.
Matt Kretman

Dear President-elect Obama,

Congratulations on your elections. It was quite the scene in the center of the University of Michigan's campus after your victory. At approximately 1 AM on the eve of your election, thousands of students converged on the "Diag," unprompted, to celebrate. People waved American flags and a small makeshift marching band played the Star Spangled Banner. People chanted "USA." It was an outpouring of spirit for our country unlike any I have experienced in my lifetime. People were proud to be Americans, and I can't say that there has been a lot of that sentiment any time in my recent memory.

In a paper I wrote for my American politics class at Michigan, I analyzed African-American success in achieving equality based upon your success in electoral politics. I concluded that though your success is a symbol of African-American gains—socially and politically—in the last half-century, there is still a long way to go. I know you addressed this in your speech about race, a historic moment of your campaign, but it is clear that we still have room to grow until we achieve a "more perfect union." As you inherit the vast economic and foreign policy issues at hand for our country, I hope that you will also focus on leveling the playing field in education for America's youth.

I wish you the best of luck.

Dear President-elect Obama:

My name is Chad Carroll and I am a sophomore at the University of Michigan in Ann Arbor.

I first of all would like to congratulate you on being elected the first black president of the United States of America. You truly have inspired millions of people and created quite a global following. In fact, here in Ann Arbor on election night there was a huge rally in the center of our campus called the "Diag" in support of your very convincing victory over Senator McCain.

Although I identify with the Republican Party, I did see you as the more astute and knowledgeable of the two presidential candidates. In fact, I myself would like to pursue a law degree of some sort and aspire myself to write for the *Harvard Law Review*.

Furthermore, I agree with your decision to field a wide-ranging and very intelligent cabinet in order to combat the serious problems of our time. You have been brought to the forefront of our nation's problems and the country is going to rely on you to see the "change" necessary to bring the U.S. back to prominence.

The United States needs the "Change" you have preached about throughout your campaign as we are in the midst of the worst economic and social disaster in the history of America. I wish you good luck with your term as president of the United States and hope you can bring this country back around.

Sincerely,
Chad Carroll
University of Michigan 2011

President Obama,

Congratulations on your historic victory! Never before have I seen a political figure capture the hearts and minds of the populace like you have, especially the demographic of young Americans. It was inspiring to me to see that Americans between the ages of 18 to 25 can have such a dramatic impact on the primary and national election process.

It is in this light that I urge you to continue to invigorate the younger voting demographic by showing us that you care. Help to show us that we not only can have an impact on who the president will be, but what policies he will implement. Please help to make it easier for any eligible student to receive the financial support they need to attend college. Furthermore, I would ask that you encourage states as well as the federal government to give a greater focus to helping public school systems. Being one of the wealthiest nations in the world means we should be able to give students the resources, facilities, and quality educators that will propel us as a nation to a higher standard for education. Without investing in the youngest generation, we will quickly run out of confident, smart, and capable leaders for our future.

On a different note, I am very excited to increase foreign support with the coming of your new administration. Having been privileged enough to travel abroad, I have heard from international students and citizens on their general distrust and dismay at our former administration. I hope you will work to improve our global image.

Thank you for giving us hope and enthusiasm for American politics again. I wish you well in your continuing efforts to provide strong and calculated leadership to our country. It is in great moments of change such as the one we are experiencing when we need firm leaders to set examples for all citizens of our country.

Sincerely,
Austin

Dear President Obama,

I cannot begin to express the joy and the relief that I have, knowing that you will lead this great country over the next four years. Your message of having hope and promoting change inspired millions, especially myself. I could not have asked for a more exciting election in which I would vote for the first time. I was able to vote for a president who I believe will do an excellent job in uniting this country by tearing down the racial, class, and party barriers. You have shown the American people that we are all one because we all share the same vision, which is to live and enjoy a country that will soon thrive again.

What I found especially intriguing about your campaign was how you appealed to the needs of everyone and how you sought to get everyone involved. I am incredibly grateful that you have listened to the concerns of the young people in this country. I am a second-year college student in the state of Michigan. With the economy struggling the way it is in my state and the higher tuition rates, paying for my education proves to be an increasingly difficult task each year. Despite some of the obstacles I face, I know that I will fulfill my dream of graduating from the University of Michigan because you have expressed a desire to help college students during these trying times. It would be a great honor to give back to my community by volunteering my time, so I can get an early start to repaying my community for the success I have had.

Thank you so much for showing the people of this country that the American dream is still alive and anyone can live that dream if they work towards it. Thank you for reminding us that we the people have a voice and that you want to hear what we have to say. I look forward to seeing the new direction in which you will lead this country. God bless you and your family.

Sincerely,
Aneisha McDole

To the President-elect Barack Obama,

I would like to congratulate you on the tremendous impact you have had on the youth of America during this election year. I have never seen my peers so enthusiastic to vote. I attended a Democrat rally at the University of Michigan, and the support you have here is incredible. I am proud to say this was the first election I was ever able to vote in. I am as proud to declare that I helped elect you to the presidency. I wish you all the luck in the world and am confident that you will lead America in the direction it needs to be led.

Yes, we can and yes, we did!

Sincerely,
Rachel Piserchia

Dear President-elect Barack Obama,

First and foremost, I want to congratulate you on the amazing election you ran, and the positive outcome you ultimately reached. It is such an amazing feat that you have accomplished, and I want you to know that I am extremely glad that you will be the next president of the United States. I am a college freshman at the University of Michigan and I was extremely excited to be able to register to vote in my first big election. I would not have taken the time and gone through that hassle if there wasn't a candidate I believed in such as you. You inspired me from the beginning to watch the news and debates and become more educated on the important topics this race would be based on. My dad would find me in the basement watching CNN or MSNBC instead of my usual MTV and VH1. It was important for me to learn about you not only as an individual but also about the issues you stood for. Once you won the Democratic nomination, I knew history would be made. You were the stronger candidate in the race, and you had a strong following of young, first-time voters, and the Democratic Party as a whole. You never faltered, and continued to stay true to yourself to throughout the campaign. I want to say thank you again ahead of time for the change that you will bring to our country in the next four years, and I know that you will not only take your job seriously, but you will also enjoy your four (and hopefully eight) years as president of the United States.

Congratulations again,
Emily Ray

President Obama,

At first I wasn't convinced. I had listened carefully to many of your speeches and was under the impression that you were simply an impressive orator with a political agenda that was not drastically different from others, and that you had rhetoric to shroud this fact. I do respect the ability and in turn I respected you, but a president, I felt, should be more.

I grew up in a home of Democrats and certainly have a liberal slant, but I was not sold on the belief that you were the person to run the country. I was certain that I wasn't going to vote for John McCain, but the 2008 election was my first to vote in and I was struggling with the idea of voting against a candidate instead of voting for one. I wanted my vote to mean that I was wholeheartedly behind that candidate rather than him being the better of two choices.

I can honestly say I no longer have such concerns. The weeks before and up until the election removed all of my doubts as I watched my college campus mobilize. I watched volunteers of all ages registering voters in an amount I haven't seen for any other election. I watched people who were never interested in politics before become passionate about the election, about your campaign. I saw no less than ten shirts with your face on them on my way to class each day.

All of this and more showed me one important thing—that you were . . . are . . . different than other politicians who tell me the things I want to hear and then do things I wouldn't want to hear about. I was convinced not because of advertising, or the debates, but by the way you truly have motivated, even energized, the people. I believe that if the four or, better yet, eight years of your presence in the White House produces anywhere close to the strength and initiative I have seen in October and November, we will be a much finer country because of it.

Thank you. Thank you for the good that I know you will do for the country. Thank you for making the first election that I participated in one in which I'm proud to have done so. And finally, thank you for inspiring so many people, a group that I can now say I am a part of. I am convinced that this is a positive turning point, and I'm convinced that you're the man to lead us around the bend.

Sincerely,
Max B.
University of Michigan
Chicago, IL

Dear President Obama,

I want to start by saying congratulations to you. I'm sure you already know this, but your election to the presidency is such an amazing accomplishment for not only you, but for African-Americans, as well as for all Americans. Our government and country is taking a step forward, and I am honored to have you lead us.

I am a white 19-year-old female attending the University of Michigan—a university whose student body has an extremely loud voice for diversity and social justice. I grew up in a typical conservative middle-class family, parents both Republican (although, my dad claims to be more of an independent), attending church every week, living in a suburb of Detroit that was once considered one of the whitest cities in the United States. I am pro-life. I am against same-sex marriage. I disagree with universal health care. Do I seem like your average supporter?

The truth is, President Obama, you do not have an average supporter. Not liberals, not Democrats, not African-Americans, and not the middle class. Everyone has the opportunity to be a so-called average supporter of you, because you stand for equality and justice. Equality is not just a word to be used when referring to minority groups or specific religions; however, it is a term to be used when referring to our government that you will lead.

I know it may not seem like much, but I want you to know that I support you. I, a young female with the opportunity to vote for the first time this year, believe in you. Thank you for being the change that this country needed.

Dear President Obama,

Congratulations on your win!
I feel very honored that the first election I got to vote in was such a historical and important election and I was delighted to cast my ballot for you.
I am really excited about your plans for educational reform.
As a current college student struggling to pay for college.
As a student who grew up in a less than perfect schooling system.
As a future teacher, hoping to make a difference in the lives of children's educational experience I look forward to a time where educational equality becomes a possibility.
I want to make my career about being a part of the movement that makes that happen.
Thank you for noticing the problems in the American education system.
Thank you even more for having the courage and boldness to begin addressing the chaos.
It is about time someone did.

Dear President Obama:

My name is Benjamin Donald Baxter. I'm white, tall, and very nice. I writing to you because I just want to.

When you take office, I hope you keep the peace flowing through the USA and the world. I wish you much luck being president. I think you're awesome and really kind. Also, I want you to do a good job as president because I'm sure it's not the easiest thing to do. Also, if it's possible, can you lower prices on game systems and video games because I'm dying to get a PS3, Xbox 360, and Nintendo Wii, but my parents think they're too expensive? Also, please lower gas prices. This would help me, my parents and the people of the USA.

Thank you so very much for reading my letter. I wish you very much luck as president. If I were old enough to vote, you would have had my vote for sure. I look forward to hearing from you.

Sincerely,
Benjamin Baxter

Dear Barack Obama,

I am writing this letter as a huge supporter of you as a person and as the next president of the United States. I am a freshman college student at the University of Michigan and I became very interested and engaged with your campaign after the More Perfect Union speech. I was truly inspired and motivated by the speech because it was so honest and straightforward. I liked that you started the speech by giving the history of the United States and began with the words "We the People." I also liked the way that you gave your own unique background with a black father from Kenya and a white mother from Kansas as well as your working-class white grandparents. That speech made me want to learn more about your life and background and led me to read your first book, *Dreams from My Father*.

At the time, you were facing criticism and scrutiny from the media in regards to Reverend Jeremiah Wright's comments but you handled the situation with dignity and class. Some people may have tried to avoid the situation by hoping that time would make people forget about it but you addressed the situation and spoke from your heart. You addressed the theme of race in America even though it was a very risky topic. Some people may have addressed the situation by completely disowning and distancing themselves from Reverend Wright but that approach would have been phony. You did disagree with Reverend Wright's comments and you did stop attending his church but you also explained the good qualities and characteristics of Reverend Wright. You also explained that you could not disown Reverend Wright in the same way that you could not disown your own white grandmother who has made some stereotypical and controversial comments of her own.

I believe that your speech was truly revolutionary because you didn't just talk about issues of race that everyone can see on the surface. Instead, you explored and talked about issues of race in America that no one else likes to talk about. Many people choose to ignore the problems of race and feel uncomfortable about it but you talked about it so eloquently. You brought these issues to the forefront of discussions and you did it in a way so everyone could relate to it regardless of race, gender, or age.

There are an endless number of great things that I could say about this speech but the best thing that I can say is that this speech gave me hope, motivation, and inspiration. I have a unique background of my own but I also see parallels between our backgrounds. I have a black father and a Mexican mother and loving, working class, immigrant Mexican grandparents that helped raise me and shape my values and morals. I was raised in inner-city Detroit but I attended one of the finest private high schools because of a full scholarship donated by a white organization and family. But my race and background is only a small piece of who I am and what I stand for. But as a young person, I have dealt with the issues discussed in your speech and it gives me hope that America will become a more perfect union by dealing with its issues of race with you as our next president.

Sincerely,
Brandon McNeal

Dear Mr. Obama,

This year marked the first presidential election I was eligible to vote in. I am a student at the University of Michigan and the energy here was amazing. I was so excited that the first presidential election I was participating in was one of such monumental proportions. I felt deep down in my bones that you would be elected. And when you were, the cheers sounded up and down my hallway. People flooded the hall and hugged and yelled and danced. I was less than excited. Even though I had a feeling you were going to carry the election, I hope you wouldn't. I suppose now would be a good time to clue you in to the fact that I am a Republican. So as others cheered I felt a strange feeling of disappointment and fear. It's not that I dislike you as a person. I don't think you're a bad guy. I don't think you have poor personality traits or anything like that. But I simply don't subscribe to the idea of candidate politics. Even though I think you're a fine person, ideologically you and I are fundamentally opposed to each other. I don't agree with your plans for health care or taxes, I'm downright scared by your ideas for withdrawal from Iraq and I can't believe you made Hillary Clinton your secretary of state. I don't think the state of affairs in the United States can get any worse than it already is, but I don't see many things that I agree with happening under your watch.

Despite all these things, your candidacy does excite me in one way. I am so glad to see that the United States has finally overcome its history of hatred and bigotry. I am so proud of my country for finally looking beyond the color of a person's skin and acting according to that person's personality and ideals. I won't lie and tell you that during the next four years I won't criticize or disagree with you. As I said you are bound to implement some policies I simply won't agree with. But ultimately, I am happy for you and as a United States citizen it is my duty to stand behind you and stand behind our country. I hope you do well the next four years.

Sincerely,
Laura Mason

Dear President Obama,

Congratulations on your victory, and thank you for inspiring so many Americans, including myself, with your campaign and promises to the nation. I must admit that a year ago I considered myself a Clinton supporter, and only after watching you give a speech in Grand Rapids last May was I finally won over to your movement. I call it a movement because that's exactly what it feels like here at the University of Michigan campus, and around the counties of mid Michigan where I grew up, and in the homes of many of my friends who up until this election paid no attention to politics or public policy in general. The enthusiasm and optimism that you have been able to generate is powerful, and I hope you use that power to make right the many flaws in our society, economy, and the world.

One issue that I hope you will begin to address shortly after you take office is the precarious state of unemployment that currently plagues the nation. Here at school I am surrounded by very smart and talented people, but the prevailing mood on campus is not one of confidence but of fear, fear over an uncertain job market and the declining state of the country (not to mention exams and grad school applications). If students at one of the most selective and prestigious universities in the country are feeling these kind of pressures then the majority of Americans must be absolutely crushed by them. I hope you encourage new industries through expanded green programs and investment in our infrastructure, while creating an economic climate that business can flourish in. I understand that to accomplish this you must first set right the current problems sapping the strength from the economy, but I hope that as you do this you look ahead to the future instead of burying your head in the sand as seems to have been the case with the former administration.

I have every faith that you will accomplish what you promised the American people this fall, and I wish you the best of luck in your endeavors.

P.S. I would very much appreciate any position you would like to offer me in your Whitehouse or a letter of recommendation to Harvard Law.

All the best.

Dear President Obama,

I first would like to congratulate you on becoming our new president! From the time you first announced that you would be running in the presidential race, my family and I have followed your campaign, and have continually been awed by your community outreach and eloquence in speaking. Not only do your academic and political successes reflect your qualifications for the position, but also your character is to be commended. You have made students and adults alike want to take part in government, and have made us all proud to be Americans. For the first time in quite a while, you have provided the country with hope. Times have been bleak in the United States, not just for the lower-class citizens, but for all of us. I feel that you have been the one to unite us during these times, proving that class should not separate us; that we are all Americans.

This was the first election in which I could vote, and I was especially excited to do so. Everyone in the country anxiously awaited the results on election day, and you gave your supporters a reason to want to travel to the polls and vote. You have provided us the hope that America will come out of the seemingly endless economic slump. During your campaign you put your faith in us to elect you, and now, that faith is being exchanged, in us believing that you may lead our country in the best way possible.

I am a freshman at the University of Michigan, and it has been incredible to see the excitement and support for you throughout the election. You have not only been the candidate that people support, but the candidate that people overwhelmingly want to vote for. Your passion has ignited hope throughout the country, thank you; you are what the country needs. I can't wait to see your plans for office.

Thank you, President Obama!

Sincerely,
Rachel Anna Brusstar

Dear President-elect Obama,

I am writing this letter to thank you. Thank you for bringing change to our nation and thank you for finally hearing the voice of the youth. On the night that your presidency was addressed, the feelings and emotions at the University of Michigan were felt throughout the campus. Celebrations were not only in the halls but they were in the streets as well. People were chanting "Yes we can" with pride as everybody knew that our future was about to change for the better. I am just writing this letter to you thanking you for showing that my voice does count, thanking you for changing my future, thanking you for helping our nation get out of a difficult time, and most importantly thanking you for making my first voting experience very memorable.

Sincerely,
Robyn Segal

Congratulations Mr. President Barack Obama! Your win was a victory for millions of souls.

I am writing this letter to you for two reasons: 1) to thank you for steeping up to the plate. I know that you will knock the ball out of the park. Also I want to thank you for putting your life and your family's lives and reputation at stake, for a better society. What a sacrifice. 2) on a more serious note, I am going to discuss the corruption of judges and the injustices they produce.

I am a freshman at the University of Michigan Ann Arbor. My concentration consists of a dual major in political science and psychology. I plan on persuing my Juris Doctorate at Harvard University School of Law, post undergraduate commencement. Then I too plan on running as in elected official to hold some office (at the moment I do not know what office I want to hold, but in due time I know God will reveal it to me). I know I am saying, "I am" a lot, but the truth of the matter is I am me, and I have been influenced and inspired by a slew of injustices that I have observed and unfortunately experienced. I have had a not so rare opportunity to personally see the injustices of the system and judges, by being a ward of the state since my ninth grade year of high school. I have seen different people of authority not do their jobs and misuse their positions, and do harm unto the people.

I am requesting that you take a close look into the creditability and character of all judges and referees on the bench. For judges are supposed to be a representation of a democratic nation. Whether just or unjust, the decisions of various judges affect everybody. The court system was intended to be a fair system that listens to the people, whether they were poor or rich, guilty or innocent. Everybody would be heard, and then the court would provide decisions that were just, and exhibited that views of both sides were taken into consideration. But like now, in my case; my voice, my mother's voice, nor the voices of my brothers and sisters are being heard because we do not have the clout or the money to have the judge to listen to our long and loud cry. I guess basically what the system is showing me through its actions is that, if one does not have the money or a high ranking in the socioeconomic system, then one is expendable and will fall between the cracks.

Finally, the product of being punished for crimes one has not committed, the product of not having one's voice heard, the product of corrupt judges, is a vile result. A result of the people giving up on a government that is supposed to be about truth and justice is the production of people relying on self to make changes come about, thus making them look like vigilantes or the product of a society that does not trust or obey its government. It makes one think, who is the government really serving? We must remember the words of former president John F. Kennedy: "Freedom is indivisible, and when one man is enslaved, all are not free." This slavery is not physically whips and chains slavery, but rather a socioeconomic slavery.

Thank you for reading my letter.

Sincerely, your sister in Christ Jesus,
Kamille

Dear President Obama,

I am an 18 year-old college student. For the past few years, it has been my dream to come to the University of Michigan, and last fall that dream became a reality. I came to school this August knowing that I would have to work as hard as I ever have to get into the Ross School of Business. However, I know that if I put in the time and effort, I will be able to reach my goal. However, with the economy the way it is, is it even worth it for me to go to business school? Am I going to be wasting $160,000 so that I get a degree for a job that I can't get? What can you, Mr. President, as the most powerful person in this country do for me, a college student looking to make the jump to the real world? Can you fix this economy so that when I graduate in 4 years I will be able to get a job? Will I be able to accomplish my dream of starting a family?

Please, Mr. President, make my dreams come true.

Good Luck,
Evan Einstein

Dear President Obama,

    Being an active member of my college community, I want to thank you for all that you have given to my generation already and all that you will offer in the future. You have inspired many young people, including myself, and you have brought excitement to the political process. I am very hopeful that you are going to make changes in this country that will hopefully bring back the value system, the trust, and the hope that America stands for. I applaud you for overcoming the obstacles to become the nation's first African-American president. You have shown this country that there is hope for change and that good things can and will come to future generations. With the economic crisis that is going on right now, I and other people my age are extremely worried about what will happen in the workforce. Many of us are graduating with specific degrees, but have no place to use our skills. As of now, it is a scary thought to know that there may not be job opportunities for us after we finish school. With this being said, it is questionable as to whether or not my generation is going to be able to support ourselves in the future. This is obviously a huge concern for everyone, but I have hope that you won't let us down. The environment is also an issue that has been a widespread concern throughout the world. I am involved in many organizations on my college campus and have taken initiative in my own life to make environmental issues an important part of my life. Nothing will be changed regarding this issue unless the world as a whole comes together. Even so, I have hope in your presidency and policies that something can be done to push back the negative effects our society has on the environment. Lastly, I feel extremely grateful to have been a part of your electoral process, by providing my first vote in a presidential election. This was a big moment for me and I am proud to say that I voted for president Barack Obama, the man who will change the future of my generation.

    Thank you so much,
Jamie

Dear President Obama,

    I am writing to express my deep gratitude and appreciation for your dedication and will during this arduous campaign on the road to the White House. I am a 19 year old from New York and was raised in a very liberal household. My parents were always interested in politics so as I grew older, I too developed an interest. I registered to vote the day I turned 18, not knowing that in just one year, I would be part of a movement that altered the course of history.

    I have always harbored a secret desire to go back and time and live in this country in the days before John F. Kennedy was elected president. His magnetism and youth made a new group of people want to be involved in their government. Not since then has the youth of America so wholeheartedly thrown their support behind a candidate until you. I believe the reason is that you truly represent change in more ways than one. It is not just a change from the past eight years of bad policies and broken politics but a change that will once again make this country great.

As a member of your organization, I feel as if last Tuesday night, I was a part of history. I helped elect you to become the president of this country. I was among thousands of students that night running around my college campus in excitement that we no longer lived in a country in which had lost our respect. President Obama, you have restored my faith in the greatness of this country and I cannot thank you enough for that. My only hope now is that these next four years can bring about the drastic change that this country is so desperate for.

Thank you again,

Allie Breslin

Dear President Obama,

After taking several political science courses at the University of Michigan I have become fascinated with the United States government and the way in which policies are created and transformed to best suit the public. I have been following current events, and your progress thus far as President-elect. It is safe to say you have impressed the nation.

Public services are the backbone to our nation's government. These civil services help organize, protect, and benefit the people of our nation by ensuring the well being of the public. Since public services hold such importance in our society, it is essential for individuals who hold political office to have the good of the people as their top priority. We need a strong leader now, more so then ever, due to the current economic struggles our nation is facing. It seems as if the definition of public service is fading as our leaders appear to be more concerned with heightening their status then bettering the lives of the millions of people that trust and depend on them. There have been far too many sensible public policy issues blocked due to partisan conflict, ulterior motives, and power struggles. That is not what public service is about. I believe that you, President Obama, have the opportunity to restore the true meaning of public service. I believe that you will do great things for this nation by bringing back morality to the United States government. Good luck.

Sincerely,
Natalie Perach

Dear President-elect Obama,

I would like to congratulate you on your amazing accomplishments. In the fall of 2007 you were my choice for the Democratic nominee, even though most had given the nomination to Senator Clinton. Yours is the first campaign I've ever donated money to, and though I wish I was able to donate more, I think you did pretty well in the end. I was very pleased with your vice-presidential choice in Joe Biden, whom I'd been hoping for. You have continued to show good judgment selecting Cabinet members, and I was happy to see you keep Secretary Gates as Secretary of Defense. After you made several choices I found an article on Fox News' Web site that made me laugh. The author was in disbelief at how moderate your choices had been. Since you've said for months this is what you'd bring to Washington, I wasn't surprised, but apparently he did not believe you. Perhaps he was expecting you to name William Ayers as Secretary of Education and Hugo Chavez as Secretary of Defense.

The night of November 4th was one of the most emotional nights of my life. I knew victory was secured when you won Ohio, but I still waited and watched until the West Coast polls closed. Right at 11 your face appeared on screen along with the words "President-elect Obama," and tears welled up in my eyes. I have never felt such a surge of patriotism like I did at that moment. I opened a window and heard people yelling from their homes and down the streets of Ann Arbor, cars honking and celebrations beginning. I ran downtown to watch your speech with my friends, making it just in time. You spoke to me personally that night, and yet you spoke to everyone in America. That night I think you won over some people still unsure, perhaps afraid of change as many are. I credit Senator McCain for his concession speech, which was more gracious than any I've ever heard. Those not convinced by you alone were perhaps willing to lend you their support after Senator McCain asked it of them. Once you and your family left the stage, we went to the center of campus and found thousands of students celebrating. American flags and Obama/Biden signs were everywhere, with cheering and chanting surely heard throughout the city. We sang the Star-Spangled Banner, chanted "U-S-A," and substituted "O-bam-a!" for "Let's Go Blue" in our school cheers. For two hours we marched through the streets, covering most of campus, and leaving us all with an election night we will never forget.

In the upcoming years, you will face a near endless list of problems. A recent political cartoon showed your to-do list, from ending the Iraq war to fixing the economy, and ending with "leap tall building in single bound." I know you are the best person for the job, but I worry things are so bad it will take more time to fix than people are willing to wait. I believe the country is ready to support you, and many who voted against you realize divisive politics need to end. I just hope they understand that any solution is going to take time; things may get worse in some areas before getting better. The 25% of the country who always think George

Bush is doing a good job as president are not likely to change their views, and you will have the same 25% disapproving of the job you are doing in office from the start. If anyone can win them over, I believe you can.

I'd like to end on a serious matter, one dear to my heart: college football. After you said we need an 8-team playoff at the end of the season, I was disappointed we don't agree on this crucial issue. You said not one "serious college football fan" you'd spoken to disagreed, so I felt compelled to ensure all voices are heard by our president-elect. College football is the only remaining sport where the regular season truly matters; a playoff system would destroy that. I attend the University of Michigan, and have been a Wolverine all my life. We had an unfortunate season, but soon Michigan will reenter the fight for one of the potential top 8 spots. The last game of our season is against an Ohio State University, our biggest rival and arguably the greatest rivalry in all of sports. Several years this game has had national championship implications, and most years it has determined the Big Ten champion. I'm afraid this game, and many others like it, would lose significance. Between Michigan and Ohio State, the loser should not be able to win the national championship, period. This could have ruined the recent SEC championship game. It was a hard fought game because each team knew the winner plays for the national championship, and the loser is out of the picture. With an 8 team playoff this game would've meant almost nothing, because both teams would still be in the top 8. The other problem is even if it's initially limited to 8 teams, like basketball it will surely be increased before long. As it grows to 16, even 32 teams, the regular season will be lost.

I wish you the best of luck in the coming 4 years, and I will be supporting you throughout.

Dear President Obama,

With this being my first election, I am very pleased to have been able to vote for you and am honored to know that you will bring about the change needed for this country.

I am a student at the University of Michigan and have always lived in Michigan. I love this state; however, everything is not as it should be. Unemployment is rising steadily and the Big Three's troubles are combining to put this state in a pretty sad situation. I have great confidence in you and I'm asking for your help.

My 75-year-old father is a retired teacher of Detroit Public Schools and has many medical problems. Blue Cross/Blue Shield insures us and he has Medicare, yet the costs of his medications are still unbelievably high. Receiving only his pension and social security for half of our family's income, we often find ourselves struggling to pay for other necessities such as either of our two mortgages, food, water, electricity, and car payments. The other half of our income is from my mother who, in her fifties, must work nearly 14 hours a day as a merchandiser, traveling across all of Southeastern Michigan to many different stores. Our two mortgages are on the house my father built in the 60s which is in Cheboygan, a town in Northern Michigan, and the one my mother has lived in her entire life in Ypsilanti, which is located in the Southeastern region. She recently had to buy a new car because the 18-year-old Toyota Camry she had finally gave out on her and she didn't feel safe driving any of her four sons around in it.

If you have any intentions of changing the way our health care system works, I urge you to do so. Recently I have been looking up health care in other countries and many people don't pay nearly as much for exactly the same drugs in other countries as we do here in America. It is things like that that nickel and dime our family so much. There is no reason he should have to pay hundreds of dollars a month for drugs that make him feel better. It should be the government's responsibility to make sure their people are healthy and happy. On another note, the problems with social security right now may bring us even greater problems. Should that supply be depleted, we would especially not be able to pay for his medications, let alone anything else.

Job security is not very good right now and my mother is feeling the effects. Employed by four different companies, her hours are constantly being cut and rearranged in ways that make it very difficult for her to complete a workweek and still make enough money to support her family. Of course she would love to be able to change careers but she can't afford to go back to school or take the time to transition.

My two older brothers have both been working since the middle of their high school careers and still live in our house in Ypsilanti. Contributing with groceries and other odd expenses, they too must pay for repairs on their used cars, insurance, school, and other things as well. Although they have been working at their jobs for quite some time, if things continue down the same path, they too may lose their jobs and be unable to afford their expenses.

I have held down two jobs since eighth grade and have been able to get by with all the costs of marching band, being in plays, and just being a high school student. Regardless of the fact that my parents were unable to assist me with those expenses, I still feel very grateful to be that young and have the chance to work, especially two jobs. I was never able to afford a car so when I was accepted to the University of Michigan; I decided I would try to live on campus. I didn't know how I was going to afford that either though. Thankfully, I was blessed with a couple scholarships from school, an unexpected and large scholarship from the U of M, and most of the rest covered by financial aid. They are providing enough so that I am able to cover the rest all by myself. If, because of the declining economy, I lose the financial aid, I will most likely be unable to finish college for a long time.

I know that you will have an enormous influence on this country during your presidency. Please, while you are prioritizing the areas you must work on, think of health care and medication, job security, and education.

Thank you,
Matthew Blinstrub

CHAPTER 10

Multiracial Citizens

Due to President Obama's biracial ethnicity, many individuals of the same such multiracial heritage and background write to the president, acknowledging the significance of this moment and offer their heartfelt thanks, encouragement, and support. They express happiness in electing a multiracial president and recognize the importance this moment will have for their children.

Dear Mr. President,

I am, like yourself, a multiracial individual. To look at me you would think I am of the white race. When people are around me the say derogatory things about other races not realizing that am multiracial. My hopes are that with you in office things will get better. I hope that on government forms we will not need to state what race we are, I really do not know how to answer that question. I just put that I am an American.

Thank you,
Judy

Dear President Barack Obama,

You are an inspiration to many citizens across the country, including myself. Many people that I know told me that you didn't stand a chance in becoming president of the United States. There were times when I had my doubts, but I supported you the whole way, and I am proud to be able to say that I voted for the first African-American president of the United States. It's not only a great thing for African-Americans but it affects everyone.

What I like most about you is that you went through a lot of things that the average or lower-class Americans have been through. You didn't grow up wealthy and you didn't have everything that you wanted; you worked hard to get where you are today. You are able to relate to many American citizens, you know how it feels to not have very much. I respect you for this because you have come a long way.

I look at what you have accomplished in your life and you give me hope that I can also accomplish my dreams. I am also multiracial; my mother is African-American and my father is Caucasian. While growing up my parents did everything they could to get my brother, my sister, and myself everything we needed and wanted. But, sometimes things did get hard and we would struggle. My parents always told me that I could be whatever I wanted; and you coming into office proves to every little boy and girl across the country that they can become anything that they set their mind to. I want to become a doctor and there are not many African-American female doctors around, but I know I can accomplish my goal is I stay focused and work hard. You stayed focused and worked hard, and know you are the first African-American president. My accomplishment will not be as great as yours was, but it will be great for me and the people I help.

When you take office I know there will be change. What the United States needs is change. One thing that I hope you can improve is the economy. We are losing jobs all over the United States and they are being sent to other countries. This is really affecting many citizens. I am also one to witness it. I am from Saginaw, Michigan, and I have seen many factories and other companies shut down leaving many people without jobs. These citizens and their families do not deserve this.

I have faith in you and your plans for the United States' future. I know there will be a change and I can't wait until you take office in January 2009. I know you will not be able to work miracles, but things will get better for Americans. There will be a lot of people out there who don't agree with what you are doing, but always do what you think is best. I wish you the best and I congratulate you for making history.

Sincerely,
Ashley Shaffer

Dear President Obama,

Autumn leaves scattered the sidewalk—orange, pink and yellow. As I walked the streets with my clipboard, the sky was a threatening slate gray. Raindrops fell gently on my face, and I wondered if in the end, people would vote for a black man. The bitter rhetoric on TV, electoral maps, and the letters to the editor in the newspaper danced through my head, but I knew that there was nothing more I could do. Whether I liked it or not, I had to embrace uncertainty.

My father's mother had skin as dark as ebony. In pictures, her teeth glisten like the ivory keys of a piano. But even in the country of my origin, India, color was a problem. Rumor has it that when my grandfather (who had curiously light, blue-gray eyes), came to see if she would be a suitable wife, the family hid her away in another room and made her play music for her suitor instead. An African gene that was traced recently in people in South India, might explain my grandmother's roots. Medical tests for my mother, on the other hand, revealed that she had a condition seen only in Eastern Europeans. Given all the relentless invasions by Turks from north of the Himalayas, I may even have some of the genes of Genghis Khan. As an Indian-American, my official racial label has evolved over the years—Asian, East Indian, and now, South Asian. To me, race often feels like an illusion, but at that moment, a few days before election night, I couldn't ignore the elephant (no pun intended) in the room.

Shelby Steel, author and columnist, called you a "bargainer" (*Wall Street Journal* March 18 2008). "Bargainers are conduits of white innocence," he said and that there was a "hunger in white America for racial innocence." But when it was announced "Barack Obama, 44th president of the United States," I didn't feel that white Americans had proved their racial innocence. I felt that Americans had ignored the issue of race and picked the best person for the job. I am grateful that people truly voted their conscience.

Winning an election is sort of like having a baby. After the pregnancy and a difficult delivery it feels as if the job is done, but as any woman who has given birth to a baby knows, boy, is it beginning. There are no real guidelines, the task is overwhelming, you have to learn as you go, and you don't get much sleep. When I look at the days ahead I see change. I see peace. I see prosperity. I see sunshine, and maybe some rain. But the best that you can do is to embrace the uncertainty. Gray skies or blue, live in the moment, because that's all you will ever have. Savor the present, good or bad. Stay true to yourself, as much as you can, because in the end, it's the journey not the destination that matters, and the driver, not the vehicle that counts.

May God bless you and your family and keep you all safe,
Lakshmi Jagannathan

Dear President Obama,

I have thought long and hard about what I would like to say to you if I was given the opportunity and now that I have it is such an honor to have you there to represent all of the people in this the greatest country in the world the United States of America. I never had any doubt that you would be our next president because you and Mrs. Obama always came from a totally believable place.

Since the announcement came that you had won the election I was especially moved by the lack of celebratory balloons and fanfare that usually follows a win. You made it a personal affair as if you were drinking in the atmosphere and could reach out and feel the ambiance of acceptance from the majority of the American People. That must have been an awesome feeling like shooting the tie breaking basket or making the winning touchdown in the final second. It was a magic moment history was made on the eve of my son's birthday which is something he will never forget. I know that those who have fought, struggled and died are beaming with pride for you and will help to guide you through the greatest journey of your life. But this is your grandest hours of ultimate promise and power. We support you 110%.

I also would like to express my feelings on how dedicated your First Lady came across. I watched several of her speeches on your behalf and if someone had any doubts she was right there to fill in the gaps. I call her the Ultimate First Mom and for the next eight years it is going to be fascinating watching your daughters grow up in the White House.

There is a sweet melody and a low warming glow that stands in the near distance, a sense of quiet pride here in Savannah, GA. People seem calmer than usual or maybe we are all afraid to exhale for fear that this is all a beautiful dream. I do know that my native New Yorkers are over whelmed by having you as our president. I have five multiracial children Natanyi, Candace, Mercedes, Fontaineskye, Demetrius and the young men of the Savannah High School Football team who did not always know if or where they belonged now it can be defined it does not matter what you are but what you can achieve no matter who you are.

Thank you for being willing to fight for and for having the courage to cause Change in this country, America. I don't know if you can save the world but the effects of the rainbows edge is always a miraculous and wondrous sight.

Now you own the DREAM.
June President Carter
Savannah State University

Dear Mr. President:

Your grace, candor and then your election have changed the lives of so many people—young and old—around the world.

Several years ago, at the age of 47, I stood in Tiananmen Square with my three sons —then 21, 10, and 8—all of us of mixed race. My older son had been studying Chinese in Beijing for the second time, while I was travelling for the first time with a passport. As I stood there I had an epiphany that each of us had different ways that the trip would be part of our life stories. I had never imagined travelling further than visiting family in the Virgin Islands, while my oldest son memorized the atlas since he was little, always wanting to travel the globe, study cultures and bridge divides. For the two younger boys it was the beginning of "where will the next trip take us to?" The world opened for them at such a young age. Their eyes were opened to possibility.

Your election brought another epiphany. Sean is now 27 and married with a child of his own—half Korean, half mixed-race American. He voted for the third time in a national election as a Democrat. His early adult years have been dominated with discussion of how American politics did not reflect his American values. His hope and optimism for his home country is now brimming over. This country now reflects him and he sees himself in the new possibilities.

And for two teenagers still at home who are also half African-American—their belief of what is possible has a new benchmark. While mine was whether anyone who wasn't white could be elected as president of this great country, your election makes that a question of the past. My children—and yours—will be setting new benchmarks that perhaps we can't yet imagine. That is the hope and possibility that your election brings.

Solving the complex social and economic problems before us won't be easy; it will require sacrifice from all of us. But the sense of possibility is a bright light calling us forward. I hope you will continue your path of being honest with the American people about what we need to do to continue moving forward. Don't listen to those who tell you to be concerned about polls, about doing what is pragmatic and achievable, or ask you to make it easy. Instead listen to those advisors who encourage you to stay true to your values and beliefs. Bono recently spoke at a Women's Conference in Long Beach California and he shared the advice he got from Warren Buffett about starting One.org.

Mr. Buffett told him:

1) Don't appeal to America's conscience, appeal to America's greatness; and

2) Don't make it easy—Americans don't like easy; make it difficult.

In our hearts we know that what is needed will take hard work and years to accomplish.

Let us know the path ahead and what it will take and we will right there ready to work alongside your vision.

Wishing you well,

Liz

President-elect Barack Obama and the World,

The New American President-elect will become the first openly African-American president, when he is inaugurated Jan 20, 2009, in American history!

This presidency while widely supported among all populations in the USA will be viewed historically by African-Americans as a step away from the chattel slavery this country was founded on in contradiction of its stated ideals and a step closer to an era of real liberation! The only way to make it a real break is to clean house on the dirty past and then move forward!!

The dawning of a new era offers a chance to rethink and redesign American Foreign Policy interests and objectives! The question arises immediately if Obama will continue to push for change having now won the Presidency or settle for the more of the same foreign policy!

If Obama is going to rethink U.S. Foreign Policy interests and objectives then and only then could critical reviews and decisions that need to be made about the USA continuing to act as the world policeman and ugly American could be made!

Currently American Foreign Policy interests revolve around making sure American capitalists can ruthlessly exploit all markets in every part of the world or changing and or replacing any regime that chooses a different type of government than the U.S. Government or a Government that is not totally considered a pro-American Government like Cuba or Venezuela!

In order to totally shed the image of the ugly American interventionist or world policeman image Obama must end the U.S. occupations of Iraq first and to also withdraw from Afghanistan as soon as possible!

To change USA Foreign Policy objectives and interests, the Obama administration must once again raise Human Rights to the top of the Foreign and Domestic Policy Agenda thus redesigning American foreign policy interests and objectives!

Promoting change as a candidate is easier than actually implementing a changing of political and or economic objectives and interests and selling those changes to the American people however under an Obama administration owes it to the American people to launch comprehensive Congressional and Administration investigations of torture in the domestic area including investigation of allegations of torture of the San Francisco 8 (former black Panthers) and the Angola 3 political prisoners as well as other Counter Intelligence Program era African-American political prisoner as who were victimized by dirty tricks of the government domestically as well as launching a comprehensive investigation of Bush administration torture in Iraq, Guantanamo, Cuba and many other countries that the USA used to carry out torture. A constitutional democracy like the USA should never be involved in torture of Americans, African-Americans, and not against any people defending their country or people so it will not happen to Americans abroad!

Once torture is studied in depth the American people can better understand how Bush acted as a rogue bully of a world policeman and then these political prisoners must be freed! These investigations should be modeled on the South African Truth Commissions and at the conclusion some of these political prisoners like the Angola 3, Mumia Abdul Jamal and the San Francisco 8 should be released. Then the USA can denounce torture as an instrument of state policy once and for all and the world will give the USA a brand new start in world affairs. Death by lynching and Taser shot deaths should also be included in these new Truth Commissions investigations so America could apologize and come clean.

These moves would show a course being chartered away from the ugly American rightwing regime changing intervention being committed against countries that may disagree with U.S. policies or interests as well as make a complete break with the dirty tricks and dirty war launched against African-American dissidents and political prisoners from the past to the present like Troy Davis. These completed investigations will also provide a basis for lifting the economic blockade of Cuba.

I also propose an African Commission be established to support of and /or implement a United States of Africa or Federated State of Africa if Africans on the continent embrace this dynamic concept. This is a time for thinking out of the box. Obama and the concept of a United States of Africa.

The concept of the United States of Africa or some form of democratically selected Federated African Continent-Wide State is that Africa needs to stand up on its own as a united continent and government as soon as it can be implemented democratically by the people who live on the African Continent!

If a Federated State of Africa can emerge, then the need for regional wars in Congo, Sudan, and Somalia will slowly but surely disappear in a united Africa. Africa as a united government and country would not need foreign assistance to feed, clothe, house, employ and develop its people and resources. President-elect Obama has to learn many new concepts, budgets and policies however Obama also needs to learn more about the concept of a United States of Africa!

I congratulate President-elect Barack Obama and his beautiful family for winning a tough election as they prepare to move into the White House!

Sincerely,
Larry Ukali Johnson-Redd

CHAPTER 11

International
Perspectives

Not all of the letter writers in this volume are Americans; several come from
Africa (like the president's father), Japan, Canada, Europe, Indonesia,
India, Korea, and Brunei, among other places. From their foreign perspectives,
we see this historic American election from a completely different worldview
and can further recognize what this event means to people of color in terms of
a global vision.

Dear Mr. President Obama,

Please permit me the honor to call you also BROTHER OBAMA:

Congratulations and welcome to the world's hottest and most admired seat in the White House.

With this historical breakthrough, you have not only revolutionized the American history but have as well succeeded in visibly placing the long forgotten and neglected black sector on the map of humanity recognition. I am also inclined to think that this remarkable incidence can also serve as a present of an ear-cleaning kit for all racists to remove the racial wax from their ears, so as to enable them properly listen and hear the birds singing their songs of freedom, justice, peace, and love and also motivate them to learn to live in a harmonious world without tears due to racial differences.

I am a descendant of a village in Sierra Leone where Semgbe Peah alias James Sinx "the Amistad revolt Hero" was born. I admire him very much as one our great pioneers who fought against slavery (injustice and maltreatments) as a tool of humiliation to our race. From my own point of view, you have continued and completed his work and laid down a mile stone in the history of mankind. You are a HERO and every person of color should be proud of you for this great moment.

May the Lord's manifold blessings, guidance, and protection be upon you, your vice president, and the entire both families in carrying out your presidential duties. I wish you more grease to your elbows and also thank you very much. Stay very strong brother. We support you.

Fraternal greetings,
Abdul A. J. Sandy

Dear President Obama,

Words cannot express how proud I am of you. As a person of African descent, I can say that our race has made great strides towards success. You have shown America that we are capable of achieving great things. However, I am glad that you decided to make your inauguration about more than race; it was not only about African-Americans, but all races. I appreciate that your campaign and inauguration transcends all races and groups. I felt that you truly unified America. As I watched your inauguration today, I saw people of all races and different walks of life joined together because of you. I have never felt so strongly about a presidential election and I look forward to your successful future.

Thank you,
Amerique Philyaw

My Letter to President Barack Obama:

This campaign is about every one of us. President Obama you have lifted the bar and put out a challenge to every citizen. The emotion of this moment is unimaginable, unbelievable, and difficult to explain. As a television journalist, I've seen a lot. But nothing has come close to the historic night on Tuesday, November 4, 2008. As someone who comes from a family of immigrants who came to this country for a better life, my family hails from Guyana, South America, a place where many people are poor and can only dream of the fortunes available to Americans. When my parents moved to America it was because it was a country filled with opportunity and possibilities. I was taught to seize that.

I found myself in television newsrooms; a place filled with a lot of type-A personalities and at times can be volatile and conflicting. And when you're the only black on-air or one of the only few black employees in an entire company, there's a weight that you carry that not many others can understand. I was introduced to part of that weight in my first on-air job when I moved to a small television market in the southern part of New Jersey. A black woman came up to me one day while I was out in the field, and said, "It's so good to see you here." At the beginning of our dialogue I had no idea where she was going. I figured she was a black woman and saw a black woman working for the local television station and she maybe felt proud. But through the conversation with her, I learned it, was much more than that for her. The woman went on to tell me why she had said what she did. She said, "For us, the black people of the Atlantic City area, when we see someone who looks like us on our local news, it makes us feel like we are a part of the community." For a certain time before that, this woman and others in the black community did not see people on their local news that looked like them. Their television sets were not reflecting an honest look at the community in which she called home. I have never forgotten that conversation and it's a responsibility I'm happy to carry, including outside of television news. On Tuesday, November 4, 2008, I understood the magnitude of what this viewer was speaking about. President Obama, for the people of this country who come from every corner of the World, you're rise is a symbol to us that we are a part of this country and we matter.

President Obama, your opponents have sometimes tried to dismiss your words and speeches as just rhetoric. But words do matter. They're the staple of many of our communities. We go to church to hear inspiring messages; we offer our condolences to others when a tragic event happens. And I personally understand the power of words and delivery from my job as an on-air reporter. I use words in my everyday life to communicate to viewers, on a variety of stories and events in our community. Words are the foundation of this nation whether on paper or in a message to rally the community to come together and give back.

My hope is that all of the people, who were inspired by you to make their voice heard, will continue to do it here on end, whether there's a black, Hispanic, or Native American candidate the next time. You are a symbol of encouragement that this is in fact the land of opportunity, if you take it.

I am a believer that God puts you to work where he needs you and I will continue to be a voice, until a new path is created for me to do the work elsewhere. Most important, I will be proud to say in the future, that I was a working journalist when this historic moment happened.

Sincerely,
Omadelle Angela Nelson

Dear President Barack Obama,

Your election to the White House in my opinion is one of the greatest progressive movements this country has seen in many decades. There are several aspects to your campaign and policies which I find extremely appealing and which I believe will work as catalysts to bring about the positive change people are looking forward to.

The first thing I noticed when I began studying in the U.S. was the extreme disparity in the public schools of inner cities and the suburbs. Over time, I have come to believe that although programs like affirmative action can make a small positive change, they are not effective enough to even out the disparity in lower level education which of course, leads to a large inequality in higher education as well. Your "No Child Left Behind" policy attempts to address this issue and deals with the problem of teacher retention, soaring college costs, and money problems for parents struggling to give their children a better education. I choose to comment on your education policy because I believe that a good education is exactly what a country needs to bring forth positive reform.

Another area in which I strongly support you and your policies is your stance on women's rights. You are the champion of several huge causes such as a woman's right to choose, addressing domestic violence, fighting for pay equity, and even addressing gender violence abroad. Women have been discriminated against for hundreds of years, and the significant effects of disenfranchisement for so many years exist even today. Sadly, many people believe that the fight for gender equality is over and that this is no longer a topic which needs to be addressed. Your stance on this issue shows your dedication to social reform and is definitely a step in the right direction toward social justice.

Social justice is like a moving walkway: if you stand and do nothing, you are simply a part of the system. I believe that you are walking the opposite way on the walkway. You as the president of the U.S. are fighting the system to bring about social change for this country which it is definitely ready for.

Thank you,
Trishya Gandhi

The Honorable Barack H. Obama
President of the United States of America

Dear Sir,

First of all I would take this opportunity to congratulate you on being elected, I am deeply impressed—impressed by the commitment, hard work and above all, dedication to make the certainly impossible, possible.

Being a patriotic Pakistani and an undergrad student in the U.S., I am writing this letter to tell you how the situation in Pakistan and Afghanistan can be controlled and that the current U.S. policies will not bring any good to U.S., Pakistan, or Afghanistan.

I have lived all my life in Pakistan and have been active in politics, local and international. I know all the areas of Pakistan, and I travelled to areas like Swat, an extremely beautiful area in North. Once a booming tourist area, it is a Taliban-held area now. Currently the U.S. is spending millions of dollars, if not billions, to curtain terrorism in Afghanistan and Pakistan and it has produced negligible results. There is no short-term solution to root out terrorism; it is long and gradual process. Those people are illiterate, do not have jobs or food, and are easily maneuvered by the Maulvis (Muslim priests) to do suicide bombings. Their minds are corrupted by the Maulvis to hate Americans and kill them wherever they find them; they are told they will go to heaven if they do suicide bombings. Islam is a religion of peace and the Maulvis have destroyed its image and made those innocent illiterate and jobless poor people take the path of terrorism.

The solution is not to bomb the villages where there are suspected Talibans or terrorists. The solution is education, build schools and give people jobs which will eventually root out terrorism. This is the only solution and current tactics will produce more terrorists than are killed. The brother, the father, the mother, or the sister of the innocent person killed in an attack on "suspected terrorist" hideout will become terrorist to revenge, giving birth to many more terrorists than are killed.

I want to say a lot more but I know you are a very busy individual so I have just written an abstract. I would really like to help U.S., Pakistan, and the entire World but do not have the resources or the opportunity, at this point in time, to do so. You have the power and the resources to do this, please CHANGE the approach, we need it.

With Prayers and Regards,
Adnan khalid

Dear President Obama,

I'd like to congratulate you on an excellent campaign and an amazing victory in 2008. You have dissolved boundaries of race, ethnicity, gender, and traditional partisanship in your election as president of the United States of America. As Former Secretary of State Colin Powell said, you truly are a "transformational figure . . . who has both style and substance." Not only have you won an election based on your merits, charisma, and new age thinking, you have displayed a sense of courage and much needed heroism that has opened windows of opportunity for hundreds of thousands of people across our great nation. I have a tremendous amount of respect for you as a decent family man, an intelligent American citizen, and our country's new leader. It is evident in your actions, especially in the way you address and engage the American public that you truly care about our nation's future. You speak with a clear understanding of the problems that lie ahead, and display an aura of wisdom in the way you offer plans of working together to address and resolve conflicts. It is evident that you are extremely passionate about the positive change you wish to bring about in our country's policies.

However, there is a massive difference between the creation and implementation of an idea, and there is a lot of work to be done in the future. One of my primary concerns is how we intend to remain Americans, and at the same time, act as citizens of the world. The way in which Americans are perceived by the other nations needs to be addressed.

Of Indian origin, British born, and now an American citizen, I consider myself somewhat cultured. I often read the international news and discuss foreign issues with my family across the seas. Even so, I hear our citizens being referred to a "dumb Americans" who have little or no knowledge of foreign affairs. The media, our public educational system, and society inform us of current events and problems in our own country, but seem to ignore or downplay the importance of issues around the world.

The problem is, international issues do concern us, and Americans should be more educated about the world as a whole. If America intends to be the "leader of the world," it is the duty and obligation of our president to lead that change. Americans need to become more educated and "worldly wise" in order to change the attitudes toward us. In order to strengthen our own nation we must work with others for social justice, economic stability, and political awareness. I hope that you will actively address this idea and make an effort to restore the American reputation to its former prestige.

Thank you for your time and consideration. Good luck with your tenure as president of the United States of America!

Sincerely,
Sharan Shokar,
Student, University of Michigan

Dear Barack:

Although I moved to the U.S. from the U.K. about a decade ago, I still find truth in words of George Bernard Shaw—that we are "two countries separated by a common language." For example, we Brits don't generally value that uniquely American, sickly sweet, sycophantic (some might even say 'fake') sort of friendliness—and yet I'm calling you by your first name because you feel like a friend to me. Absurd of course, and yet clearly I'm not alone. Because while perhaps none of us know the real Barack Obama—we feel as though we do. More than that, you feel like not just any old friend, but an old and trusted friend; the best kind.

As one of the world's truest, die-hard cynics, I have been trying to put my finger on why I feel this way about a politician. Perhaps the affection we feel for you has something to do with the fact that you are not only a bright and an educated man, but also carry yourself with an air of calm and dignity. You seem trustworthy, humble, dependable and honest—unique qualities in anyone—but especially rare in politics.

And yet there's more to it. You seem to offer the one thing we truly desire. Hope. Hope that you might be capable of rising above the hypocrisy of Washington to do the right thing. So many of us never imagined we would ever feel that sort of hope with respect to politics. We'd given up—sold out—believing that this is "just the way it is." We accept that our government is self serving and corrupt. We accept they don't really care about anything but their administration. Disillusioned, we accept second best.

But for the first time I found myself voting for a candidate with genuine enthusiasm, rather than just accepting the mediocrity that was on offer.

Barack, you've energized the entire world—which has experienced a collective sigh of relief. It seems that the United States—a frightful, petulant teenager for too long—has finally entered adulthood. For a decade, the United States has been surviving on an outdated reputation that it is numero uno—with it seems only Americans believing it. Perhaps now America can start behaving again like the world leader it has long claimed to be.

And although you may suffer from the sort of over-expectation that curses any Messiah, if you are even half the man you appear to be, you will bring change to not only a country but to a world that is in desperately need of it. Because although so many of us have given up on the world and on each other, deep down most of us want change. We want to believe. We want to believe that life is possible without war; we want to believe that the destruction of our planet is not inevitable—that our human foolishness can be curbed.

Washington will undoubtedly take its toll. But while it will drain you, cause premature grayness, and compromise your family life, what I really want to say is: Don't change. Don't let the hypocrites beat you down. Don't let the new job warp the man you are today; the man that won our hearts and minds; the man who captured the imagination of the world—who made us believe that change may just be possible.

We are rooting for you. Because in rooting for you, we are rooting for a better country—and a better world.

No pressure, ok?

Dear Mr. President,

My name is Eugenia and I am an Italian exchange student at the University of Michigan, for the winter semester 2009.

I am very happy to be living in the United States in this period.

In my country, when it comes to talk about the United States, there are two different kinds of reactions: some people are enthusiastic and think that everything in the States is perfect, just because they consider your country as a political hub and the place where there is richness and democracy. Some others deeply dislike the United States, mostly because of the past political actions that were led by your country.

I don't share these extremist opinions. I have been studying Political Science for 5 years, and I consider myself still ignorant on the political issues in the world.

Studying what is happening around us from an academic perspective, is a relevant matter. But sometimes I ask myself if what I study at university could give me the sufficient tools to face what the reality is.

As far as I know, the answer to my question is negative. I have always be interested in the relations between Europe and the United States, and when I did an internship at NATO HQ in Brussels, Belgium, I felt blessed. I had the opportunity to see from the inside how the political machine works. But I also felt how small I was, compared to the greatness of the political issues that were discussed during the committees.

Today I had to write an assignment for my course in American politics, on the importance of Martin Luther King Jr. Day for that course itself. In the paragraph I wrote, I talked about you.

I think that the dream that Martin Luther King had, has been now partly fulfilled. Thanks to you. And thanks to those people who believed in you. When I watched the inauguration, I almost cried. I never cry when I watch movies, but I cry when I see that a country like the United States elects a black president.

I was in Chicago last weekend, and everything was a reminder of your presence there.

I feel like you will be a turning point not only in the American history, but also in the world's history.

During your speech, you said, "The world has changed. And we must change with it." I agree with you, Mr. President. I agree with what you said later, "All are equal, all are free, and all deserve to pursue happiness." I think that sometimes we forget about the word happiness, because we take everything for granted. But happiness is something that shouldn't be forgotten, because everyone deserves it.

Dear Mr. President, I could have written about terrorism, about the financial crisis, about the environmental emergency.

I didn't.

I would like to wish you the best for your presidency and I am sure you will do well, because you know how much responsibility you have.

I am proud of living here in the States for the following months, and part of my pride is due to you.

Eugenia

Dear Mr. President,

I'm a 23-year-old girl from Italy. I'm writing not only to congratulate you for the victory, but also to thank you. I've never thought I could get involved in something like this: the world's changing, and I want to be part of this change. I've always wanted to find the way to express ideas of hope, unity, respect, and change. I never thought I could find someone who was able to keep my attention that much, able to make me feel responsible for the change I was looking for. I started following your speeches from the primary elections, despite the jokes from my family and friends. Everybody said it was meaningless to stay up at night to listen to someone who was on the other side of the world, but I didn't give up. I started talking with friends, relatives, and colleagues, but most of them laughing at me when I said that there was a man overseas who was about to make story, about to start and change the world.

As time went by, I wanted to go deeper, to discover all the aspects of your ideas and I started reading your books (in original language, as I wanted to catch every word) and the more I read the more my ideas got stronger, and myself with them.

Last week I spent two nights up to follow the elections, I hoped and I cried. I felt part of something so far from me in space but so close in feelings.

I've never thought I could write a letter to a president of the United States but things have changed.

I'm writing to thank you Mr. President for giving me the hope for a better world, for helping me seeing that it's not only up to others to make things go better but it's up to me first. Thanks for reawakening in me feelings of responsibility about our world and our lives. Thanks for giving me the power of facing people thinking I'm a fool in believing in change and hope. Thanks for giving me the chance to believe that I can hope for a better world.

I'm sure I'll be there, in the first line when you'll come to Italy (even if people say it's dangerous), I can't miss the occasion to hear you speaking in person. One of my dreams would be to talk to you, just for a while, to shake hands and try and get your spirit and your courage and, of course, to thank you again.

Dear President Obama,

I am an international student currently attending one of the most diverse universities in America, the University of Michigan. I did not have a right to vote in the States but I had an opportunity to participate in this dynamic election by reading campaign books for each candidate and by analyzing the election poll and the result while I attended the school. My first experience as a foreign student in America was a most amazing and unforgettable one, especially since I was from a country which recently became a democratic one by the free election. Republic of Korea has been the powerful and consistent ally of the United States since the Korean Conflict. And as a beneficiary of the American foreign policy of spreading the capitalism and democracy, Korea has become one of the leading economically developed countries in the world. I, as a natural-born citizen of Korea, also was a prime beneficiary of the generous economic and military aid from the U.S foreign policy. I was excited to see the peaceful transition of the government especially during the war time. People say that the 2008 election was a historical moment because it is the first time that the African-American became the president of America. I think the different. African-Americans since of the Civil War has always been the citizens of the United States. Rather emphasizing the fact that African-American citizen became the first president, we should praise the fact that every citizen has the right to participate in politics and anyone could speak out for himself on behalf of the Americans and under the American Constitution. Mr. President, America is now facing multiple difficulties in its own economy, the world economy, war in Iraq, and terrorism. As a leading herald of the democracy and capitalism, and as a sole supreme power of the world, The United States need to adjust to the new international system and should fight for what it has been standing for. Mr. President, with your unique background of ethnic, academia and political experiences, I have a confidence in you to lead the world with respect and love.

Thank you.

Dear President Obama,

I am an international student from Korea and I have studied in the United States for 5 years. I must admit, when I first came here only five years ago, I could never imagine I would see the black president during my stay. I thought the barrier and invisible curtain in America was still too strong to break.

Therefore, I congratulate you because your achievement is simply astonishing and groundbreaking. You have shown that American can change and the nation's future in the 21st century is indeed hopeful.

On a more personal level, I should say I was greatly inspired by you. I've always wanted to become a politician one day, and I learned a lot from you. Like you have the dreams and visions for America, I have them too for my country. I hope I will be able to have such passion and determination when I go back to Korea and start working for my country.

America is going through many crises—actually, not just the United States but the entire world—and many people, including myself, have high expectation that you will solve these problems. In the election Americans showed you that they can change. Now is the time for YOU to not only change America, but also fix real problems this country and the world currently carry. I certainly do believe you will be able to do that.

What you showed during the election inspired me to make you as my role model. I hope I continue to see you as such role model even after your presidency.

Dear President Barack Obama,

With a week left until the inauguration, I would like to first congratulate you.

As a "foreigner" (I am an international student at the University of Michigan) perhaps it isn't necessary to participate so actively in American politics but I think this time, your election will change the world and having lived in the United States for years, I have become to love this country and for that reason I look forward to the new changes.

I am thrilled to see the United States having reached another level in history.

It is definitely time for change and something to be accomplished that was considered impossible in the past. I think Americans have gained trust and hope from this experience.

I wish you the best of luck at the White House, sir.

Sincerely,
Haeyeon Roh

Dear President Obama,

I am an exchange student from Japan. I was very impressed by your triumph in the election. I watched the moment with my American friends. Some friends started crying when you won, because they were so delighted. I was surprised because many students in Japan don't have interest in election. I don't know about your policy very much and I am not sure whether I support you or not, but I was impressed by your charisma which attracts so many young people.

One of the most interesting issues for me is tuition for university. Why is it so expensive? In Japan, tuition for private university is as expensive as the United States. However, those of public university are cheapest. In the United States, public university is so expensive that my family can't afford it. If I hadn't had an opportunity to use an exchange program, I couldn't have studied in the United States.

I believe that tuition for public university should be cheaper. It would enable young people all over the world to study in very good American university. Moreover, if the United States could have more foreign students who study hard, it would contribute to develop American society.

Sincerely
Yuki Igarashi

President Obama,

I can never feel more than blessed to be in America at what you call "a defining moment." Your victory, a precedent from which change will gain ground and evolve for the better, defined the moment that America and the world has been waiting for. This is the beginning of undying hope—the very core of human survival and the strength to persevere in peril, the very same adage that will get anyone where we want to be.

It has always been one of my biggest dreams to go to America. I am fascinated with the idea of America: a place where people from different walks of life, be it national origin, creed for that matter, will eventually find a place where they would belong. Coming from Brunei, a small country in Southeast Asia, I know my transition to a different way of life, being away from home, would be challenging. Besides kicking off my college life when the presidential election fires on, I know that this would mean a lot of changes and facing trying times on my part. But that is just the tip of the iceberg. Your determination and perseverance are immense and all the more contagious. Your victory is wonderful inspiration for a person with high expectations and aspirations for a better future. A better life, if not more.

The rest of the world acknowledges America's challenges just like you do. The world anticipates change, and with you as the president, I hope that the changes you have pledged will be America's reality to live and the world's as well.

I live by these wise words of yours:

"Change is always possible when you're willing to work for it, and fight for it, and, above all, believe in it."

Those worlds served justice for my transition here and I admit to feeling a greater change in my own life. Thank you for the inspiration you gave, President Obama, not just to me but also for the rest of those who dream, who aspire. Your story gives me the confidence and faith I need to achieve great things in life, just like you do.

Dear Mr. President Barack Hussein Obama,

We are West Papuan and are very glad to hear you have taken an opportunity to become a president. It means that we black people over the world have awakened from a deep sleep to protecting our right as human beings who were created by God.

Let us deliver our request about West Papuans and the real bad conditions under the struggling political situation.

1. Human rights problems

2. Education

3. Economics

4. Health

Special autonomy was given by the central government in Jakarta but it FAILED 7 years later.

We greatly appreciate your protecting us as West Papuan.We knew more about your profiles, we also hope you have time to visit us in West Papua. We also request, if possible, could you give us an opportunity to attend on January 20, 2009 in Washington, D.C.

Hope you will write me back as soon as you can.

May Jesus Christ our Savior bless you.

Our prayers be with you always.

Sincerely Yours,
Samuel Tabuni
The West Papuan Students Association supporting Barack Obama

Dear President Obama,

Today I am proud to be an American. I am proud to call this land my home. I am proud of the leader of my country. I am proud of the direction in which we are headed. Today, as you raised your hand and took your oath to become the 44th president of the United States, I found hope and pride for my country.

I too lived in Indonesia; I have had international experience among those who believed American politics and leaders were a joke. I have been embarrassed by American actions, American arrogance, and American ignorance. There have been moments in my life where even as a child, I was ashamed to call myself an American. But today we took the first step towards a new future. Today, change has finally come to America.

This was the first election that I was able to vote in, and I cast my ballot proudly, ready to exercise the best right that I have. And I cast my vote for you because it is time for things to be different here, and you are the one who will lead us to be the country we are meant to be: a country of peace and tolerance for all.

You mentioned challenges that we are facing today, and that we will meet them head on. It is clear that you are ready to fight through the difficulties facing you, and that you have a clear and definite plan. Not only that, but you are calling on all Americans to stand beside you and fight for what they believe in. As a whole, we can be the country we want to be, divided and quarreling, we will surely fall.

On top of all of this, you are a real person. You are a family man, a caring man, an average man. You did not have a particularly privileged childhood; you were not coddled. You did not have opportunities handed to you. You had to have determination and perseverance to get where you are today. I place my trust in you that you will be able to shoulder the enormous responsibility that you are now faced with. I am proud to call you my president and to have taken part in this momentous, historical day.

Sincerely,
Erika Mayer
University of Michigan '12

Dear President Obama,

In Canada we have received refugees from the States: blacks during slavery, war objectors during the Vietnam and now Iraq wars, and gay couples wishing to form legally accepted families.

We hope this exodus need not continue, through greater racial equity, avoiding foolish military conflicts, and granting equal rights to all, in the United States.

One of the most effective ways of ensuring this, I suspect, is by prophetic appointments to the U.S. Supreme Court, such as exemplified by Justice Thurgood Marshall. Ms Hillary Clinton strikes me as a possible appointee. Like Justice Marshall, she is a trained lawyer who has attempted to ameliorate American society.

Sincerely,
"Mac"

Dear President Obama:

We were touched and very impressed at the inauguration ceremonies!

How wonderful it is to have a U.S. president with the courage to publically and unequivocally promote the major foundation upon which the country was based . . . i.e., the Christian faith; an obviously active Christian faith at that!

What a witness to North America and the rest of the world! Thank you and we sense that God will use you mightily in His service globally, and we keep the safety of you and your family in prayer regularly. God bless you!

And with the current situation of the present government trying to stave off a possible coalition government, our question is this: could the president of the United States also be the Prime Minister of Canada? The Overseer of the North American government? No doubt your current task is more than daunting, but more assuredly is that through your faith, God through Christ will give you the strength you need. So what about considering leadership for all of North America? We could still be two countries, but with the same leader.

If your answer is that you would consider this, please let us know, and we would try to start a petition to the House of Commons to this effect. Seriously. Through Him all things are possible.

With continued prayers for you and your family,

In Christian brotherhood,
Paul and Tammy Zimmerman

Yes We Can Too,

I felt that sweet-bitter pain of joy with goose pumps running through my body when the president-elect gave his remarkable Yes We Can speech.

But I couldn't help but envision the same for us . . . us being the Arab world.

For it is about time to say Yes We Can TOO. We have been dormant for a very long time and bottled up for a very long time, enraged volcanoes with the lava burning our hearts for a very long time . . . giving the keys of our children's destiny to corrupt political leaders and feel bad and oppressed about it for a very long time. We have lost generations and generations of men who were oppressed to silence and suffer from their dignity being suppressed for a very long time

But it's about time to Raise Our Heads Up High . . . be Proud of our Passion. And say "Yes We Can," too

The awful game of nurturing blame and blaming everything on other people and systems out of our influence areas, thinking and dreaming about immigration and adopting the American dream of living has to be stopped

For finally we understand together with the whole world that plastic money is not money it's just plastic that the stock market can base prices on fake supply and demand and that this whole game of a dream is in fact just a nightmare . . . We have to wake up.

And remember that unless it serves the purpose of humanity and the whole universe it wouldn't work. So now we know the game can't go on and we can stop it. Yes We Can.

The media manipulation!!! Well that's another coat hanger we chose to believe in and sedate our fears for decades. Now I can write this, you can read it, you have at least 50 TV channels at home and the Internet and we know the game there is no excuse any more . . . and we can stop it . . . Yes We Can.

Palestinians . . . being massacred . . . butchered . . . denied of basic human rights when they are not directly being slaughtered infront of our own eyes . . . children . . . women . . . and our honored elderlies . . . tears are not enough . . . being enraged is not enough . . . glued to couches and exchanging points of views are not enough . . . for if we chose we cant . . . then we can't . . . but if we choose, we can. Then Yes We Can.

The American people are now at the ending scene of the *Truman Show* movie that was imposed upon them to be the heroes of . . . they know there turned out to be no nuclear weapons in Iraq . . . that the little girl dying and bleeding in her father's arms . . . died in vain. That people in the Arab world who chose to express some anger . . . have actually been hurt . . . alot . . . and that it's just a reaction . . . That the United States' game of being the strongest allies of Israeli terrorism, manipulation and destruction . . . is what the American people are paying the price for . . . and they too don't deserve it . . .

They have stopped and said Yes We Can.

And us too . . . It's our turn . . . it's our responsibility . . . it's our obligation . . . Yes We Can. Muntather Al Zaidy . . . is an Arab Man who said ENOUGH . . . and used his shoes to say He

Can . . . but his name is the sign to all of us . . . Muntather: Awaiting . . . awaiting us saying Yes We Can Too . . . If those children in horror . . . crying at the enormity of horrendous human abuse . . . the blood of children and elderly poured down on hospital floors . . . lit by a candle . . . the screams pain . . . is not moving you now to action . . .

Then What Can?

Move beyond action.

A Personal Letter to President Obama

Initially I did not want to write a letter to you, Mr. President. I did not feel that I wanted to say anything to the public. After some time, I changed my mind. This was because of some things that I picked up from a Martin Luther King Junior speech and comments about him from a talk that was delivered at Sage Chapel at Cornell in 2008. The title of his speech was "Martin Luther King Junior, the vision, the way the movement. After he spoke, I went to listen to my CD of Martin Luther King Junior speeches. A message of hope arose way inside me and I decided that I would embrace his understanding of what I came to do in this world.

Your election has assured me that Americans are a great people because they live by the principles that are in the constitution. I had become skeptical of democracies. I still am, but at this moment, I want to shelve my skepticism and begin to dream. Your election gave me no excuse to hide behind being black when I am supposed to do things that I came to do in this world. I decided to revisit the speech that I listened to at Sage Chapel.

I realized that I needed to rearticulate the vision, the way and the movement. I felt that many people had spoken about this. Pastor Dave Williams, the Michigan Pastor of Mount Hope Church, had spoken about the same topic and tied it to each and every person's understanding of what real success and creative accomplishment means. He had said, "God was speaking a new Civil Rights Movement." Since he is a white pastor, I did not understand what he said as having a meaning for all of us. I listened to the message and surprisingly took notes. I have thought about this election and felt that I should rearticulate what I heard in these two speeches. I know that I am not a world thinker and these two gentlemen are great philosophers. If they can take the words of Martin Luther King and bring out something in me, it means they are also great teachers. I do take credit for the title of being the most unteachable person. I think this is obvious from this letter.

I have decided to share with you how I have personally interpreted what they have said and what it means to us. I learned this from a speech by Sister Souljah when she gave a speech at Michigan State University in the nineties. She said that it is important to take what people say and translate it to one's life. I want to share that I have decided to redefine my vision and ask myself what it is. What is the vision, the way, and the movement that we are supposed to be working towards as people? I have come to conclude that we have to strive to see love more through color-blind eyes and do it (love) like never before. It means agreeing to go into service even when we are not sure what we will bring, believing that we will articulate the way forward with the people we work with. It means a lot more than that, but let us leave it here for now.

It also means being focused on the wrongs of the past and being willing to fix them. At a time like this, when the present sitting on us with a pressure that makes it difficult for us to breathe, we need to look through the fog, and see the light that shines into every wrong and changes it to a right. For humanity this has always been difficult. Our emotions and wanting to have more than one's neighbor have made it very difficult. At a national level, one fails to imagine the wrongs we have wrought on ourselves in trying to fix a wrong. We have ended up doing more wrongs because of the difficulty of understanding what is right. I trust that people who are lawyers like you are people who have all the knowledge and understand how difficult the struggle for truth, right and wrong etc is. Yet this is what we are still resolved to do in this new dawn.

I have decided that it means defining success both at the individual and national level in a way that encompasses the success of others besides myself. I am not sure what that means right now, but I feel that I am committed to asking myself the question, "What does my writing this letter mean to the reader who is the president, those who have no health insurance, those who have lost their homes, my children and my neighbor especially Jack the plumber?" (If I may use an analogy that came into vogue with the elections of 2008.) How will we define the success of this nation during and after the Obama years? How will I define my personal success if it means doing for myself and others? That is deep! I have learned this expression from my African-American friends.

I have decided that it is a time to embrace Africa and African-American creativity and take it to more of the world. This is because I feel that it will put my story at the center of global issues. I am not sure what to take with me on the journey of embracing my creativity. I just believe that I lived and walked as a person who could create. Some people laugh at my creativity, as you will laugh at this letter, but what can I do. It is what God gave me and I am taking the whole baggage to the creative places of this world, including your mind, Mr. President.

As I have alluded to the level of my creativity, you can see that it is not much, but what is good is that it is a personal gift. I am appealing to those who are like me to please join me in our personal venture to use this era in our lives to understand, embrace and appreciate the gift we have to create. Whatever you do with your hands never fail to believe that it will bless the next person if it comes from a heart that has the light—I hope you know that I mean a heart that has love.

This is a time of boldness in talking about our beliefs about what hurts us, what we like, what our future hopes are because being alive is about hurting, healing, hoping, and going on and never giving up. It is a time to believe we can. This is what I believe President Obama's election taught all of us. It taught us that we are a nation of people who believe they can. Hence the slogan, "Yes We Can." It must not just end here. It is time for it to go deep inside us and awaken that which made us. It is a time to look at the nothing that we were before we were born and see it miraculously coming into being, standing and saying, "Yes I Can" more with words of encouragement to each other and the president and also the environment around us.

For those of us who live in poverty, it is time to know that poverty is a state that can be changed. As a nation we cannot go on without addressing this malady. We need to think together and know that people do not invite poverty. It arises out of circumstances and man was given power to transform situations and not be changed by them. We need to look out for each other and shine a light into this darkness.

Mr. President, those who know me know that I have the gift of the garb. I like to joke even when people are serious. Please do believe that you have inspired even the likes of me to take the pen and share their interpretation of what you mean to us. I have been amazed by how I have gone back to the church in trying to write this letter. Most academics do not do that because they fear being called demagogues, bigots and the like. I had to speak the truth as it came to me. I am happy that the writers of this book gave us a chance to express ourselves. YOU WILL DO US PROUD. YOU ARE OUR PRIDE!

Sarah Mkhonza

CHAPTER 12

Opposition and Apprehension

It would be unrealistic to think, based on the previous letters, that nearly everyone in America and abroad either supported and/or voted for the new president. Although Democratic Barack Obama beat Republican John McCain by nearly seven percentage points, his actual vote total was 53 percent of the total votes cast. This indicates that he had substantial opposition in both the primaries and the general election. In this chapter, letters writers indicate their opposition to him and divulge their apprehension about Obama's ability to effectively run the American government.

Dear Mr. President Obama,

Today is January 20, 2009. It is a day that will forever change America. It is the day that American citizens formally accepted you as its first African-American president. The time has finally arrived for an African-American to be able to say "the most sacred oath."

While I consider myself to be fairly conservative, I have to admit that I am now excited for what your administration will accomplish in the future. This excitement appears to be contagious, for many Americans are almost giddy when they speak about you. What is most exciting is that American citizens seem to finally adore their new leader. Instead of past elections when people voted for what they thought to be "the lesser evil" in the political realm, America made it loud and clear that they are overjoyed to have you as president. It is relieving to know that many Americans already feel so much devotion and hope for their future. This sense of unity and patriotism seemed to diminish a little while after 9/11. I like that this has been restored.

While I still have my doubts and reservations about your administration, I think that you have already made many strides to bridge the gap between liberals and conservatives. This is a wonderful beginning, and something that I truly admire about you. After your inauguration speech, one of the first actions you performed was going and giving former President Bush a hug. You even mentioned your gratitude for him in your speech. You also invited former presidential candidate John McCain to join you at a dinner. I think it takes tremendous courage to do these things in a country where there is constant war between the two political parties. These actions demonstrate your dedication to America as a whole, and not just the Democratic Party.

This sense of unity is something that our country desperately needs. The United States is in a time of great adversity and challenge. I applaud you for your attempts and intentions to have our nation forget about the petty Democratic vs. Republican debate, and focus on the common goal of bringing America back on her feet. Thank you for inspiring so much hope for our nation. And like you have said, if we can work together as a nation, "Yes We Can!"

Sincerely,
Shannon O

Mr. President,

As a young Republican attending the University of Michigan, I never personally supported your quest to become the next president of the United States. We often seemed to share different views and I found that I was closer linked to Senator McCain. That being said, I have tried to fully embrace you as our country's president and my president.

Your election night was one of the most amazing things I have ever experienced as I joined a large group of fellow students and Ann Arborites on the streets in celebration.

While it was a bittersweet moment for myself, it was exciting, as a political science student, to see so many people rally behind a political figure. Now, even though an entire country seems behind you, there are many challenges that you and we are going to have to face. The economy is on the downswing, unemployment is on the rise, and unresolved foreign conflicts are abundant. As my president, I fully hope that you will succeed in the many tasks you set you to accomplish, knowing that it will be for the betterment of my country, my state, my hometown and my planet. Anyways, that is all I can think of to say right now. Good luck in your upcoming four or eight years and God bless.

Sincerely,
Timothy H. Shields
University of Michigan
Political Science Major

Dear President Obama,

I must begin by telling you that I voted for Senator McCain. But that is no longer an important issue. Voters have put their faith and their confidence in you. It is now necessary for Americans to come together during these uncertain times despite their differences.

I would like to commend you on a couple of things that you have done in the months since the election—first, your acknowledgment of the fact that you can't immediately begin to pull all of the troops out of Iraq and second, your choice to surround yourself with people who will be vocal and not always agree with you.

I think that you made a poor choice in picking Joe Biden as your vice president. He did a complete 180 on some of the things he was saying during the primaries when he joined your campaign. His one redeeming quality is his history serving on the Senate Committee on Foreign Relations and the connections gained from this that will be of great help to you during the next four years.

I think that now is a good time for you to use the charisma and oratory skills that helped you win office to effectively increase the flow of information to your constituents. The State of the Union addresses over the last eight years have been insufficient. A good State of the Union address should not leave people feeling like they are missing critical information. I feel that thorough your speeches and public addresses you can give more Americans the ability to feel confident in their leader and government.

I wish you the best of luck during the next four years; you will undoubtedly face trials and criticism but always remember the faith and hope people have in you that got you to this point.

Sincerely,
Katherine Eleanor Dertz
University of Michigan '12

Dear President Obama,

I am proud to call you my president. The ironic thing about that is the fact that I didn't vote for you. I was very undecided until the final few days of the campaign. I was skeptical of both candidates. I thought what Senator McCain was promising was feasible, yet yours were a little far fetched. Change is something I do think you are capable of, but to what extent? The people of the United States have wants and needs beyond your reach. You have a mere four years to give them these things or otherwise they will not be happy. I think your approval rating will suffer because you cannot make change happen quickly enough. This would be true of any president coming into office at this time. My fear is people will lose hope. You have been a beacon of light to many. I have watched with my own eyes the emotions you evoke in people and it is overwhelming. I wish you the best of luck these next troublesome years. Continue to shine.

Sincerely,
Samantha

Dear President Obama,

When you began running your campaign, you said that you believed in change. However, many of your actions seem to contradict your statements. You claim that you are an honest politician, yet you broke a promise with Senator John McCain and did not take government campaign funds. Many of your cabinet picks appear to be suspect at best. For the secretary of the interior you chose Senator Ken Salazar, who has a history of opening public lands for cattle ranchers. This seems to go against your "green" policy even if he is pro alternative energy. For the secretary of education, you chose Duncan, who is in charge of the WORST public school system in the nation, the Chicago public schools. I am from Chicago and live close to University of Chicago's campus and the surrounding neighborhood and I can tell you that I am not impressed with the work that you have done with that area, with the exception of the fact that you did shut down some of the floundering schools in the area. I, like most Americans, want to see a change for the better in our nation and to rectify the mistakes of our previous leaders. My issues are not with your policies (which I support for the most part), but your track record. How can you persuade skeptics like me that you aren't another corrupt Chicago politician?

Dear President-elect Obama,

Congratulations on your victory over John McCain for the White House. Although I did not vote for you, I believe your campaign tactics and efforts were efficient to mobilize a substantial amount of the population to support you. Your victory is unprecedented and will go down in history as a significant election. I hope that while in office you will be able to address to economic issues our country is facing without raising taxes too much. As a fiscal conservative I am apprehensive about some of your proposed legislation including universal health care. However, I agree with your stance on the environment and the necessity to "go green." I hope that you like you predecessor will continue to show strong support for the state of Israel, and even when you open diplomatic relations to countries like Iran I hope you consider Israel's interest as well as our own. I wish you much luck and success for your term in office.

Sincerely,
Ryan Garber

Dear President-elect Barack Obama,

First and foremost I congratulate you on your recent victory. However, much like the Pennsylvanians who cling to guns, for me your victory was a bitter one. For I spent my entire summer working against you this election cycle. I worked in Senator McCain's War Room. During this time, I monitored you and occasionally attacked you. In fact, I watched and listened to almost every speech you and all of your surrogates made for a good three months. I know your speaking tendencies, your favorites jokes (yes Dick Cheney won't be in the White House next year), and most importantly your promises. I am extremely doubtful this letter will ever reach your hands, perhaps some intern will read it, but in case it ever does I hope you heed and take into account my advice.

It is widely known that one of your favorite books is *Team of Rivals*. You said that once elected you would build your own "Team of Rivals." While, you have given Senator Clinton a position in your cabinet, you have yet to appoint a republican to a prominent position. Perhaps you will, I guess you could say that after this election I have become disenchanted by "hope." You advocated "change" your entire campaign. However, you have picked primarily Washington insiders from the Clinton era. I must inquire; if the people wanted Clinton insiders why didn't the democrats just elect Senator Clinton herself. While I am quick to criticize, I must give credit where credit is due and praise your decision of Rahm Emanuel to Chief of Staff, who is quite the pragmatic.

President-elect Obama, I agree with you on a lot of issues, I think the whole country does, but I think the disagreement stems on how these issues should be solved. I am sure you have heard every argument against your policy and its implementation, so I won't waste space and time repeating arguments. But I will urge and implore you to be respectful of the other point of view and not attempt to jam radical left wing legislation through Congress. You may very well get a filibuster-proof Congress, and in the event, I can only hope that you will not let the tyranny of the majority infringe on the rights and liberties of the minority.

While I worry about much, I believe that you can't do much worse than our former president. There are two wars at hand and a failing economy. A lot is on the table. However, this means there are more opportunities then ever to do the right thing. You have been presented with the opportunity for greatness. Let us reach for the greatness.

While I may be a Republican, I am also an American. I wish you the best of luck in your presidency.

Best of Luck,
Brian Wangling

Dear President-elect Obama,

Congratulations on winning the 2008 presidential election. Hopefully you will be able to make a change large enough to strengthen America and bring it out of the mess it is in. Our country needs a president whose ideas, opinions, and actions will make a difference and lead our country in the right direction. Obviously, the citizens of the United States are confident that you can make the right decisions to change our economy, education, and health care for the better. As an eighteen-year-old, voting in my first election, I was very involved in learning about all of the issues between you and candidate John McCain. Personally, I chose to vote for McCain, because I was nervous that your actions would turn our country towards socialism. Hopefully, you will be able to prove me wrong and meet the expectations of all the citizens of the United States. I find elections to be very frustrating, because of how political the campaigns become. Candidates tell their country what they want to hear during their campaign, but do not fulfill their promises once they are in office. You need to actually do what you promised and fulfill the changes majority of America supported you for. America elected you for a reason and your actions can and hopefully will make a change. I will support you as my president and hopefully in exchange you will provide a safe, strong country for me as an American.

Sincerely,
Shelby Ambrose

Dear President-elect Obama,

I am a 19-year-old Democrat, studying political science at the University of Michigan. I never voted for you. On February 5, 2008, I voted for Senator Hillary Clinton in the Massachusetts Democratic Primary. I voted for John McCain on November 4, 2008. There were a number of times throughout the campaign when I disagreed strongly with your decisions. That said, I always believed you had the potential to be a great president. I voted against you because I did not know who you were and I refused to gamble with the presidency. I hope that you prove me wrong. So far you have.

Not only have you taken a stance in favor of a college football playoff (an issue I wholeheartedly support you on), but also your selections for government jobs have been outstanding. Joe Biden was a terrific choice for vice president. Hillary will be a great secretary of state. Robert Gates will continue to be a good secretary of defense. I believe you know what it takes to be a great president. You need to be honest and straightforward with us.

There is one thing that made me almost vote for you. The fact that you have inspired so many people is not irrelevant. People are getting engaged in the process because of you. My neighbor used to say to me she would move to Washington and work in an Obama White House. You have inspired a generation and the fate of this generation's political involvement lies in your hands. Let them down and they won't believe in government and politicians for decades. Prove them right and you will have mobilized millions of Americans to take part in this process once again.

I wish you all the best. There are tough times ahead, but with wisdom, humility, and courage, you can meet every challenge.

All the best,
Anthony W. Mariano

Dear Mr. Obama,

Please don't infringe on my right to bear arms. This right has been created and protected by our fore fathers for hundreds of years; it is one of the most fundamental rights given to me by the constitution and the bill of rights. I hope that you choose to do the right thing and not infringe upon my right to protect myself and my family.

President Obama,

I just wanted to let you know that I didn't vote for you. I am from one of those small towns that you talk so strongly about and I would just like to let you know that I will cling to my guns and my religion because that is my culture and, unlike your opinion, does not express any bitterness or racism. I encourage you to visit some small rural towns and get to know the people before you talk about them or make laws that may affect their deep culture. Also remember guns don't kill people, people kill people. Bans on guns will do nothing but bring more violence. The people who are getting guns legally in this country do not plan to use them for violence they are simply using them for recreation. People who still want to get guns for violence will still get them whether there are bans or not. In my hometown we take pride in our guns it is a collectors sport and we use part of our collection for hunting. We enjoy owning a variety of guns whether we use them for hunting, target practice or just something to show off to our buddies. There is a sense of pride in killing what you are going to eat for dinner and growing the food that America survives on. Farming, hunting, and Christianity are my heritage and any candidate who does not support those things does not deserve my vote. Despite this I congratulate you on your presidency and hope that all is well with you and your family. I also thought that it would be interesting to point out that your daughter and I share the same name only mine is not spelled in the traditional Hawaiian way. God bless you and your family.

Dear Mr. President,

It has been a long standing tradition in the United States that people have been able to protect themselves and family members from harm and oppression by being able to bear arms. However, it has come to my attention that you are an advocate of gun control and the disarmament of the American people. Your actions in Illinois, I am speaking of your support of the ban of handguns and assault weapons, has laid ill on my mind for quite some time now. I am afraid of what measures you may take as president to extend this tyrannical action to the entirety of our nation. Why do you believe that disarming the people will bring about better days in the United States?

Sincerely,
John Van Hoot

President Obama,

I am writing this letter to inform you of my concerns for your views on gun control. I am well aware of your actions in Illinois, and can honestly say that I do not agree with your thoughts that getting rid of guns in the state of Illinois will reduce crime and be advantageous to human prosperity. Although Illinois is only one out of the 50 states in this nation, you are now in a very favorable position to push your views and potential regulations on the rest of the United States. Please do not try to take away our rights to own and use weapons further than the United States government's already constricting regulations. The government system does benefit the people, but the government cannot be everywhere all the time, therefore people need another way to protect themselves. In your views and preferences, guns increase crime, but even without guns, people would find other ways of committing the same crimes. Knives, rope, eating utensils, chopsticks; the possibilities are endless. It is a matter of if a crime can be committed or not. It is not a matter of what someone commits it with.

John Van Hoot

Dear President Obama,

First of all, congratulations on being elected the 44th president of the United States of America.

It is a great accomplishment. You won the support of millions. I however, do not agree with all of your policies and your stances on certain issues.

I do not support your plan for health care. I don't think that taking a step towards communism or socialism is the answer. Yes, Americans should be covered, but I believe that you should be working or somehow contributing to society to receive these benefits.

Also, I don't feel that abortion is morally right. Just because a mother doesn't want her baby, does not mean she should take a human life. In extreme cases such as rape or where the mother will not survive, then abortion should be used if it is absolutely necessary. However, an ignorant teenager who becomes pregnant due to not being safe or prepared should not be allowed to have an abortion.

I also do not believe that pulling the troops out of Iraq would be the best move for the United States. By pulling out of Iraq, the United States would look inefficient and incapable of finishing the job. We need to finish our work in Iraq if we still want to remain one of the world's supreme powers.

I know that you cannot please everyone, but if you would at least consider some of what I said it would be greatly appreciated.

Thank you for your time,
Danielle Wurth

Dear President Obama,

First and foremost, I congratulate you on a historic win. However, for two months I worked vivaciously to defeat your campaign. As you could imagine, the loss was heartbreaking. In all honesty, the campaign has left me bitter and somewhat disenfranchised, as I have now become a minority. I come from one of the most Democratic districts and I attend an extremely liberal university. However, I am ironically not persecuted for my ethnicity or skin color, but rather for my political stances. Politics tends to divide our country more than it does unite us. I can only hope that, like Lincoln, you will strive to unite our country, rather than play partisan politics.

I must concede that I have been impressed on your ability to reach out to members across party lines. When Senator Lindsay Graham, comments that "many of these appointments he (Senator McCain) would have made himself," it is very admirable. While, we may have different views on how to do things, I believe we share the same common goals as Americans. America faces two wars and the economy in the worst shape since The Great Depression. However, daunting the challenges are I hope that you will remain optimistic and remember history, as some of your predecessors had much more difficult tasks like preventing secession from the union or curing the Great Depression.

I don't expect one man to fix all the problems, but I hope you can bring us together to overcome these difficult times. I will try and do my part and act as a constant gadfly buzzing in your ear, hoping to remind you of the voice of the minority. I can only hope for the best and wish you the best of luck in your future endeavors, as it is in all our best interests.

Cordially,
Brian Wanglin

Dear President Obama,

I just saw you get sworn in as the 44th president on television today. Congratulations. This year was the first presidential election in which I was eligible to vote. However, I did not vote for you. I believe strongly in a limited government and free market politics.

In watching you since the election, however, I have come to greatly admire you. I think that you will be a positive force in bringing our country together. Our country needs a strong leader at this time. People are really disillusioned with the way things are going. More than anything please help get our economy on the right track. Please set up regulations for Wall Street, so that they can no longer take advantage of hard working citizens. I hope that the policies of yours I disagree with surprise me. I hope you are able to end the conflict with other countries. Most importantly, I hope that you can restore my faith in America.

Sincerely,
Ellen Deters Melville

Dear President Obama,

I can't say that I voted for you in this election because I did not. I am worried that you are not experienced enough to deal with the large economic problems this country will see in the very near future. I think that this is a time in our country when experience is a lot more needed than making history. The majority of the country, however, doesn't seem to agree with me. I hope, for the sake of the country, that I am incorrect in my assessment of you, and that you will lead our country out of this economic depression that seems inevitable. I also am worried that terrorists will try to test you in the near future. Try to see just how weak you are and if you are capable of protecting this country. So I ask you, what are you prepared to do if that happens?

To the President-elect Barack Obama,

I would like to congratulate you on winning the most powerful and respected position in the world, the presidency of the United States. Although I did not vote for you, I hope that under your leadership my concerns about the country will be addressed.

As a student, I am worried with the potential long-term economic downturn. The main area which concerns me is the job market. Upon graduation, every student wishes to utilize their education in the professional environment. However, the current economic crisis hinders the availability of jobs for not only recent graduates but of experienced professionals as well. I would like your administration to focus on expanding the economy in order to create more opportunities in the job market.

I wish you the best of luck and look forward to a change in the United States. I believe that your administration under your leadership will bring the United States the respect and prosperity it deserves.

Dear Mr. Obama,

Congratulations on being elected to United States presidency. Though I did not vote for you I look forward to seeing what changes you plan to make in D.C. You made many promises during your campaign and due to recent economic events I was wondering how you plan to implement the promises you made in regards to welfare services, especially when the government is currently looking at bailing out the U.S. auto industry now too? I realize you will probably not be able to implement all the plans you hoped to, which is why I was also wondering which plans you feel deserve the most immediate attention? I look forward to receiving your response and wish you all the luck in the forth coming years.

Sincerely,
Eric Vorenberg
University of Michigan 2011

Dear President Obama,

Congratulations on your recent inauguration! I do have a few specific concerns I would like to bring to your attention as a conservative thinking voter.

First, as you well know, America is now faced with an enormous deficit due to the recent recession, the war in Iraq, and many other factors. I am greatly concerned with how you plan to eradicate this debt (or at least diminish it substantially) while also authorizing an $850 billion stimulus package and almost a trillion dollars worth of new spending for "green" jobs. At the end of the day, how do you plan to help a country with such a debt as ours while authorizing nearly two trillion dollars worth of new spending?

Second, I struggle with the point that not only you, but most Democratic Congress people and your friend's make that we must tax the big corporations more and more. How will that improve the economy when all the corporations will do is raise prices and shift the burden to the general public? Or worse, jump ship and relocate to Europe or Asia erasing thousands, if not hundreds of thousands of jobs? With all due respect, President Obama, that is simple economics. If a government introduces a higher tax on a producer, the producer will increase the price of the good, forcing the consumers to bear most of the burden. Not only will there be losses for consumers, but producer surplus will also take a hit, because fewer consumers will buy the product. These shifts cause a dead-weight loss, money that could be made by producers, or kept by consumers that is lost and benefits no one.

I am also curious as to how do you plan to fix health care? We can plainly see from Canada that completely public health care hurts those that can actually pay for it, and even those who cannot by creating insurmountable waiting lists for surgeries. By forcing hospitals to treat everyone, the incentive to be devoted to the highest standards of professionalism are lost. I propose a mixed system. Provide a minimum amount of health care for people who are unable to afford any, but allow those who can to seek their own health care and be healed. As cold-hearted as it may or may not seem, that is the nature of our country, President Obama. Our free market society still has people immigrating legally and illegally to live here. Our country remains strong, no matter how much the media or Democratic party leaders tell us our last president failed us. Some of us understand that. Keep that in mind.

All of that to say, I implore you not to hurt our country by hindering it with government regulation. Sadly, the fact is that government never really runs anything at maximum capacity. Even leading economists, such as N. Gregory Mankiw of Harvard University, believe that "when policy makers set prices by legal decree, they obscure the signals that normally guide the allocation of society's resources." I wish you all the best in your endeavors to do what you believe is right for the American public. While I am, and continue to be conservatively minded, I have faith that you will do the best that you can for our country and thank you for that.

Best wishes,
Domenic Anthony Sessa
The University of Michigan–Ann Arbor
Freshman in Literature, Science, and the Arts

Dear President Obama,

Although I did not vote for you in the 2008 presidential election I feel we both understand that this country is in need of change. Some of your policies have good intentions but they need to be worked on.

As a member of the struggling middle class my dream for this country would be for unemployment to decrease and are economy to strengthen. Many families are going through hard times and aid for those families would be very helpful.

Your choice for a universal health care system will work if and only if the program is made fair for everyone and is organized properly. It cannot benefit any specific class to the extent that people wait hours and hours for help while others with the same condition are able to be seen right away.

The war in Iraq is obviously a touchy issue with many Americans. We definitely have overstayed are welcome but if you remove everyone in a fast process and not leave any type of force behind, everything we have accomplished will fall apart. A large portion of money has been put into Iraq and many lives have been lost. If we just pack up and leave, all of the hard work and dedication will have been for nothing. I agree removal of troops is needed but we should not just up and run from loyal Iraqis.

Congratulations on an excellent campaign. You made many Americans feel the need to voice their vote and you inspired many young Americans to vote as well. You will go down in history as the first African-American president, but is that enough for you? Work hard to repair this country for it is being handed to you in a weakened state. Protect this country and listen to everyone's opinion, not just one, and don't give Americans any reason to distrust their government more than they already do. By doing so you will be an excellent leader and not only go down in history for who you are, but for what you did for your country!

Dear President Obama,

Although I was not one of you supporters in the 2008 election, I am still proud to acknowledge this historical moment in the United States. I was very proud to say that I am an American when I watched your victory and I would like to congratulate you and your family, as you embark on this long journey together. For our country, I hope that we will soon see better economic times and an end to the war that has taken so many of our brave men and women from us. I know that you are ready for the job and I hope that you will take the United States to groundbreaking successes in the future.

God bless,
Maria Gronda

Dear Mr. President,

Although I campaigned and even voted against you, I am very proud that I was able to watch you elected president of the United States and that I saw history being made. I wish you the best of luck in office; please don't turn our country socialist.

Dear Sir,

I am sorry that you are so deceitful and tell so many lies. I am even sorrier for the American people who have been deceived and will have to put up with you for four years minimum.

If you believe so much in the redistribution of wealth, when are you going to capitalize your assets and share them with the people who have been mesmerized by you?

Barbara Day

To the Honorable President Obama,

First of all, congratulations on being elected president of the United States. While I did not vote for you in this election, I do believe that you are a good candidate for the job and will do a great job.

I must ask though, that you deeply consider the options for the removal of troops in Iraq. I do believe that the troop surge in Iraq helped trememdously in calming the terrorist activity in the region and I must strong object to a timeline removal. To do so would essentially waste the efforts of thousands of men and women who have fought and even given their lives to free the citizens of Iraq for a terrible dictator. The men and women who lead our Armed Forces are the most intelligent people I have had the pleasure of speaking with and I ask that you please listen to their advice.

I wish you all of the best and Godspeed.

January 21, 2009
Dear Mr. President Barack Obama,

May I first start out by congratulating you on your historic election to the office of the presidency of the United States of America. Your victory was not only a victory for you and the Democratic Party, but for America as a whole. Your election shows that anyone in America can achieve anything that they set their mind to and they no longer restricted by their race or background.

As a young conservative, I identify myself primarily with the Republican Party and their values. The things that concern me most in terms of public policy are in the areas of foreign policy, national security, and the economy. As the current president of the United States, I am hoping for you to continue in building our nations reputation overseas. At the current moment multiple countries seem to view us in a bad light do to certain foreign policies that were enacted under the Bush administration. I feel that these certain countries are crucial allies to America and we need to maintain strong relationships with them.

Regarding the Iraq War, I feel that we need to stay until the job is done. The job will not be completed until the Iraqi government can take complete control of their government and country without any protest from those against a democratic government in Iraq. As the sitting president, the citizens of America look to you to do what is right for the American soldiers and bring them home safely. However, if we leave the country too early more Iraqi civilian lives could be lost and this could lead to a bigger uphill battle.

I feel that one of the top priorities of any president is to keep our nation safe from the harm of others. I feel that one of the strong points of the Bush administration was their increase in national security. As you proceeded in your job as president I hope to see you maintain a high level of national security and enact policies to keep our nation secure from terrorists and those who want to see harm done to the United States.

Finally, as a current college student at the University of Michigan, I am starting to see the affects of the current state of the economy. In less than four years I will be pursuing a career in the job market. I am hoping by that time the job market and the economy will be stable. In terms of government intervention in the economy, I am hoping for less than what we currently have today. I feel that we need to start holding banks, businesses, and people responsible for their actions. If banks are willing to give out risky loans, they should have to suffer the consequences of their actions. Holding people more accountable and eliminating the level of government bailouts, will teach people to become more responsible. By bailing banks and businesses out after every mistake they make could cause them to rely too much on the government and this will not lead them to make the necessary changes needed in their companies to restructure their business.

As I conclude this letter, I want to wish you the best of luck. Even though I a member of the opposite political party, you are my president and I give you my full support for the next four years. May God bless you, your family, and may God bless America.

Sincerely,
Angela Pijper

President-elect Obama,

Writing to you as someone that did not vote for you, but rather for your opponent, I wanted to first, offer you my congratulations. I also want to you to know that I sincerely hope that you find success in the next four years. I pray that you keep our country safe, and continue to spread freedom across the world. If these things are done, I may change my mind, and vote for you in 2012. God bless you, and I hope that you and our country find success in the next four years.

President Obama,

I must admit that I am a dedicated Republican, however I am extremely excited to see the nation's first African-American president. While I don't actually agree with your policies (most notably your stimulus package) I think it is a major step in the United States of America's history to elect a black president. I think it is amazing that our nation is finally starting to see real equality and I believe it will only lead to greater things for this country, after all we are an incredibly diverse nation. I also think it proves to minorities that they can accomplish anything if they set their mind to it and race does not have to be the force holding you back. Good luck in your upcoming four years and I truly hope you can accomplish all that you set out to do!

Thanks,
Ashley Kuehne

Dear President Obama,

I would like to congratulate you on your victory. While I personally did not vote for you I place a great deal of confidence in your ability to lead the country. It is my hope that you will overlook the celebrity-like status you have amassed and challenge yourself to do what is best for the country while ignoring the public's critical eye. I wish nothing but the best for you and your family as you embark on what could be the best years of your life.

God Bless,
Christie

Dear President Obama,

Congratulations on becoming our 44th president. Although I do not agree with some of your policies, I feel that you have America going in the right direction and I wish you the best of luck. I am a college student and a lot of decisions you will be making in the next term will be affecting me, so I obviously have a vested interest in your policies. Again, good luck and I look forward to seeing some crucial changes.

Mr. Obama,

I did not vote for you or for McCain. I do not trust you, the Democratic Party, or the Republican Party. These institutions have long records of immoral behavior, war crimes, and corruption that could shame the Caesars.

That said, you now have the chance to "change" things, as your hollow slogan did imply during the election fanfare.

So change this:

1) A global network of military bases in other people's countries must be closed down (more than 760 bases). No American would tolerate foreign troops running bases here in the USA. Why is this double standard acceptable to Washington, D.C.?

2) Illegal wars of aggression must cease immediately. Failure to do so means that you, President Obama, become a war criminal too, the same as Bush, the same as Saddam, the same as many a despot who came before.

3) Restore the rule of law, and prosecute all government misconduct—including that of the Central Intelligence Agency and any other "black" agency operating outside of the law. Massive narco-trafficking is ongoing and rampant, and no one is even attempting to stop it.

4) Fully disclose the facts of the 9/11 attacks, including the role of the "foreign governments" which provided assistance and financing to alleged hijackers. Prosecute the former administration for the cover up of this reality and for "treason" in giving "aid and comfort" to the facilitators of the 9/11 attacks on America.

5) Fully disclose other treasonous U.S. government activity, including: Oklahoma City bombing, 1993 World Trade Center attacks, Iran/Contra, BCCI, the global illicit drug trade, covert support for terrorist networks, the assassinations of JFK, RFK, and Dr. Martin Luther King, Jr., among others.

6) Purge the government of lunatics, foreign assets, spies, and anyone who places the interests of a foreign power above the interests of the People of the United States.

7) Reform the election system completely, guaranteeing every American the right and opportunity to vote, and securing the counting of votes in a transparent, open-sourced publicly controlled system of the highest integrity.

8) Reform the campaign finance system so that the biggest money-raiser does not buy the election. Use public funds to finance third parties and mandate substantial free prime time public airwaves to political candidates and parties during the election periods.

9) Create a permanent independent prosecutor to monitor executive branch felonies and violations of the Constitution with subpoena power, and the mission to enforce the laws of the land without regard to the individuals occupying the offices.

10) Create a public health system that operates more efficiently and effectively than the current dismal failure. If a tiny island nation like Cuba can educate enough doctors to export them to numerous other nations, then certainly the United States can do similarly. The problem is there is no priority to do so. Health care should be a right, not a privilege, as should some minimal access to food, clothing and shelter. A basic minimum floor for our citizens should be acknowledged as a hallmark of a civilization that is worthy of the name.

Mr. Obama, much has been made about the label of "Muslim" or "Christian," even when describing you as a candidate. As a self-identified "Christian" you should be well acquainted with the following passage: (Matthew 5:43) "You have heard that it was said, 'Love your neighbor and hate your enemy.' (44) But I tell you: Love your enemies and pray for those who persecute you, (45) that you may be sons of your Father in heaven."

And similarly, this passage:

(Luke 6:27) "But I say to you who hear, love your enemies, do good to those who hate you, (28) bless those who curse you, pray for those who mistreat you. (29) "Whoever hits you on the cheek, offer him the other also; and whoever takes away your coat, do not withhold your shirt from him either. (30) "Give to everyone who asks of you, and whoever takes away what is yours, do not demand it back. (31) "Treat others the same way you want them to treat you."

America has never behaved this way, despite the empty rhetoric from the right wing about a "Christian nation." Our nation's blood stained history is one of an aggressor, involved in numerous conflicts in all corners of the world. Our taxes have gone to illegal wars of aggression (Crimes Against the Peace), to the undermining and overthrowing of legitimate, duly elected leaders of other lands (violations of the UN Charter), to outright terrorism and the sponsoring of "death squads," giving arms and money to "dictators" and numerous other shameful practices, which they call "statecraft."

Will America ever behave in a moral fashion in the future?

Are the "Christians" of America capable of understanding the words of Jesus?

Let's start with the office of the president, Mr. Obama, and clarify matters of morality and the rule of law, matters of right and wrong.

Dear Barack Hussein Obama:

Congratulations on single-handedly brainwashing millions of people across the country. Your pre-arranged speeches and love from the media that claims to be non-partisan has inspired many. People are completely oblivious to how cruel and sadistic of a man that you are. You ran a successful campaign that exploited the unnecessary factors in the election by questioning the wrong things. You are not fit to be president and it is sad to see that so many people can be so idiotic to want to have you run their country.

First of all how can a country elect a pro-death baby killer? You have consistently said that you would pass the worst act ever created, the Freedom of Choice Act. This act will end any regulations on abortions. Never should a baby be allowed to be killed, especially partial-birth abortions. The FOCA will not only allow partial-birth abortions, but it will allow thirteen-year-old girls to get abortions without parental consent. That is so sickening and no person in their right mind should ever pass something like this.

Secondly, how could our country elect not only a racist, but a man with proven terrorist relations? I cannot believe that people would actually believe that you were unaware of your preacher's (if that's what you want to call him) views after being a member of the racist church for twenty years. Obama, I have gone to church for many years and I am well aware of all of my pastor's views. Let me jog your memory, "God bless America—no God Damn America." If he does not like our country he needs to get out. Does anybody honestly believe that the government created AIDS to keep the black population down? That is ridiculous and way out of hand. Bill Ayers is a great friend of yours, along with many other terrorists. How can somebody honestly vote for a man who is friends with a terrorist?

You talk about pulling out of Iraq, but then you say we need more troops in Afghanistan. Are you out of your mind? Let's tell the terrorists the day that we will pull our troops out so they can come right in and take things over again. Great idea, Mr. Obama, you are a football fan right? That would be like the coach one team walking across the field and showing the other coach the team's playbook and telling him all the plays the team will run. Makes a lot of sense right? Think about it, the idea of pulling out immediately is completely idiotic. Believe it or not, Mr. Obama, but we are actually winning the war.

Mr. Obama, you tell the country what you plan to do (even though it changes every day and depends on who you are talking to) but what have you done? The answer is nothing.

As a senator you did not have a single accomplishment. You constantly voted "present." Mr. Obama, even I can go to Capitol Hill and vote "present." You were in charge of one committee that never met; that shows great leadership.

You do a great job of reading a teleprompter but your true feelings are shown when the teleprompter leaves. People actually voted for you after you told them they were a bunch of low life's that cling to their guns and religion. You tried to play the race card and you divided America because of this.

Are you truly proud to be an American? I do not think this is true. You did not put your hand over your heart for the pledge of allegiance. You refused to wear an American flag pin on your lapel. You listened to Reverend Wright blast America for twenty years. How can people think for one second that you would be fit to be president?

How can any American believe that your policies can actually work? Do you even realize what you say sometimes? You said that you wanted to "spread the wealth." Mr. Obama, that's called socialism. You even said your tax plans would bankrupt our coal industry. Your health care plan will never work. Why would we want the same health care as a third world country? Joe the Plumber was 100% correct with his statements. Instead of questioning his statements about your policies, you chose to find dirt on his personal life.

You think that the laws on drug dealers are too harsh. How can you honestly believe that? Maybe it's because you admitted to the use of marijuana and cocaine when you were in college. Our country elected somebody who has a history of drugs. You want to make things easier for illegal immigrants. Did you catch the key word? ILLEGAL. There is no reason to make things easier for illegal immigrants. They broke the rules and they should be punished, not rewarded.

Mr. Obama you are not fit to be president of the United States. You talk about "change" but you never specifically say you reasons for change. Change for the sake of change is not always best. Mr. Obama, I fear for our country. I fear for our economy. I fear for my safety. The worst of all is that you have lied to the American people. You ran a campaign on lies, fake promises, and with no respect to your opponents, and succeeded.

Chapter 13

Congratulations

Many citizens simply wanted to offer their best wishes, thanks, and hearty congratulations to the new president. Here, in these letters, individuals pour out their personal feelings of gratitude. Many of their sentiments are quite moving.

Congratulations President Obama,

Mr. President, your victory in the Democratic primary and in the presidential election was a political and monumental accomplishment for this country. Moreover, when the state of Ohio put you over the top for the presidency, I cried because I had been waiting for this moment in history. Furthermore, I believe that your victory will inspire more minorities and women to believe that they too can aspire to become the president of the United States of America.

When I realized that you had won, I reflected for a moment and thought about the many African-Americans and white Americans who risked and gave their lives to make this country a better place to live in and to provide opportunity for all in the United States. Mr. President, I think of the individuals who lost or gave their lives for freedom and secure the civil rights laws and voting and rights laws for this generation and so that future generations could enjoy these freedoms—the freedom to vote without intimidation from mobs seeking to prevent them from exercising their right to vote. Furthermore, I reflect again on the individuals who gave up their lives for the freedoms that most U.S. citizens take for granted today. The names that I recall risked their lives to protect our voting rights and freedoms that we possess as citizens of the U.S. regardless of race, class, or gender. The individuals who gave their lives must be identified and recognized such as Emmett Till, Mrs. Viola Liuzzo, James Chaney, Martin Luther King, Jr., Medgar Evers, Andy Goodman, Addie Mae Collins, Carole Roberson, Denise McNair, Cynthia Wesley, Mickey Schwerner, and the terrible beating that Mrs. Fannie Lou Hamer endured to gain the right to vote. The list of individuals that died for freedom is much longer than the list that I have identified. But, the known and unknown foot soldiers are celebrating a victory that they envisioned when we did not.

To those who sacrificed for this moment, I thank you. To those who were not born during that era, I say to you many individuals sacrificed their lives to provide you with freedom, and the right to dream and become a mayor of a major metropolitan city, governors of a state, state senators and state representatives, a member of the U.S. Congress and a U.S. Senator, and yes, the ultimate prize: the president of the United States. Mr. President, your victory in winning the U.S. presidency in 2008 will encourage many minorities and women to achieve what some thought was the impossible, however, President Obama, your victory made this objective obtainable and made this goal a reality in our lifetime.

Sincerely,
Dr. Lewis A. Randolph, Ph.D.
Professor, Department of Political Science
Ohio University

President Obama,

CONGRATULATIONS, President Barack Obama, on becoming the 44th president of the United States of America. Who would believe that in times like these we would have an African-American elected as President?

I am so proud of you and even prouder of how you ran your campaign. As I watched the returns, I was praying for you to continue to get the electoral votes needed to be elected president—and I can say at the 11th hour of the 11th month of the year, you captured the highest office in these United States. What an exciting time for all people of every race!!

Your acceptance speech was brilliant and inclusive of everyone, even for those who did not vote for you. I know that after you take office everything will not be peaches and cream, but the challenge is before us to reach for the sky—because there is no limit to what we as a people can accomplish—you proved that by being elected the 44th president of the United States.

Congratulations again.

President Obama,

I've never thought that one person could make a difference, that one person could change the world. I've never really been a believer in the power of the individual, or even the power of the people as a whole.

My senior year in high school was when I first became interested in politics and a teacher of mine suggested the book *The Audacity of Hope* to me. I was very skeptical; I had read similar books before and was never impressed, why should this one be any different. However, after I was finished I have to admit I was intrigued. The things you had to say were interesting, inspirational, and made me think (something that doesn't often happen in high school).

The 2008 election was the first I have been eligible to vote in. Until recently I was never passionate about voting. I thought, if the president is truly elected by the Electoral College, why am I even voting? Even so, if I do vote, what difference does one vote make in the scheme of things? Then I thought about that same high school teacher who lent me your book. What would he say? He would be ashamed, that one of his favorite government students wasn't going "to exercise her right as a citizen, and fulfill her civic duty".

Now two years after I first read that book, here we are. You are about to become president of the United States, and I am a recently declared Political Science major at the University of Michigan. I have realized the politics is my passion and no matter what people say, one person can make a difference. Whether it's a high school teacher, a college student, or a young politician with a vision, the individual makes a difference.

The young, the old, the rich, the poor, the conservative, the liberal, all believe in you. It's time for a change in America and you're the perfect person to lead us into that change.

Congratulations and good luck!
Brittany Selmi

President Obama,

My heart swells with pride as I type this letter addressed not to a Senator, not to a president-elect, not even to a president, but to a fellow American, one who I particularly admire and who has inspired me time and time again. Your eloquent inaugural address delivered earlier this morning was one such time; it was moving and earth-shattering, deliberate and transcending of the moment. The best I can do is thank you. For the changes you have already brought to my country, and for the changes you have promised me will come. The way you carry yourself with dignity and conviction has a profound inspirational effect on American youth, and I say this because I witness it every day, in myself and in my classmates on the campus of the University of Michigan in Ann Arbor. You have spread a sweeping wave of optimism I have never, and will probably never again, witness. People believe in what you can do. They believe our country will be improved in your hands. You deserve this glorious burden, and we deserve you.

I never thought a period of time would be more rewarding than was October and November of 2005, which as I'm sure I needn't remind you, was the sweet triumph of OUR Chicago White Sox! However, the excitement I feel now in January of 2009, and felt during the election in November of 2008, may very well have proven me wrong.

I thank you on behalf of the millions of young Americans, who will never forget where they were today,

Martin Armstrong, Jr.

Dear President Barack Obama,

It is an absolute honor to have you leading our country for the next four years. The inspiration and revolutionary spirit that you have revived in the American people is amazing to watch and be a part of at this specific time, all odds against America. As a senior undergraduate student about to graduate in a matter of months, I have felt the negative impacts of our economy and current state of our job market. It is awful to see fellow overly-qualified students struggle like no other class has before to make a mark in the job market.

From my understanding unemployment rates are sky-rocketing and people are losing their jobs at an increasingly fast-paced race. It is upsetting to witness and be victim to this terrible phenomenon, and it is my sincerest hope that your administration will be able to alter the path of employment for graduating students and to allow those who are employed to be more secure in their jobs. Thank you for inspiring Americans for a better America, and best of luck to you.

Sincerely,
Rupa Ramadurai

From: Senthil Kumar Kurunthachalam
Dear President Obama:

Congratulations. You registered your name in a history record book. Your black diamond body (including yours wife and beautiful daughters) going to beautify White House in another 4 years but I wish you should continue even after 4 years 2013–2017 even after with your perfect regime. I admire your determination, your cool answers, your policy, your style and the way you talk. There is no doubt that you going to be one of potential strong leader to the states. I wish that you should fulfill all the promises you made especially on economic policy. I would love you even if you withdraw all the war forces sitting in Afghanistan and Iraq. It is not shame but I consider as a wise move.

May GOD bless you and support you in each and every good step you take. Please wipe the tears of many middle class peoples and poor community.

Please also have a very good relation with INDIA only other democratic country in the world. You would admire so many things from India if you visit and make some INDO-US collaborative economical schemes. I wish you all the best and my support will always for you.

God bless you and God bless America.

President Obama:

I would like to thank you for the enthusiasm and energy you have brought to my generation, and restored in my parents' generation. I am so proud to be an American at this time, as we have shown that it is still a very special nation. I wish you the best of luck and I understand that things will probably get worse before they get better. And since you played with the UNC basketball team last year, I feel obliged to say, Go Heels!

Best,
Scott Strogatz

President Barack H. Obama,

I would like to express my sincere gratitude to you and all of the achievements you have accomplished. I find it so remarkable how far we have come as a nation in such a short time. I still find it hard to believe that we have finally elected a black president. Even a few years ago, I believed that we would only accomplish this feat twenty to thirty years from now. You truly are an inspiration to all Americans and all people around the world. I honestly thought America was heading into one of its darkest times in history but you have clearly demonstrated that we are still a great nation and are still capable of truly remarkable things. I have not felt so good about the direction this country was heading since the catastrophe of the 2000 elections. You are a beacon of hope to all Americans and are a prime example of achieving the American dream. Even though we are facing very tough times ahead I am certain you will lead this country through them and we will emerge stronger and more united than ever. The American people have called for true change and you are answering that call. You have made history President Obama and I am so proud to have been able to witness it. I wish you the best of luck in these next four years and I am certain you will be called upon again by the American people to continue your noble service to the United States in 2012.

With my highest regards,
Kevin Lane

President Obama

I have to say I am very pleased to see more diversity in the White House. I am also happy to see that there is a president who believes in government work programs, and a redistribution of wealth. Whether or not you agree, I feel it imperative to make the United States more like the rest of the Western world. By saying that I'm implying that although as you said in your inaugural speech we are and will continue to be innovators and leaders in thought and technology around the world, I believe we are still too greedy. To reallocate the wealth to those who work hard in the middle class would really help take away the image of a greedy America. A humanist view is additionally something that has been lost in America in the last few years, especially with obvious torture cases at Abu Graihb and, yes, other facilities during the War on Terror. I wish you the best and hope that after the third year of your presidency Americans are still on your side and comprehend that true change takes time.

Thank you for a minute of your time,
Eric

Dear President Obama,

You go down in history, not only as the 44th president of the United States of America, but also as the first African-American president. I am proud to say that we have come such a long way in a short period of time. It shows that the youth of America has changed to be more open-minded, and no longer see the color of skin differently. It is evident that people stand for their beliefs in a new era and are able to disagree with their elders and acknowledge that the color of skin determine the competency of a person, but it is the person within.

Congratulations and thank you for having the courage to step up and make a change in a country that begs for change. I look forward to having you as my president and am excited to see the good that you can do for this country and the positive that will come out in both the near future and in the future afar.

Sincerely,
Amanda Roberts

Dear President Obama,

First of all, it is with great pleasure that I am able to acknowledge you as president of the United States. I believe you will do extraordinary things for our country with your outstanding determination and ability to reach out to all races, religions, and people of varying political opinions. This, combined with your seemingly sincere desire to do what is right, will make for a successful eight years as president. Please do not let the political scene of Washington lower the high standards to which you currently hold yourself.

Mr. President, perhaps your greatest strength is your positive leadership and inspirational words. Your "Yes We Can" campaign slogan summarizes exactly who you are. You believe in yourself, your family, your friends, and the United States. Instead of pretending problems don't exist like many politicians, you acknowledge the problems and explain how we as Americans can fix them. In doing this, you always instill the power of change in the people. With your positive, honest leadership, Americans can look forward to a new era of economic prosperity, energy independence, international respect, self-reliance, and pride.

I will rest easy tonight knowing that you are at the helm, President Obama. Now you must put your appealing words of campaigning into action and lead the United States into a new era, one in which the American dream is redefined and achieved.

Dear Mr. President:

I am a senior citizen who has memory of presidents since Eisenhower. How differently I feel at this time. I feel ownership. You are "My President." I have high expectations of you. I expect that you will respect me as well as all of the other people of this great country. I expect nothing less than your best and anticipate receiving that. Good luck, Mr. President. My prayers are with you in these times of major issues.

Thank you Mr. President and God Bless America,
Barbara

Dear President Obama,

As your term begins, there is a great deal of unrest around the globe. Problems such as the conflict between Israel and Palestine, the genocide in Darfur, and the looming economic crisis (and the underlying problem of addressing the instability of capitalism) will make your presidency a critical one. It will also make it incredibly difficult. I understand that you cannot combat these problems alone, and that progress will be slow if any true change for the good is to be made on any front. But most of America probably won't. And that is why I am writing to you today.

You will quite possibly be under the most scrutiny of any president in history. Every false step you make will be on the headline news. Along with the media, anyone with any reasonable or unreasonable grudge against you will be after you. Basically, you're going to be under intense pressure from everyone.

What I would like to ask of you, Mr. Obama, is to ignore all of the upcoming pressure and hype and stay true to your beliefs (and focused on the job that lies ahead). When I first watched you announce that you were running for president, I saw a genuine and passionate figure make a fantastic speech. I saw a man who honestly cared for those less fortunate then himself. And this was very exciting. But all too often, exciting figures such as yourself never live up to their potential as politicians. They get jaded and warped by corruption and failure within the system. But please, don't fall into this trap that most politicians fall into and lose yourself to your job. Avoid the temptations of money and power. Avoid being a corporate jockey. Avoid the ignorance and pressure that leads to violence and destruction. Instead, stay true to the values of peace and equality that you have stressed so well in your campaign. I assure you, that if you do this, nobody has any legitimate reason to criticize you. If you can honestly say that you're the one defining your presidency (and not the other way around) while you serve our country, your job will be alright with me. So please, stay true to yourself, and don't let anyone push you around. That's all any good citizen of the United States can ask for.

With humanity in mind,
John Oltean

Dear President Obama,

I just finished reading *Obama* by David Mendell, and your story inspired me to further pursue a career in political science! After reading about your struggle through school and in Illinois politics, I am now more interested than ever to continue to law school, and hopefully work as a politician some day!

To President-elect Barack Obama:

Hello my name is Alexandra Lynne and I am a student at the University of Michigan.

Over the past year I have been following your campaign closely and I have waited for change to come to America.

In October, I attended a local concert by Bruce Springsteen to rally support for your cause.

As I listened to the acoustic tunes of the Boss on a tranquil fall evening, I felt in my heart that the next president of the United States will move beyond just being a number; he will solidify a unique place in history.

Now, one day before you take office, I truly believe that change has indeed come to America. Mr. Obama you have made history by being the first African-American man to be elected to office, and I expect your presidential term to succeed the election with the same prestige.

Mr. Obama, you are a unique individual that serves as a source of inspiration for many Americans including myself.

At a time when our country is emblazoned in turmoil, I believe that you have the tenacity, courage, determination, intellect, and intuition to revive our nation.

Good luck and congratulations on being the next president of the United States of America.

Sincerely,
Alexandra Lynne

Dear President Obama,

Congratulations. I am very excited to say that I had a stake in such a historic election and as a nineteen-year-old first-time voter; I could not have chosen a more exciting election to be my first to participate in.

I am both nervous and excited for your upcoming term in office, mostly because of the current economic situation and the status of our troops overseas, but I am fairly confident that you and your administration will be able to handle it. It can't be handled much worse than it had been for the last eight years anyway . . .

Good luck.

Sincerely,
Katie Rosenberg

Dear President Obama,

You are inspiration not only for me, but for millions of others across the nation and the world. It is because of you that I am going to law school and potentially into politics. I will never forget the chills that went down my spine when you were elected president. It was at that moment that it was made so blatantly clear that the American dream was still alive and well for everyone. I just want to ask that you keep a strong commitment to curb global warming and climate change. I sincerely believe you when you speak of creating millions of new green jobs. I will keep my commitment to lowering my carbon footprint, and can only hope that you do the same from your position of power.

Thank you for being such an inspiration,
Chris Blain

President Obama,

Throughout your campaign, you inspired millions to believe in change. You publicly denounced the corruption and injustices in our country, among other things, and therein achieved superstar status in our political system. Surrounded by what seems to be annual scandals in Washington, you pursued the selfless road of service with your morals in your pocket. Still, some would love to steer you off course, and even more would love to witness it. Whether or not you save the world (as much of the public may expect), know that I will be overjoyed if all you do is execute your duties with honesty and decorum.

David Taylor
Rockville, MD

Dear President Obama,

Congratulations on winning the election and becoming a symbol for so many Americans of a nation progressing toward positive change. In a country in which inequality is still so prevalent—merely disguised and ignored—it was amazing to watch the degree of political mobilization that occurred this past November as the public came forward in tremendous numbers to exercise what I see as freedom of choice. And their choice was you, exemplifying a significant step in truly embracing diversity; their choice was to turn around the disappointing direction that this nation has traveled in under the administration of the past eight years.

I have great faith in your ability to exert an impact upon this country for the better, and am proud to be part of the generation to see you into office.

Again, congratulations, and best wishes to you and your family.

Jennifer Z.

Dear President-elect Obama,

I am counting down the minutes until your inauguration! It seems as though Bush's final year of his presidency has been interminable, and I think I speak for a great many Americans in saying that your administration will certainly prove to be a much-needed breath of fresh air for our citizens. After volunteering on your campaign in the policy department of one of your Michigan offices, I became fully engrossed with the campaign and have greatly enjoyed watching you mold your policies and follow through on your promises. Further, it has been a thrill to follow you as you fill up your cabinet and create such a "valedictocracy"; I have nothing short of the utmost confidence in your cabinet's ability to pull this country out of the mire that we are currently in.

OBAMA '12!
Best regards,
Hannah

Dear President Obama,

With your victory comes a sense of speechlessness so profound that I can only be reminded of the voices of our ancestors whose blood, sweat, and tears were overcome by their strength, resilience, and bravery, so that you and WE could live to see this day. All Americans are better for this moment.

One of the wonderful things about you is that you recognize that this moment is bigger than yourself. You bring both an acknowledgement of America's dark past with a renewed sense of foresight into a future with bright possibilities that recognize their tragic point of departure. For the thousands of Americans lost in the middle of this trajectory to a better, more inclusive America, you have been the missing link so many have been waiting for. This is not simply because you are black, but because of the black American you have chosen to become one that genuinely cares about uniting the marginalized with those who have set the margins and with others who may have never cared either way in the first place. You are a proud American who is a friend of all of America. Everyone wants to hold your hand and through you we are holding each others.

The symbolic value of president Barack Obama is essentially not about you—Barack Obama—but about America and its potential to be the beautiful America that we envision in our dreams, speak of in our hearts, and read about in our history books. Your election as America's first black president brings us closer to the perfect union.

Many have made you out to be an exceptional American with a diverse background and educational experience that has uniquely positioned you to lead the United States at this critical moment in American and world history. I consider you extraordinary precisely because your life experience can be so easily traced to the common man or woman. You are exceptional because you have ordinary beginnings from which Americans from all different walks of life can identify.

At Oberlin College, our motto was, "Think one person can change the world? We Do." It is unrealistic to assume one man can change the world, but at Oberlin we never thought it unrealistic to try.

President Obama, we certainly do not expect that you will solve America's deep-rooted problems in education, race relations, global warfare, the environment, health care, etc., but we expect that you approach these issues with the vigor, open-mindedness and steady hand as if you, with our help, can positively change America and the world. Your example inspires me and the world to work harder, care more and together make the world better by each doing our own part.

You are one person, but with us, you are America's face. Thank God I'm fortunate enough to look in the mirror and see the reflection of America a little more clearly.

America needs you, the world needs you, and most importantly, WE ARE WITH YOU.

Peace and Blessings,
Menna

President Obama,

First of all, let me congratulate you on the election. I am very excited and comforted knowing that you are our next president. I feel at ease knowing that you and I both share a passion for universal health care and I am looking forward to your policies regarding health care. I look forward to seeing all of the positives steps our country will not be taking with you as our leader. I am once again, proud to be an American! I hope the transition into the white house with your family is a pleasant one.

Thank you for your time and support,

Sincerely with great gratitude,
Carly Constantino
MSW Student
P.S. I saw you on *Ellen*. You do dance better than McCain, however, Michelle has you beat!

Dear President-elect Obama,

I would like to start off telling you how much you have inspired me. I have read both of your books and find your life story truly amazing. I wanted to wish you good luck with your presidency because this will be one of the most difficult starts to a presidency in American history. I think you are just as fit or more fit for this then any other president we have had. I hope you have the ability to turn things around in the economy that is at its lowest point since the Great Depression. The American people need a strong leader now more then ever and you have been chosen to be that leader.

Best,
Kevin

Dear President-elect Obama,

Let me start by congratulating you on your victory. I must say that it is not a victory shared by only you, but by the entire nation. This was the first time I have been able to vote and it was definitely an experience I will never forget. Our country is in dire need of change and I truly believe that you can revitalize not only our economic situation but also our spirit. Your passion and strength prove that you are truly devoted and have taken on this position because of your undying love for our country. It certainly will not be an easy feat but I think you are the most capable to accept the challenge. Watching the results come in on election day brought tears to my eyes. Seeing how many people were smiling and crying when you won was moving. I have absolute faith in you and I know that you will do your best to pick this nation's head up in a time of need. I commend you for your bravery and commitment.

Thank you for believing in us,
Allison L.

Dear President-elect Obama,

First off I'd like to congratulate you on winning the presidency. November 4, 2008 will forever be a historical date and marks a great advancement towards the end of racism in our country. Although I consider myself fairly conservative you should know I greatly respect you as a person and will stand behind you as the leader of the world's greatest nation, no matter your political affiliation. I feel we as a country are too concerned with political parties and are missing out on many important issues. Being a Republican, Democrat, or third party member shouldn't matter, at the end of the day your decisions still affect nearly 300 million Americans. All I ask is that you live up to your promises and strive to better society as a whole. I hope you always keep the American citizens in mind and make decisions not just to please the Democratic Party, but to benefit our country.

You're considered a hero to many Mr. Obama. Please don't let us down.

Sincerely,
Nick Sattelberg

Dear President Obama,

I'm sure that I am not the first to say this, but congratulations on your historic and inspiring presidential election. While many people have said this election is important because of your race, I am thankful for your victory because of who you are. To my generation, you are a symbol of hope and change, and as a Democrat, you bring welcome relief from the last eight years. I implore you however, to not fall short of your rhetoric and promises, and to deliver the leadership and guidance this nation needs, especially in these difficult times. We understand that some unpopular decisions will need to be made, and I am confident that you will make them on their merit not on political strategy. I believe you are a man of supreme intelligence and judgment and I hope that your term in office will be as historic as your election.

Good luck!

All the best,
Alex Leikin

Dear President Obama,

First off, congratulations, congratulations, for being chosen as the instrument of change for a nation in need. More than congratulations in being chosen to fulfill the most powerful position of this country, I would like to say good luck. Good luck to you for the next assumed eight years. You have been called upon on a basis of statements and promises and the values you stood behind during your campaign period. Good luck in your quest to fulfill these words of change and to provide the American people with exactly what you promised. America expects a lot from you; I expect a lot from you. The fact that you won this election not only obligates you to your platform, but also you have just become the role model, and symbol of the African-American people. Now that is something that should put you to sleep with a smile on your face each and every night. You are the American people, you are what they want, and you are the African-American people, you are change, and you are the next American president.

Good luck!

Cheers,
Devin McGahey

Dear President Obama,

I want to congratulate you on your election to office. These have been hard times on our country as of late. I know that you will do your best to put our great nation back on track. We need a change from the status quo—you are our answer. Please do not let us down.

Growing up as a first generation Asian American, I was not originally that interested in politics. My parents didn't feel that even with citizenship they understood enough about the issues at stake to vote.

Thus, up until high school history class, I had no intention of breaking from their course of action to be an active participant in politics. Through my education, I was enthralled by the prospect of my vote making a difference. I think that the election of the year 2000 confirmed that one vote does count—and I'm glad that I was able to voice my vote this year.

You are an inspiration to the young and a beacon of light for our generation. We need change, and we are looking for you to bring it.

All the best,
Jenny Leung

December 2, 2008
Dear President-elect Obama,

Two things:
First, congratulations on your election to the presidency.
Second, there is a verse from the Christian Bible I would like to share with you. In the past few months, this verse has encouraged, challenged, and guided me in being a leader. I hope it encourages, challenges, and guides you as you lead our nation.

Psalm 78:72
And David shepherded them with integrity of heart;
with skillful hands he led them.

Please lead our nation with integrity of heart and skillful hands.

Sincerely,
Joshua Z. Symes

Dear President-elect Obama,

First of all, I want to congratulate you on your amazing achievement. The perseverance and determination you exuded throughout the campaign was inspirational, and filled American's hearts with confidence. This triumphant sense of confidence made people realize that you, the next American leader, will bring about monumental change to restore the greatness that once was associated with America.

Additionally, I wanted to thank you for making my first voting experience as great as it could possibly be. It was an honor to be able to vote for you, knowing that when you won, I would support your administration to the fullest, along with having a great feeling about being an American. The support that you had throughout the campaign was historic, and that speaks to what you were able to do over the last four years. Witnessing history, as you spoke in Grant Park, was a feeling I have never had before. I was proud to be an American, and to have you as our representative of America, and everything it stands for.

Finally, I wish you the best of luck. I, along with millions of other Americans, have the utmost confidence in you and your administration. Knowing that you, President-elect Obama, will run our country I am confident that we are moving in a great direction. Thank you for all you endured throughout the campaign, and I wish you and your entire family all the best.

Thank You,
Brian Gutman

Dear President Obama,

First of all, congratulations on being the next president. It's a big accomplishment. I know the next four years are going to be difficult due to the destructive policies of your predecessor, George W. Bush. I'm sure that an Obama administration will be able to get America headed in the right direction though. I just wanted to discuss a few issues that are important to me, and in part why I voted for the Obama/Biden ticket.

For my entire life, there has either been a Clinton or a Bush in the White House and it is nice to have something different. Nothing against the Clinton family, but personally I felt as though David Axelrod, David Plouffe, and you just ran a better campaign. And we all know about the divisive "Rovian" tactics of the Bush administration, so thanks for staying above the fray and not being like Karl Rove. Essentially, that was one of my main reasons for supporting you and the other was your opposition to the war in Iraq from the beginning. Clearly, that has not gone well for the United States and has only lowered our standing in the eyes of other countries.

As for the important issues for the next four years, obviously the economy is the United States' top priority, as evidenced by your support of the necessary bailout package. Without a solid economy, the United States will not be able to fight issues like global warming or alternative energy, which are serious topics facing my generation. I'm really looking forward to your plan of creating green jobs and putting more hybrids on the road, but the economy is still more important and should have greater importance than any other issue at the moment.

Sincerely,
Steven Geelhoed

Dear President Obama,

Since that beautiful night in 2004, the Keynote Address that inspired a movement, your destiny was clear. The next day, the chorus grew strong with quiet whispers of, "He could be our president someday." Now here we are, four years later with a destiny fulfilled.

To paraphrase your words, "You are what we've been waiting for," President Obama. It's no longer a whisper, it is a loud roar shouted from mountain tops around the world. I pray that your presidency will be blessed and you will steady the state of our nation and our relationships around the world. It is with great pride that I can call you my president.

Sincerely,
Sedonia Cochran
Everett, WA

Dear President Obama,

I admit that I did not support you at first. In fact, I did not support anyone at first. At the beginning of the primary season, there seemed to be no stand-out candidate that would be the answer that so many American's had been looking for after 8 years of with President Bush. Neither Democrat nor Republican seemed like a good fit. But then, my father watched a speech you gave and mentioned you to me, a freshman in college at the time. My father said, "That Barack, I like him. There's something about him that just makes me want to trust him. I'll vote for him." This was after one speech, and from the mouth of a life-long moderate Republican. If anyone could make my father seemingly switch parties after one speech, I knew I had to investigate. I watched the debates and various speeches that were available, and I have to say I saw what my father saw: you truly gave hope to the people. For my father and me, you gave us the hope that our country could once again be the great nation that we know it is. The bad economy, the unnecessary war in Iraq, and the out-of-control unemployment rate (felt especially hard here in my home state of Michigan) are just a few of the issues that cemented my belief that you were exactly what the country needed. I know that my father did vote for you, as did my mother, my sister, and I. We all look forward to seeing you take command and be the leader you seem to have been born to be. I offer my congratulations on your historic victory and send good wishes towards you and your family. As for the 2012 election, should you decide to run, I can guarantee you that you have my vote from the get-go.

Sincerely,
Jessica

Dear President Obama,

Congratulations on winning your hard fought campaign for the presidency. I admired your clear and articulate message of hope and unity for the nation. We as a nation will need the consistency of this message as we face the challenges ahead of us, as the "greatest" generation begins to slowly leave us, and those of my generation who faced the challenges of the Korean Conflict begin to slip away, it is urgent that the torch be passed to our young and diverse citizenry with tact and diplomacy.

Some are calling us an entitlement nation. I do not believe this, and feel that most Americans wish to earn their living and the rewards of democracy. However in recent decades it seems the only hallmarks of success are conspicuous consumption and the accumulation of wealth. I do not believe Americans begrudge anyone great financial success as long as it is not borne on the backs of poorly paid employees. Every decent, hard working, honest and reliable employee deserves a living wage regardless of job description. How else can they exist beyond survival status?

Hopefully, Mr. President, you can foster a more compassionate culture where the measure of character is worth more than the measure of wealth.

I have many more thoughts and dreams about your presidency, but I have said enough. I'm sure much more will be covered by other writers. Thank you for the opportunity to share my ideas. God bless you, your family, and the nation.

Sincerely,
Dennis Hoppenstedt, age 78
Lynnwood, WA

Dear President Obama:

Heartfelt CONGRATULATIONS!!! You are truly an enormous inspiration to millions not just in America but all over the world as evident in the public support and well wishes you have received. I, like so many others, have shed tears of faith, joy, hope, peace, unity, and of dreams fulfilled as a result of your victory—that country's victory.

It is my personal belief that you have been chosen by God. It is by His Divine intervention you are where you are today and my family and I are so grateful. You and your beautiful family will have His shield of protection at all times. Continue to keep Him first and foremost in all you do, no matter how small or insignificant. Continue to model His teachings as recorded in the Holy Bible and pray much.

We love you!

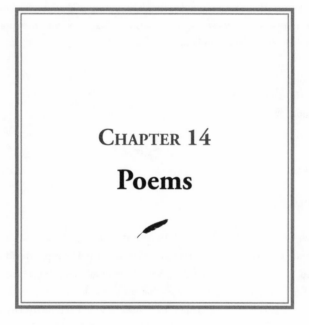

CHAPTER 14

Poems

Not every word of appreciation, joy, and support came in the form of a standard letter. Several came in a poetic form and these people, just like the prose writers, have inventive, colorful, and innovative ways of expressing themselves. All congratulate the new president and talk of the inspiration they feel in his leadership. Perhaps poetry is the best way to describe this historic moment.

"Yes We Can and Yes We Did"
"Yes we can and yes we did"
So it seems,
Rising up as a nation on the promise
Of the Constitution at hand across
The land
Yes we can
Believe in one,
Take the challenges of the world
And work to resolve the
Problems at birth or behind the
American Wall
Yes we can
Exchange power from one hand to another hand
Change gender as one believes
Look beyond the race and color of skin
But
Accept the Executive Power of Change
For our land
Yes we can
Move our struggles around the energy crisis, economic problems,
the Financial downfall, mortgage loss and
Unemployment plus do not forget!
Fallen heroes on foreign streets
And Wall Street let down as the Dow goes down
Crime on the rise who will take the time
Education needs changes
But our struggle is not over yet
Yes we can
Become one nation overcoming
Our failures
Rising to our problems
Solving our issues
Reviewing our policies and making wise decisions
Yes We Can and Yes We did
We can take our Changes
And our belief in Change
To the Destination and Proclaim
Our Reign on Democracy for All

And
Democracy for our
"Cause from home to abroad."
Vera M. Grant

Savannah, GA.
Dear Mr. President,
You are a remarkable person.
Do remarkable things.
With hope and prayer in my heart,

Rosie Ullman
P.S. May we please leave our shoes on now?

God's Greatest Creation
by Tamara Shepard
Sitting in a corner with a pad in your hand
Staring out the window pondering on what you
Once had . . .
Lost it all—It happened in a blink of an eye.
Head slumped low rehearsing the reasons why try
What changes can occur that can pull you out
Of your rut . . .
Voices fill your head of all the negative words
Saying your never going to amount to nothing
Before you convince yourself your life is over
and those words are true.
Meditate on the success of the ones before you . . .
Rosa Parks took the stand,
Martin Luther King made the walk.
Oprah decided her fate was to talk . . .
Not enough Tupac decided rap was his way . . .
Over the top, there is more to say . . .
Take a look at Jennifer Hudson struck down as an Idol
But look at what God did—her future couldn't be brighter . . .
Let's also take a look at history today—

The law abolishes slavery but the symbolic chains remain—
Until a senator by the name of Barack Obama talked about change.
Now in 2009 we will have our first black president . . .
So how can you wonder about your life and time
and how it should be spent . . .
Stop your pity party and start your celebrations . . .
You too are a star and one of God's greatest creations.

Step up to the plate
Citizen of the planet
Everybody has a point of view
So what are we going to do?
Track your carbon footprints
Take conservation hints
Tread gently on the earth
Reevaluate worlds' worth.
Make plans for the future
Say the scientific tutors'
Conserve water, oil and gas
Are we up to this task?
Counting carbon emissions
Making daily decisions
Our legacy the earth to save
From the cradle to grave.
Step up to the plate
Citizen of the planet
Everybody has a point of view
So what are we going to do?
MINUTES TO MIDNIGHT
MINUTES TO MIDNIGHT
Here beauty and truth,
Stretched out ahead
As we strolled a path
To greet the dead.
Our minds were sharp

Six senses keen
We traveled light
The years were lean.
Man's greatest pride
To feed the poor
Strike out terror
End genocide.
Mankind one with nature
Idolized our Creator
Our inner creativity
Drew society to diversity.
For the principle of honor
We used military power
World problems we'd mend
With justice and valor.

Vintage Shadows of my Aspirations—
I was mesmerized by the shadows on my Brazilian wooded floors.
They were not shadows of fear or desperation but of (something).
You could tell when the gusts of wind would stop to inhale there would be a brief pause
as the shadows returned to equilibrium.
These shadow were brazen, carrying no baggage or guilt.
They defied their label of shadow.
They were defined, bold, dark, poised.
They were created in a time of quality, a time of political meaning.
They were the eyes of a revolution.
They were the eyes of a new beginning,
They were the eyes of a hundred women.

Dear President Obama,

   I wrote that poem in a time of confusion a time when I, like so many Americans, were suffering from the harsh realities in our world. I wrote of my hopes and dreams: of my aspirations that are vintage in a time not yet experienced: a time of equality. I continually pray for this equality in all aspects of life, learning, and living for there is no hierarchy of oppression. Audre Lorde stated that an attack on one's social identity is an attack on all social identities. I firmly believe this, but thus, must also believe that by defeating the odds of our targeted identities we all rise together.

I want to thank you President Obama for defeating these odds and helping us all rise up. You have given young minds the dedication, drive and fueled our passion to constantly strive for the very concepts our founding fathers created. It will be our differences that define us, and at times separate us, but it will be these very differences that defy the odds.

Thank you for all that you have done and will do for our Nation.

Democratically yours,
Sunethra Muralidhara
Sophomore, University of Michigan

Dear Mr. President,

I write to you as a person who has had a difficult time in making a decision during this campaigning season. I finally made my decision for YOU, Obama, last week. Here is what I wish for OUR America. I wish first for Change, change to bring our sons and daughters home from war. I have no children over there in Iraq; however, I have friends that have children over there. That would be my first request. Secondly, being raised in some part of my life in an orphanage I know the great power of America and would like America to be once again, THE LAND OF OPPORTUNITY. I believe in you Obama. Thirdly, I want to wish you protection for the God that watches over each and every one of us. At this time I want YOUR family to stay safe. As, tears flow from my eyes, and my heart beats rapidly, it is with this I endorse who you are. This is not a race of color this is a race for survival. Our country is in such hot water that we really need someone who will come through with promises. Palin was recently in Carolina, at a college, Elon, in which my niece Kristina attends. I asked her what she thought as she had phoned me last week. "Auntie," she said, "she was full of empty promises and said things anyone could say." "There are a lot of Republicans down here," Kristina went on. "So, I am voting for Obama!!" she said. I thought what a smart young women. There was no talk of race for she had chosen whom she thought was the best person for the job and she is a smart kid!! An honor student. Someone YOU would want on YOUR team OBAMA! So out of the mouth of babes and OUR future, OUR children are choosing YOU!

Work hard for us for we represent the FAMILY of America! Let's get it back! Let's not forget 9/11 either as it is time for the quote "LET'S ROLL" to reappear in YOUR campaign speech! Say these words with respect and dignity as you are talking of many peoples family and friends we have lost. Three being from my home town.

I have made my decision and I place my future and the future of my daughter and my future grandchildren in YOUR hands, Obama! As, I have decided on YOU for a change to remember what America once was and what it can become again. Better and more Hopeful! DON'T FORGET ABOUT IT Obama! Love and change are important for OUR FUTURE.

May God bless you and keep you and your family safe.

Always,
Summer A. McLaughlin

January 20, 2009
Dear President Obama,

Sometimes, the Truth cries out for Grand Guignol (the shocking theater tool) to be its partner, a crucial ally in Truth's desperate plea to be heard, acknowledged as the only way for Reason and Hope to breathe again, prevail—your brave promise and intention for All, not the Few. You are to be honored, and given people's patience, sacrifice, total involvement. I'm an octogenarian composer, novelist, and poet who has lived through, witnessed, wild, ungodly times, heartbreaking times, magical emboldening times in the history of our species, with its singular talents of inspiration and imagination, and despite its repetitive pattern of two steps forward, three steps back. I pray; even atheists are trying prayer on for size, these potentially Armageddon days of the twenty-first century. I pray that you and We the People successfully join in a common dream of healing the frighteningly injured, glorious experiment in Community and Democracy called the United States of America, succeed for our people, for the world's people, for the very Planet. I embrace you with these words:

"Infame!"

I keep thinking in my room:
I should listen more to Mozart,
reread de Tocqueville on Democracy,
after Socrates and Plato, Engels, Marx, of course.
Take a swig of Verdi; no, bel canto's not enough.
You'll need a long gulp of Bach
before walking out that door.
To where?
Out there, to stop the chaos

With Reason, deadly accurate.
Like Voltaire, pussycat.
So why can't I?
Murder by Word! Murder by Idea!
Both quick as bullets to the heart.

I keep thinking all of that
in my room, and more . . .
Kavoom! Ta-da!
Watch the sucking carnivores flee
when Reason and the Word outraged,
with frying pan in hand,
chase them off the earth,
right over the damn moon!
Count me in! I can yell "Infame!"
I own a cast-iron frying pan,
I'm here! I'm here!

    No, I'm not (here) after all of that.
    I'm stuck with fingering my rosary.
    Rubbing thin my worry-piece of jade.
    Trying still to peek up Mama's skirt
    and Papa's pants. Splaying down to Allah
    till my joints hurt. Wrapping
    my phylacteries in all the wrong places.
    Until I look like what? A failed comedi-anne?

I open the door for a breath of air.
Slam! I can't get back! Kerr-ist!
What in the name of God is going on out there?
A stew of bodies floating in cold grease!
Again?
Swelling velvet skin, tender chests
Tattooed with holes! Again?
Abandoned babies hung in trees,
Flickering out like dying stars.
The streets are screaming: "Murder! War!"
    I reel, I faint,
    I hear a mocking voice:
"Hey you, writer, over there.
Cat got your tongue?

Your epiglottis closing, heart contracting?
Did you bring your weapons with you?
You'd better had!
The wilding ones are back and raging,
Raping, killing, de-de-humanizing.
"And Poetry?
That seeming tinsel, fragile creature?
They think she's crucial. Why?
She's always the first to know, to go.
See her over there on the rubble hill?
The beautiful one with the popping eyes,
contused and bloodied, legs spread wide,
still alive?"

    Fear bubbles in my mouth
    As if I'd drunk detergent.
    "What weapons?" I yell
    across the keening square.

This anonymous, mocking answer comes
From I know not where . . .
"The ones you twirled, lying like an odalisque,
a eunuch in the harem of your brain.
'Reason . . . Idea . . . the Word.
All quick as bullets to the heart,' you say?"

    In disbelief,
    My head is shaking no, no,
    like a metronome.

"Ah, but now, here you are,
clad in nothing but your id,
and the door has locked behind you.
The locksmith's dead. You can't go back.
You shiver?
Find a sweater for your soul.
Take it off a corpse.
Now that you are here, know this:
either join with us or die inside.
Start cooking, Writer!
The stew is spoiled.
The cook's gone mad. Again.

Start shouting, you,
you with your pen and brain."
"Infame! Infame! Infame!" I try.
"No, Writer, louder, louder!
Breathe! Deep!
Exercise your lungs!
The streets are lungs!
The streets are going deaf
from pain! 2,3,4.
March
your heart
and soul! 2,3,4.
Left! Right! Left! Right!
Louder Writer, louder!
1-2! 1-2! 1-2! 1-2!"

Doris Schwerin

Dear President Barack Obama:

I offer my congratulations and best wishes for success as our first African-American president of the United States of America. Teaching at a HBCU, I had an opportunity to witness how your political campaign has been the catalyst of hope/change in government for a generation of young voters—Generation Y. Today, your accomplishment as president is an inspiration for all Americans.

In spite of my belief that this dream could not be realized in the United States today, I voted for you. Your victory is nothing short of a political tsunami. I pray that your legacy after leaving this office will inspire hope for future generations as well.

One of the most important responsibilities of the president is to exercise the charge of the commander in chief. I hope that your administration will break from the past, and embrace humility as well as compassion for all nationalities of people. A sense of humanity should not stop at the American border.

As a political scientist, I believe that all great leaders are truly compassionate humanitarians. We the people of the United States hope that you will be remembered in American history as one of our great leaders like Dr. Martin Luther King. He stated that: "Those people who practice Christianity have not only a moral obligation to do what is right. They have a moral obligation also to speak out against what they know to be wrong."

In U.S. foreign policy we cannot afford to be silent when either our allies or adversaries fail to show compassion toward civilians. Human laws should incorporate natural laws including respect for life, liberty, and pursuit of happiness (property).

It is important that you never forget the faith and hope that we have placed in your administration during these challenging times ahead. Americans are praying for your success and the safety of your beautiful family. Hope has defined your presidency. We have responsibilities as citizens to continue to participate in this process of change. In providing good leadership, may God grant you the wisdom to do what is best for our nation.

Sincerely,
Larry L. Wright, Ph. D.

"ONE BLOOD"

Come America, let us sing the song of ourselves—
The signature hymn whose tune was once but a wispy
Breath that danced on the lips enslaved brethren, of the underprivileged,
Those of a second-tier—the song of a separate but unequal people—
A hymn! Birthed by a suffrage booth.
Raise up your voice America and let the song of Change be heard.
Hear and Believe—Hear and feel—Hear and be inspired.
Let us bathe in the refreshing cool of ourselves the newborn babe.
Democracy and Unity; united we have proved to be.
United we stand in our return as the beaconing light on the horizon of Hope.
Oh America, rejoice as we prove our good with brotherhood
From sea to shining sea!
Come America, let us sing the song of ourselves—
A song that only we know the words; a song only we can sing.
Hark! Listen, to the once silenced chain gang children of this nation—
For they sing a joyous tune, like the sweet nothings whispered by Aeneus to Dido.
The rapture of it Tickles at the Conscience of our Soul and resounds!
Inoculating Freedom and Equality from the paralytic disease.
America, We have unearthed the Democratic ideal of Union
The democratic Dream in limbo—dormant—not perished:
It smoldered in the cooling ash and promised: "Soon! Soon! We shall overcome!"
And behold America, we have indeed overcome and Oh!

America, look and see what lies before you:

Oh beautiful, for spacious skies!

Come America, let us sing the song of ourselves

For we can see! We can see! We out cried for Change for so long

Lamenting that he had gone from this country, and like a new Great Father,

Change heard our cries. Change has held the Union. Change has come.

My brother and my sister, together we make this journey; the quest

To trample out the vengeance that those grapes of our shackled history have stored.

All aboard! All aboard! The new Conductor calls to us

Singing the inspirational whistling of our Call to Arms: Yes We Can!

Hear the call and we cannot but join in together

as one voice; one people, one soul, one country—One Dream no longer deferred.

Alas! Hark! Lo!—The Gatekeeper tears down his guarded wall and Angels cry unto us:

Oh America, welcome home to the Promised Land of the Free, the Brave, and the Equal!

CHAPTER 15

Hope

Letters in this category call upon the new president to revive, renew, and reactivate America's "can do" spirit. These letter writers ask that Obama act not only for citizens of this country but also for those all over the globe. Others inform the president of how he has given them great personal hope, a hope they can embrace in their lives and futures.

Dear Mr. President,

Congratulations on your victorious presidential campaign. The next four years will come and go faster than we can imagine and I hope your time is well spent and you make the most of your position both in this country and around the world.

I hope for you safety, both personally and for your extended family.

I hope for you an easy transition from Illinois to Washington.

I hope for you a strong cabinet and board of advisors as they assist you through your term.

I hope for you a clear mind in which to make the best decisions for the country.

I hope for you wisdom as times will prove tough and you will question your position.

I hope for you strength for leading the military both on home soil and far from.

I hope for you a trust in the American people as hard working individuals who need a government to support, not burden them.

I hope for you joy as you travel the world and shake hands with fellow leaders creating lasting friendships and peace.

I hope for you success as the 44th president of the United States.

Alyssa Doster
University of Michigan

Dear Mr. President Obama:

How thrilled my family was when you were elected president of the United States of America. It was the most glorious day of our lives. My dad is 83 years old and to see him cry tears of joy was a touching moment for our family. For we never thought that we would see such an accomplishment in our lifetime. Our pastor said, "Rosa Parks had to sit down so that Martin Luther King could rise up; Martin Luther King stood up so that Jesse could run and Jesse ran so that Obama could win." You have given us all a hope for the future. Our prayers will forever be with you because the weight of the world is on your shoulders and all eyes are on you.

Let me just tell you this, that the Bible does not promise any of us exemption from hardship, even the chosen of God. In fact, it warns us of the inevitability of suffering and takes such for granted. We're in a fallen world, and all who live here experience the effects. However, God made a promise that gives us victory over all we experience: "I will be with you." In the very midst of our trials God offers this safety; He is with us; and this security: "He will never leave us." God's presence makes even our sorrows smile. We love you and your family and wish only the best for you all. "May the love of God and the sweet communion of the Holy Spirit, rest rule and abide with you henceforth now and forever."

Peace be with you,
Marilyn L. Felder

President Obama,

Thank you for giving our country hope in a time where every single person has some sort of concern about our future. I believe that we must be inspired to change in order to achieve sufficient change, and you have provided that inspiration. I am optimistic about our future, and so are many other young people. We are the future, and it is up to us to change our country for the better. Thank you for giving us this realization. I am sure that you will become one of our country's greatest presidents, and I am proud to say that I helped elect you into this high office.

Good luck,
Lyndsey

Dear President Obama,

I could not be more ecstatic that you will be our next president. My middle name is Hope and I've always felt that hope is the most important thing to possess in every facet of life. I believe that you will be the most dynamic and inspiring president our country has had thus far. I feel extremely fortunate to not only have you as president, but also be a part of history with you. Thank you for giving this country hope and showing the world how the American people can come together and use our civic duties to make necessary changes.

President Obama,

You provide hope in this great country in a time where hope is surely needed. This nation needs a facelift, and I believe you are the man capable of giving that facelift. End the corrupt and counterproductive drug war, reform education, and patch up our diplomatic relationships abroad. You have restored my generation's interest in politics. We are proud to be Americans now more than ever before. Continue to lead us with your unwavering confidence and optimism.

God Bless You,
John Pitcher, Jr.

Dear President Obama,

I simply wanted to write this letter to thank you. I want to thank you for giving me hope. I know you campaigned on having hope for our country as a whole, and although you have inspired that within me and so many around me, that is not exactly what I am talking about. I want to thank you for giving me hope for me. Although I am not sure I will ever be able to explain why, when I see what you have accomplished it gives me hope for what I can accomplish. When I watched your inaugural speech I felt that I had it in me to change things or affect something or someone for the better. I say explaining why would be difficult because there seems to be little that relates me to you. We are of different gender, race, age and background, but the hope is still there. So again, thank you. Thank you for allowing me to feel and hope that I can be and do better. I wish you all the luck, courage and hope that you have inspired in others to guide you through your presidency.

Wishing you the best,
EKC

Dear Obama,

I just want to share with you that I have nothing but hope of success for you. I voted for you because the words you spoke were genuinely spoken. Our nation is in a desperate time of need, we can do nothing but go up. Staying focused on your plan is what you shall do and cast out all negative moods. It is your time to shine, make the United States of America proud.

Good Luck,
Your Constituent

President Obama,

Your election comes at a very dangerous and important part in our country's history. The honeymoon for winning the Cold War is over and now there are many other influential actors on the international stage. Also, our domestic economy is struggling worse than it has in over 50 years.

I was impressed and inspired with how your election galvanized the population. I hope you can use this popular support to institute programs and initiatives that create real progress for our economy. I also hope you, along with Secretary of State Clinton, can manage to keep our country safe from our enemies. Please do not underestimate the evil, resolve, or abilities of the countries and people that wish ill against us.

The pressure you are under must be immense. I ask that whenever faced with a difficult question, you look towards our constitution and our history, because those are the two most powerful resources a president has at his disposal. Our country was the first democracy, and we still exist because our presidents have, for the most part, always acted in accordance with the founding fathers' beliefs. I have no doubt you will do the same.

Good luck Mr. President,
Ben Cook

Dear President Obama,

There isn't much that I want to say that I'm sure you haven't already heard millions of times over from people like me all around the country. I would like to make this short and sweet in hopes that this letter reaches you and my voice can be heard. You have restored my faith in the federal government. For the past eight years—the majority of my young adult life—I have seen our form of government abused and the constitution ignored. I have always wanted to be a politician and everyone always tells me not to because everyone in Washington is corrupt. Well I'm glad to say I can now prove them wrong and point to the new administration for a renewed sense of faith in America. I know in these tough times you will prove to the country what it means to be a true leader and bring prosperity and safety back to the nation.

Thank you.

President Obama,

Red, white, and blue. You have made me proud to be covered by the colors of this great country. You have spoken of Hope, I have decorated my campus with the word Hope, seen Hope in the faces of those in the Nation's Capital, and spent endless nights lying awake contemplating the power that Hope does possess. You have shared with this Nation your hopes for us, now I'd like to share my hopes for you.

I hope you know what lies ahead, because I can't grasp the vastness. I hope you know how many hearts you hold, because I can't even begin to comprehend the mass. I hope you know how you've inspired me—guided the past year of my life toward setting standards for my future higher than I can reach. I hope you know that I did my best to help, spending months campaigning motivated by potential for there to be actual change. I hope you know how proud your family is, as the media captures Malia and Sasha's eyes glisten as they see their father conquer mountains. I hope you know I realize the "we" in "Yes We Can" includes me, and I plan on doing my best to fulfill my end of the deal. I hope you know that the country's prayers are with you, and millions of heads are held high because of you.

Wishing you all the best,
Nicole Livanos

President Obama,

Congratulations! Today, January 20, you were sworn in as the president of the United States of America. Pressure, anxiety, pride, nervousness, and many other emotions must be circulating through your body as you plan to attack the current state of the United States. We are currently experiencing a recession, our national image and security are more questionable than ever, and the overall quality of life continues to drop among United States citizens. However, as they say, "the night is darkest right before the dawn," and I believe your passion and love for this country will guides us out of the darkness. Your policies, you cabinet, your decisions are all vital to our nation's turnaround, however, I believe your charisma and image that you project to the rest of the world will enormously help us in our foreign affairs. I look forward to your presidency and I wish you the best of luck.

Sam

Dear President-elect Obama,

I want to personally congratulate you on your victory last November and I, like so many other Americans, look forward to what you and your administration will be doing for our country in the coming years. Despite the many hardships we as Americans have faced over the past seven to eight years, I have become motivated and have developed a strong need to learn more and become involved in our government. Over the last 2 years, I have followed your campaign, learned about your positions on issues, and immersed myself in political thought, as well as the 2008 presidential race. Your devotion and passion for America has truly redeveloped my own passion for our country and has inspired me to major in political science here at the University of Michigan. You are what we as Americans need now in this time of economic, international, and environmental uncertainty. You give the depressed hope, and the fearful courage. You can change America forever, and start us all on a track that will lead us through the next several decades. I ask only one thing of you during your presidency—that you never go one moment, make any speech, or a single decision without remembering the everyday American who works tirelessly, day in and day out, who strives for a better future, and who puts their dreams of a more peaceful world and stronger America in your hands. From the bottom of my heart, thank you for everything you do and I wish you only the best in the job ahead of you.

Sincerely,
Steve McKenzie

President Obama,

Prior to the 2008 election, I had never really followed politics. It was not that the material was too dense for me or not relatable, but I just felt that it was not very interesting and it was not going to affect me whether or not I tuned into a political debate or kept up to date on candidates' political platforms.

As a college student voting in my first presidential election, however, I began to sense the buzz around me as people were getting more and more excited about the possibilities for the future of our country. So many parts of the election were targeting new ideas, breaking new boundaries, and becoming youth-focused. I started peeking at the political news, and turning up the volume when newscasters delivered the latest campaign updates. Soon, I realized that this election was an exciting mixture of getting strong ideas across to the masses, countering negativity, and standing strong. It was inspiring.

Your campaign more than anything has inspired me to never lose hope and to keep forging through what may seem like impossible obstacles. It can't be difficult to try to influence public opinion when billions of people are watching your every move. I am amazed at how much support you have gained within such a short amount of time, and not only that, but how strongly your supporters feel about you being our president.

What I am inspired by most though, is that throughout all the publicity and events in your life, you remain a down-to-earth person, a loving husband, and a good father. These are values that I feel transcend politics. It is nice to have someone to look up to who remains himself despite a complete whirlwind of a year. Of course, you talk about positive change for our country, but your moral character is something that I hope never changes!

Best,
Vickie Hwang

Dear President Obama,

I am pleased that you have been elected our newest president. I have high hopes that you will help take our country out of its poor current situation. I am pleased that you have already created and have begun to implement plans to help our economy and create new jobs. I wish you the best! Good luck!

Best,
Anita Gebralter

Dear President-elect,

You embody change and fill so many people's hearts with optimism! I know things will not be perfect in your administration, but I trust your judgment in the face of adversity. I want you to know that I will be praying for you and your family constantly as I am sure this will be a very big change for everyone involved.

Best,
Olushola A. Samuel

Dear President-elect Obama,

It is truly remarkable what you have been able to accomplish. As the first minority president of the United States of America, you provide hope to ALL Americans. Only 50 years ago, what you have accomplished would have been unimaginable. Even though you are an inspiration to all Americans, the hardest part is yet to come. With our country facing a number of challenging issues like: the state of the economy, terrorism, and a dependence on foreign oil we need a true leader who can unite both Democrats AND Republicans and lead our country through these troubling times, and not just a charismatic leader.

Good luck,
Mark

President Obama,

You are such an inspiration, and words cannot express how proud and happy I am that you will be our president. I wish you all the success in the world, and I know that this country and the world will benefit greatly from your presidency. You will remain in my prayers.

Sincerely,
Lauren

Dear President Obama,

The integrity of public and private institutions in the United States has eroded. From government distortion of scientific findings to outrageous compensation of CEOs, the rich and powerful have become accustomed to abusing their positions. I grew up in a generation committed to making the world a better place, was disillusioned to see those ideals trampled in a deceitful war in Vietnam, and have been further disheartened by the current War on Terrorism. I watched my son join in the infantry full of idealism, serve in Afghanistan, and return disillusioned. Much of my retirement savings has been swallowed by Wall Street greed. I feel cheated, angry and demoralized. I desperately want to have a country that I can believe in—and depend upon.

Principled leadership, beginning with you, is needed to restore ethical standards for public conduct. The work required to resurrect our economy and deal with the environmental challenges posed by a still growing world population are daunting. Nonetheless, your greatest legacy could be the restoration of integrity throughout this country sparked by your presidential leadership and vision.

John Guckenheimer

Dear President Obama:

Congratulations on becoming the 44th president of the United States. Your historical election is affirmation to the progressive vision of the people of our country. You have much work ahead of you in your first term in office. I am encouraged and hope that you remember that building stronger ties with the global community and unified action is highly important in dealing with the multitude of issues that we face today. Bringing our allies to the table when making decisions will go a long way towards creating a positive global climate into the future. Whether dealing with economic policy or foreign policy, if we have a strong coalition of nations behind us your plans will be most easily and successfully executed. I believe that the best possible future of the world lies when countries share common goals to a common end. Creating a climate of global cooperation and goodwill should be high on your list of your priorities, for it will pay great dividends now and into the future. Best wishes in your first term in office.

Respectfully,
Jordan Schwartz

Dear President Obama,

Your election has been an inspiration to me. Though I am white I, too, have overcome great adversity to achieve all that I have and have hope for the future. I can only assume that your skin color and ethnicity have raised eyebrows all through your career, closing some doors to you and, probably, opening several others. As a half-Jew, I have had a taste of the animosity you have dealt with forever. My legitimacy as a moral, spiritual, and ethnic human being has been questioned by some Christians and rejected by some Jews. Caught in the middle, I lost touch with myself and was open to predators and harm.

During the last several years I have turned the corner, so to speak, and am able to envision myself as a contributing, respected, and valued member of society. Though I must credit my associates with helping me thus far, your election affirms my belief in myself and what I can accomplish. I am reaching, just as you have, the level of confidence in my position, abilities, and future that I can open my eyes to those I see struggling with personal and institutional impediments to progress. I have decided to pursue a career in public service with the aim to influence policy and change through policy and music. Policy facilitates upward mobility and expression gives the soul the energy and commitment to make it.

Thank you, President Obama, for the hope you have brought me and countless others. I do not expect you to solve the incredible issues facing our great nation, but I do see your presidency as critical in domestic equity and international tranquility. Please continue to remove the barriers to individual progress; you have already given us the energy and commitment to succeed.

In sincerity and admiration,
Jonathan Hulting-Cohen

Dear President Obama,

First of all, congratulations on achieving one of the most defining moments in American history. It is unfortunate to still have to say in our current time that this is such a monumental achievement for the African-American community, but it certainly is. Your achievement is an uplifting message that although racism still inherently exists, the playing field is slowly becoming more level. Although you have broken the whites-only barrier that the White House has maintained for the first time, hopefully in years to come crossing that barrier will be celebrated as much as the election of a white president; clearly, a President-elect has never been a milestone for being white, because it has been the norm. We can only hope for this outcome in the future.

Secondly, I recently read the novel by Frank Rich entitled *The Greatest Story Ever Sold*. It was about the selling of the Iraq War by the Bush administration. If I was not forced to write a research paper on the book itself, I do not think I could have finished reading it. The lies and propaganda that the administration spread to the American public were absurd. It is incredible that a democratic government that is supposed to derive its fundamental power from the people could be run in ways such that democracy was thrown out the window and the people were tricked into giving their support. I have always had a fundamental distrust of government in an age where power and money prevail over everything, and this book simply reinforced my views. I extremely dislike this book for depleting my faith in something I know I should be passionate about, but in the end, it is not the author's fault that our administration has truly committed these atrocities . . . He is simply expounding them for the public's sake.

PLEASE give me something to believe in. Through this election you have, and I hope that you will continue to do so when in office. The entire American public has been let down by the Bush administration, and we could all use an honest, ethical administration (or at least as honest and ethical as politicians can be). Be straightforward, do not deceive us, and do not allow corruption to take place at any level of government. I truly believe you are levelheaded, but you know the old saying about how power corrupts. We do not expect you to be perfect, but we expect you to do your best. Prove to the world that under your leadership the United States is headed back towards a positive direction and worthy of respect. I believe you are more than competent enough to achieve this, and I anxiously await your first term as president of the United States of America. Good luck.

Sincerely,
Lauren Dominick

Dear President Obama,

The American people elected you because they have hope for the future. Much of that hope was based on faith that you would do the right thing. However, we don't know where you stand on many issues or what policies you will implement to address problems or issues facing us, because your campaign focused on vague generalities and platitudes, rather than a specific plan of action. As you said yourself in one of your campaign commercials, "Change to what?"

The only change we need is change that will move us forward, not set us back. We don't need change that will tie the hands of those serving to protect us domestically and abroad, that will overburden large and small businesses that create and provide jobs for people, that will reduce the ability of families to do good for themselves and others, and that will increase government's power over us. We don't want to be burdened with taxes, government regulation and debt that will stifle our economy, our growth, and ourselves. We want to be empowered to do for ourselves, and not have a nanny state that financially supports us and thus decides what is best for us. We want to keep our hard earned money, not have the government decide who gets to benefit from the fruits of our own ingenuity and hard work. We don't want the government intruding into every aspect of our everyday lives. Our government exists to serve us, not the other way around, and we want to keep it that way.

The United States of America has been the envy of the world for more than two centuries because we enjoy the blessings of liberty and we are willing to fight for those blessings for ourselves and for others. We hope that your presidency will continue policies that will keep us safe from threats to our national security and ensure our collective prosperity so that we can continue to be a beacon of hope for everyone around the world.

I wish you the best of luck, and am excited to see what you will bring to the future of our great nation.

God Bless,
Erin

Dear President Obama,

I would like to first and foremost congratulate you on reaching a milestone in history. You have given hope for many of those out there, Americans and people all around the world. Dreams are always possible if you have the drive and the capacity for success.

What this country needs is change. Out of anyone who can turn this country around, it is you. It is you who can bring change to a country that needs it now more than ever. Your vision for a new and better America is not only feasible, it will be achieved. Your dreams for a new America give people hope. In one of the hardest times this country has ever endured, your aspirations encourage people to not give up.

I am proud to witness such an important event in the history of the United States of America and cannot wait to see change for this country. Change for the better, change for the people, change or the future.

God Bless,
Tanya

President Obama,

It is hard to put into words how happy I am that you are president. I hope you will be a breath of fresh air to the United States and that you really will be the change that this country needs. I'm a very optimistic person, but I have many friends who are cynical and think that your words will be only that—words. Please don't let this be the case. Please prove them wrong. Honesty is something that needs to be more evident in politics because I feel that currently that value is sorely lacking.

Keep your promises President Obama, America has put its trust in you.

Sarah Wulbrecht

Dear Mr. President-elect,

My sons attended "award-winning" schools. It soon became obvious that these schools were also "award-seeking" schools. I would rather they were simply schools that cared about the students first. That is why I am reassured by things I've heard about you recently. I am reassured that someone said you were a mediocre senator, that someone else saw you as a small town mayor. I find this reassuring, since you were obviously focused on something that mattered more than getting noticed.

I was born and raised in the heart of a community that was built on cooperative ventures. My heart's desire as a girl, was to grow up there and raise a family. Today, I am a recently divorced woman who has lived or worked in 23 different places around the world. I am a mother, a musician, a seminary graduate, and founder of a non-profit, in that order. I partnered with artists and professionals to reconnect people in systems of all sizes with their own authentic processes, in ways that lead to creative solutions. Because of moves, a non-supportive marriage, and lack of funding, I gave up working. Now I am beginning to recover what it means to be a member of a small community near where I grew up.

I know what it means to build community and find partners, but so many young people have no idea how that feels. I am writing out of concern for my sons, who I raised as my parents raised us; to care about each other and everything around us; to be honest, to work and play, to share and learn, and most of all, to appreciate what we can, and to let go of the rest.

My oldest son was described as a genius when he was five, because of his ability to describe what was around him and what his perspective on things was. He used to compose music as fast as he could think, but has worked since he was 18 as a programmer. My middle son was happy from the moment he was born. By the time he was 9 he started bringing up possible explanations for why he felt sad; maybe it was too much milk, maybe no one else had a sense of humor, maybe no one knew who they were. He told us once, "You always are who you're going to be. You just don't know it yet." He is trying to start his own business in a city where he and others got out more votes, percentage-wise, than any other city in the country in 2004. My youngest is a bit of a cynic, having seen the results of his brothers' efforts. They have all "hunkered down" to earn a lot of money as programmers.

They wondered if the world really is as callous as it seemed until you were elected. You have given the world hope and we are energized by knowing our country finally had the combination of heart and good sense to elect someone with a vision who still has the energy to express it. Someone who has been able to navigate around the obstacles, to jump the hurdles, to see a way through the disappointment and rejection of a single-minded and opaque culture that hoards its resources while going after those of others.

I remember an earlier time of cooperation, when farmers worked together, when late-night and weekend deliveries were made from businesses to help someone finish an outdoor job before winter set in. Every day, newscasters instill fear by broadcasting scarcity. The stock market does not dictate reality unless we believe CEOs really deserve the wealth created for them by employees. The wealth of this country lies wherever people live and work toward something. There is an abundance of resources for development by anyone with the energy to motivate mutuality, partnership, cooperation. More important than that is the enrichment we get through the exchange of our resources and efforts.

Children and young adults and all of us need to feel the support of community again and experience the potential of human understanding and finding a common vision.

I wonder what sustains you in this country, to carry you beyond the misperceptions and reactions of others? Is it something your family instilled or your international experiences beyond our country? Show us how to stand up to the culture of greed, competition, ego, and scarcity.

CHAPTER 16

Praise for America

Beyond expressions of exuberance and excitement for President Obama's brilliant political achievement, several of the letter writers are similarly ecstatic about seeing America live up to its promise and to the great ideals that are expressed in the formative documents of the nation. The results of this election affirm the nation's strong belief in the doctrine of equal opportunities for all.

Dear President Obama:

My father was a Holocaust survivor. As a boy, he lost his father to genocide and spent two years in a Nazi concentration camp. He came to America with nothing, just the hope that America would offer him a chance at a new life. He got that and more.

He ran a thriving business. He married a nice American girl. He bought a home. He raised two sons and sent them to college. He skied. He golfed. He took his boys to the World Series. He drove a Cadillac. He lived the American dream. He was proud of his life, his family, and his country.

Though he died in 1985, if he were here today, he would be reveling in your election. He would point to your father's story and say it was just like his story. He would say it was true that that in America anyone can become anything they want to be, if they work hard and want it enough. Seeing you elected president would have validated so much of what he believed.

Now, you have the tough task of living up to his aspirations and to mine. I know your job will be tough, nearly impossible. However, if you stay true to your beliefs, and always strive to make the American dream a reality for as many citizens as possible, I know that you will succeed, and I will take pride in my father's dream, and in your father's dream.

Best of luck, Mr. President.
—Bill Wolfsthal,
New York, NY

To President-elect Barack Obama and our new first lady Michelle Obama—

I am white. I am a woman. I am 65. I have no land line, communicating only by cell and Internet. I am a retired professional. I do not seem to be reflected in the polls; in this, I suspect, I am not alone, as tonight's election results may suggest.

In the sixties I demonstrated for free speech. I marched passionately for civil rights, fought with conviction for women's rights, and stood up to end the war in Vietnam. To the dismay of all who stood together in these righteous battles, hatred emerged from our commitment to peace and equality. Division rather than unity resulted: between men and women, soldiers and citizens, black and white, Republican and Democrat.

Before I turned thirty every great leader of my lifetime had been assassinated or imprisoned: Mahatma Gandhi, killed a few years after my birth, became an icon shaping my early thinking. The assassinations of John F. Kennedy, Martin Luther King, Malcolm X,

Robert F. Kennedy, and the silencing of Nelson Mandela—too soon yet to be seen as symbols, these were among the better known casualties contributing to the failed hopes of an entire generation of dedicated activists. Even John Lennon's murder in the street at a time when music was the only thing keeping our hearts from despair combined finally to break the path of our determination. Our future died.

A generation of bright-eyed idealists succumbed to drugs and apathy, decades later emerging as yuppies focused on individual materialism and new agers focused on inner growth and individual enlightenment. Though not entirely socialized, our passion for social reform had been successfully sublimated.

This week's election victory was not only a triumph for black citizens and minorities. You, sir, stand for so much more than the color of your skin. You reflect what we can be when we are at our best. You demonstrate, not the idealism to which I sacrificed my youth, but the pragmatism of wisdom upon which real change may be founded. For the first time in my life, I am proud of America! (It took me a little longer than you Madame First Lady, for I am sorry to say Mr. President, I no longer dared to hope.)

Now, on this incredible night of history, with my family, and through sporadic tears and shouts of wonder, I rejoice.

Dear Barack Obama,

The death of hope is a fearsome thing. And because nature really does abhor a vacuum, fear, cynicism, and despair rush in to fill the void that the absence of hope had left. We became, I became, more comfortable living in negativity than confronting the losses and lacks in life. To give these up, to trust again, to have hope again required a leap of faith that was terrifying to contemplate.

Yet somehow beneath the rage, below the cynicism, under the despair still flowed a trickle of hope. And that is what you have touched. Through the power of your words, through the consistency of your behavior, and through the clarity of your spirit, you have bored holes through our defenses and reached our deepest, most protected sense of the possible. Slowly, in spite of our reluctance and our terror, that trickle of hope rose up to become a freshlet, a stream, a river of belief that things could be different. Slowly, disbelief turned to hope and terror to trust.

But that was not enough.

A nation is composed of people loosely bound together by shared dreams and visions, united by a shared sense of purpose and underlying belief. It was not enough that I began to hope, I had to see that hope shared by others. By myself a raindrop, linked to others I become a flood, a torrent rushing to change the tide from apathy and cynicism to hope, trust and belief.

So your gift to us was not just the reawakening of our own inner faith in possibility but also our individual connection to our collective awareness that change was not just vaguely possible but real and tangible and trustable. You restored nothing less than our collective psyche, our unified belief in the decency of Americans. You drew us up individually, united us in a common awareness of our shared vision and created a mandate for change. Fueled by our hunger and yearning, we trusted, not just you, but ourselves and each other.

That is your legacy, the restoration of the shared belief in the decency of America. Reagan's "shining city on the hill" is not a mirage, not even a vision, but a tangible place within reach of our very hands. It is that, not the power of your ideas or the clarity of your policies that has won our hearts. You have given us back our very selves and thus, the soul of our country.

With deep gratitude,
Jody Morrison

Dear President Obama,

This may sound a bit odd, but I would like to thank you. By taking the presidency, you reaffirm the advancement of America's culture. Our country voted to have you, an African-American, take the most powerful position in the world. Only several decades ago, blacks were widely discriminated against and did not even share equal rights as whites. Now, you show that blacks are capable of ANYTHING. This is a great step for the United States and I wish you the best of luck. Thank you!

Brian

Dear President Obama,

I want to write to you about you: your family, your place in this world, your place in history. I feel like I know you. I feel like I know your lovely, intelligent, well-grounded wife. Your daughters, your mother-in-law, your grandmother all seem like people that I have met and had discussions with regarding topics both big and small. Your mother seems like an amazing woman, more of an angelic presence in your life, and your father almost a mythical character. I have read so much about you and your family, but here is what strikes me most: the love and respect you have for each other is immense. Michelle will guide your family through these very public years. She will keep you real and honest and strong. Your daughters will keep you humble. Your mother-in-law will put your life and great works into the perspective of a life that has seen a lot of changes in this country.

When your grandmother was gravely ill and you flew to her side, at the pinnacle of the campaign, I could not have been more proud of you. I am your age, but feel in some ways motherly towards you, in some ways like your friend and colleague. Your visit to your grandmother gave you time you could never get back. I was so grateful that you had the perspective and appreciation for the importance of seeing her and saying goodbye on your own terms. I cannot even imagine how proud she must have been of you. I am sure that, until your daughters bring you grandchildren, you cannot imagine the love she had for you or how you filled her heart with immeasurable joy and pride.

Your place in history as the first African-American president is obviously immense. It is also obvious. What is less obvious, however, is your place in history as a person who brings together different views, different perspectives, different passions, to solve problems. Your mark will be as one who gets things done. A president who does not mince words, but who uses words wisely, thoughtfully, intelligently, and precisely. You do not do things by accident; yet you are not a cold, calculating person. You are warm, loving and full of life. Your mom, stepdad, grandmother, friends, have molded you into someone who cares and someone who is acting for the best interests of everyone involved in a situation. Your intelligence has been well-noted, but more than book-smarts are the street-smarts that you have acquired over the years. You understand people, what motivates them and what they need and want.

I am proud to live in a country that values intelligence, perseverance, and motivation. I am proud to live in a country that recognized that the smartest man was the most capable man to run the country. I am proud that the man I voted for respected his opponent and recognized the contributions that he made to our country. I am proud to have voted for a man who respects his wife immensely. I am proud to have voted for a man of whose sincerity I have no doubt. That is hard to say of a politician, of this or any age. You remind me of Abraham Lincoln or Jimmy Carter. Both of these men were sincere and uncompromising. Jimmy Carter may not have the reputation of strength of some of our more illustrious presidents, but history will prove that his honesty and integrity were among the highest of men in his position. He also came from a strong, loving background.

I wish you all the best during your presidency. I support you unconditionally because I trust the man that you are. And, besides, I know that Michelle and the girls will keep you in line!

Sincerely and Truly Yours,
Leslie Ragsdale

Dear President Obama,

Congratulations on your incredible victory. I would just like to take the time to point out what the results on that historic 4th of November meant to me. It was not that I agree entirely with your polices and viewpoints, or that I believe that you will be able to pull our country out of the disarray that we find ourselves in today. I did not celebrate and find myself elated because I knew you would be able to change the country in exactly the way you promised. One person by him/herself cannot drastically alter a nation in the ways which you are attempting to. You require the cooperation of thousands upon thousands of people, and they may falter.

However, the possibility that you could do all these things and more exists, and that is why I cheered. The very possibility, that glimmer of sunshine breaking through the clouds was enough for me to vote for you. For you see, you represent hope, something we have been without for some time. To me, you personify hope; you could fail in your endeavor to lower students tuition, for example, but there is a chance that you may not. Inside of my cynical political heart there is a beat, beating in time to your footsteps as we advance closer to your inauguration. I may just be a student who is learning what it takes to survive as an adult, but I am able to recognize a leader when I see one, and President Obama you are obviously a fantastic leader.

Your victory also allowed dreams to soar. I did not think that a minority president would be elected for a very long time, if ever; and yet you beat the odds and are now on your way to proving so many people wrong. If Vegas had odds on who would win the presidency a few years ago, whoever put even a dollar on you is now a very rich person. If you could defeat the critics, the naysayers, and all the obstacles then what is to stop any citizen from achieving their highest ambition? Anything is accomplishable for so many more people, simply by doing something that many people thought was impossible. You set a new bar for what can be done, and everyone is better for it.

Yet even this hope does not completely explain my euphoria. The fact that this country was willing to elect an African-American to one of the most important positions in the world speaks volumes about where we are as a nation. Forty years ago minorities were struggling to get the same basic rights that whites had, a century after the civil war had ended. Twenty years ago they legally had these rights, yet many refused to give in to civil rights laws, going down fighting with all they had. Even today prejudice against minorities has not gone away completely, but by electing you president this country is attempting to wash its hands of prejudices and embrace countries where all ethnicities have equal importance. I guess I was also so ecstatic on that day because I was proud of this nation and the progress that we have all made.

Thank you for your time, I wish you nothing but the best luck heading into the next few years. Even if you do not accomplish all that you want, I hope you know that you filled at least this writer with two of the greatest emotions we have: hope and pride.

Sincerely,
Sid Mitra

"Rosa sat, so Martin could walk, so Obama could lead . . . " Written by a child, on poster board with markers, at home somewhere in Teaneck, NJ, on November 4, 2008.

To start—In the United States we're now on the cusp of a Brave New World, a New World Order, of sorts. On November 4, 2008—a mere 143 years since he could have been owned via slavery—Barack H. Obama was clearly, definitely, no-glitches or miscounts, elected the 44th president of these United States of America.

Can I get an Amen!?

So let's discuss the human interest of this story—the element that makes it a people story. We have to take stock in how far we have finally come. We have to acknowledge the ebb and flow of emotions now penetrating the core of our nation because of this quantum leap. We have to pat ourselves on the back to have made it to this long-delayed change.

I admit that I was not for Obama from the start. Like all good forward-thinking females, I was a staunch Hillary supporter. I was well aware that when she occupied the White House with Bill Clinton, it was she who wore one leg of the pants. I knew that Hillary had quite a bit to do with the direction the country took back then. And while I won't say it was the perfect ideal, it certainly was better than the perfect storm we are in now.

My cousin was an Obama supporter from the start. He was always after me to join the ObamaNation—claiming aloud that it would be an "abomination if we did not end up with an ObamaNation." Well, thankfully, we have landed in the highly fabled ObamaNation. The former Hillary follower proclaims herself an Obama Mama!

The election of Barack Obama came at the time it needed to come. Some may argue it came just in the nick of time to get our sorry national butt out of the place it's been sliding into for the last eight painful years. Today, the United States finds itself weary, beaten down, despised by global neighbors, in a seemingly never-ending and ill-explained war, and on the verge of a corrupt, self-inflicted bankruptcy—some say unseen since the days of the Great Depression.

Enter Obama—a man whose very presence inspired millions, but incited race chatter all about, too. A man who unwillingly fell into checked boxes and categories he should never have been in to begin with. Here was a man running for the highest office in our government and African-Americans and minorities in droves clung shamelessly to him as the last great hope for them. Is he a first black president? Is he a first African-American president? No.

With Obama it should never have been about race. It should have been about how amazing it is for the nation to find a man with a white mother and a black father to bring the nation a first president who is able to be both sides at once without apologizing to any one group. It should have been about the poorly healed wounds of slavery, bigotry, and civil rights violations finding closure through him. It should have been about facing ourselves and owning up to election mistakes of the past. Admitting through action that we could redeem ourselves. There is something calming about Obama. Knowing he IS now the President-elect gives people a desire to look forward. There is hopefulness in knowing that through one man all men and women can come together.

Barack Obama is a citizen of the world. His place of birth is Hawaii, but that is merely geography. His true home is planet Earth. It means he can hang his coat anywhere and be welcomed. All over the globe, he was hailed and cheered when, at 11 PM EST, it was pretty much a given that as a nation we had collectively gotten past the bigotry of years and elected Barack Obama.

I stayed up to watch his speech. I felt connected to my global neighbors. I knew that where a television flickered, Obama was being heard graciously and without a hint of arrogance, making his historic victory speech. People were awed and moved. Mostly, people were thinking: "Damn! It's about time."

I was trying to mentally transport myself to Grant Park in Chicago. I was trying to be a part of that happy, hopeful sea of people that were not one color, but all colors looking one way. I saw them cry and cheer and hug and kiss and look up in awe. I couldn't help it. I teared up, as well.

I was not around when John F. Kennedy was president or for his tragic death. However, I recall countless photographs and grainy videos of his presidency. The kind of hope and awe I saw on the faces of Americans then is the same kind I see for Barack Obama now. It reflects a kind of hopefulness and trust that has been lacking between us (the people) and them (the governing bodies) for years. Call me sentimental, but I can only pray that we are indeed heading to that greater good, to that place of lost trust and less cynicism. I am neither idealist, nor realist—I prefer a middle ground to both. I think Barack Obama, in many more ways that we have yet to see, is that middle of the road for all of us.

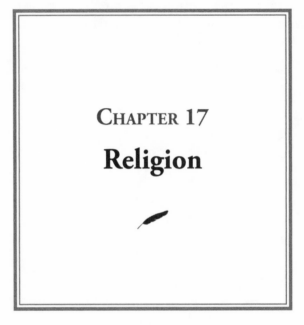

CHAPTER 17

Religion

Given that the ministerial leadership of the recent civil rights movement invoked morality as a justification for both its political protest and its successes, several saw President Obama's election as a consequence of their civil and religious efforts. They have reacted to his election in light of these beliefs.

President Barack Obama
The White House
Washington, D. C.

Dear Mr. President:

I join with many others who are dismayed that you chose Rick Warren to give the Invocation at your Inauguration. Many Afro-American clergy are saying, *How could you?* It is a fact that almost everyone, including yourself, is aware that an African-American would not even be considered as a *nominee* for president had there not been a revolution to destroy segregation and racism in the United States if it had not been for the huge involvement of black preachers across this nation, North and South, especially, like Fred Shuttlesworth of Birmingham, Billy Kyles of Memphis, and Jim Lawson of Los Angeles; Milton Reid of Virginia and C.K. Steele of Tallahassee; Jeremiah Wright of Chicago and myself of Harlem, NY. The list could go on and on. To my knowledge, Rick Warren NEVER was involved in that struggle *to redeem the soul of America!*

During your campaign for president you made much of your judgment, such as your opposition to the war in Iraq, etc. Your judgment was terribly flawed on this one. Many of us literally put our lives on the line in that struggle along with the safety of our families. There were many times I left my wife and children with the prospect that I would never see them again. That was true of all of us who I have mentioned. We all lost our friend and leader in an assassination that we all believe was orchestrated by J. Edgar Hoover, the director of this nation's FBI.

I too ask: *How could you?* I do not know what counsel to give you.

This was a horrific error in judgment. This was a poor judgment *politically.* Before your first term ends, you will need us again! A superior choice would have been congressman John Lewis who was almost killed crossing the Edmund Pettis Bridge in Selma on Bloody Sunday who is an ordained Baptist minister or Joseph Lowery. What makes it horrific is that Rick Warren did not publicly give you his endorsement. Did you get seized by selective amnesia?

Your servant and His disciple,
Wyatt Tee Walker
P. S. You may not know me; I suggest you Google me on the Internet.

Dear President Obama,

Congratulations on your historic election. I am confident you will be able to lead this country skillfully and wisely through the next four years. This will not be easy as the nation faces some difficult situations abroad and at home. Take care to keep American interests as the primary motivation for all your actions as president. Thanks for choosing Rick Warren to lead the prayer at your inauguration ceremony. He is a great representative for the whole Christian community. Good luck in the next four years, and you have the support of the American people behind you.

Sincerely,
Brad Walvort
P.S. Keep playing basketball. It is a great stress release!

To the Honorable President Obama,

Congratulations on your epic victory! Your leadership is desperately needed and I have full confidence that your will efforts will be fruitful. Your recent triumph has created a sense of unity and euphoria, among Americans, so palpable it is impossible to deny.

Despite the obvious liberal and progressive nature of your success, I unfortunately believe that it has brought about an unintended, yet very real conservative feel to your election, and I am frightened by the possible and unintended negative consequences that it may potentially yield.

To explain, I feel this way because African-American parents are now telling their children that they can do or be anything that they want, they can even be the next president. And, although, there is no doubt that your efforts, and profound victory has paved the way for so many, I feel very strongly that we, as a nation, and you and your administration, do not forget or ignore the social, economic, and political forces at play, those that yield an unequal distribution of resources, especially education, and the perpetual cycle of inequality, are at the root of the issue. Without adequately and effectively addressing the root of the issue the extreme inequality evidenced in the United States will persist. Vast discrepancies among our nations' social classes will remain; the demographic composition occupying each social class will go unchanged, ultimately yielding no real sign of change, equality and progress that your victory represents; and upward mobility among ALL Americans will remain next to impossible, resulting in a false sense of hope and equality, for not only African-Americans, but for all American citizens.

While your victory has left me ecstatic, and I have, am, and will continue to celebrate the progress and success African-Americans and all citizens of the United States have achieved, I feel it essential to remember, and place the much needed and deserved emphasis on what is really keeping people of all races, ethnicities, and genders from achieving the American dream.

Sincerely,
Meredith Coppola

CHAPTER 18

The Inaugural Events

N ot only are the letter writers in this volume eyewitness to the events surrounding this historic election, but more than a few were active participants in many different facets of Obama's campaign and election. Most of the letter writers in this chapter went to the presidential inauguration on January 20, 2009. They describe this event and explain the emotions they felt as the day's events unfolded. These remarkable observations will provide current and future readers with an up-close and personal portrait of this moment in the nation's history.

Dear President Obama,

I am a political science major at the University of Michigan. I had the privilege to attend your historic inauguration. It was an honor and a great experience to attend the inauguration of the first president for whom I have voted. I was amazed at the sheer number of people who traveled to Washington, D.C. in full support of you. Your speech was amazing and gave me great hope for your vision of the future for our country. You have a great task ahead of you in fixing the problems that have plagued this country. I agree that no matter big or small, the most important aspect of government is that it works. I hope you can follow through with fixing the effectiveness of our government. You are facing a daunting task with a struggling economy and many conflicts around the world. I hope that you can fix these problems for although you are not the only person in government working on these issue, our success as a nation will be riding on you. I hope you have the strength and composure for this task. I think you will. Good luck.

Sincerely,
Zachary Sullivan-Pickett

Dear President Obama,

Congratulations on your monumental win. I am so proud to be among the millions of Americans who voted for you. You are a truly amazing man and I am so excited to see what you can accomplish in the next four years. You led a very respectable campaign when faced with negative attention from both McCain and Clinton. You are truly a leader. I have framed your inauguration speech upon my wall as it was one of the most inspiring moments of my life so far. I was fortunate to attend in Washington, D.C. on January 20, 2009 and will remember that day with honor for the rest of my life. When tackling the challenges America faces, I know you will do it with both dignity and grace. You have inspired a nation to move past their outer judgments. Your position as leader of our country will force all Americans to look beyond color and race, religion, sexual orientation, and disability. We chose you not for the color of your skin, but for your character. As you struggle through the next four years of recession and war, hold your head up high knowing you have changed the lives of many. You have made this young girl from Ann Arbor Michigan to look beyond the preconceived notion of how things are or should be. Yes we can, I know we can and most of all, yes you can. You are the change we can believe in and I look forward to your days in office as a new turn for America. I thank you tremendously for giving yourself to helping others and our country.

Sincerely,
Megan Frasier

President Obama,

Congratulations! I just finished watching your inauguration speech and it gave me the chills. It was truly incredible and inspirational. In your speech, you discussed values that bring people all over the world together. President Obama, you have given hope to all Americans that there will be a bright future and you will lead us there. I am very excited and looking forward to all the new changes and programs that will change America forever. I believe in your abilities to do what is right for the American people. I would like to wish you and your family good luck in the White House and hope in the next four years America will transform back into the most powerful and prosperous nation in the world.

Thank you,
Robert Feinland

Dear President Obama,

Watching the inauguration ceremony today was something remarkable and truly historic. This election is something that I will carry with me for the rest of my life, and hopefully pass on to my children and grandchildren. I've been anticipating this day ever since I was a freshman in high school. My American government teacher had a picture of you on his desk. One day I asked him who the person in that picture was, and he said, "Nick, this man will one day be the next great president of the United States who will bring collective and constructive change to this country." That was seven years ago. When my teacher promised me that, I thought he was crazy. I asked him "Do you really think the American electorate will elect an African-American to serve as president?" He replied, "Just wait and see how this man will unite the country." As I reflect on that conversation with my teacher, it is amazing how he foreshadowed these events. President Obama, what you did during the course of your campaign is something this country needed. We needed someone who could bring all Americans together, regardless of race or political ideology. If race and ideology persist as barriers in our society, then change can never be implemented, and you got the Americans to believe in this notion. We trust and believe in you; we know that there is no better candidate in this country who can effectively reform the status quo. I wish you and your family the best of luck during your tenure as the president of the United States, and offer my unrelenting support of your presidency. Thank you for what you have accomplished already, but this is only the beginning.

Sincerely,
Nicholas Camilleri

Dear President Obama,

I was at the inauguration today and I know I am young at only 20 years of age, but I can truly say this was and will be one of the most memorable experiences of my life. The joy and utter excitement expressed on all the faces today was something I have never seen and hope stays with us throughout your time leading us. I am excited for what is to come and I hope that people begin to truly hear your words and not just listen to them. "Your people will judge you by what you can build, not by what you can destroy," is the quote that resonates most with me and the quote that I will never forget hearing come from your mouth on this day. I hope you can truly get people to understand this and move not only our nation, but the world, to a better place. Thanks for everything and I am excited to embark on your journey with you.

Best Wishes and Congratulations,
Danny Gutman

Dear President Obama,

Today I witnessed a most historic event: your inauguration. As a 19-year-old, this was the first, and probably the most life changing, election that I have had the privilege of participating in. I have found hope and inspiration in your words, your economic and foreign policy, and your refreshing humility and plans for the common American. With the turmoil that our country is in overseas and economically, I can see that the task set out in front of you will not be easy, nor can we expect as a people to see immediate, easy solutions to such a daunting task in this financial crisis. Times are changing, and with that America must too, and you stated that so eloquently in your inauguration speech. I felt proud to be able to rally in the streets of Ann Arbor on the night of election day in November, and couldn't help but sit back and take a mental photograph of the climate of the times. All the young people around me were filled with a passion and an engagement in politics that I rarely see in my own hometown environment or everyday life. We really believe that you have a vision to take America into a world beyond the constrictions of conservative domination, of the post Cold War egoist tendencies, and really use the powers bestowed upon you to incorporate diplomacy and innovational ideas into the American tradition to change how we move into this next decade. With a Democratic House of Representatives and Senate I know you can begin to make some fundamental changes to boost up the economy and more importantly, to begin to change the frameworks of the way we view our government and the role it can play to our generation positively. Your words today were bold, and I have every confidence that your actions will be bold as well. The support and inspiration you have shown to me has helped me see politics in a new light, as well as the options we have as a country to change. Yes WE CAN. I really have faith in that slogan.

Sincerely,
Marissa Fellows

Dear President Obama,

As I sit here and write this, some three hours after your inauguration, it still brought a great deal of emotion to the surface to refer to you by your new title. A self-admitted political junkie, I have tremendously enjoyed observing the electoral cycle over the years, but have never been particularly comfortable with actually engaging myself in its workings. And as with many others, I have been moved to action by your candidacy and its place in America's historical narrative. Given the tremendous damage that has been done to America's international reputation and standing over the past eight years, I feel that your elevation to the national consciousness was particularly well timed. In a sense you were the perfect candidate; liberal enough to satisfy both hardcore Democrats and disenchanted Republicans, and intelligent and grounded enough to be able to effectively deflect many of the criticisms frequently levelled against our nation's leaders. It is evident from the tone you have used in the majority of your public comments since the election that you are fully cognizant of what challenges face us as a nation and while you back down from no one, the gravity of our current predicament certainly weighs on every decision you make. Because of all I have stated, I have complete confidence in your abilities to effectively serve this great nation, and best of luck in living up to all of the promise we, the Democratic faithful, have seen in you for years.

President Obama,

Congratulations on your inauguration today as the 44th president of the United States. I watched today as you made history in a charismatic, passionate, and focused manner. I believe that your presidency truly does mark the end of one era, and the beginning of a new one that is filled with hope and prosperity. I'd like to thank you for all that you have done already, and for all that you plan on accomplishing in the future. We will all be waiting and watching patiently as you attack the burdensome tasks that face your presidency. We all have extreme faith and support in you and can finally say that we are proud of our country and her leader.

Dear President Obama,

Today, I, with millions of other Americans, watched history be made as your took your inaugural oath. Although I wished I could be part of the millions that watched you in person, I can truly say that a tear came to my eye as I watched on my television at home. At age 20, this was the first inauguration of a president that really took my interest. I was amazed to see the millions of votes and countless hours you spent on your campaign materializing into what I consider one of the greatest aspects of our democracy today; the peaceful transfer of power. I felt a sense of my own efficacy in this large country for the first time. I was a part of what put you in office and I cannot say that I could have been any prouder. I think you are going to be what it takes to turn our country around and take us out of this recession. You made it known that we have many obstacles to overcome, but with a president with the attitude and abilities that you possess, I know that you will be the leader that pushes us to surpass the hurdles in our path. Thank you for being the catalyst for the positive change that is coming and for being the inspiration for so many. I truly look forward to the coming years with you as our commander in chief.

Sincerely,
Rebecca House

President Obama,

The inauguration ceremony yesterday was absolutely beautiful. The speakers and musicians selected to show their support of you did a tremendous job. However, what I found most impressive was your inauguration speech, specifically your acknowledgment of non-believers when mentioning different religions. I've never heard another politician address non-believers at all, let alone with such an accepting and kind tone. While I was excited for your presidency already, especially because of your health care plans and higher education goals, I am now completely convinced that you will be successful not only legislatively but also in inspiring the world to see the America it should see: a country who is accepting of all of its citizens regardless of religion, race, sex, you name it.

Much love and my best wishes,
Christina Bertrand

President Obama,

Congratulations on becoming the 44th president of the United States. I, as a college student who often wonders if the good political fight can be won, hope that you and your administration can serve as an example of government that is both deaf to lobbyists and outside interests to my generation. Unfortunately, the presidential office and most of government for that matter has been tarnished by the constant suspicion of outside motives. Although there are a lot of specific goals I hope and believe you and your administration can achieve, my biggest hope is that you can restore faith in our government, and practice in "the light of day" as you orated on your inauguration day.

Best Wishes,
Elliot

President Obama,

I just want to say that I was at inauguration and witnessed firsthand your unbelievable ability to bring people together from across the world. It is a testament you as a leader, as well as the United States and its ideals. You are an inspiration to millions. Congratulations.

Matt Kretman

Dear Senator Obama,

I will make this letter brief, because you are probably receiving thousands of letters and because this letter is time sensitive. I have two main concerns that I hope you will address.

First, I am concerned about how you plan to govern based on the election results. When you ran for president and won the election, your platform was a slightly left-of-center to left platform. However, since you won you have said that you will govern from the center, despite the fact that your electoral college results as well as the overall election results indicated a landslide in favor of moderately left-wing policies at least and left-wing policies at most. Because of this, I hope you will govern at least slightly to the left.

Second, and more personally, I really want to attend the inauguration, but there are so few tickets available. I was wondering if you could release more tickets, or even move the inauguration site, to allow more of the American citizenry to watch the inauguration live. If possible, you should even consider a Jacksonian-style inauguration with a large barbeque on the White House front lawn. While I realize this is unlikely, it would be a great symbol of the rebirth of American democracy.

Thank you for listening to my thoughts.
Andrew Rabenstein

Dear President-elect Obama;

Over the past year, just as many others did, I watched carefully and undecided about who I would vote for as leader of this nation. I have been very discouraged with our government's inability to do what they were elected to do, and that is govern. This past administration has been one of no substance or commitment to promises made to the Latino community. After the attacks of 9/11, our president allowed anti-immigrant groups to literally bombard our airways and local communities with hate rhetoric and the injustice that has been done to our Latino communities has been catastrophic on our families. CNN has been one of the worst during this whole time, literally daily overwhelming our airways with the negative images of Latinos. I have yet to see them have a forum where neutral heads prevail and perhaps allowing someone to dispute the half-facts they report. I am an Hispanic American, a United States citizen who lives and interacts daily with Latinos who may or may not be undocumented. They go to my church, their children go to school with my children, parents attend PT conferences as I do, they play sports, etc. The raids that the government has allowed to take place only to cover the fact that Mr. Bush has failed atrociously at finding the terrorists who are really responsible for our country's attack, have devastated our communities, dividing families, small children from their parents. I have witnessed law enforcement authorities' unjust behavior to someone in my family solely on the basis that his skin was brown. I witnessed an officer toss a family member's credentials to the street, and tell him to return to his country; he was not wanted here. These things are happening on a daily basis, and it has to stop. It is time to understand that all Latinos are not criminals. Many of these immigrants have been forced to leave their country and families in order to see that their wives and children have basic human needs fulfilled. Many of them are here lonely and wanting for their families and the sacrifice they make is so unselfish, placing their needs to the side. I voted for you because you seemed to be a person who will allow common sense to prevail, and look for ways to work across the aisle. I believe that you will not be pressured by politicians but do what is right. I am asking you to look for a way to provide legal status for the millions of undocumented people who are here and doing the right thing. Those who have stayed out of trouble, and contribute to this country on a daily basis with hard work. Please do not disappoint us. Immigration reform is something that has to happen as soon as possible so that these families stop suffering the injustices done to them on a daily basis. Congratulations on your election, and we all are hoping for a people's administration, not a bought administration.

Dear Future President Obama,

I would like to start out by simply saying congratulations! What you have done is a huge milestone in American history and I feel honored to have been here to see it happen. I know you probably get millions of letters everyday saying congratulations but I hope by getting one more it will enforce the fact that you are well deserving of the position and you have given my family and I high hopes for the future. I hope you follow through with making strong changes to strengthen our country's weaknesses.

There is one problem I would like to comment on, however. In the economic state that our country is in today it seems wild to be spending so much money on multiple inaugural balls. Although some tickets are more inexpensive than others, I believe that the inaugural ball appeals to the elite class. I think there should be one public party that is low key and more down to earth that will appeal to more than just the upper class. I think this would be a bold statement to not only the United States but the rest of the world as well.

I cannot wait to see what new and exciting changes will take place during your presidency!

Sincerely,
Danielle Portnoy

CHAPTER 19

Vice President Biden, Hillary Clinton, and the Cabinet

S ince presidents, no matter how intelligent, well-trained, and skilled, do not serve alone, some of the letter writers took this opportunity to comment on President Obama's vice presidential choice, Joseph Biden, as well as presidential primary rival, former first lady and New York senator, Hillary Clinton, whom he named secretary of state. Other letters, while not mentioning specific individuals, did also reflect more generally on the cabinet.

President Obama,

Your election is a momentous occasion. Your first term should be historic and revolutionary at least. I have full faith in your decision making and praise you excessively for the choice of Joseph Biden as your vice president. He is without a doubt the best man for the job. I only ask that you choose wisely for the eventual Supreme Court Justice appointments. Their decisions often set precedent and effectively change laws. Social issues may be on the back burner with the s__tstorm that is the economy, and the ongoing war in Iraq, but they matter to some people more than anything else. Choose wisely, use Joe as a compass and crutch, and don't lose sight of the big picture.

Everybody's watching.

Dear President-elect Barack Obama,

My name is Patricia Ceccarelli and I am a sophomore studying political science and peace & social justice at the University of Michigan. I am originally from Westchester, New York, which, as I am sure you know, is the county in which Hillary Clinton lives. I should start off by saying I love Hillary Clinton. I love her as a senator, a wife, a mother, a policy maker, as a strong woman and as any other label one might use for her. I traveled from Ann Arbor to Detroit at 5 AM last year in order to see her at a rally. Because I had arrived so early with my friend Josh, I even got to meet and take a picture with her.

Suffice it to say, although I voted for you, I was bitter when you defeated Hillary. As a young, intelligent, independent woman I feel that there are not very many positive female role models for young girls to look up to. Hillary is one of those few that I can honestly say I would be proud of to have not only represent our country but also the female gender. For this reason I am glad you were able to award her secretary of state although I can't help but feel it is somewhat of a consolation prize. I can only hope that in my lifetime I will see a woman elected as president of this country, my greatest hope being that I would be elected as president one day.

You can imagine my distaste at the idea of Sarah Palin being second in succession to run this country. I honestly have no words to express the rage I feel when I imagined her eternalized as the first woman as the United States vice president. This was one of the first reasons that I considered voting for you. But, as I learned more about you, and fell in love with Joe Biden, I could see that you were the right choice. I am sincerely impressed that you were able to defeat Hillary and your story is inspirational. I was watching *The Colbert Report* and a member of the band Wilco was asked by Stephen if he would be attending the inauguration. He said he had once asked you that and that you had responded, "If Hillary invites us." I guess that just goes to show the amazing feat you were able to accomplish by becoming the Democratic nominee and president-elect and I congratulate you and your family.

As you probably know, many locations around this country, and world, rejoiced at your election. Ann Arbor was one of them. I ran and cheered in the streets just like many of my peers. Election night was one of the most meaningful moments in my college career. Seeing students singing "God Bless America" at 1 AM, completely sober I might add, on the steps of our Student Union was reminiscent of the 1960s, a time in which young and old alike were able to mobilize for social change. It was amazing for me, a self-proclaimed sunshine patriot, to see other students act on their renewed love for America. Thank you for allowing us to have this moment for it will shape us for the rest of our lives.

In conclusion, I would just like to again congratulate you on your being president-elect. I have great faith that you will surround yourself with good people, as it seems you already have, and I look forward to living in a world of change. I wouldn't say by a long shot that I am an optimist but I love America and everything it stands for. I believe that you will be able to uphold everything that is true and great about our country and I wish you the best of luck. People will expect a lot of you, which I am sure you know, but we will try to be patient since you will have to undo a lot of bad before you are able to make some good. Take care President-elect Obama and enjoy your holiday season.

Sincerely,
Patricia Ceccarelli

Dear President Obama,

I would like to address my concerns about your choice to elect the UN ambassador as your cabinet member. I know Bill Clinton did the same thing but I question your motives for such an action. What do you feel are the benefits for having the UN ambassador as your cabinet member? I am curious how other countries feel about such a move. The UN's purpose is to serve the best for everyone, not just the U.S. Do you think the UN ambassador's role will impact the UN's opinion of us? Also, how does Hillary Clinton feel about this and how will you divide the roles between the secretary of state and the UN ambassador?

I wish you the best of luck in the next four years.

With respect,
Yoon Choi

Mr. President,

I would like to praise your swiftness of action in assembling a team immediately following your election as president. Announcing nominations for cabinet positions and other pertinent public offices as early as November 5 proved you are ready to get to work immediately and will not prolong the honeymoon period as previous administrations have. For example, it took President Clinton nearly three months to complete this very task, which invariably postponed the progress of the nation in the interim. However, President Clinton did not inherit a nation in peril as you have, and though he should have acted swifter, he could afford the delay. Today, with an economy in shambles and the United States engulfed in a two-front war, no time can be wasted, a reality you clearly understand.

Sincerely,
Brittany Keller

November 5, 2008
Dear President Obama:

My husband and I are overjoyed at your election. It was a huge victory for all: young people not only registered but voted, once again we can be proud of our country, the world joins us in that pride, and for at least four years the constitution, the Geneva Convention, the Kyoto Accord and our Bill of Rights will no longer be optional.

My hope is that you continue to inspire us to do our best with your intellect, temperament, and equanimity under pressure that you exhibited during the campaign.

You have already kept your first promise: a new puppy for the White House. Some may snicker, but all promises, big and small are important. They may be small to some but highly significant to others.

I am writing this letter before you have announced your choices for the 3,000 men and women you appoint to government office. My hope is that your promise of "crossing the aisle" is kept and that these appointees will serve the public rather than padding their resumes.

I don't have the ability to suggest what should be done with the economy, the environment, health care, the wars, etc., but what you have espoused resonated with me. Your exhortation in March in Philadelphia is good enough for me. "In the end, then, what is called for is nothing more, and nothing less, than what all the world's great religions demand: that we do unto others as we would have them do unto us . . . and let our politics reflect that spirit as well."

So after years of distrust, I look forward to our country seizing this moment of unity and reconciliation, with you as our leader, to forge a "more perfect union" not only within these United States of America but globally as well.

Thank you for your dedication!

Sincerely,
Alice B. Acheson

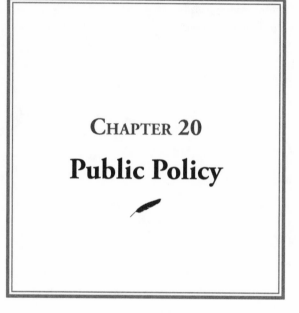

CHAPTER 20

Public Policy

Some letter writers took the occasion to offer advice on specific public policy issues, like the economic crisis, universal health care, climate change, child care, abortion, a college football play-off championship, housing costs and home mortgages, gay marriage, small businesses, video games, and a variety of other policy matters. Americans, particularly in this election, were concerned with a variety of issues and wanted the new president to address them.

Dear President Obama,

I remember when I was a child growing up in Ithaca, New York as a person of color, my mother would tell me that you have to be twice as good to gain the same recognition. Even though this reality is the symptom of a racist history, even though it was uttered before you could be imagined, I nevertheless want to pass this sentiment on to you. As you must know, people, particularly progressive people, young people, people on the left, those who voted for you without hesitation, have higher expectations for your presidency. While many have already become cynical once again or said things like, "We shouldn't expect too much," or "The job of the presidency itself constrains," or "Becoming president of the United States means firing bombs on others," I hope that you will prove these sentiments incorrect. Please surprise us. Please do more than we expected. While building on the work of those who have preceded you, please be much better.

Please end the war in Afghanistan also. Please put a stop to the prison industrial complex. Please help to rehabilitate and reintegrate all of those who are in prison now. I appreciate your sentiment about the need to renovate and rebuild school infrastructures. Please also help to invent new systems of possibility for those who, for the first time in a long time, again have hope. Please use your hip-hop affect to connect with failing schools in West Oakland, or even schools in Ithaca, New York, that help the elite get to the best colleges, but also reproduce the same impossibility for so many others, like African-American kids, or the children of low-income rural residents.

Israel/Palestine is an obvious site of much-needed attention. I am glad that you are beginning to do something there. Please make it happen this time, not only because the U.S. is a powerful country, but also because some of those bombs landing on the heads of Palestinian children in Gaza were made in and financed by the United States.

Finally, your presidency is an obvious opportunity to do something about the environment and our impact on it. Regulate. Make the automakers better than they would be on their own. Force us as voters and consumers to be less wasteful and more efficient. Since 1989, I have been in and out of Germany, sometimes living here for extended periods. When I first came, I was immediately struck by the greater attention to the human impact on our planet. I was amazed not only by the recycling programs, but also by the fact that people here often work during the day with their lights off in their offices and classrooms. The escalators only run, for the most part, when people are actually using them. On the underground train in Berlin and above ground trains throughout the country, when the train stops, the doors only open for those who need to get out, or those who need to get in. Gas prices are high, and the public transportation system, at least in Berlin (a city of only 3.5 million) is filled with people. There are bike paths everywhere and many actually use bicycles as their primary mode of transportation. I won't go on, but you get the point. Please let's do something drastic here.

In the end, it is clear to me that your success will be based in part on our continued vigilance, not to let you fail, and to give pushes when pushes are necessary. Sometimes, we may even need to shout. When those times occur, please don't take offense. Please remember that our hope is also embedded in those shouts.

We love you.

Peace,
Damani J. Partridge
January 25, 2009
Berlin, Germany

Letter to President Obama November, 2008

Campaign

You ran a well-organized and disciplined campaign. You demonstrated your intelligence, calmness, thoughtfulness, insight, determination and leadership. Your campaign will probably go down in history as one of the greatest campaign in America. Congratulations!

Political Policies

I think with your political policies, the United States will again regain the respect that it deserves around the world. I trust that you will change some of the negative perceptions that seem to be present. Hopefully, the intelligence and insight that you used in the campaign will guide you in your political policies for us in America and around the world.

Economic Crisis and the American Families

Many American families are facing multiple challenges. Unemployment has continued to increase. Your stimulus package for new jobs would lower unemployment and assist the economy to recover more quickly. Jobs are difficult to find. Wages appear to be rising slowly or not at all. The value of homes is decreasing in many areas of the United States. Many homes are in foreclosure. Health insurance is not available for many, or in many cases insufficient for necessary good health treatment. Insurance premiums seem to be higher without families getting better health care. College tuition and other cost related to a good college education seem to be rising faster than wages or other incomes in the family. Interest on certificates of deposits is dropping. In October, the value of many individual stocks and mutual funds fell, wiping out a sufficient amount of savings invested in stocks and mutual funds. Gas prices have continued to go higher. Before the bailout of the financial institutions many families in the country were fearful of their financial security, especially those that are retired or planning on retirement. As though these challenges were not enough, the tax structure we have now seems to be against the hard working families as well as the past hard working families. The tax structure should be beneficial to all Americans, not just the upper few Americans. Could some taxes be on luxury items? An example of a luxury item would be a private airplanes or a luxury boat.

It seems some of the economic crisis in families can be reversed with the creation of jobs in America, your new tax structure, your provisions for financial assistance in educational opportunities, your health policies and changes in housing regulations. Also families could benefit from the reduction of money used for the Iraq War. This money could be spent on jobs, reduction of health cost, or education.

Thank you for giving many Americans hope and inspiration. I will be looking for change in policies to improve the lives of us. May God continue to bless you, your family, and all of us.

Lois Deskins

Dear Mr. President,

There needs to be a voice broadly for prison reform in this country. Despite the difficulty of prying open the hearts and minds of the majority of Americans about imprisonment as the institutional default position for addressing infractions against our society's social contract, the bully pulpit would provide the voice broadly needed to strengthen the political will and influence the way we think about the prohibitively high economic and social costs of current sentencing laws and imprisonment as the only way to address our society's collective need to right infractions against its social contract.

You and your family are settling into the nation's capital on the heels of the December 27, 2008, *Washington Post article*, "In Prison at the 'End of the Earth'," followed two days later by the December 29 *Washington Post* article "Webb Sets His Sights on Prison Reform." Although the downwardly spiraling economic situation rivets our daily attention, the December 27 article that "more than 6,500 District inmates . . . are scattered in more than 70 federal prisons across the country, wherever the Bureau of Prisons can find space" is a jarring reminder of the racial disparities in our criminal justice system. The nation's capital has a population of approximately 592,000 and 56 percent of that population is listed by the U.S. Census Bureau as African-American. More than 6,500 or 11 percent of that population as prison inmates scattered across the country in different federal prisons because of prison overcrowding is alarming. This prison overcrowding is a reminder of the country's mindset (reflected in its sentencing laws) that we can imprison our way out of society's collective need to right wrongs against its social contract.

The absence of prison reform will continue to rend the economic and social fabric of this society in ways not readily apparent to the naked eye—the hidden direct and indirect costs of incarceration such as lost wages to the individual and lost tax revenue to the county and state while simultaneously tapping into tax revenue to house prisoners. An upside to this grim reality was the December 29 article informing us that "this spring, Webb (D-Va.) plans to introduce legislation on a long-standing passion of his: reforming the U.S. prison system. Jails teem with young black men who later struggle to rejoin society," he says. It was encouraging to read that Senator Webb's office plans to "introduce legislation that creates a national panel to recommend ways to overhaul the criminal justice system." This announcement means that Senator Webb's voice joins the voices of the list of experts in the field of prison reform, many with decades-long professional and personal commitments to writing and challenging the nation's sentencing laws and disparities in how justice is meted out. In addition, some states, including California and some cities, including Newark, New Jersey, have ushered in dialogue led by experts in criminal justice about economic alternatives to long-term incarceration.

My suggestion is that the Obama administration get ahead of the curve on this issue by calling for a national panel on prison reform at the executive office level. A dedicated senior position in the West Wing advocating for prison reform would be at the discretion of the president. The primary responsibility of this senior position would be to create and manage the agenda, activities, and actionable recommendations of a national panel committed to getting us beyond the level of only study, research, talk, meetings, conferences, etc., to the level of some concrete action. Prison reform is a challenging economic and social problem about which America may not be ready to focus attention, but it is a problem deserving of as much attention as possible, especially during this period when states and cities are facing increasing financial crises. Trimming the waste will be an essential element in the climb back to increased national and local economic and financial prosperity.

Consequently, the person in this senior position would be someone who has earned the trust of mayors, governors, criminal justice professionals, and other legislators, as well as representatives of religious and community organizations. The proposed panel, drawn from offices of mayors and governors; religious and community organizations; university and adult training institutions; criminal justice institutions; and private sector representatives, would be responsible for crafting the communications and dialogue that would reflect the nation's concern about spending federal dollars on high impact change such as prison reform.

Although the Obama administration's Urban Policy platform appropriately calls for the creation of a White House Office of Urban Policy that will develop a strategy for America's urban challenges, including commitments to crime and law enforcement; recidivism and ex-offender support; the cycle of youth violence; gun violence in cities; and racial profiling, I believe the issue of prison reform should be elevated to a place of priority attention—perhaps under the Urban Policy umbrella, but not subsumed under either of the critical symptoms listed above under the Urban Policy, each of which is the result of the absence of prison reform.

Since the challenge of prison reform is a combination of deeply ingrained socio-cultural values and emotions about penalties for infractions against society and the politics of sentencing laws within the criminal justice system, moving it out of the shadows into the light will require the attention of the bully pulpit. This issue needs the attention of a proactive senior office.

It is understood that at this time in the history of our country many crises demand the full attention of the Office of the President. Consequently, it is hoped that in time there will be room to consider this letter's request of a voice broadly for prison reform.

Respectfully yours,
Dr. Theresa A. Ware
Adjunct Associate Professor
University of Maryland University College

Dear President Obama,

I would like to congratulate you on a job well done. I wish your mother and grandmother could have seen you win the presidency. All the late nights studying has really paid off for you. You have so many different characteristics of different people it is scary, for example, Dr. Martin Luther King, Jr., Senator Robert F. Kennedy, and Malcom X.

I have two issues that I hope you can address. The first issue is offering affordable health insurance. The way the economy is these days, it is hard to afford good health insurance. Cancer medication is very expensive. Cancer medication can cost you more than $100 dollars for a thirty-day supply of pills. There are no generic medications available. The second issue is offering affordable education. If I put money aside for my children's education, it still will not be enough. I know that student loans are offered, but they take forever to pay off. I could use my retirement money, but with stock market going bad, my retirement money is still not enough to get the children their education.

Please stay true to yourself and your word for a change.

Yours truly,
Cheryl Sparks

Dear President Obama,

Congratulations on your election, and best of luck as you begin to tackle some of the biggest economic and national security challenges our nation has ever faced. The feeling of hopefulness and optimism that you bring to the country in this time of great challenge is truly inspiring. I teach political science and communication studies at the University of Michigan. In particular, I am excited to see your administration's plans for restoring the public's faith in science. Several of your cabinet appointments give me every reason to be hopeful. As an educator, I have noticed a decline in the motivation of our nation's young people to embrace the scientific method not only in their professional work but in their approach to life. We have, I fear, traded evidence for ideology as the guiding light for an entire generation. Our nation should be a place where rigorous science guides our public policies. Your greatest contribution and legacy will be to restore that tradition. It will represent a giant step toward regaining our respect as an honest broker in the world. Thank you for your service and best to you, Michelle, and your beautiful children.

Sincerely,
Nicholas A. Valentino
Associate Professor of Communication Studies and Political Science
Institute for Social Research
University of Michigan

Dear Mr. President,

I am aware that there are many important issues that the administration must address. The three main issues that I believe are paramount to the success of our country right now are the energy crisis, Social Security problems, and a financial crisis. These core issues are affecting each and every American every day and I don't think we can keep pushing back the dates on these vital matters. The only way we can achieve success is if we become independent from countries that don't have our best interests at heart.

The energy crisis is a problem I feel that has been delayed for way too long. Why hasn't our country done more to solve this key dilemma that is affecting our Earth as well as keeping us dependent on countries in the Middle East? There are many other sources of energy such as solar, nuclear, and geothermal and there is no reason we should be reliant on fossil fuels. The new administration needs to subsidize an incentive program for research and development of greener energy sources and more fuel efficient cars, homes, and businesses.

Social Security is another crucial topic that needs to be addressed by you and your administration. The Social Security program is unsustainable and something needs to be done. When the baby boomer generation begins to retire there will be more old people taking out of the system than young people putting money into the system. The government has already spent the money that was paid into the system by the baby boomers. This means the government will either be forced to increase taxes or raise the retirement age. Addressing Social Security should be one of your top priorities.

Our financial situation is horrible. Close to eight percent of the American population is unemployed at this time. Some of the major automotive industries are going under and if this problem is not dealt with severe consequences like further layoffs and bankruptcies will take place. I think your new administration needs to come up with a new financial plan because the economy is in a volatile state. Stricter regulations are needed to make sure that past financial misdeeds will not be repeated.

These major issues facing our country will not be solved overnight but I believe that a lot more can be done. You and your new administration have to take very strong and positive steps to show the American people that they can make changes. This will get everyone back on the right track and get our economy rolling.

Zack Bender

Dear Mr. President

You will have a lot to accomplish in his first weeks and months as president. Our country is in the state of a recession, people are losing jobs at incredible rate, and losing money faster than it comes in. On top of the large national debt that you will be inheriting, the nation has developed high standards that I hope you will live up to. Three points that I feel should be some of your first priorities focuses on are putting in tighter regulations on how corporations spend and deal with money, lowering the price of health care, and regulating or adjusting the price of education.

Regulations need to be put in that standardize how bailout money is spent in large corporations. The packages given to the companies were meant to help everyone involved, not just help the heads of the companies. I believe you should make a standardized method for how the bailout and any future government funds should be handled by these corporations. The money should not be put into the pockets of the CEOs who got their companies in trouble to start. There should also be a limit put in place on how large retirement packages for heads of companies can be.

Another issue you should address is the high cost of health care. For far too many citizens, it is too expensive to afford the health care plan that will benefit them the most. It is a horrible situation to be in because not only are medical bills too expensive without health care, but for many, health care itself is too expensive. You must take care of this problem immediately so that families can live with the peace of mind and assurance that they will be protected if the need arises.

The other issue that I think you need to address within your first few months in office is the high price of a college education. The youth of this nation are its future and they need affordable education. Too many excellent schools have too high tuition prices. Many brilliant high school students aren't able to continue their education at the best school for them because of the high tuition prices. Harvard, for example, has an undergraduate tuition that totals about $50,000. For many families with bright children, this is far too expensive to even consider. Harvard advertises on their Web site that they give over 50 percent of their undergrad students need-based financial aide, which comes from their large endowment fund. Even though they claim to assist so many students, the massive amount of funds available seems to be barely touched. Why not give more to students or make every student's tuition lower by using endowment funds? Why not help out the future leaders of America have affordable college education so that they can continue to make our country a better place? You have much to consider in your first months as president, and I believe these causes should be some at the top of his list.

From,
Emily Bell

Dear President Obama,

It is very difficult to choose just three things to ask you to work on in your first hundred days in office because of the trying times we live in. It is my hope that in these first one hundred days as president you will work hard to better our country. Three things that I think you should address, sooner than later, are: land border security, developing energy resources on American soil, and saving the auto industry.

By improving land border security we will make it harder for crime, people smuggling, drug smuggling, and terrorism to occur in our country. Illegal immigrants take jobs away from the American people and increase school expenses and make health care costs in hospitals and emergency rooms skyrocket because they don't pay taxes and don't have health insurance. The taxpaying citizens are punished by having to pay these unpaid bills. Guarding our land borders and building whatever walls and fences are necessary will create new jobs for people during a time when it's hard to find one. More importantly, though, it will help to stop enemy cells from penetrating our country and the acts of terrorism they plan to perform on American soil. Tightened border security would deter drug smuggling from South American countries.

Energy has been a big concern for our country for many years. We are at the mercy of the countries from which we purchase oil. Importing oil severely affects our home heating bills, gas at the pump, price of airline tickets, the price of trucking consumer goods to the stores where we shop, and many other aspects of our lives. We need to drill on American soil, harness wind energy, and build more nuclear plants.

Again, this would create many new jobs for people.

The auto industry needs to be saved from bankruptcy because if we don't a massive number of people will lose their jobs. We must take into account that it is not only the autoworkers but also the companies and the employees of the related industries that provide goods to the car manufacturing plants that will be negatively impacted by the auto industry's bankruptcy. The experts warn that if the auto industry goes down our country could find itself in a full-blown depression.

I did not vote for you but I have faith that you will do a good job of improving our country during your term as president and as a patriotic American I give you full support of your policies and decisions. I respect the upcoming choices you will have to make and know you will do what's best for our country.

From,

Lida Bard

Dear President Obama,

It is with a great feeling of hope and optimistic anticipation that I look toward your inauguration into the office of the presidency. As an American and an inhabitant of the state of New Jersey, there are several issues that are extremely important to me. I'm a to-the-point kind of guy so I'll cut to the chase. Within the first hundred days of taking office, there are a couple things you have to do. First of all, something needs to be done about the war: end it, set out a timetable for ending it, bring home twenty guys every other day, whatever it takes to get the ball rolling for real.

Secondly, I think we need to restore America's image in the world. I think your inauguration helps to some degree, but there is still work to be done. We need to begin taking steps toward returning America's reputation to the way it was ten to fifteen years ago. Foreign relations over the past eight years have been sub-par to say the least. I feel like our government has become somewhat of a mockery in recent years, but I really feel like you can help turn that around. Also we have to work to restore America on the home front. Too many people are losing their homes to the banks, people don't trust their neighbors anymore, the media keeps everyone afraid to do anything from going out at night to driving with the radio on, and people have reacted accordingly. I believe that the spirit of America has not been lost, but temporarily misplaced. We need to seek out that spirit and restore our own belief in our great nation.

Finally, I think the thing that's really been on everyone's mind recently is the economy. The multibillion dollar bailouts pretty much say it all: we may be in trouble. Of course this may be part of the normal economic cycle, but nonetheless it is still frightening. I know I don't want my generation to end up keeping their money in their mattresses out of the fear of some massive bank collapse like our grandparents' parents did during the Depression. I know that we will make it through this rough patch, but the real question is when? I think that once all of this is taken care of it gives us the opportunity to really begin changing the U.S., and the world, for the better.

Sincerely,
Jon Weiss

President Obama:

There has been a lot of talk about what you represent to this nation, as our first African-American president. But I didn't vote for you because of what you represent. I didn't vote for you because of your race, or your age, or your slogans. I voted for you because I am sick of the way this country has been run lately. I am sick of pointless wars and I am sick of secret prisons. I am sick of a president who ignores laws whenever he finds it expedient, who ignores the will of the Congress, who ignores the judgments of the Supreme Court, and who ignores his own people.

I voted for you, Barack Obama, not because I liked the T-shirts or the music videos, and not because I care about breaking barriers, but because I like the idea of a Constitutional scholar in the White House, and because I care about having a leader who understands the importance of protecting the values this country was founded on.

Our national leadership has relied for too long on fear to motivate and unify this country. If there is one Change you can bring to government, I hope that it will be to have faith that the strength and fortitude of the hope that got you elected will see you through the difficulties you are about to face.

Dear President-elect Barack Obama,

I share my deepest congratulations as you prepare to enter the most powerful position in our country's government. I am truly proud, as an 18-year-old, to be able to see a black president in office so early in my life. I believe this is a large step in the ongoing and painfully slow process of attempting to create equal opportunities for all races.

I do not wish to write you a letter about your amazing accomplishment though I am writing to address a concern. My concern is your ability to abuse power through signing statements.

I am about as politically liberal as one can get, but I am opposed to any president, regardless of political party, abusing power. I would like to specifically address your power of the signing statement.

Congress was designed to create bills under the Constitution and it is your right, as president, to sign, veto, or pocket veto. I must place emphasis on the fact that it is not your right to modify, by means "interpreting" a bill. I have already sadly witnessed your predecessor abuse this power.

In essence, the signing statement is equivalent to a line item veto. This is unconstitutional under *Clinton v. City of New York*. I am asking you as the leader of our declining country to limit, if not abolish, this power. It is a shame that most American citizens are not informed enough to understand this precursor to autocracy. I hope that you hold the personal responsibility to run this country in a fair and efficient matter.

The majority of the country is incredibly apathetic, ignorant, and indifferent towards the political system, but having the ability to get away with an abuse of power does not give justification. I ask, as an informed citizen, that you please stay true to your understanding of checks and balances. Please do not run this country unchecked.

Sincerely,
Peter Gibson Kotvis

Dear President-elect Obama,

Congratulations on being elected our 44th President. I was moved and proud that so many Americans spoke so strongly that it was you that we wanted as our president. Thank you for rising to the challenge of our exhausting campaign and electoral process to run for president. Your wise, thoughtful, analytical abilities are especially needed at this time in our history.

Since I work as a public health nurse with young families, I most typically write to elected officials advocating for funding for services for children, youth, and families. I'm certain that you will receive letters with all manner of requests. My request at this time has more to do with the core principles of our democracy—the balance of powers across the executive, legislative, and judicial branches of our government. I know that you, as a professor of Constitutional law, have a deep understanding of the checks and balances that were developed by our founding fathers to protect our country from an overly strong executive. Over the last 8 years, I've become increasingly concerned about the erosion of those checks and balances. My greatest hope is that you will restore the balance of power even though at this point in time, the erosion gives you exceptional power to do as you please.

This link to a Frontline episode from October 2007 outlines with great lucidity the nature of the erosion: www.pbs.org/wgbh/pages/frontline/cheney/. It speaks extensively about the enhanced presidential powers that have been claimed over the last 8 years. These expanded powers have led to approval of warrantless wiretapping and have narrowed the definition of torture. The current use of Signing Statements by the President have undermined the power of Congress to exercise its' legislative powers. Last year, we saw the Vice-President refuse to respond to congressional subpoenas by claiming executive privilege. Because democracy is a precious and fragile system, I urge you to strengthen and restore the balance of powers that was intended by our founding fathers and that have served our country well for over 200 years.

I'm looking forward to the leadership that you will provide for our country over the next 4 years. I believe that you've already begun to restore the image of America across the planet.

Good luck on this new journey.

Sincerely,
Karen Brozovich

President Obama,

Congratulations on your new office.

As a member of the artistic community, I urge you to not let attention to the fine and performing arts go to the wayside. Public funding and support of the arts allows us to continue to create, entertain, and question without fear. In dire times, it's even more important for the public to engage in a mode of expression and discourse. Please consider support of the arts to help get our country out of this financial turmoil. Not only by revitalizing current institutions and programs, but fostering new ones for future generations.

Thank you for your time.

Sincerely,
Kathryn

Dear President Obama,

Your FCC transition team of Susan Crawford and Kevin Werbach are strong proponents of Net Neutrality and expediting the broadband rollout in the United States. Those two issues affect the public's equal and unfettered use of the Internet and how the country will be able to keep up with the rest of the world with inexpensive access to the internet. What kind of policies will you and your FCC Chairman implement to ensure Net Neutrality and expand the broadband infrastructure in the United States?

Best regards,
Harriman C. Lee

November 19, 2008
Dear Mr. President,

I was hoping that you could think about an idea that I have had to make our streets and our children safer. I am an individual that prides myself on being creative to find solutions to problems. I have an idea that I hope you think would be worthy of addressing during your presidency.

I was thinking why not use our driver's licenses to keep people who have committed crimes in connection with drugs and alcohol from purchasing these items? If all stores that sell any drug (over the counter) with ingredients that are in question and all places whom sale alcohol products are required to check ID of everyone, not just kids, then this gives us an avenue to limit its use. If a person has not been responsible with these items, say alcohol problems with DUI or domestic abuse that has alcohol involved, they would be entered into the system to not be allowed to purchase alcohol. AND so the next thing to take care of is persons buying alcohol/drugs for them. Well then take away their privileges. I know this may require a new law that makes it illegal to purchase these items for someone whom is being restricted, but that could come along later if needed. Let's get the ball rolling with limiting the actual offender. This is not going to be a cure all for everything that can come up. It would be placed upon the judge to make this new tool part of their punishment and to determine the length of being prohibited from these privileges. AND LET ME SAY THEY ARE PRIVELEGES THAT SHOULD BE GIVEN ONLY TO THOSE RESPONSIBLE ENOUGH TO NOT ABUSE THEM.

I believe that this could be reasonably easy to put into action. I am not sure if all states have codes on the back of driver's licenses that can be scanned but, it seems reasonable that during your presidency this could easily be accomplished. Just think of all the crimes we have now that may be lessened or eliminated by this. I think it should be given further thought and my hopes are that you do too. I know that normally this should be handled by senators and congressmen but I hope by bypassing them and going to you a lot of time can be saved.

Congratulations on the election and I look forward to the changes I am sure we will see during your 8 years. I am an optimist.

Wendy Owen

Dear President Barack H. Obama,

It's not easy being a person who follows her heart in a sea of skeptics.

I've always prided myself on my ability to reason something out; when life is confusing, I take a moment, take a breath, and weigh the choices. Political arguments can be formed with clever uses of our language from people who, perhaps, read more about current events and have a head for the details of a voting record, a promise or word made years ago, or a line-by-line budget proposal. I've seen the sway of the loudest voice who can talk the longest. Successful sellers of miracle elixirs came out of this same mold. But sometimes I don't have the words for "knowing" what's right.

I can bring out the facts and figures, but honestly, it's that bottom line of just knowing, in my heart of hearts, what's right. My self-doubt has been reduced and my faith in our culture has been somewhat restored. I have been convinced that it's good there are people like you who follow their own hearts even when the tide turns. Steadfast loyalty to a personal mission—generally, one of the betterment of the human condition—is periodically challenged in a variety of ways.

Your commitment to remember—what it feels like to anticipate, to fear, to hope, and to have those hopes crash and cast aside—is crucial to your leadership. Many people hesitate going to the mailbox, not because of some anthrax scare, but because there may be an overdue bill or a rejection from a job application.

I am a librarian without a library. I have seen the demise of public, special, and school libraries and the abrupt halting of needed construction for some existing libraries as funding is suspended. Educators of all calibers are affected. Information literacy, the freedom of information, and the impact of a lack of access to accurate, age-appropriate, freely available information through trained information specialists (librarians) is becoming a luxury. The digital divide is widening ever so rapidly.

Libraries are committed to their communities, to bringing programs and workshops that partner with schools and enhance education. Intergenerational focuses give grandmothers ways to learn about how to e-mail and send or open photographs of their children and children's children, as well as teenagers an important role as mentors for younger children. Outreach programs touch lives of the homebound and incarcerated. After school and on those days when schools are not in session, libraries are filled with students who have nowhere else to go. They are a refuge from commercialism. Librarians work with patrons online through chat and e-mail reference, on the telephones, in person, and through their Web sites to help each one find the information they seek. Libraries are filled with dedicated professionals who create an environment that supports continued education through a variety of ways.

In your dedication to education, please remember libraries as an essential part of this plan. I would be happy to set you up with a tour of any library you'd like to visit, to find out more about this valuable resource. They are a central place in any educational or information gathering. I may not have a library job today, but I am still dedicated to the profession and am still proud to say, "I am a librarian." I am hopeful that you will remember the importance of libraries and the role librarians play with education and with the exchange of information. We are (maybe too quietly and thereby unnoticed) at your service.

Sincerely yours,
Cathay Crosby
Librarian

Dear President-elect Obama,

It was a happy day for me when you were voted the next president of this country. The reason I was jumping up and down in front of the television was because I knew you were going to make positive changes, as you promised us. The question is this: will you keep your promises? I have a few issues that I definitely want you to stick to.

Firstly, I would hope that you would not raise our taxes, and will give the middle class tax cuts, even though I do believe you will keep your word. As a member of a middle class family, I know my parents worry about keeping my sisters in university. If you raise taxes, our family and most others will be balancing on the point of a knife, waiting to be impaled.

The next issue I will bring up is health care. Please, Mr. President, improve the health care system, so that everybody can afford medical attention. Every family needs to be able to have their children vaccinated and treated when they are ill. It just wouldn't be fair, you know, if the wealthier class was healthy and the rest suffered.

This last subject is the one I find most important to me. It is education. Elementary, junior high, and high schools are (in my eyes) falling behind the rest of the world. Those in authority keep experimenting with the systems instead of fine-tuning those that work. In fact, there is no standardized system of education across the U.S., as there is in other countries, like Singapore. I hope you will improve this.

With any luck, when you are at the head of our nation, every living soul will believe that you were truthful in your campaign—that you will bring change for the better.

Best Regards,
Isabel S.

Dear President Barack Obama,

First and foremost the obvious congratulations are in order. Congratulations on winning the presidency. Now I just hope that you are up for all the responsibility that it entails.

That is what my letter will focus on—the change that you promised this nation. I do not wish to sound like a pessimist, but the path that I have seen this country go down not only the past few months, but much of the past decade, has left me with a pessimistic view of the government. I know that the reason you won the presidency had nothing to do with your race, but the promises that you made this great nation, and I am very grateful for that. I am glad that the people of this country could look beyond the color of your skin and actually listen to your words. With that said, I wish that you did not say those things just because you knew that was what we wanted to hear, but rather because you intend on actually carrying out such things.

Let's start with the war: get our men and women, mothers and fathers, brothers and sisters, family and friends back home. This war may have been the right path at some point, but that no longer appears to be the case. Do not just say that it is in your plan, but actually do something about it. Do not give us some vague sense of the future and the change that will happen in it, but set dates, give the American people a time line. We are running on our last bit of hope that things will get better in the future and we want things to be better in the present.

Which brings me to the economy—do all you can to fix this. People do not like to use the words like "recession" or "depression" or "panic" or anything that may cause a negative reaction, but that is exactly how it will be referred to in the history books, so we should not avoid it. Do not look to blame people for what has happened, because the fact is that it has happened and we need to move on from pointing fingers. Blame never solved anything. What we need to do is get some faith back in the American economy. We need to create jobs and get the economy moving again. Create public works programs and employ the unemployed. I had a friend that gave me what I consider to be a great suggestion as a way to collect some money that I do not think the American people will be opposed to. Currently gas prices are the lowest they have been in years, whereas just this summer they were the highest they have been in this country. Put a tax on gas, raising it fifty cents, which would place it at about $2.30 a gallon, which is still well below what it was this summer by about two dollars, and use that fifty cents from every gallon to pay off some of this nation's deficit or to circulate the money back into the pockets of Americans, then that would help to get the economy going again.

People may be angry at first that they are being taxed on gas prices, but I truly believe that they will understand if the reasoning is explained to them. It is not as bad as it was this summer, raising the price to over four dollars, and the money will go back to improve things for them. It seems like a win-win situation.

That is just a suggestion, of course. There are so many other things you could do, and you need to do, to get this country going again. Please do not hesitate in doing so. This country needs you to get things done and get them done as quickly as possible. This is a lot of pressure, but as a country we obviously feel as if you are up for the job.

Congratulations again and all I ask is that you please keep your promise of change.

Stacey

Mr. President-elect,

Congratulations on your recent victory. This election season proved to be long and challenging, but your demeanor constantly provided reassurance to Americans everywhere.

As you begin your tenure in office there are several challenges you will most certainly face as the United States continues to work towards a more promising future. I would like to urge you to carefully examine the current economic situation and the conflict in Iraq.

The global economy is currently in a very difficult situation and we must act carefully to avoid the situation from worsening in the future. Bailouts will only lead to a higher national debt and simply provide temporary financial relief. We must weigh the future against the present to determine what the best course of action.

The current conflict in Iraq will also be a critical issue for your administration. Despite what personal ideological beliefs you may possess, we must continue our mission in Iraq to ensure those who have died have not done so in vain. I believe your decision to keep Secretary Gates on will help ensure you are able to continue this noble goal and to bring stability and peace to the region.

Congratulations on your election and best wishes for a smooth transition and productive tenure in office.

Best wishes,
Kyle Swanson

Dear President Obama,

The presidential race that you have just recently won represents a critical milestone in today's civil rights movement for all individuals. I am hopeful that the future is bright as all people of color, gender, and sexual orientation have the chance for advancement not only in the economic market, but in equal rights legislation as well. Personally, your historic presidential win represents what America is today—a diverse nation full of hope and optimism. One topic I would like to touch on is the Iraq War. I know you have committed to removing troops from the war overseas, but I would like to know at what rate you will be removing troops. And how long do you predict the entire removal of soldiers will take? Also I would like to know how you intend to deal with the recession that is currently taking place. What financial moves are you considering? Once again I would like to wish you the best in leading our country back to prominence.

Sincerely,
Brian

President Obama,

You enter office tomorrow amidst economic, political, and international dilemmas, and the job ahead of you is not an easy one. The presidency that you are inheriting comes with loads of responsibility, sound judgment, and difficult decision-making, but I believe you have the necessary qualifications to be successful in leading our nation through these troubling times.

It is important that during the course of your presidency, you do not forget the important resources that America has at its disposal. As the leading economic power in the world, we must stabilize the American financial markets so that there will be a fervent supply of jobs, capital for investment, and value behind the American dollar. As the leading military power in the world, we must use our troops when necessary to maintain world order and keep peace around the world. Furthermore, we must work with democratic nations and our allies to prevent despotic rulers and terrorist regimes from staying in power and threatening our existence.

There is nothing more sacred in the American ideals on which our country was founded than the right to peacefully exist and to express your own ideas. No group or individual should be denied these rights. At present, Israel is threatened by Iran and many rogue groups within its neighboring Arab nations. As president, one of your most important priorities should be on protecting Israel's right to exist, and to keep peace in that region at all costs. The Jewish people suffered for centuries to have their own home, and to forget the only democracy in the Middle East would be a grave mistake.

Lastly, do not ever forget that despite belonging to the Democratic Party, you now belong to all Americans. It takes a good amount of fortitude to stand up to your own party when you do not agree with their policies, and there will be times ahead when that is the case. We, as Americans, are tired of the political bickering amongst both parties, and we all would like to see all politicians work together for the betterment of our country as a whole. It's time for you to bring the change to Washington that you promised in your campaign, and do not forget the concerns of your colleagues from across the aisle.

I have the utmost faith that you will do what it takes to lead our country back to its prominence economically, politically, and militarily. I wish you the best of luck.

Sincerely,
Jason Vaupen

Dear President Obama,

I am writing to you as one of your fellow minority citizens. And as a minority citizen, I often ponder our role in society and whether it has truly increased and made an impact in society today. Although certain legislation has been passed in order to ensure "equal opportunity" and to ensure that certain civil rights are protected, sometimes it still feels like there is still injustice in the United States, despite all the steps we have taken forward. My question to you is: Will you push for any legislation that will reinforce this? Coming from the state of Michigan I know that affirmative action has already been reversed, and I fear that similar legislation will follow suit. What do you foresee for minorities in the future?

Sincerely,
Judia Chang

Dear President Obama,

First, I would like to congratulate you on your successful presidential campaign and inauguration into the office of the president of the United States of America. This is a historic time for yourself, our country, and its citizens as we are embarking on a new era of both change and equality. While not a Democrat myself, I recognize the urgent need for change in our government that will hopefully foster change within the country and its people. These times of unease and turmoil in both the economy and the confidence of the people of the U.S.

must be met with strong resolve and passion in order for the appropriate change to be made. It is almost impossible for any single person to understand both the pressure on yourself during these times as our executor of change, and the importance of which this position of 44th president of the United States of America holds during this turning point in the path of our country. In this endeavor I wish you the best of both luck and the strength to prevail in times where changes may not happen in a time scale with which people are happy. I hope that we as citizens can be mindful of the monumental task before you and react to you policies with an open mind and patience.

Next, I would like to offer you, as I am confident many have some areas with which I have a personal concern as a citizen of this country. I hope that you will understand the strong need for bipartisan relations during these times. I realize that each president is a member of a political party which brings with it its own personal agenda and that this agenda is sometimes put at the forefront of the presidential agenda upon assuming office. I urge you to remember the words of our first president and founding father George Washington, where he warned in his farewell address of the potential danger involved with political parties and their agendas. I further hope that you can use this bipartisan means of executing change to bring an end to the current war in a manner with which both the least amount of blood will be shed and the most peace will be preserved where our troops are present and helping. This war has the potential to end in a manner where all citizens can be happy with the results and additionally in a manner where we can continue to show that terrorist activity both at home and abroad will not be tolerated. I hope that you will show an equal treatment and consideration for all those classes in our country from poor to rich, as the possession of money does not necessarily equate to having less concerns about the path our country is headed down. Please take note of all voices of concern from slums to suburbs, as both the rich and poor are citizens and as a citizen our right to a voice is equal. Please also keep an open yet cautious mind toward the technological innovations that we are developing on a daily basis. We are a brilliant country, and as such, we are privileged to the opportunity to expand our technological horizons such that cures for terminal diseases and more efficient means of fuel and electricity are mere days from becoming realities. I hope that as the president, you actively seek out opportunities to expand peaceful relations and alliances with countries who we are currently friendly and those who we may not have yet befriended. I hope that you can realize the unique and historical opportunity you have now as the president during these times and use that power in its most efficient way, such that after your four years in office, we can look back and truly say we are better off as a country for having elected you to this prestigious office.

Finally, I would like to wish you the best of luck in balancing your duties and opportunities as president, with the importance of your family life and its health. This is no doubt a difficult task, but it is of paramount importance as without the love and support of your family, your presidency will be nearly unsurvivable. Know that you have the backing of an entire nation of supporters who are hopeful for four years of continued success and change for the better. I am confident that the tides will turn soon, and I hope that you can see as I do, the light beaming at the end of the tunnel and run to it with the utmost of urgency.

Congratulations again, and good luck with your coming four years in office.

Sincerely,
Christopher William Weigand

Dear President Obama,

On the day of your inauguration, I can remind myself that I am fortunate to live in a country which can conduct free and safe elections, as well as a country that is capable of breaking free from the traditions of past injustices. Furthermore, as someone who voted for you, I like to believe that I had at least a small part in your victory.

I am not sure what to expect in the next four years. I listened to your campaign promises to reform the health care system, end Iraqi occupation, and reduce dependence on oil. I am confident that you meant these things; however, I am aware that the political realities in Washington are such that the interests with the most money often win. President Obama, I hope that you have the fortitude to make decisions based on the ideals of democracy and social justice rather than the interests of powerful corporations and Washington elites. In a time of financial crisis, the poor and unemployed of America will need effective government support to survive.

In terms of foreign policy, I hope that you make an effort to undo the damage caused by President Bush as well as President Clinton. Dropping bombs is not an effective means of negotiation and the United States needs to set a better precedent for all nations worldwide. Additionally, I hope you take a stand against Israel's assault on the Palestinian people and work with the United Nations as well as the Israeli and Palestinian governments to help bring about a solution to this conflict.

Finally, I would like to congratulate you on your election to the presidency and wish you luck during your term in office.

Sincerely,
Kevin Green

President Obama,

I, like many Americans, am against a partisan government and thus am not biased towards either Republican or Democratic ideals. I am a 24-year-old masters student of engineering at the University of Michigan–Ann Arbor. I know that you are already implementing your economic stimulus plans and that our economic situation is your top priority. Although I have more of a laissez-faire attitude towards economy I am in agreement that our present situation should not go unchallenged by government intervention. I do however have my own set of beliefs that I am interested in and I would like to know your plans of action for the following issues:

1) Abortion: I am pro-choice. I believe that conception is only in the eye of the beholder and religious belief need not play a role in one's decision so long as they are of sound mind and judgment. I also feel that governmental financial aid should only be provided in cases of absolute need (e.g., rape, incest, extreme destitution).

2) Gay marriage: I am against gay marriage. I do not believe that it is healthy for the next generations of our society to be forced to comprehend such mature decisions so early in life via gay adoption. I believe that it can be detrimental to the natural order of life in our country and that such a decision should coincide with other maturities in that they are prohibited by law until the person is at least 18 years of age.

3) Legalization of marijuana: I support the legalization of marijuana. I do not use the substance personally but I believe that it is a major opportunity of economic stimulus in our country and that the benefits far outweigh the detriments. I also feel that it should be nationally accepted because of the many suffering patients in states where medicinal marijuana is still illegal.

4) Big 3 bailout: As a "Michigander" I feel that the government would more effectively help the U.S. auto industry by offering a temporary tax relief rather than supplying funds with control mechanisms attached to them.

5) Stem cell research: Corresponding with my beliefs on abortion, to waste unused or potential stem cells is unnecessary when they can so positively educate our society.

6) Gun protection: I believe that the already stringent measures for owning a carry weapon are enough to warrant allowing personal protection.

7) Minimum wage increase: I am for the minimum wage increase as the current rate has people remaining in poverty without comfortable living conditions especially with our inflated economic conditions.

8) Universal health care: I think universal health care will only serve to make the poor poorer and extremely lower the quality of health care for those who have it. Other methods/plans should be developed in place to help those who cannot afford it.

9) Censorship: I believe that there is entirely too much effort and funding supporting organizational efforts on censorship. Censorship should be the responsibility of the

parent and that the naivety of the FCC for what children are exposed to rivals that of archaic puritan ideals. If censorship of such levels continues then all involved organizations' priorities for censored materials need extreme reevaluation.

10) Iraq War: I am in full support of what you decide for the troops in Iraq. I trust that you will fix Bush's incompetent and inconsiderate mistakes in handling this matter in a proper way.

11) Homeland Security: I do not believe that anyone has the right to physically torture any other human. "Embarrassment" forms of torture seem humane and thus I am in support of them. I am a firm believer in protecting one's right to privacy so I am against any efforts to violate that civil right no matter what the consequences or risks may be.

Thank you for hearing me I know you are busy and this will probably only reach as far as one of your staff but I care a great deal about the condition of our country and hope to one day leave my mark on our improvement.

Sincerely,
Daniel James Dabrowski
BSE Naval Architecture and Marine Engineering
President, UM: Autonomy Autonomous Surface Vehicle Team
University of Michigan–Ann Arbor

Dear President Obama,

Congratulations on your election to the presidency. I am excited about the future of our great nation and its people. You bring great hope to the American people and I hope that you will be able to fulfill your promises of prosperity. I am hopeful that you will govern as a centrist as you have promised to do. You have done a good job surrounding yourself with qualified people and I believe you will make informed decisions. I hope you don't spend too much money on the stimulus package and I also hope you don't waste money on tax credits. Studies show that people save 2/3 of the tax credit, so it is a very inefficient allocation of taxpayer money.

Good Luck,
Lawrence Joseph

January 20, 2009

Dear President Obama,

Congratulations on your groundbreaking, history-making election as the 44th president of the United States. Unfortunately, you were not my choice for the job, but now that you have proven to be America's choice, I offer my wholehearted support. I sincerely hope that you keep some of the promises you have made throughout the campaign, such as actively pursuing a bipartisan government because as you well know, democracy entails representation of the entire nation. Yet, I hope some of your other campaign promises remain unfulfilled.

As a young person, I recognize the need to increase the national debt in order to begin the economic recovery that our country desperately needs. However, I want to be sure that the programs you and your administration create will deliver future benefits because the taxes I will be paying will be the taxes used to repay this debt. Furthermore, I hope you keep in mind the importance of maintaining the free market system and capitalism when jump-starting domestic economic development. I worry about the ease with which you discussed middle and lower class tax cuts during your campaign for many who are not subject to federal tax. Such a system of tax cuts is in reality an income redistribution system. If your true goal is taxing wealth, then I hope you consider taxing wealth (i.e. dividends, interest, and net worth) rather than wages and other earned compensation.

Similarly, I believe that small businesses will be the foundation for our economic recovery. Intrusive government regulation on these businesses, I fear, will kill ingenuity and ambition—two American business characteristics imperative for stimulating and maintaining future job growth. Because you are an advocate of hope, I ask that you not implement tax and regulatory policies that would stifle the dreams of many Americans who hope to start businesses or those currently struggling to build and maintain businesses. Further, the current bailout craze for the financial and auto sectors is in many ways nationalizing these industries—I hope you see the potential pitfalls of industry nationalization and put an end to the bailouts of inefficient and unprofitable companies.

Following the economy, the war in Iraq is the next most critical issue facing our nation. I think that a democratic Iraq could help stabilize that entire region. With that said, I fear that a premature withdrawal of U.S. troops (using your campaign pledge of a 16-month timetable for withdrawal) could potentially lead to a regression in the progress made thus far. Prior to a complete withdrawal, we must ensure that the Iraqi army is equipped to adequately maintain Iraq's national defense and that the democratically elected Iraqi government is able to rule without U.S. aid.

Finally, because you are an advocate of national health care, I ask you to consider the consequences of such a system. Looking at Canada's national health care system and other similar systems, I cannot help but notice their inefficiency. I consider the United States to have the best health care system in the world, and I would love to keep it that way.

So as you begin to translate your campaign promises of hope and change into concrete foreign and domestic policy, please remember that the U.S. has always been a land of hope and change sometimes comes with unintended, adverse consequences.

Respectfully,
Lauren Lewis

Dear President Obama,

Two of the biggest challenges our nation faces are reducing our dependence on (foreign) oil and mitigating climate change by reducing our carbon emissions. One often-discussed route to achieving these goals is improving the gasoline mileage of automobiles or running them on biofuels/hydrogen/batteries.

While those are important steps I believe they are a long-term solution with limited short-term potential. A quicker way to dramatically cut oil usage and emissions in 2 to 4 years is to focus on a handful of cities with severe traffic problems and SOLVE those woes by dramatically improving the access to and reliability of public transportation there. According to *Forbes* magazine, Atlanta, Dallas, Houston, Los Angeles, and Miami are all examples of big cities with inadequate mass transit and constant gridlock. Using the Bus Rapid Transit model pioneered in Brazil we could offer a fast, efficient, and reliable transit system for any of those cities and spend less than a month of the war in Iraq costs.

Decades of underfunding have given mass transit a bad name to many Americans. I believe targeted use of sufficient resources in one or more of the previously mentioned cities would create a success story which could help build support for extending public transit and increasing ridership throughout our nation. The potential for saving oil and reducing emissions is immense.

Dear Mr. Barack Obama:

My name is Twanice Jones and I am a sophomore student at the University of Michigan. I come from a relatively large family, and I am the first one to leave home to start my life. I am the oldest of six children; one of which, my youngest brother, has been diagnosed with an autism spectrum disorder. I have read your stance on the issue and I appreciate your willingness to work for those who cannot do so for themselves. These disorders are usually not at the forefront of political issues, and this race has been no different. I am writing to first thank you for your involvement, and encourage you to remember those who suffer from this disease in midst of everything else that you have on your plate.

Respectfully Submitted,
Twanice Jones

Dear President Obama,

During the presidential debates, as well as throughout the fight for office, autism became a major issue due to vice presidential candidate Sarah Palin and her son. Autism is a growing form of mental retardation. More and more children are diagnosed with autism everyday, therefore new techniques and medicines need to become available to these individuals. New facilities are needed in order to help autistic children develop and learn new skills. This is a pressing issue that needs to be addressed. Funds must become available for research, new programs must be opened to train individuals in order to help those with autism as well as their families, and doctors need training in how to diagnose individuals along with to prescribe the correct medications and lead families to the right treatment facilities. These are just a few easily named things that are necessary in order to help ease the process for those whose children are diagnosed with autism.

In the final debate, Republican candidate McCain and you both spoke about the pressing issue that Americans faced with the growing numbers of those diagnosed with autism. Therefore, I would like to know what you and your administration plan to do during your term to deal with autism and the other forms of mental retardation that affect the families throughout the United States and the rest of the world? This country can no longer wait for action to be made in the field of autism. Individuals with autism, and their families not only want, but need progress to be made to ensure a better tomorrow for those who live with autism every day.

Thank you for your time,
Jennifer Beitner

Dear President Obama,

Congratulations on winning the election and for the opportunity to change America. We look forward to the change for our children's future. I am writing to simply ask for help. I am 31 years old; I have resided here in the U.S. since 1996 and have been a permanent resident since. I am originally from the Philippines and I have lived in Germany for a while but this country is unique and has provides opportunity and chances to those who wants to succeed. I was married to an American at such a young age and had two girls, now 12 and 8 years of age. We divorced after 9 years of marriage. And it has been very challenging as a single mom to raise two kids and work. Moreover, I decided to go back to school and refused to depend on child support. But working full-time to get by and get through school has been a journey for me. I had to get my GED and to find a sitter is not easy since I don't get much help. On a personal note, I was in a relationship that failed and had another daughter. I am not asking for pity but help on behalf of all the single parents. I was laid off after my maternity leave due to the economic crisis. And now to get to the Department of Labor to claim unemployment is also a fight and I was denied, because I couldn't make it for the seminars they require, which do not allow children. I have three girls that depend on me on a daily basis, how is it possible for me to get to where there are no kids allowed? I still haven't found any work. I am asking for assistance for us single parents. Just a hand as we go to school to further our careers and to be able to provide for our children. Maybe a scholarship program or reduced childcare as we go to school could be provided. Temporary help is needed. Childcare is an issue as a single parent. My wish is to have help in this area.

Thank you!

Sincerely,
Ruth Ladd

January 11, 2009
Dear President Obama,

I know that by the time you receive this, IF you receive it at all, you will be leading our country. First, please know that you are in my daily prayers that God will show you the wisdom to lead our America in the right direction for progress, safety, and moral standing in the world.

This letter is written primarily to ask on behalf of many of my colleagues that you re-consider the abortion issue. Regardless of what the media tells the people of America, the approval of the killing of unborn babies IS the major issue that made many people vote Republican, instead of Democrat. Because we know that an unborn baby has a separate heartbeat than the mother, and that if there is any possibility that God would regard the killing of this precious innocent life as murder, why would we advocate doing it?

The reason abortion is advocated by some is that abortion clinics get paid well for their services by desperate women who do not know that they have other more positive choices. Elliot Institute spokesperson Amy Solby reported that one study found 64 percent of women who had abortions reported they felt pressured to abort by others. "Something like 80 percent of them said that they didn't get the counseling they needed to make a good decision, that often they were not given counseling at all, or that the counseling they had was inadequate," she explains.

Instead of pouring funds we do not really have into abortion clinics that kill babies, could we not provide support to counseling facilities that enable mothers to see the value of every human life and give them other options, such as adoption, if they really do decide that they cannot love their children or do not have the financial means to support them?

What if the parents of our Heisman Trophy winner in football, Tim Tebow, had been aborted when a doctor told his mother that he should be because of complications? What if other people, like Einstein, with learning disabilities, had been aborted? A list of no fewer than 100 well-known celebrities is found on the internet of people who were adopted instead of aborted. Many American couples who wish to adopt now have to go to Russia or Romania to find children to adopt. We do not have to kill our babies. People want to love them. And, even though you say that you "would not want your daughters to be punished if they were to become pregnant out of wedlock" or something to that effect, abortion IS punishment, and as a prospective grandparent, I would hope that you would see that precious life differently.

Our church, the First Baptist of Euless, Texas, supports a pregnancy center that provides women with better alternatives than killing that separate life that is within them. Please help us support these programs, instead of those that kill our babies. Think what God would want you to do. What if your mother had decided that you could not be born?

Thank you for thinking about it when people who have no regard for life ask for funds to support the killing of our babies.

Patricia Walters, EdD

Mr. Barack Obama,

My earliest recollection of learning American history in grade school sparks memories of words like "manifest destiny," stories of Abraham Lincoln and his humble log-cabin upbringing, concepts like the self-made man, and images of glory from the American Revolution. As American children, we have been conditioned to associate our history and heritage with morality, equality, justice, peace, and all the words sprinkled throughout the Constitution that symbolize the goal and purpose of the United States of America. I was taught to believe that my basic rights as an American citizen were to life, liberty, and the pursuit of happiness.

When I was 13, my father was rushed to the hospital for having a dangerously low blood count. He was diagnosed with acute leukemia and before I even had the chance to absorb reality, he fell into a terminal coma and died a few days later. My father had been sick all his life. He had been victim to a severe liver disease, had cancerous growths in his neck, had to undergo chemotherapy and radiation, and was eventually diagnosed with the acute leukemia that was responsible for taking his life. For years he struggled with getting medical insurance. After his first sickness private insurance companies were constantly denying him coverage. When he passed away, my mother was left with a hospital bill that was insurmountable. To top it off, the bank to which my father paid mortgage life insurance for 22 years refused to pay off the mortgage on our house that should have been taken care of after his death. As a result of the bank's disorganization and carelessness, my mother, now left alone with no family to help her, was responsible for the cost of our house as well as the hospital bill that covered the 10 days of my father's intensive care before he eventually died on Halloween in 2002.

As a young middle school student with an even younger sister, I found myself and my in a downward spiral that we could not escape. Not only had my life as I knew it been destroyed, but I was stripped of all liberty to pursue life and happiness. It only got worse when my mother was diagnosed with cancer a few years later. For the second time in our experience, the health insurance companies refused coverage for the surgery necessary for my mother to have the cancer removed.

My mother was born in Scotland, a country in which health, education, and welfare is a right, not just a privilege. I have come to realize that in America, life, liberty, and the pursuit of happiness are not in any way guaranteed. These have become a privilege, for those who have the stability, the support, and the means to achieve them. If America is going to be a land of equality and justice, the right to live without being destroyed by corporate giants or insurance companies needs to be something that is guaranteed to all citizens, regardless of who they are.

Part of the reason I was so drawn to you as a candidate for the presidency was your belief in the fact that the American people should have access to affordable health care that won't severely financially burden American families. I believe this is something that is absolutely necessary in this country, as people's lives are destroyed on a daily basis not only emotionally, but also financially, when family members are faced with a terminal illness, which they cannot afford to treat.

Sincerely,
Siobhan

First of all I just wanted to congratulate you on becoming the 44th president of the United States of America. By winning this election you have given me hope that nothing is impossible to overcome. I am from Gurnee, Illinois, and I followed your senate race very closely. I was taken away by your ability to articulate things in a manner that made me want to get involved at some level. I am a firm believer in the mantra that you must be the change that you want to see in the world, and your victory is proof that this mantra is worth believing in.

I am particularly interested in what you are going to do with health care and education. My mother has colon cancer, and the amount of help we are getting from the American health care system is very close to nothing. I am a student at the University of Michigan, so helping her and making sure that she is being taken care of is my first priority. Hopefully, you are going to be able to improve the ability of American health care to help the people. Furthermore, I hope that you are able to improve the educational opportunities that many Americans are deprived of. I was fortunate to attend a prestigious university, but many of my peers were unable to do so due to the lack of educational opportunities they had.

Best of luck in the White House, President Obama, and I hope that you are able to accomplish everything that you want and more.

Thank you,
Remit Sony

Mr. President:

A week before the 2008 election, I went home from college for a routine eye doctor's appointment. By the time I was back in Ann Arbor, I was on four different types of vitamins and medications which aim to slow down the progression of a degenerative retinal disease (retinitis pigmentosa) which exists in both of my eyes. Before I left the doctor, he told me that I was lucky; thirty years ago, I would have been told to prepare for a life of blindness within ten years. Today, doctors have made great strides. I will not go blind for another 30 years, but I do not anticipate being able to see my grandchildren. I do not anticipate being able to function normally at the age of 50. I do not anticipate being able to live out my dream of being a sports broadcaster—a silly dream perhaps, but a dream nonetheless. The doctor told me that the best thing I could do to try and give myself a chance of living a normal life was to vote for you. He told me that your ideas with regards to stem cell treatment could transform the way that retinitis pigmentosa patients look at life. He told me that, if you were elected, I would be taking medicine not to merely slow the progression of a disease, but to buy me time before a cure was discovered. Mr. President, I am thankful that you are energizing my generation and changing the course of this country. I am proud, today, to call myself an American. But, most importantly, I am hopeful that someday I will live the life that I had planned on three months ago.

Sincerely,
Jeremy Kreisberg
University of Michigan

Dear President Obama,

First of all let me say that you have made me hopeful for the future of our country. As a student at the University of Michigan I have studied the governments of many other countries, and at times have questioned whether or not the United States is the right fit for me. But with your election I feel proud again to be an American because I feel that finally everything won't seem so bad.

I am mostly looking forward to see the health care changes you implement. Though my family is middle class our health care coverage is very bad, and because of that I suffer through more chronic pain than I really should. Hopefully Congress will support the policies you propose so then people like me can get help when they are suffering through pain.

I hope you understand how much hope you are giving the country. And I feel this not because of your ethnicity, but because you are actually putting yourself in a vulnerable position with your strong initiative to make change.

Good luck in office, and thank you for making me happy to be a citizen of the United States of America.

Sincerely,
Elle Mastenbrook

Dear Mr. President,

I am very grateful to have experienced such an important 2008 presidential election for my first time voting. I respected both candidates, but I proudly voted for you, president Barack Obama. I understand the world is facing many types of problems today. One such problem, you plan to address, is the issue of health care in America, which has concerned me for quite a while now. I am a first generation Albanian-American, a student at the University of Michigan, and part of a low-middle class family living in the United States. After three years of my family's residence in the U.S., we had to make the decision that we could no longer afford the medical insurance provided by mother's employer. So we simply hoped to not suffer any health issues and thus far we have been blessed as my parents, my little sister, and I have all been pretty healthy. However, as we struggle to pay for my school's tuition, we have become greatly skeptical about visiting any hospitals or doctors. I do not want to put any more financial burden on my family, so when I do get hurt or sick, I have learned to deal with it my own way, and again I am fortunate to be in really good health.

My love for sports has put me into a few unpleasant situations, when I have suffered semi-severe injuries while playing them. One of my latest injuries happened a few months ago when I was accidentally hit by an elbow, while playing basketball, and got a bad cut on my eyebrow. Everyone was immediately asking to get an ambulance, but I immediately refused such help because I did not have any medical insurance and feared the great costs associated with the emergency room. I do not forget the moment when I entered the emergency the night I hurt my eye. The first words said by the receptionist were not "Are you all right?" Instead she wanted to interrogate me on my identity before I received any medical treatment. This upset me, as in my eyes this seemed like a compassionless gesture. And it was not directed towards the receptionist, but the health care system itself. One where we care more about how the medical treatment provided will be paid for instead of the person's suffering at the time. I immediately discovered my student status did not cover any treatment and walked out, still bleeding. A friend later helped me carefully bandage my cut, and I managed to recover in a few weeks.

What's interesting is that my good friend, who helped me, inspires to be a millionaire someday. And one of his career choices to help him achieve such inspiration is to become a doctor. I often tell him my perspective as I think he should pursue a medical career to help others in need and not solely to make good money. Don't get me wrong, I know the feeling of wanting to be richer but at the same time I would rather care more about people than about money.

In the midst of this election, I have learned many things about you and built great respect towards you as a person. I admired how instead of accepting a fancy lawyer job, after Harvard, you went back to your community and helped them with their issues. I also admire your message of hope and change. And this bring me to my question, how do we attempt to shift the love of money or personal greed many people in our society have towards caring about others around us, which I believe would make the world a much better place for everyone?

Sincerely,

Alban Rushiti

P.S. I realize you have enormous work ahead as you transition to the presidency, but I hope to someday receive a response from you.

Dear President Obama,

Throughout your election I thought that you supported gay rights. I was shocked when I heard Biden state in one of the vice presidential debates that you do not support gay marriage. I suppose that although you do support gays, you do not wish to legalize gay marriage, but isn't this contradictory? I strongly oppose this viewpoint. This topic is a pressing one, especially in recent light of what happened in California with Proposal 8. What happens to all the people that were married beforehand? Are they still legally wed? Wouldn't it be in opposition of Proposal 8 if they are? Proposal 8 is a violation of the equal protection clause. How is not allowing certain people to get married equal protection? Everyone should have the same benefits. Obviously, it is clear that people are being discriminated against. I just hope that this is sorted out and that everyone will get the chance to love and marry freely, a right that should not be so hard to come by.

Dear President Obama,

First let me extend to you my deepest congratulations on your victory this past November. As many have said before and will continue to say for years to come, it was a historic day that I wasn't sure I would ever see in my lifetime. I followed your campaign fairly closely for almost a year prior to your victory and have supported many of your stances on numerous issues. However, one issue that I often did not hear about was one that is moving to the forefront of debate in our country: the issue of gay marriage. As I'm sure you are aware, on the same night as your victory Proposal 8 was passed in California, banning the recently legalized gay marriage. I find this sort of proposal appalling and am shocked that it was able to pass. There is one person who I believe can truly help this situation, and that is you.

I know that gay marriage is one of those hot button topics that few people like to discuss, but it's one that affects millions of people every day. And it doesn't just affect the people who are trying to obtain a marriage; it also affects their family and friends who have to watch them suffer from this type of discrimination simply because others do not agree with something they cannot control. People may claim that gay marriage goes against the Bible's teachings, but we're living in the United States of America, a country where our founding fathers provided us with the religious freedom they themselves were not so lucky to receive in England. We are free to practice whatever religion we so please, and just because the majority of the country is Christian does not mean that we all are. Therefore the entire country should not have to follow the rules of one religious book simply because the majority believes in its teachings.

While I'm aware that this is a very controversial topic, I urge you to consider the other side of the spectrum here. As difficult as it may be, try for one minute to put yourself in their shoes. Think of the pain these people must feel because they fell in love with someone of the same sex and are not allowed to marry that person in the majority of the 50 states. It's time for true equality to come out and I believe that you are the one person who can make it happen, whether it be through forcing California to repeal Proposal 8 or creating a constitutional amendment legalizing gay marriage. This issue is not going away and it's time that we do something to help it along.

Sincerely,
Emily Fogelsonger

Dear President Obama,

I want to begin by saying that I was not a supporter of yours in the primary. But I did actively support you in the general election. I now believe that you have the opportunity to become a great president.

Our world is at a crossroads and the United States has the opportunity to lead it constructively into the 21st century. We must remake the image of our country into one that is respected across the globe. The American people are basically a good people. We have always been a melting pot welcoming those to our shores who want to live a free and better life. We must once again live up to that vision and showcase the creativity of the American people as we rebuild our economy and help to rebuild the worlds.

At home we need to become a forward-looking nation. We must be a nation that values human and civil rights both in our nation and around the world. We need to work to enable all people to live a productive life and achieve to their full potential.

As a gay man I look to you to lead in achieving equality for the GLBT community. I want us to have the right to live free of hate, work and live without discrimination, and have the right to give our lives for our country in service to our military. I want us to have the right to live in peace with our partners and our children and to share all the rights and responsibilities that all other couples have.

I want you to use the bully pulpit of the presidency to encourage teaching our children about the diversity that makes our nation great. To encourage schools to teach young people about the religions of the world and why we need to respect each other's religion. To make it possible and encourage young people to volunteer in their communities and to share their thoughts and ideas with others without fear of retribution.

I hope that you will speak out and support the ARTS. That the United States will be a leader in the world in educating our children to appreciate the world or art, theater, music, and that no child will be able to graduate from high school without being exposed to the ARTS.

I look forward to the positive impact you and your family will have on our nation and the world and I will do everything in my power as an individual to support you as you move forward to rebuild our nation.

Congratulations, Mr. Barack Obama, to you and your family. There comes, every once in a blue moon, a human being who can unite, enlighten and lead people across all nationalities and creeds. Your soul has been blessed to become one of these great human beings.

I didn't pay much attention to the Democratic election process at first. Being a lesbian, I had planned to vote for Hillary Clinton, on principle alone. Even after I realized that you were running against her, I still thought Clinton. I did not want to vote for you just because you were black. So I started listening to your rhetoric, you hopes, your visions for the future of America. Truth be told, they didn't sound like anything I'd heard in the past 8 years. This was a good thing. The American people had been so ignored. You sounded more like a grassroots politician, here for the good of the American people—and who had heard of that in a while, outside of fiction novels that is.

I began to listen to your political stand; I began to listen to my friends, coworkers, and family. I watched as people who did not share the color of my skin, rallied around you. Somewhere in there I realized that I was willing to take my lesbian vote and do the right thing.

Melissa Etheridge has a song on her album, and one of the phrases says, "I believe a woman can work hard, and be the president." I attended her concert in July of 2008, and when she sang the song she changed it to "I believe a black man can work hard, and be the president." There wasn't a whole lot of enthusiasm in that largely white, largely lesbian WaMu Theater audience. I began to realize that maybe there was no hope for you, Mr. Obama. I feared for your life, and that of your family. I didn't want to feel guilty about putting you in a position to be assassinated. These are things that went through my mind. I prayed, I looked deep within, I wished I could do something to change this suffering country of ours—I voted for you. Twice.

Last year was a tumultuous year, and an historical time in all of our lives. Four hundred–odd years is quite a long time. For that much time we, as an African-American race, were enslaved, raped, hung, and stripped of our families, our humane rights—for 400 years legally. After we were "freed" we weren't treated much better for the next 200 odd years if truth be told. I grew up believing that it was illegal for anyone but a Caucasian protestant to be the president of our country. As an adult, I just assumed that a black man/woman would never become president. I am proud to be a part of that history with my vote.

My expectations are this: that you heal our America. Turn within and heal us within. Make us a strong country, make us the big brother that we falsely boast to be. How can we be a good big brother when we haven't kept our "family" cohesive? I expect you to get us our forty acres and a mule in the form of a waiver of all tax liabilities for the next 10 years for any African-American. (This can be offset by taxing everyone—everyone whose yearly income is above a million dollars). I challenge you to a better education for our children, more environmental protection so that these same children of all races will have a viable place in which to succeed and achieve.

Health care can and should be better regulated. Hospitals should not be advertising on TV and radio. This alone states that some hospitals are better than others—translation—some of us can't afford to get good health care. But I digress, and I apologize. I simply want to say to you, President-elect Barack H. Obama, do the right thing! We are, all of America, behind you! Congratulations Mr. President!

Dear President,

I was very pleased with the election outcome. I voted for you and your party for many reasons. However there was one issue that stood out to me. You position on rights for same-sex couples could change the lives of people all over the country. As a young homosexual it is comforting to know that there are people in our government fighting for the rights of all minorities. I have faith in you and your party and look forward to the changes that have been long overdue.

Sincerely,
Hopeful Citizen

Dear Mr. President,

During your election I noticed that there were many issues that you tried not to get into because of the controversy that they cause for the public. Understanding of course that you are/were a politician and had to play to everyone's side in order to get their vote I still wonder today where you stand two very important issues. First issue would have to be abortion. I recall watching an interview of you where you were asked about homosexual marriage and you decided to state that the nation was to focus on what we agree on not what we disagree on and may cause tension and separation. I know that you being a president indeed means that you are THE American citizen and must represent the nation as a whole. Not being able to choose whether you want to represent the straight, homosexual, Christians, non-Christians, but every American. However, at one point a decision must be made. Do you or do you not agree with abortion and homosexual marriage? My concern with allowing homosexual marriage in this country is as follows: people say that declaring that "straight marriage" is the "norm" is giving this group privilege. I do not disagree with that statement. However, if we are to allow homosexual marriage is that not giving it privilege as well? My concern is not that gays marry, but where do we draw the line? Will there be regulations made that say one is allowed and the other not? What if there are some who claim that marrying an animal is all right? Will that be allowed? This may seem silly to you, but I do feel as though it is something that will arise if America is to allow everyone to marry who they want and agree not oppress sexual orientations.

Another thing that I observed is that you appear to be a man of family. Yet it is okay to you for 14-year-old girls to have abortions without their parents' knowledge? Is that not contradicting? My concern for this nation is where it is going morally. Everyday we are pushing for something new to be allowed in society. Where will this end? You too claim to be a religious man? Are you not concerned about where this country is going morally? Will we allow our youth to have these abortions and to continuously kill babies? Or will you take a stand against the majority of most liberals and defend the faith that you claim to belong to?

I congratulate you on your win. I hope to see these great changes that America has waited and voted for. Praying for you and for your family.

God Bless.

Dear Mr. Obama,

Thank you from the depths of our hearts! You already have shown yourself to be a real representative of the people. We worked long hours to make sure that you were elected. We are elated!

We realize that your attention will be demanded from all directions. We are pleased that you realize the importance of having experts from all fields offer guidance and help you make important decisions. "Two heads are better than one" is even more relevant now than before. We have endured eight years of the opposite philosophy.

We are thrilled that you put such a great value on conserving our earth. We will be behind you 100% in your efforts to conserve and heal this earth, the only home we have.

Please call on us to do our part!
J. R. Butler and F. F. Butler

Dear President-elect Obama,

I am a college student extremely concerned about the preservation of the environment. I supported and voted for you in hopes that you and your administration will take steps to preserve the environment and embark on a long road to undo the spiral begun by the Bush administration towards further degradation of our environment.

I have been studying the impacts of global warming on our planet and am extremely concerned with the pace that the ice at the poles is melting and the beginning of the breaking up of the ice in Greenland. If the ice there and at the poles continues to melt, much of Manhattan, coastal California, and other low-lying parts of the country will be underwater in addition to many other parts of the world currently home to millions of people. If we continue in our current pattern of pollution, such is inevitable, will be dealing with a catastrophe much larger than any previous one. Although such a catastrophe may not occur in your time as president, we must all think ahead and make educated decisions knowing that what we do tomorrow and in the next four years will have lasting effects on our country and on the entire world.

I hope that as president you tighten environmental standards and adopt a strict version of the Kyoto Protocol in addition to preserving any wilderness habitat we have left. I also believe strongly in a future where green energy drives our nation and the entire world. Investing in green technology today will pay off in the years to come when the United States is the leading producer of green technology and energy. As other countries follow, they will pour capital into the U.S., stimulating the economy, as they buy and study our new technology and energy.

Thank you so much for your time. I am excited to see what the future holds when you are president of the United States.

Congratulations and good luck.

Sincerely,
Amy Scarano

Dear President Obama,

I am sure that you will receive thousands upon thousands of letters commending you for your achievement and celebrating how historic the journey has been. My letter is partially meant to do the same, and so I congratulate you. But I do so not only on the fact that you are our country's first African-American president, but also on the movement that you created. I am a student, and you motivated the student population of our country in a way that has not been seen since the Vietnam era. You gave voice to a segment of our population that usually is too apathetic and uncaring to speak out.

With all of these grand, idealistic thoughts out of the way, I want to address something more pragmatic. I voted for you in part because of your eloquence and your historic campaign, but your policy is what my decision really hinged upon. I urge you to keep your campaign promises, especially in the areas of education and the environment. Our county is dying without the jobs we could use from researching and implementing green energy plans, and our next generation of children is being held back by the policies that have arisen from the terrible standards set by No Child Left Behind. Remember what you promised. You have a new kind of role in government right now, in the time between your election and your inauguration. You have a period in time where lobbyists cannot affect your decisions, because they don't have an outlet in your administration yet; you have appointed no one to hear them. This is the time when you and your team can draft legislation unfettered by any kind of obligations beyond the promises you made to the American people in your campaign. This is the time when you can affect true change.

Congratulations on your historic victory,
Seth Buchsbaum

Dear President-elect Obama

With the economy tanking and other countries not purchasing the bank withholdings of our nation's debt, the only thing that keeps Americans distracted enough not to move to Canada is college football. Along with other collegiate and professional sports also captivating nearly the entire population, college football is a cornerstone to national unity and pride. I am very grateful that our nation doesn't revolve around soccer or rugby. Football is the greatest thing in the world and the Super Bowl proves this. However, to maintain interest in college football, I along with many other Americans, believe a playoff is necessary for the FBS subdivision of college football. A vast majority of Americans support this ideal. According to definition of democracy, the elected officials are to represent the logical views of its citizens. This is a perfect calling to fix the mess not only in the BCS but also in the Big 12 South. Texas and Oklahoma would have a shot to prove who, if either of them, is the best team in the country.

Thank you for your time. Also, please have sympathy for all of my fellow Michiganders—Lions, Tigers, Wolverine football, and the failing auto industry; we have little to look forward to. We have been struggling for a decade now, more so than most states, so please do us a favor. Do not appoint Ms. Jennifer Granholm to a cabinet position. She may be a personable and intelligent woman, but the country doesn't deserve to be put under the burden that she created for my state.

Good luck in office, thanks for your time, but most of all, GO BLUE!

Best,
John Jack Patrick McNally

Dear President-elect Obama,

It is indeed appropriate to start out by wishing you congratulations on your victory in November's election. To your millions of supporters, you are a beacon of hope, youth, and progression. To those who did not support you, you are an unproven, unreliable candidate. Now is the time to prove that you are indeed capable of taking this country on your shoulders and continuing to make America the greatest country on earth. With great power comes great responsibility, and being the most powerful man in the world, you now have the responsibility to direct an entire nation. I personally believe that you are fully capable to leading this country in the right direction.

Your victory in this election may be the culmination of the civil rights movement. Though racism may always exist somewhere in the world, you have proven that race does not affect a man's character or his potential to do something great with his life. It was claimed by Thomas Jefferson in the Declaration of Independence that all men are created equal, and your victory has added additional proof to this point. African-Americans have made tremendous steps since the beginning of the civil rights movement and this is yet another of these steps. I recall a few years back the significance of Super Bowl XLI. The Indianapolis Colts were playing your Chicago Bears. Before the game I remember watching the show *Pardon the Interruption*. The topic came up of the two coaches, Lovie Smith and Tony Dungy, being the first two African-American coaches to ever reach the Super Bowl. This was a newsworthy accomplishment. Michael Wilbon said something in that show that I will never forget. He said that it was indeed an accomplishment and was newsworthy that two black coaches had made it to the Super Bowl, but said he dreamed of a day where this wouldn't be news; a day where the achievements of blacks were not heralded as monumental advancements, but a commonplace achievement for blacks of that day. We are undoubtedly nearing that day. Wilbon's dream is certainly one worth shooting towards, and your victory is a step in the right direction to the achievement of that dream. You have the weight of not only the African-American population, but the entire nation on your shoulders. Your victory was celebrated worldwide, and at times, you may have seemed too good to be true. Stay focused on your strategies and do not lose sight of the ultimate responsibility of your victory: to lead the greatest nation on earth.

I wish you good luck, Mr. Obama. You are respected all throughout the country and around the world, and I have full confidence that you will not disappoint. Good luck, and Godspeed.

Sincerely,
Steven J. Stefanko

Dear President Obama,

I'm writing you to ask for justice. My best friends son just died on the 28th of this month from a house fire. On the 17th, he his wife, and children were sleeping and their dog threw a blanket over the space heater and the house caught fire. He got his wife out. Then went back into the fire for his children. Wrapped a blanket round his children and went back through the fire which he caught a blaze. He got the kids out safely but he was engulfed in flames and it was too late when the fireman got to him. He survived and they rushed him to Georgia burn unit in Augusta. Over 80% of his body was burned and he was a very handsome young man. As I said he passed this friday. His family has no insurance and the hospital told them they cannot move his body until they have $6000. To take him to a funeral home.

The hospital told them that if they didn't have the money by Monday that they were gonna burn his body in the incinerator at the hospital. They are a poor family and we've done everything we can to come up with the money but it is impossible. What I'm trying to say is how can the lottery companies say they are collecting money for schools and to fix roads when every road in my hometown has big potholes and I don't see any progress in our schools? If the people of the United States are supporting the lottery why can't they set up some kind of fund where if someone dies and cant afford to bury a loved one they could help at least to make sure that they had a good funeral? Not a fancy one but just one that could ease the minds of the families that fought in the wars, worked all their lives, and supported everyone in the goverment. Seems like we the people are the only ones that are giving and the goverment is the one that is taking.

I am so glad you got to be president and I pray you can make a difference in this world. God bless you and your family and happy holidays.

Ms. Lorene Jerandes

Dear Mr. President:

Congratulations! I am encouraged by the election that made you the 44th president of the United States and the respect around the world for our country due to your election. I am motivated by a "can do spirit" due to your victory and swift and decisive actions, from announcing your cabinet members to deploying our nation's "peacemakers" to the Middle East during your second week in office. Your signing of the Lilly Ledbetter Fair Pay Act days later is a turning point in achieving pay equity.

However, I believe that bailing out big business by issuing blank checks directly to them has been proven a dismal failure. I believe that our economic recovery should begin at ground zero. In my mind, public, funds should be administered and monitored by public stewards. If businesses need a bailout, my recommendation is that they appeal to the communities in which they operate. The local governments of the businesses have the organizational structures and levels of accountability already in place to quickly implement your economic initiatives and keep businesses in check. Collaboration between residents, public and private sectors is how local governments are established to operate. Also, local governments have and some are in the process of establishing, economic development programs in their communities. Tight budgets and dwindling tax revenues have forced local governments to carefully examine their expenditures while improving the local economy and the quality of life of their residents. Local governments are by no means perfect. Measurable improvements should be required for federal commitment of public funds in areas, such as, but not limited to:

Economic development

Creating and keeping jobs

Drug and crime free neighborhoods

Reducing jail populations and recidivism

Youth development

Affordable housing

You have accomplished much in your first three weeks in the White House. Again, God Bless and I congratulate you and your family on your historic journey to the White House.

Sincerely,

Linda J. Haynes, MA in public adminstration

CHAPTER 21

Economic Policy

Wall Street began to crumble on September 15, 2008, with the collapse of the investment firm, Lehman Brothers. This was followed by its almost complete demise on September 23 and, overnight, the economy became the number one issue for the American electorate. Thus, for many of the letter writers, this public policy issue became an important issue when writing to the new president. Here numerous ideas are put forward by American citizens.

Dear President Obama,

First off, I would like to say congratulations on your amazing victory. I know that you and your family may need some time to adjust to your new life, but this country needs to be helped, and we can make a change, with your help. My parents are both Real estate agents, and as you well know the economy is really struggling right now, and my family is struggling right now as well. With so little money coming in, there is barely enough money for the things we need. Please, get things back to where we will be able to say we are proud to call America our country again.

Sincerely,
Jennifer Griffith

President Obama,

There is obviously something very wrong with this picture.

My parents bought a house that they could afford, not necessarily the one of their dreams. They paid for it on time, every time, and eventually in full.

They did this at the same time they paid bills on time, sent and are currently sending children to college, and have always lived within their means.

They did NOT buy more houses than I could pay for, they did NOT buy things they could not pay for and they did NOT take trips and enjoy dinners using a credit card they could not afford to pay off every month.

Yet it seems that everyone who did the aforementioned things and can't pay for them is being rewarded with new/lower interest rates on their mortgages; some of the amounts being forgiven completely. They are being financially rewarded for their gross fiscal irresponsibility!

If these rewards are intended to help our economy, then let my parents help out too. Give them some type of financial reward for being fiscally responsible! We would love to have more disposable income to help enhance the economy ourselves.

There is something wrong with this picture!

Dear Mr. President,

Although I cannot say that I voted for you in this past election, I do feel that you will perform well in this office. The main concern that I had that kept me from voting for you were your plans on how to deal with the economy. My family is part of the upper-middle class from a suburb outside of Chicago, and I am currently enrolled at the University of Michigan. My dad is a real estate developer and his business has been affected by the poor economy and the stock market failures. He is extremely concerned about your philosophy on increasing taxes for the upper-middle class because he feels that this will end up hurting the economy even more because these people will then begin to lay-off workers in order to compensate for the increase in taxes. I do agree with him on this point because I feel that jobs are available because of the companies these types of people started and if they are taxed more, some people will lose their jobs.

One thing that has impressed me however, has been the selection of your cabinet and economic advisors which has given you a good balance between conservatives and liberals. You seem to have a good plan in effect as of right now, which I find impressive. I sincerely hope that the fears I have about the economy will be proven false and that it does in fact improve under your term. I also hope that your election to the office of president will also help Chicago win the bid to host the 2016 Olympic games. Good luck the next four years in office and depending on how things go, I may vote for you if you choose to run for reelection.

Sincerely,
Vince Lucchese

Dear President-elect,

Congratulations on your victorious win. You ran one hell of a campaign and made history for the United States. You probably are swamped with letters having the same introduction as this, but I want to let you know that you worked hard during this race and it definitely paid off at the end. I cannot wait to see what you and your administration will bring for the next four years. My main concern during this presidential election has not only been the economy, but the housing crisis that is sweeping across the nation.

My father is a landlord and owns apartments in Southwest Michigan. He has had first-hand experience of people having trouble paying rent. With this, he has to evict people or families. He doesn't like to do that and has made a few adjustments for families, but if they are unable to pay the rent, then what is he suppose to do? Therefore, within my family, we are not making too much money from my dad's business and are more reliant on my mother. She is a radiology nurse that has to obtain three jobs in order to make payments on the bills and pay tuition for two. My sister is will be graduating from high school this upcoming spring and my mother is now really tied up and not knowing how many loans she may have to take out. We are fortunate to not have our home foreclose, but we have seen members in the community who have suffered this great loss.

A home is a place everyone deserves. It is a place where families can come together and talk about what happened during the day. It is a place you can call your own, where you can get away from your problems and relax and maybe watch a few re-runs of your favorite TV show. People who are forced to have foreclosures do not deserve this. They all are employed, but are unable to make payments due to their salaries.

Once you are sworn into office, not only should you focus on the economy, you should also focus on the housing crisis. Those two go hand-in-hand, and maybe you can solve this particular problem. You may not obtain the final results in your first term of presidency, but I want to see progress and effort. I want to turn on CNN and see that your administration is working on this problem. I want to see people being able to afford their homes like they use to eight years ago.

Again, congratulations and I wish the best of luck for you, your family, your staff, and departments.

Olivia

Dear President Obama,

I was raised by my mother, a Republican, and my dad, a Democrat. They didn't always agree on candidates and issues. However, they believed in America. My mother was a homemaker and my father worked a humble job as a scrap material sorter for the government. They taught me to be proud of my heritage; to believe in America and that if I was honest and worked hard, I could accomplish anything in this great land. After the death of my parents, I was going through papers they had stored in a garage. I found evidence that, during the 60s, my father had been shorted a small amount of pay from his job. He took his grievance to a Nevada congressman and this man advocated for my father. His lost wages were re-instated. I was happy to see that the America of my youth still stood for "the little guy."

In past years, when I heard the "Star-Spangled Banner," my tears would flow in gratitude for this great land. However, now they flow in sadness; I weep for America. The economy is in shambles. The federal government is far too involved in local and foreign affairs. Three years ago I was prosperous, lived in a beautiful home, was part owner of a business, had real estate investments and worked for a company that paid my health insurance. I was living the

American dream. Now, the business and real estate investments are gone. I work part-time. I earn a fraction of what I earned previously. I am uninsured. Where is my bailout? Well to be honest I wouldn't dream of asking because I believe I should work for and earn whatever income or benefits I receive.

Where is the America of my youth? I grieve for Her. Bring America back, President Obama. Help us recover. Care about the average citizen again. End corruption and special interests that do not further the common good. Help us be respected around the world again. It's time.

Regards,
Sethina

Dear President Obama,

I am writing to you concerning your talks of a new economic stimulus package. In recent news, you have stated that you will approve a stimulus plan for Americans from anywhere between $300 and $600 billion. You state that this package will reinstate American confidence in consumer markets across the country. I find it hard to believe that such a stimulus plan would do this.

Looking back on the Economic Stimulus Act of 2008, we can see how such a plan would have little to no effect on today's consumer markets. An empirical study conducted by Professor Matthew D. Shapiro and Professor Joel Slemrod of the University of Michigan concluded that national saving increased by nearly exactly that of the stimulus payments. The article highlighting the results is titled "Economists: Most Stimulus Went Into Savings" and appeared in the *Wall Street Journal* on August 7, 2008. This clearly shows that Americans placed their stimulus checks into savings and used hardly any for consumption.

Looking into today's economy, I can only assume that the correlation between national savings and economic stimulus payments would only be greater. With credit becoming tighter across the country, Americans are deleveraging themselves against their debt, as their revolving credit from banks is shrinking. For consumers to avoid a substantial decrease in their standards of living, they have no choice but to now save a larger proportion of their income. This shows that, more now than ever, Americans would save a stimulus check rather than use it for additional consumption.

It is understandable that such an economic stimulus plan would garner you great praise and support from the majority of the American people. However, what is politically popular is not always what will benefit the economy. The credit bubble that was experienced during the past few years allowed Americans and businesses to borrow and spend much more than they should have been able have otherwise. When the real risk of such high leverage was finally realized with massive losses from banks, lending levels dropped significantly, to a more practical level. It would be unnatural to attempt to bring consumer spending to where it was in 2007 because that was based on unrealistic and unsustaining credit levels. In time credit markets will improve, as banks begin to decrease their balance sheets and reduce their risks elsewhere. Revolving credit will return to its previous levels over time, businesses and consumers will receive the funds they need, and consumer markets will begin to rise naturally.

I will be interested in hearing about your positions on the economy in the future and wish you a healthy and most successful presidency.

Thank you.

Sincerely,
Ryan Businski
University of Michigan

Dear President Obama,

Congratulations on winning the presidency. I am currently a sophomore at the University of Michigan. As a student in political science, the current issues facing our country have been the topic of discussion. I was currently discussing our economic problems with my father and an issue came up. I was wondering why it is that the leaders of our country only advise high-profile CEOs of major companies. My dad is a senior vice president of a small family-owned metal company. We were talking about how it could be beneficial to talk to people like my dad regarding issues facing our economy. This would provide you with a different perspective.

Anyways, I hope this is helpful. Thank you for taking the time to get feedback from the people who elected you into office. Good luck with the presidency, I am sure you will do great things.

Sincerely,
Jennifer Entin

Dear President Obama,

I am writing to you today concerning your idea of an economic stimulus package. I am concerned that an economic stimulus package will be ineffective in alleviating the economic problems of our country. I understand that it is an attempt to prolong any future economic issues from directly affecting the average American. However, throughout history, there have been very few stimulus packages that have reached their full potential. Just last year, President Bush enacted a stimulus package that was designed to have consumers invest the money they received from the government directly back into the economy, to give a jumpstart to the struggling businesses. This has proven to have no economic effect.

I am not insinuating that an economic stimulus package cannot be successful if implemented with the proper provisions. My underlying question is: What would be different about your stimulus package as opposed to others before it? Would you have certain provisions in it that demanded it be spent a certain way? Would you include a rebate check or more of a gift certificate? How specifically will you implement this, and what specific effects do you see coming from this?

My other concern regarding the stimulus package is the financial piece of it, from a budget perspective. You have announced that you plan to implement a stimulus package of over 100 billion dollars that is entirely separate from the financial bailout that was approved during the election. Where is this funding of this stimulus coming from? How do you plan on managing this stimulus package along with the financial rescue plan with the government essentially distributing over 850 billion dollars across America? I understand there is a need to spend money now that we are in these dire straights, but to what extent do you draw the line? This is perhaps the biggest financial crisis America has faced since the Great Depression and these questions are vital not only to a successful stimulus package but to America's success in regaining our economic strength and prosperity.

This is of course one issue, and I think that this new time in America will represent resiliency as much as it will represent change. As much as I am concerned about the stimulus package, I do have tremendous confidence that this administration will do everything it can to help America restore itself in this tremendously difficult time. I appreciate everything you have done, and your tremendous dedication to this country, and I look forward to the next four years with as much excitement as I do trepidation.

Thank you for your time, and all the best.

Sincerely,
Brian Rappaport

Dear Mr. President,

We live in a country that is stronger than other countries, but there are many problems with our country. I believe that the largest problem with our country at this time is the economy. I do not believe that it is going to be an easy task to repair the economy; nevertheless, I understand that it is going to be very difficult to make a change in this great nation. I am also aware that you do not have a lot of experience, but I expect that you can remove to our country out of these hard times. I believe that upon ending the war in Iraq, the welfare of our country is going to improve. Ending the war and bringing the troops home will affect all the other problems of the country. I am a Republican, therefore I believe in the war but I know that this war has caused too much pain to too many people.

I think that the plan to give to the large companies 700 billion dollars is a complicated and very controversial idea. It is a good idea to obtain the economy stimulated but is unjust to give him to the companies more money. The president now, President Bush, says that the plan goes to help 1.2 million. I doubt that it will work. In the past the government has tried to utilize a similar plan, and it worked. But I do not know if the history can be repeated again. Our national debt has exceeded amounts of any in the past, and that is a large problem for many people.

Another problem with our economy is the labor market. I understand that there are not jobs in the United States and that affects many families. Children are hungry in the night because their parents do not have a sufficient amount of income. That is a large problem. The families cannot pay their mortgages and they are losing their houses. The United States has many problems, but the largest problem is the economy. Finishing the war in Iraq will cause the economy to begin to improve. Therefore, doing this causes all the other problems also to disappear.

Thank you for taking time to listen my thoughts and opinions.

Tisheka L. Allen

Dear President Obama,

I am writing to you as a concerned citizen about the state of the economy. The government bailout is taking money from hardworking American tax payers and giving it back to the executives who have repeatedly made horrible business decisions without considering the implications of their actions on everyone's pocketbooks. The bailout sends the wrong message to Americans and promotes irresponsibility and careless spending as seen by the auto industries attempts at also receiving a bailout. I would like to know what you plan on doing about this situation and how you will restore faith in the American government and institutions, as well as businesses. Lastly, good luck cleaning up the many messes and failures of the Bush administration. Thank you.

Sincerely,

Jen

Dear President Obama,

I want to congratulate you on your inauguration earlier this afternoon. Unfortunately, I was not able to be in Washington, D.C., but I did watch it on television. Indeed, it was the first presidential inauguration that I have ever tuned in to watch.

Watching you take the presidential oath gave me hope in regard to the future of every American, as well as my own. I am a junior at the University of Michigan, and I aspire to go to law school after I graduate. A former law school student, you know how much of a burden paying for college can be. With three younger siblings, all close in age, this burden will be even greater for my family.

Indeed, my family was one of those affected by the economic crisis in 2008. In a matter of months, I watched in astonishment as my father's business failed, and my mother became both homemaker and bread winner. Unable to face this harsh reality, my father attempted suicide. Watching both of my parents spiral into depression due to this crisis was one of the hardest things I have ever had to overcome.

My parents are both doing better, but the fear is still there. Will 2009 bring fortune to our nation or will the events of the previous year repeat themselves?

Months before the election in November, I prayed to God that He would bring change that would lead our nation out of chaos. Well, He answered my prayers. That change is you President Obama. Like many other Americans, my hope lies with you.

I must confess that I have never been more proud to be an American than when I watched you deliver your inauguration speech. You told Americans "Yes we can," but I tell you "Yes we did."

God bless,

Christy

Dear Mr. President,

You, your inauguration speech, and everything you represent inspire me to do everything I can to serve my country and to serve those who protect, preserve, and defend this great nation.

As a small-business owner making positive contributions toward protecting people, facilities, and high-profile assets from acts of terrorism, this selfless commitment comes with endless challenges. If I may make but one request, please establish a path for small-business owners to gain access to information and the necessary support to help close security gaps and counter evolving terrorist threats.

Thank you for permitting this platform for letter submissions and for your service to our country.

Very Respectfully,
Grant Haber CEO, American Innovations, Inc.

Dear President Obama,

Congratulations on your recent win in the 2008 election. You and your campaign team worked very hard and deserved to win the presidency. I will be honest with you. I disagree with a lot of your ideals and policies. I trust that you will lead this country in the right direction but I hope you do so wisely and with all American citizens in mind.

In this recent election, I have had some concerns about your policies. My father is a small-business owner in the Detroit metro area. The auto industry directly affects his business, due to the fact that his patients are autoworkers. When their benefits are cut, or their jobs are lost, dentistry is the first area they decide to cut back on. Because of this, my father's business is slow. I am concerned that because he makes enough money to qualify in your "higher" tax bracket, that he will be unfairly taxed. His practice makes a lot more money than he himself brings home, but he will be taxed based on his practice. This will hurt my family and community and put unfair pressure on our finances. Your tax plan would severely impact my family, so I think you should rethink your cut off income level for tax brackets. I would suggest looking at income after taxes to get a fair look at what the exact amount each household actually has, rather than the business he or she runs.

Another area that concerns me is your foreign policy. I believe that going into Iraq was a mistake, and that it is time for us to pull out of the Middle East. However, with the recent India attack, I am concerned about homeland security. You need to address the nation on your plans for keeping America safe, because, as a scared citizen, that is one area I need guidance on.

Thank you for your time, Mr. President.

Yours truly,
Victoria Jennings

President-elect Obama,

With the economy in shambles as of now, many thoughts are circulating through people's minds. I think people need to remain calm and society cannot become chaotic because the market always finds itself back into a competitive equilibrium. With regards to the auto industry, it is their problem and their issue to overcome and resolve. Other people should not suffer economically for their obvious wrongdoings and mistakes. A laissez-faire economy must be prevalent and in order during your presidential term. With the government at the wheel interfering with the economy, more chaotic times will be ahead and there will be unjust circumstances with businesses to follow. With plans already in place to cut taxes for people making less than $250,000 a year, a policy of deregulation must exist. I am against this decrease in taxes for that particular tax bracket, but I cannot think of any alternative solution to circumvent this problem that exists today. It is an unjust tax cut to this tax bracket, but the upper tax bracket in the United States will have to carry the bulk of the load, more than they usually do. We preach everyone is equal and that we follow a great and powerful democracy, but there are obvious flaws that cannot go unnoticed. Most of the higher tax bracket made their money through hard work and dedication and to punish them for achieving the American dream is thoroughly wrong. Less price-fixing subsidies as well as other price controls need to be limited so competition can still exist on its own within markets and money can still circulate within a specific market. Laissez-faire and deregulation are two concepts that need to be implemented and remain constant policies with regards to the economy in the present and future.

Best of Luck,
Andrew H.

President Obama:

Congratulations on your position!

I am close to graduating from the University Of Michigan with a degree in Engineering. I also live in the state of Michigan, so job searching is intimidating with our economy!

Anyways, I am very excited for your tenure guiding the best nation in the world! I think you did an excellent job with everything you've done so far, and you should have the utmost confidence in yourself and our nation!

One concern I have is with Social Security. I know this is an impossible issue to please but here is my concern:

My generation (I am 21 years old) is what I might call the "college era" because a college education is almost required to find a good job. My point is that a lot of us have HUGE student loans because of the cost of tuition and room and board. Therefore when we go out in the real world, we are already close to $100,000 behind. THEN, when we try to retire, I'm nervous we will be missing out on any Social Security that we have been paying for in all of our "college jobs." I just feel we are at a big disadvantage compared to previous generations.

But I look forward to the next few years and the great changes we have ahead of us!

Dear Mr. President:

As a college student, I watch my peers and myself slave over countless readings and homework assignments and invest thousands of dollars into this institution, knowing full and well that the well-paying, rewarding jobs that we rightly deserve may in this economic state be out of our reach when we enter the job market in a few years. This reason, among others, is why I believe that the youth vote came out in droves this election in your favor. But as you have said, our work has just begun.

The university student condition, though not to be mistaken as more miserable than the extensive poverty and human injustice that still plagues this and other countries, is clearly evidence of the fiscal irresponsibility of a government that renders pork gathering a greater responsibility of their representatives than productive legislative work. Education has, and should always be, a responsibility of the states, but with the budgetary restrictions currently placed on state governments, it is clear that the educational system is hurting as a result. In these difficult financial times, I see no greater investment than in the education of future generations, for it is to these citizens, sir, that you have promised prosperity and a better America.

As a fervid follower of current events, I realize the enormous task you must take on in the following weeks, months, and years to get the United States functioning again both domestically and on the international stage, and I have full faith in your ability to do so. I write this only to request that you remember us: the generation that hopes to carry this nation forward through the values of civic duty and common good that were instilled in us by an educational system and society that fervently believe in the American ethos. This socialization as well as the current conditions, I believe, are what inspired us to take faith in the democratic process and elect the right man into office.

To you, sir, I send my hope and prayers, but I and my peers recognize that the difficult situation facing the United States today cannot be solved by one man alone, and that we have a duty to our nation to step up and work for the greater good of our country. It is a promise that I vow to fulfill.

Sincerely,
Amy K Richardson
University of Michigan, 2012

President Obama,

Congratulations on your victory over Senator McCain in the November election.

I look forward to the next four years being better than the last eight.

One of the reasons that I am writing is that I am concerned about the economy. I am a second-year college student and since high school, I have been hearing that when I graduate from college it is going to be difficult to find a job. This is rather discouraging, especially since the total cost of attendance for a year at the University of Michigan is more than $25,000. I am lucky enough to have scholarship money to cover most of the cost; unfortunately, many of my friends are not.

Although, your economic plan provides a nice start, more money needs to be put towards education on all levels, pre–k, k–12 and post-secondary.

College is hard enough without having to worry about finances. Furthermore, in the end the government will come out ahead. To get a good job a high school diploma is not enough anymore, which means more people, are unemployed and relying on government assistance. If we invest in people while they are young and help them get an education, we will have more people in the work force to feed the economy and hopefully stop the trend of welfare generations.

Sincerely,
Brittany Smith

Dear President Obama,

As a new voter this past fall, I was very attuned to the debates between yourself and Senator McCain. In looking at your policies pertaining to the economy, though, a few questions have arisen. As a college student looking to enter the work force in the next couple of years, I am glad to see that you are looking to increase funding to scientific research, as this creates a plethora of available new jobs. It is conceivable that this money will come from the influx of taxes from the upper class; however, it is unclear to me where this research will be funded from. Also, looking through your economic policy, I saw that you are looking to increase the minimum wage. The reasoning behind minimum wage works in theory, but minimum wage is a major factor in driving up production costs, forcing companies to look overseas to employ cheaper labor. While wages are remaining stagnant and creating a period of stagflation, which poses a threat to the current outlook on the economy, raising the minimum wage does not do much to combat this issue. Thus, I am wondering what you plan to do to truly revitalize our economy. I wish you good luck in your term in office.

Sincerely,
Alyce Robelli

Dear President Obama,

Congratulations on your election. It was a very exciting election year for me because it was my first time voting in a presidential election. I am a freshman at the University of Michigan and the atmosphere on campus was unbelievable throughout the majority of the fall. I have lived in Michigan my entire life and for the past several years have watched businesses continually close in the Lansing area where I live. I was considering working in Michigan after I graduate, but the opportunities seem slim. I love the state of Michigan. Its economy needs your help more than ever. I believe you are the right person to turn Michigan's economy around.

Sincerely,
J. Crim

Dear President Obama,

I would just like to make certain that some important issues are addressed in the near future. The most prevalent problem in our society today is the state of our economy. My friends and I have had long, almost tearful discussions at the tragedy that is our current economic situation. I find that although I am not severely impacted by the recession, as I think it should be classified, there are many many other less fortunate citizens who are feeling the impact of our economy too much. I wonder what plans to remedy or at least ameliorate these issues. I want to make sure that we will not find ourselves in an even worse position, which I believe could certainly happen without action, or without the right kind of action. So, I don't want to preach, I would just like to emphasize the importance of the issue to the American people. You have the power to help us all and I hope that you can make the change happen.

Sincerely,
Rachel Bruce

Dear President Obama,

You now have one of the most important jobs in the country since winning the election. Now, we have to ask the question of what are you going to do with the power that you now have.

I would really like to point out that our economy is getting worse and worse and if something isn't done really soon, we will have another depression that the government won't be able to prevent from happening. As president, you need to make sure you solve this problem before it keeps getting worse and worse. Also, you need to have more government involvement in the banking systems. I know that in the past, the presidents disagreed that the government should play a huge role in the banking system, but at this point, the government needs to step up and protect the people and manage things right. The banks had too much power that was used to make bad loans to people which was a major downfall that led to the stock market crisis we are now experiencing.

As president, you need to help get this country out of debt, or else significantly reduce the debt that has been built up by the war in Iraq. The war really was useless to our country but has put us in so much debt because of all the money we are spending over there. It is putting our citizens at risk because they really don't need to be fighting this war at this point and they are dying in Iraq. This is not good and needs to be fixed as soon as possible which you are president. You need to make up for the mistakes Bush made while in office but I have faith that you will be able to help out at least a little bit.

Obama, you have a lot expected of you at this point and people are counting on you to turn our country around for the better. I wish you luck with your presidency and hope you will make life better for us all.

Dear President-elect Obama,

I am writing with regards to the many economic issues facing the United States of America. The economic crisis you must address includes unprecedented economic and political challenges, but I am confident in your ability to guide America through this economic storm.

Current economic conditions require immediate action. You must prioritize economic policy and begin rebuilding our economy the moment you take office as president of the United States. I was pleased to read and learn about the economic team you have assembled, and I am confident in their ability to address economic issues with speed and prudence.

In my opinion, our economy needs an aggressive fiscal stimulus in addition to the monetary policy already conducted by the Federal Reserve. With the target federal funds rate hovering near zero, the Fed has nearly exhausted its ability to conduct monetary policy and should not risk a liquidity trap. Instead, the federal government must now espouse expansionary fiscal policy. I encourage you to increase government expenditures and create new jobs by supporting massive infrastructure and alternative energy improvements. Such projects will help alleviate current economic conditions and promote long-term stability.

Above all, trust the many experienced economic advisors by your side. Sound economic analysis and appropriate policy implementation can resolve the crisis we face.

Good luck and God speed.

Dear President Obama,

Congratulations on your presidency! Although this is a very exciting time, you will be faced with many challenges and obstacles. Our country is in a huge economic crisis and we are counting on you to help the United States reestablish our torn economy.

I feel that your ideas in order to jumpstart the economy will be very beneficial. For instance, your plan to provide tax cuts to working families and small businesses. The promised $1000 a year on permanent tax relief will help people be able to spend more money in order to get the economy moving again. Also, I feel that your idea to provide $50 billion to jumpstart the economy and prevent the losing of jobs is exactly what our country needs.

Finally, while president, you need to take into consideration that not all Americans support your views. American citizens will express their opinions to you and, as a leader of the country, you need to appreciate and respect all views. Once again, I am so happy that you have won the election. I know that you will make a great president and I can't wait to see all the improvements you will make to the United States.

I noticed in the news that you may not up the taxes for the rich. One way to handle this is to stop companies from paying upper management's taxes through "gross ups."

Talk to your CPA and you will find out that this is done for bonuses and extra money with this method. Once grossed up, the company pays the tax. This is not so for union employees.

I know this to be true, I worked in payroll.

Thanks
Lowell Griffith

Dear President Obama,

I had heard months ago about your plan to create a tax credit for all college-age students who conduct more than 100 hours of community service and sure enough I found something to that extent on your Web site, but it was not quite what I imagined. According to the new official White House Web site you plan to: "Create the American Opportunity Tax Credit, which will make college affordable for all Americans by creating a new American Opportunity Tax Credit. This universal and fully refundable credit will ensure that the first $4,000 of a college education is completely free for most Americans, and will cover two-thirds the cost of tuition at the average public college or university and make community college tuition completely free for most students. Recipients of the credit will be required to conduct 100 hours of community service." As an Eagle Scout and a member of Alpha Phi Omega (a national co-ed service fraternity), I am curious if this "universal" tax credit will be available to all students. I ask this because I already do more than a hundred hours of community service each year, but I have been ineligible for any financial aid beyond federal loans for the past two years. It would be nice to know part of my college tuition would legitimately be paid by the government, as opposed to a loan that would leave me indebted to the government.

Obviously, you won't be responding directly to this message, but I think that you should definitely think about how far reaching this program will be, because if more students are eligible, more students will get involved. In addition, while there are many issues plaguing the country (i.e., the economy), I think it is important that you not back down from this pledge because it was college students who registered and voted in record numbers to ensure the best man for the job (you) got it. We would greatly appreciate any help we can get during our journey to adulthood, and this program will ensure that even more students can make this journey. Thank you.

Marty Cozzola
University of Michigan, 2011

President Obama,

First of all, congratulations on becoming the first African-American president this great nation has ever had. People never thought the day would come when someone from an historically oppressed race in this country could rise to the greatest leadership position the United States has to offer.

I would like to tell you that I am in strong favor of your proposed tax policy in which you would grant tax breaks for all those who make less than $250,000 per year and would raise taxes for the few who do make more than that. Coming from a family with a father and mother who have both been unemployed for two and five years, respectively, this just makes economic sense. No longer can they continue to pay high taxes when they are trying to pay my way through college and help my older sister purchase items that she cannot necessarily afford by herself.

To those who complain about their taxes being raised because they are in that extreme minority, I would say, "So what? You of all people can definitely afford to pay a little more." Unless they were planning on giving that extra money to a charity or non-profit organization, I see no reason why that extra money couldn't be given to the U.S. government. After all, in order for you, Mr. President, to truly make a difference in this country, you will need money— that is no secret. But for the betterment of Americans' lives, these payments are a necessary step to bring about the change we need.

Kevin Parker

President Obama,

Congratulations on becoming the 44th president of the United States of America.

Health care reform is no doubt needed in this country. However, I warn against socialized medicine as the United States is founded on competition and this competition in the heath care industry would disappear with a government-run program. If you reflect on the question "what does the government do better than the private sector?" I think even yourself would have difficulty compiling a list. Please, President Obama, keep health care private.

Sincerely
Bill Schnittman
University of Michigan '10

Dear President Barack H. Obama,

I am writing this letter as a form of gratitude towards your inspiring presidential campaign and historic victory. Throughout the primary season, I grew attached to your strong will to fight through potential adversity and remain steadfast in your promises to help reform the political system in the United States of America. Your promises of help for college students in need of aid for school and health care reform struck a chord in me.

I come from a fairly low-income family, and throughout high school, I was consistently worried with how I might finance higher education. Gaining a college degree was always a goal of mine, as I would be the first in my family to achieve such an accomplishment. As of this writing, I am a sophomore at the University of Michigan. I have received a fairly generous financial aid package, which helps me to get by with the help of a part-time job. With your platform of aid for college students, I am hopeful not for myself, as I have found a way to survive, but for my younger brother and others in our situation to be able to afford higher education when the time for them to achieve greater learning is at hand.

On the subject of health care reform, I am particularly hopeful that there will be a chance for my recently retired grandparents to gain affordable health care. Like you, my childhood was spent in the comfort of my grandparents. My mother was constantly working, so I was raised in their care. My grandfather has just recently retired from Pratt and Whitney, for whom he had worked for 43 years. In recent years, my grandfather has had a hip replacement, and my grandmother is suffering from dementia, which is increasingly limiting her motor functions. I worry that without my grandfather working, they will be unable to afford health care, which would be crippling to them, as they rely on insurance to cover their medical bills and help to pay for their prescription medicines. It is my hope that you, in conjunction with our congressional leaders, will fight to change America's health care system and make it more affordable for people like my grandparents, who should be able to retire in peace and not with constant worry over medical expenses.

In closing, I just want to say that I wish you the best in your first term as president of the United States. You are facing monumental challenges with the current financial crisis and the unrest in the Middle East. You have shown glimpses of your judgment and clarity of mind in decisive times, and I hope that you will continue to work hard for the American people.

Thank you and good luck,
Scott House

Dear President Obama,

Please don't turn this country into a socialist nation. As John Micklethwait said, the worst thing to happen to the world is the Marxist movement. Just let the markets do what they do best.

Thanks,
A concerned citizen

Mr. Obama,

While you may be congratulated on your victory in the presidential election, there are certain things that you must always remember. First, despite what many of your supporters believe, you are only one man. Additionally, you ran for the office of the president, not God. Despite what some people believe, the president does not have powers sufficient to fix any crisis, particularly economic ones.

You have stated that this economic crisis will take five years to fix. Personally, I find this thought disturbing, as it will mean that should the economy still be in the gutter in 2012, you can say that there has been insufficient time. The truth is that government is the last thing we need to fix this crisis. Need I remind you that it was government that encouraged home ownership, convincing banks to take on incredibly risky loans, which left a ticking time bomb that could explode at any time? The government is only capable of placing chains on free enterprise, slowing it down in hopes of certain perceived moral gains, such as, for example, "worker's rights." Katrina and its aftermath have shown us how inefficient government can be. After all, this problem was not a problem with any one party, but with the government in general.

Calvin Coolidge once said that "collecting more taxes than is absolutely necessary is legalized robbery." This country has an obligation to spend these tax dollars wisely. Unfortunately, nearly half of the voting public does not even pay taxes, meaning they don't care about such inefficient spending because it doesn't come out of their pockets. This disturbing fact is a recipe for disaster. Al has no moral obligation to pay for Bob's health insurance. When can we have a day where health insurance could be shopped for as we shop for car insurance?

Additionally, I have reservations regarding the closing of Guantanamo Bay. As it is, the Supreme Court has once again rewritten the Constitution to provide certain privileges to these captured prisoners that this country has no obligation to do. It is necessary that we have the tools to fight this War on Terror and Guantanamo Bay is one of these tools. We also need enhanced interrogation, not for confessions to be used in a court of law, but for discovering information that can be used to prevent the murder of innocent American lives. This is a battle that must be won, and against an opponent that does not play fair. Remember, these are enemy combatants captured on a foreign field fighting for an organization that did not sign the Geneva Convention.

Again, though I feel you have the potential to be the worst president since Jimmy Carter, if not worse, I would like to congratulate you once again on your victory and I hope that time are good, even if such times are inaccurately attributed to you.

CHAPTER 22

Automobile Industry Policy

During the current economic crisis, the big three American automobile makers fell upon hard times and two of them asked the federal government to bail them out. Many individuals and students have parents and/or other family members working for these industries. They write letters seeking relief and providing advice to the new president about what to do in terms of this industry.

Dear President-elect Obama,

I am writing to inform you of the danger of bailing out the U.S. auto industry. America is facing a terrible financial crisis that has plagued nearly ever corner of the economy. Consumer spending, industry, and banking are all under enormous pressure. Drastic times call for drastic measures, and I think, given the circumstances, the $700 billion bailout for banking was necessary. Many commercial and investment banks, as a result of poor management and greed, were highly leveraged and sitting on very volatile assets, such as sub-prime mortgage loans. Although their poor decision-making is not deserving of a bailout, there is far more risk to the rest of America and the world if these banks are allowed to go under. Banking affects everybody, but American automotive companies do not. As I am writing to you, the chief executive officers of Ford, General Motors, and Chrysler are lobbying for a $34 billion dollar bailout to save their companies and the several million jobs that are related to the U.S. auto industry. These companies, however, are built on unprofitable business models, and giving them money to stay running will only prolong their inevitable fall into bankruptcy. These companies will quickly burn through the bailout and return in the spring asking for more money. It is hard allow the employees of these companies to lose their jobs, but giving away $34 billion in taxpayer money to these companies is an exercise in futility. When running a country of 300 million people, it is often necessary to choose the lesser of two evils. These are trying times, and I wish you the best in your approach to the adversities this country is facing.

Sincerely,
Michael Koeneke

Dear Mr. President,

As a fellow American, I would like to congratulate you on making history in becoming the 44th president of the United States. As a student at the politically active campus of the University of Michigan, I witnessed democracy flourishing. Students were encouraging others to educate themselves about the issues and encouraging them to register to vote.

This election was the first one I was eligible to vote in and I will never forget that moment for as long as I live. Congratulations on a hard-fought and well-deserved victory. You proved that democracy is still a vital part of American society, which was inspiring to witness.

I hope that you continue to demonstrate the strength of the American spirit and how elected officials can come together, cross party lines, and put the needs of the American people above everything else. As president, you will be the leader to help facilitate this meeting. It is vital to breathe life back into the economy and give hard-working citizens who are suffering from the recession a decent source of income. Most of my relatives have worked in the automotive industry for years and have been struggling to live with an unstable working environment, inevitable layoffs and living on unemployment while trying to find new jobs. I have seen the truly generous and caring spirit of Americans in times of tragedy and crisis. Now we have to come together again and support our own interests and I hope you will support solutions that favor American companies over foreign ones by giving incentives in the form of tax credits to the American people. These American companies, as the Big 3 proved, are important to the national economy and affect many jobs (at least one in every ten).

I look forward to the changes you have proposed during your campaign and even more recently as the President-elect. May God bless you and your family and may God continue to bless America.

Sincerely,
Tiffany Burrows

Dear President Obama,

Congratulations on your successful campaign for the White House. Although I may not agree with your policies and beliefs, I do wish you the best of luck throughout your term. With your cabinet appointments thus far, you have demonstrated that you are willing to work with the opposition to accomplish what is best for the country. Please do what is best for the country throughout your presidency and not what is the most popular with the electorate. I urge you to turn your attention to Michigan because we have the worst unemployment in the country and we have suffered for years with the decline of the auto industry and the lack of diversity in our economy. My father works for Chrysler, so everyday my family has to worry about the future and whether or not my dad will have a job. Once again, congratulations on your victory and good luck. There is a lot of work ahead of us as we try to turn our country out of this recession.

Dear President Obama,

One of my concerns about keeping America on top and relevant is foreign relations. You will have to improve relations with countries throughout the world. Relations have been strained with some of our allies and are poor with much of the world.

Please remain upbeat in your speeches. Your inauguration speech promoted American patriotism, which will be vital to navigating the economic crisis.

While it is important to regulate the capital markets, it is equally important to allow progress. You mentioned this in your inaugural speech a bit. We must harshly punish investment fraud, as high-profile scam artists dissuade the public from investing in honest investments.

The American auto industry has not been competitive for many years. We have to emerge from the auto industry turmoil poised to succeed not only by selling American cars domestically, but by selling abroad. We can compete internationally but the big 3 will have to scrap their business plans of old. They are proven failures. It is not impossible for our cars to compete with foreign autos. Take Audi for example. Their cars were notoriously poor throughout the 1980s but through resilient leadership who made critically important decisions they have risen through the ranks. Audi sold more A4s in Germany than BMW sold 3 series. This could never have been forecasted ten years ago. Audi used proven formulas over at BMW, put their own twist on the new Audis, and eventually improved on some of BMW's philosophies, establishing their own identity along the way. It will not happen overnight, but it must happen.

I will save the rest for my next installment.

Best wishes,
Rob Furst

Dear President Obama:

How are you doing? I want to congratulate you on your victory of becoming the president of the United States of America. America is surely blessed to have a president like you.

The current economic status of this country, as you already know, is not so good. Day by day, it is becoming very difficult to live in this country. My Father is currently working for Ford Motor Company, and my Mother is working as an independent business owner for the body shop. My younger brother and I are currently studying at two different universities. The Big Three motor companies are in a mess and are in need of some financial support. If they do not get this support, it will not only affect the motor companies, but it will also affect many families. It is getting really difficult to pay the bills, and my parents do not know what will happen in the future. Not only is it getting difficult to pay the bills, but it is also almost impossible to pay off all other debt. This year alone, I will have to pay back over $10,000 in student loans. By the time I graduate in about 2.5 years, I will have a debt of over $30,000. Why do universities have to cost so much? Isn't it humane to provide an affordable education? After

I graduate, I will want to start a new life. However, I wouldn't be able to do that, as I will have so much to pay back.

Health care isn't cheap either. Although my family has good insurance, we all have to pay a co-pay of $25. At the pharmacy, prescriptions can cost us anywhere from $10 to $25 each. When will all of this stop? Is it possible that we can have universal health care like Canada? That could easily solve the problem.

While most families save and think of the future, my family only thinks about what will happen tomorrow. We feel blessed if we can make it to the next day; the future is too far away.

This horrible economic state leaves me no choice but to do one thing. In the summer of 2009, I will hopefully go to Mumbai, India, to try my luck in Indian television and Bollywood films. If acting doesn't work at first, I will go for singing platforms such as "Indian Idol." Perhaps my interest in acting and singing will help my family and me in this horrible economic state. Not only will I be able to help my parents with all of our debt, but I will also be able to provide a great life ahead for my younger brother. This will also solve my loans problem for school tuition. The cost of tuition for one year at the University of Michigan, where I study, is more than enough to pay for the entire four years at any reputable university in Mumbai, India. In this state of high costs, why wouldn't I go to Mumbai and try my luck? Although other family members tell me that my dreams are either too difficult or almost impossible to accomplish, I will take all the risks for the sake of my family. I know that I will succeed because every impossible has an "I" "M" "Possible" in it. I also know that GOD is always on my side, and he will help me along my way. This will definitely be better for my family and me.

I understand that you are very busy, sir, but I know that you are also a family man. You not only understand how hard it is to pay back student loans, but also understand how to survive in this world. Please do take a moment, and think about my problems. May GOD bless you and your family.

Sincerely,
Pawan P Janveja

Barack Obama,

I would first like to extend my congratulations to you regarding your victory on election day and your excellently run campaign; I agree with almost all of your policies and with the direction you intend to take our country. However, there is one position that I must respectfully disagree with you on. You have graciously extended your support to the American automakers, a noble and honorable gesture, yet unfortunately one that I feel is misguided. My feelings on this issue, by the way, are far from ideological (politically, at least); rather, as an automobile fanatic, my feelings are simply realistic. The automakers simply don't need billions of dollars from our government; instead, they need the massive restructuring that would come from bankruptcy. I know this seems like a cold response to an emotional issue, and I can assure you that in a political science class I am currently enrolled in, I took some fire from a fellow student whose enrollment in college depended on her father keeping his job at General Motors, but it is reality in my eyes. These sentiments, by the way, seem to be compounding the problem—of course no one, least of all me, wants to see any of our country's automakers fail, because we are led to believe that upon filing for bankruptcy, a lot of good, hardworking people are going to be out of a job, and it is this sentiment that I feel is clouding people's judgment on this issue.

Unfortunately, the reality of it is that even with a huge bailout of our automakers, the sort of restructuring they require in order to be competitive again would shed nearly as many jobs as bankruptcy, while saving the Federal Reserve some critical money. Bankruptcy will allow the "Big Three" to re-negotiate their labor contracts and benefits plans to match those of foreign automakers who operate factories here in America. This is a critical part of a critical restructuring of our automakers; they boast some of the best pensions, benefits, and pay in the industry, a fantastic program when the companies were doing well but an anchor in these hard times. We either keep trying to pay out these pensions with bailout money, and have the companies die later anyway, or file for bankruptcy and allow the companies to opt out of these obligations for their survival and save the U.S. the money. Another reason I have trouble justifying such a large sum of money to the companies is the question of who gets what? Some of the Big Three need the money more than others—for example, GM really needs the money, whereas Ford will likely survive this mess due to their thriving European operations (the only profitable arm of Ford in the last few years) and the fact that they are shifting said operations to the U.S. (finally!). Chrysler definitely needs some major, yet doable, streamlining; for example, Chrysler should make the cars, Dodge should make the trucks, and Jeep should make the SUVs. So with Ford's initiation of restructuring, and Chrysler's relatively straightforward restructuring, this leaves GM, whose restructuring will have to be massive, and expensive, and here's why: GM has too many brands under its name-Saturn, Chevy, Buick, Cadillac, Saab, GMC, Pontiac, and of course, Hummer. Part of GM's problem is that for every Chevy, there is a Pontiac or a Saturn that is the same basic car, just slightly restyled, rebadged, and sold at the same dealership, so that essentially they are competing with themselves, and when the car you just copied wasn't exactly great to begin with, where does that leave you? So the simple solution would be to kill several of these unnecessary brands, right? That is right, except that with this approach, GM would have to settle with all of the dealerships of the brands they killed; this is not cheap, as GM's laying to rest of Oldsmobile a few years ago shows. This alone could possibly take a large part of the bailout money. So if GM needs most of the money, how do you can you justify giving more to one company than the other without disrupting the spirit of competition? Therefore, I pose this question to you, Mr. Obama: are you willing to make a hard decision that may not be all that popular in order to save an industry, instead of trying to throw money at a problem in a way that will only delay the inevitable? It may be a more popular and hopeful decision to back a bailout of these companies, but isn't it a more responsible, if tougher, decision to let them go into bankruptcy if it means that they will go through restructuring that may not happen if they are (temporarily) saved with billions of dollars? I hope you will choose the latter though I will support any approach you choose, since you probably have much smarter people on this than a college kid who may be spending more of his time following the car industry and reading automotive publications than he should be.

Sincerely,
Alexander Stoklosa

Dear President Obama,

Lately I have been really troubled about the problems surrounding the auto industry. My uncle owns many car dealerships, and my whole family works for the family business. I'm really hoping that Congress can pass the bailout for GM as soon as possible. I hope they make progress before you take office in January, but if not, please help The Big Three!

Thanks,
Brigid

Dear President Obama,

First and foremost I would like to congratulate you on becoming the United States' 44th president. Your election was unique in the fact that you are the first African-American to become president, but also the turnout in this election was higher than in any other recent presidential election. This increase in the amount of voters this year reflects how Americans are looking for a change in the coming years. Currently our country is paying millions of dollars and thousands of American lives to fight two wars, and on the homefront our nation is suffering from high unemployment levels, struggling economy, and dwindling education. Americans are starting to feel defeated. Our nation needs a change and a hero—something and someone that every American regardless of age, race, or religious can believe in, a beam of hope for the future.

It must be an honor to know that Americans put our faith in you. You are the hero we elected, the one we need who will have the responsibility of reforming our nation. Your vitality, composure, strength, and poise are qualities that Americans hope will bring change to our country. You need to be that hope for America. The hope for families with loved ones in the war. Hope for single-family homes where individuals are working multiple minimum paying jobs with no health care benefits to support their families. Hope for companies, the economy, and all unemployed persons looking for a way to use their talents. Hope for all oppressed persons around the world who cannot express their opinions without facing persecution and are looking for help. And hope for the American youth, so that they may always be provided a strong education so that they can have a secure future, secure freedoms, and always have faith their country.

However, a symbol of hope and inspiration can only offer so much to the American people. Instead you must also change policy and strengthen programs to truly provide hope of a better future for all Americans. In order to do this it is essential that we reduce unemployment and have our economy gain steam again. Living in Detroit, MI, I have watched many friends and my dad experience layoffs from automotive companies. Now these companies are asking for a bailout, but are arriving to Washington, D.C. in their private jets. I think it is important for the auto industries to be strengthened, but it is unwise to just bail them out with a blank, no-strings-attached check. That money will go straight to the top of the chain and will just hold off on the failure of the company for a few months. Instead, the companies need to work with economic consultants to discuss reforms in the companies that will make them more competitive and efficient (also it would be a good idea to enforce the need for environmentally friendly companies now, and offer a tax break if they alter their systems to decrease pollution, because we need to also protect our environment), and it should be necessary that they have a definite plan for how the money will be used. This format should also be used for other companies across the nation. The United States is not struggling economically because Americans are not as highly educated as other countries; it is because we have settled into a rut. We need to be more creative, innovative, to make products for the changing times, and already look ahead and predict society's needs for the future. This is just one suggestion, but I think it is important to get the economy rolling again to decrease the unemployment rate. When citizens have job security they feel better about their situation and then it is easier to look at other problems and to gain support on other issues.

The citizens of the United States of America need a hero and source of hope. They need changes to their nation and an enthusiastic leader that will bring back faith to the country.

Peace be with you.

Sincerely,
Lindsay Hagan

President Obama,

In these trying times—politically, economically, socially—I, as an American citizen, thank you for your beacon of hope through the dark clouds. Your message of "Yes we can" resonated farther than your aims for the White House and was reflected in your eloquent inaugural address. America will face all of its struggles and not back down, you said, and with the conviction that makes us hope that you will follow through on this statement, you passed along to us once more the motivation to work to make America a better place.

America HAS faced troubles before, and has risen from ashes to be even stronger. Every single one of us must rise from the obstacles and work to make America the nation of integrity and hard work that you described. Your campaign made so many believe in the possibility of politics that rises above partisan divisions to the belief in a better America, and I ask that you stay committed to these goals of surpassing the conflicts and arguments that have plagued politics for so long.

In your leadership, consider the common man. Consider the auto worker that rises at 4 AM to provide the country's manufacturing base, and help the Big Three to rise back to their feet rather than letting Michigan falter. Do not forget us, and do not underestimate us. We have the intellect, the talent, and above all else, the will to do the work that you describe to improve America—do not forget us. Help us, rather than simply punishing a company for its past mistakes—and in so doing, take the country along a path to renewable energy and help us prevent future global warming. Let America be a steward to the world, considering people of all countries and resources of all lands in your political decisions.

Your ability to motivate Americans and excite citizens about politics is truly remarkable—and inspirational. What we witnessed in the past election season was groundbreaking, and perhaps sets the stage for a new age of American politics. With your election, continue that support, that motivation, that excitement—except now, let that excitement be directed to the America that we know and love.

Thank you.

Dear President Obama,

I would like to take this opportunity to write to you on behalf of my thoughts on our country's transportation issues. The drop in gas prices in the recent few weeks has been more than efficient enough for our citizens' wallets. Being able to afford traveling to see family has been absolutely wonderful over this Thanksgiving. However, how long is this fairness in price/gallon of gas going to continue? This I fear and this is why I am writing to you today.

In Europe, they have high-powered trains that can zip you from one country to the next. Why can't we initiate the same thing or at least the same idea throughout North America? I understand we used to have a more efficient train or trolley system in cities, in the past. I know General Motors paid major money to buy these well-liked systems up and replace them with polluting, smelly, and non-liked buses. Hence, then became the problem with traffic, expansion of roads, and pollution of our free air in this country. So we have lived, learned, and experienced, what can be done or has been done instead of jumping in a gas-guzzling vehicle and inefficiently getting from point A to point B.

In the 1970s, General Motors came out with the first electric car. What a hit! People like Tom Hanks and other movie stars all went out and bought one of these efficient and fun vehicles to become more and more efficient with every day to day driving needs. Well, what happened to the idea of making America efficient, safe, and affordable? The oil companies!! WE allowed them to press lawsuits against OUR COUNTRY'S car industries in order to make a few more billion dollars a year! WE allowed them to make these false accusations that they would go out of business if the government continued to allow research into making these MIRACLES on wheels for OUR CITIZENS to drive around! FIRST of all, do you think ANYONE cares about the oil companies making a few more BILLION dollars a year? NO!! And let me just lay on the line what CAN be accomplished here if we do end up BAILNG out these auto companies today that have only screwed themselves:

Go ahead and give 20 billion dollars to the Big Three but make DARN sure that someone OTHER than their own higher-ups manages what this money goes toward. And it should ONLY be put forth toward research and IMMEDIATE development of not just more efficient vehicles but MUCH more efficient vehicles.

In order to accomplish creating these "MUCH" more efficient vehicles, we need to not look toward how much power we can throw into them and THEN make it get good gas mileage; you have to make it get good gas mileage and THEN add power to accommodate going 0 to 60 miles per hour in 3 seconds. This brings up a good point, WHY do we need to go 0 to WHATEVER in such a short amount of time? I realize that I myself LOVE punching it as I get on the expressway, but recently, I have found myself more and more NOT doing that because of the high cost in gas! THEREFORE, there is no reason to do it and by tuning down the power or acceleration in vehicles by even just a little bit will get us a LONG ways in efficiency.

The idea of immediately making ALL vehicles more efficient is out of the question. However, using our world's less and less oil supply to have one person drive a Hummer H2 around is not exactly what I want accomplished either. Why not limit the use of oil to more industry-needed purposes like semi transportation for power needed, large trucks needed for businesses to accomplish daily needs, and air transportation. What I am saying is if a vehicle is being used only for transportation of people, than why not make it a more efficient way of doing so? Yes, this transformation will take a long time and a lot of people may not be very happy with it because those are the people who have the money to throw around with unnecessary means.

California is becoming more and more unsafe by every vehicle that transmits gas emissions into their air supply. WHY not replace at least HALF of those vehicles with more efficient cars like General Motors (OUR NATION'S JOBS) electric cars that they ALREADY HAD in the 1970s? Why not push for this form of technology and use oil more efficiently through already used means like heating our citizens' homes, fueling our businesses through ONLY large amounts of transportation, etc?

Mr. President, the bottom line is that we do have the ability and technology to make our country's transportation means MUCH more efficient and we hide behind the idea of anyone standing up to the little oil companies who control, manipulate, and rob the pockets of OUR COUNTRY'S CITIZENS' pockets!! We can NO longer stand it, we CAN do something about it, and we WILL prevail through this need of change. The change you have given us in our minds to become more idealists and fight for what is right for our citizens of the United States of America.

Sincerely,
Matthew Buhr

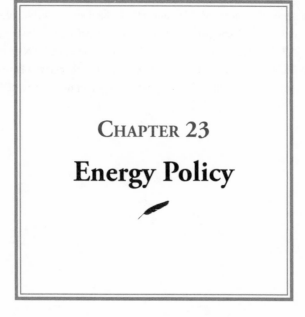

CHAPTER 23

Energy Policy

Throughout the presidential primaries, the national conventions, and the general election, gasoline prices continued to rise until they reached a national average of more than four dollars a gallon. In fact, the gas prices, along with the banking and mortgage crises, helped to contribute to the Wall Street meltdown. Hence, finding alternate sources of energy became a major campaign issue. Thus, we find in these letters not only discussions about what is needed to provide the country with a solution to rising energy costs, but also advice on how to go about solving this national problem.

Dear President Obama:

I am a resident of Long Island, New York, and commute with my wife by car into New York City. This is a 50-mile round-trip commute that we make about 200 times per year.

When the price of gasoline was over four dollars a gallon, the cost of the commute was equal to the cost of taking the Long Island Railroad, the local commuter train service. The cost for wife and me to take the train is approximately $420 per month.

Now that the cost of gasoline has dropped to $1.80 a gallon the cost of commuting by car is now far cheaper than commuting by train. Also, due to decreased revenues caused by the recession, the price of a monthly train ticket may rise as much as ten percent.

My personal situation demonstrates the urgent need for a coherent, logical energy policy. Mass transportation must be encouraged and driving discouraged to end our dependence on foreign oil and save our environment. The only way this can be achieved is by the imposition of a new gasoline tax and a large federal subsidy to local and state governments to lessen the cost of mass transportation. We also need a high-speed rail service. To offset the burden of the gasoline tax on low and middle income families, a payroll tax credit should be imposed.

You ran a great campaign and transition. There is enormous goodwill toward your upcoming presidency. People would be willing to sacrifice more now than since World War II. Don't waste this opportunity—fight for a rational energy policy no matter what the special interests want or do.

Good luck Mr. President. We're all pulling for you.

Sincerely,
Ed Friedman

Dear President Obama,

First off I would just like to tell you that I believe in you. That is not to say that we agree on everything, because there are some matters of policy on which we do not share the same views. However I can soundly say for myself, and for my peers, that you have inspired us. You have inspired us through your immaculate orations, your calm demeanor, and your strong character. In a time of such nationwide turmoil, where economic and foreign policy crises dominate the American media, you instill a positive attitude in us, one truly anticipating that somehow, someway, you are going to get us out of this.

You speak a lot about change, and you specifically speak about changing our country's habits of dependence on foreign oil. During my summer internship, I worked extensively on a project designed to handicap the success of each type of renewable energy, and along the way, I developed a very strong opinion, much like the one you expressed during the debates, about the importance of renewable energy both for political and environmental reasons. In my research, I found that this task, while not insurmountable, will be a hefty one. While there has been significant progress in several fields, ample progress is left to be made. The difficulty in transporting wind energy, the dangers of nuclear waste, and the high expense of solar energy all present sizeable obstacles to our goal. However, I want to advise you not to give up on this goal, whatever it takes. While it may take several years to complete, its positive consequences, including the creation of environmentally friendly sources of energy and our independence of the corrupt oil producers of the Middle East, make the accomplishment well worth the journey. I encourage you to call on the young engineers and business leaders of tomorrow to help you with this task. They will be ready and willing; the theme of this semester at my school, the University of Michigan, is energy futures, so all of my classmates are currently gearing up to help you out with this enormously important task. Yes it is big. But like I said, we believe in you.

Thank you so much for being such an inspiration to us all, and remember to call on us, because we will all be ready to help you. I know I will.

Sincerely,
Jonathan Hornstein
University of Michigan Class of 2012
Future Owner of Hornstein Biofuels and Co.

Dear President Obama,

My name is Dino Ruggeri and I am currently attending the University of Michigan. I am deeply concerned with our energy crisis and I'm a big proponent for further research in alternative energy. America is addicted to energy and we cannot continue using it at the rates we do if we wish to sustain ourselves in the near future. Climate is being affected more than ever, landscapes are being blown apart to mine coal to power our homes, and we use more petroleum than any other country on earth. Your energy policy earned my vote as it proves that you're striving to get the United States to utilize more alternative energy sources while at the same time creating millions of green collar jobs. By creating more jobs through green enterprises you gain more support from the people as they see how solving our energy crisis can also solve our labor crisis. Other components of your policy, such as getting plug-in hybrids on the road and utilizing alternative sources of energy in the near future, are extremely practical and should have been looked into years ago. So please keep America's energy crisis at the top of your agenda because we need to find an answer to this problem soon if we wish to protect our economy as well as the environment.

Sincerely,
Dino Ruggeri

Dear President Obama,

Congratulations on your election to the White House. You are the hope and change that this country needs in the difficult times that face us. We are all responsible to take a stand and start working towards a more positive future. There are many urgent issues that need to be addressed, but I feel that the most important are issues pertaining to the environment.

We are in a new age of technology, and just stepping into the Green Revolution. We need to put our minds and resources together to form a plan of action to save the planet we call home. Your New Energy Plan for America is the first step in the right direction. By creating new jobs to build a clean energy future, you are not only giving the economy a boost, but making a permanent change to the way we live our lives. It should be made possible for all Americans to make small changes for a better, cleaner way of living.

We need to concentrate on new technologies to research all aspects of green energy and leave no stone unturned. Technologies like hybrid cars and solar and wind energy alternatives need to be made a reality for every family in America. Already we can see small changes across the country in countless households from reusable grocery bags to more efficient light bulbs to increased recycling. We need to make the Green Revolution a way of life instead of a choice.

Your Cap and Trade program is a great start to making the necessary changes to our green house gas emissions. This will open up a door for companies and families alike to really get involved and feel like they are doing their part to help save the environment. Countries around the world are making the vital changes towards clean energy and green living. We need to follow in their steps, but rise up and become a leader in all things sustainable.

The Earth is threatened by global warming, rising sea levels, and an overall degradation of the atmosphere. We started this downward spiral with the Industrial Revolution. It is our time to take responsibility of our actions and work to provide a clean and useable environment for those to follow. The only way to put this in reverse is to act now and act strongly.

Thank you,
Caitlin Lowery

Dear President Obama,

Your first hundred days in the presidency may go by fast, but you have to take advantage of these days and not let them slip by. Here is the opportunity to set the tone of your presidency and show the people of America what you are all about. In these first hundred days there is a certain energy that is given off that keeps the American people intrigued on what you are going to do for our country. Make sure that you define the biggest thing that will change our country. I believe that in your first hundred days in the presidency you should address America's dependence on oil. America will eventually have to depend on some alternative resources to power itself, why not start that search now? If you are successful in discovering this new energy source, you would benefit America's security and economy as well. America would not have to deal with hostile countries to retrieve its oil and also America would profit from being the first to discover an alternative energy source.

Another issue that you should address in the first hundred days of your presidency is the troops that are stationed in Iraq. You should make it very clear what will be your course of action in ending the war in Iraq and removing our troops safely. I believe this to be in your benefit because it has been one of the citizens' worries for a long time now. Alleviating their uncertainties by bringing our troops home safely as soon as possible would be in your best interest.

Doing all three of these things during the first hundred days of your presidency will set you out on the right foot for the rest of your presidency. It will set the tone and let the people of America know what Barack Obama is all about.

Guy Perez
New York

CHAPTER 24

Educational Policy

Since this project was based at the University of Michigan, it should be clear why some of the letters raise questions and concerns about jobs and employment opportunities after graduation, as well as how the impending economic crisis might very well eliminate the possibility of getting a college education for many of today's young people who are currently enrolled. These letters are quite poignant and offer critiques and recommendations.

Dear President-elect Barack Obama,

When I was in kindergarten, I dreamed of being president of the United States of America. As time went on, I abandoned my dream, and decided instead to become a teacher instead. You held the same dream I once had, and your dream has come true. I just ask that you don't forget the classrooms that you first had that dream in. Don't forget the children of America and the teachers who foster those children.

Good luck these next four years,
Jessica Stokes

Dear Mr. President,

I am a product of public school education and an undergraduate college student with hopes of attending graduate school. Therefore, the decreased value and functioning of public school systems and the increasing costs of higher education are issues very close to my heart. And so I am writing this letter to show both my appreciation and support of the planned reforms for both. The "Zero to Five" plan, which is designed to offer early care and education for young children, provides a solution to an issue that has preoccupied me for awhile. At times, in urban neighborhoods, there arises the mentality that education is unnecessary, that there is no escape. Being educated from a very young age, being instilled with an appreciation and yearning, could dispel all negative mentalities. I am also interested in the plans to better train the teachers because good teachers are hard to find but indispensable, especially in a public system. But most pressing for me, and for which I am most grateful, are the American Opportunity tax credit and the simplification of applying for financial aid. Thank you so much President Obama for endeavoring to provide quality education and, consequentially, a better way of life for all American citizens.

Dear Barack Obama,

My name is Anna Pierre, from Bushwick School for Social Justice, and I'm writing this letter to congratulate you on being the president of the United States. I don't think that the country could have made a better decision. I look up to you because I've read all the things you've been through and you still made it to the top. Knowing that you are our president makes me see a brighter future for us.

I hope in the future you will run again. So you can be reelected, and so I can vote for you. I feel more proud to be an African-American now since I know the way we have a say in this country. I've noticed that you try to bring whites and blacks together, unlike McCain. I've watched McCain on television talking about whites this and the blacks that. But I never heard of him talk about us as equals. I've watched McCain bad mouth you so many times but never once I heard you talk bad about him and that's what's up.

I really hope that you will end the war because I know you see how it is hurting people and killing them. I know that you are smart. After all, you did graduate from Harvard Law School. And I know you know what it's like in the low-income neighborhood. And I know you'll do your best to help the hood by lowering prices on houses. Then we can spend that money on food and gas.

Some people can't go to college because it's too much money. Please give us the chance you had. I believe in you and so does America. We believe that you'll do everything in your power to change America. The best is yet to come.

You said people who came on a boat didn't have to go back, but they do have to pay a fine. When I heard you say that it made me so happy because I know that you are thinking about us. We don't do anything bad. We just came to America to have a better life, for us and for our kids.

I enjoyed your speech so much that I have everything you said on paper. And when I get home, I'm going to hang it up on my wall then I'm going to write on top of it, "The 44th president is black." I'm proud to say "BARACK OBAMA IS MY PRESIDENT!!!!" I'm sorry to hear about your grandmother but I know she's in heaven smiling down at you saying "That's my boy." And that she's very proud of you.

Love,
Anna Pierre
P.S. Yes We Can!!!

Dear Barack Obama,

It is a pleasure for me to write this letter to the new African-American president of the United States. I feel proud of you and I believe in some of your goals to improve the United States. I think that you are a positive person and strong. I also think that you can make our dreams to become true. We all want to change the United States. And with your help we all say "Yes We Can." Well, me as a student, I think each one of us will walk with you to make our dreams to become alive. And if you walk with us we will walk together to a new direction where we can find peace and love for everyone. We don't want any more war and I know that you don't want this to continue too. So, I think that we are on the same page. I know that you worked hard to be where you are and I think you are where you belong. You are an example for us to follow. We will do our best to study to become someone in life just like you did, now that you are president. Help us because we want to have better rights. I think that it is time to put some color in the United States' White House because that's how gardens are made. If all the flowers are the same color, a garden wouldn't be as beautiful.

I also want to know if you can help us to go to college. Well, me as an immigrant, I would like to become someone important in life to help my parents. I am the only child so I have to take care of my father and mother when they get old. So my responsibility is to work hard and reach my goals. I think that maybe you can make new school laws. I hope you help immigrant students to go to college because you know that we have to pay a lot of money to go to college. I also want to remind you about the economy. Also to increase the amount of money that immigrants are paid for their work. Well, for now these are some of my words to you and again congratulations once again. Take care and

God bless you and your family.

Sincerely,
Wendy Perez

Dear President Obama,

Congratulations on your win for president. I'm very happy because I voted for you and support you to be the president of the USA because I know you being the president, our futures are going to be better and our education is going to improve. I know that you are going to stop the war and save all that money to help people that really need it.

I suggest you pick up your pants and fix this country and talk to all the police officers around here because they are going too hard with us. No one ever thought about having a black president before but now they do because people that vote for you really know that we are going to have a better future. Like my grandfather used to say, "Our future is in your hands."

I hope you make this country better.
Adrian Marmalejos

Dear Mr. Obama,

I want to tell you congratulations for being president of the United States of America. I hope you be a better president. Some suggestions on what you should do as president is to stop the war, help the poor people, and to help all the immigrants. You could help the poor people like give them food and a place to live. You could also stop the war in Iraq. Another thing is that you should be a nice person and don't be racist to other people. Good luck being a President and help the people who voted for you.

Sincerely,
Andres Tepepa

Dear Barack Obama,

I wanted to congratulate you for being nominated as the president of the United States. It is my honor to say that you have made a huge change in the United States history of presidents. But, how does it feel to be known as the first African-American president? I do believe that being president for the first time is a hard job indeed. So my question to you would be, "What are some changes you want to make so that the Unites States can be a better country? Since as of now you know that we are going through a huge crisis and the economy is really bad, what's your plan?"

I think that a good thing to do as a president is to put down the food prices because it's not fair that the lower and middle class have to suffer to eat because the prices are really high. Also, more medical insurance that is eligible for mostly anyone who really needs it. I also think that another good suggestion would be to make more programs for kids who need help in school and make it more fun. That way gang members can get off the street and actually get an education without leaving the classroom because it's boring. Well, these are some of my suggestions to you as far as what I think needs to be changed for the better.

Once again congratulations on earning the title of the first African-American president and to be the honorable president of the United States. Now that you are the new president you could end the war. Dr. King's dream has come true and the new president is an African-American. Nobody expected this but it is true. Back in the days, there were a lot of racist people.

Sincerely,
Samuel Vasquez

Dear President Obama,

    As a twenty-year-old university student from Michigan, I wanted to write you in order to offer my support for your upcoming plan concerning education. I was always on the college track while in high school but I recognize the issue that many students are not. I think your idea to implement intervention strategies early on in middle school will help less students drop out later. From my own personal experience in high school, we started off with a freshman class of 400 and graduated with only 360. I think the best way to attack the dropout crisis would be to have more future planning earlier in the student's career, such as in middle school. This could be accomplished through more students and counselor interaction because I know that at my school, the only way a student talked to their counselor about their future was by him or her taking the initiative. Perhaps if more schools enforced direct student/counselor interaction more students would be able to start planning their futures at a younger age. I also think that your Make College a Reality initiative would help more students attend college. At my high school, not very many AP courses were offered and not very many students took them. Out of about 800 juniors and seniors eligible to take these classes, there were never more than around 15 of the same students in each of the six AP classes offered. Now as a student at the University of Michigan, I realized that I missed out on a lot of learning opportunities because of the lack of AP courses offered at my high school. I believe that if more AP courses were offered at more public high schools like the one I attended, more students would be able to take them and therefore be more motivated to attend a university. And as a college student, I wish I could be applicable for your American Opportunity Tax Credit. I think it is important to create as many opportunities as possible to get young people to college and this initiative would help both those who can attend big universities or smaller community colleges. I also support the aspect of this initiative that students would need to complete community service hours in order to receive the credit. Interacting with one's community and working for others is good experience for many young people and getting help toward paying for college would encourage more students to get involved. I know that now the future is in the hands of my generation and these education acts would help us all make the future what all Americans want it to be. I hope to see many of your education initiatives going into effect so that even more young people will be able to get the education they need and deserve. Thank you for your time and good luck in your upcoming administration.

    Sincerely,
    Jane Burke

Dear President Obama,

After watching the inauguration today, I can say with certainty that I am so proud to be a part of this amazing time in the history of the United States. Watching your speech gave me chills, the same chills I had on election night. I thought that being a college student, it would be relevant to discuss my support for your education policies. I support your goal to reform the No Child Left Behind policy, because I know from personal experience that test taking in no way determines the intelligence or potential of a student. I know that I did not score as highly on the SATs as I would have expected, but I was mostly a straight A student all through high school. Children should be learning life skills and other important skills they will need for future studies and their future in general, not simply learning what will be on a standardized test or strategies for taking one. As a college student, I especially support your plan to make college affordable for everyone. The $4,000 will go a long way in helping many families who feel hopeless, thinking that college may be out of reach. Not only that, but community service in return will help the student's community as well as the nation as a whole, and teach the student the value of money and giving back. I also fully support the plan to make applying for financial aid easier, as I think the current FAFSA form is rather complicated, and many families who have never been in a situation to fill out such forms may be overwhelmed or unaware of how to correctly apply. It would be completely absurd for a student to be unable to receive financial aid simply because the paperwork was too complicated. In closing, I just want to reiterate my support for not only your educational policies, but your policies on the economy, environment, health care, and others. I think you will do a great job, Mr. President! Thank you for your hard work, and I look forward to seeing what the future holds.

Dear President Obama:

Congratulations on your victory of becoming the president of the USA, as well as the first African-American president. As an African-American, it truly warms my heart and fills my soul with pride to see you become the leader of the free world.

Additionally, this was the first presidential election that I got involved in beyond voting. Your platform for change, your commitment to improving early childhood education, ending the senseless war in Iraq, improving our economy, restoring our country's damaged reputation in the world, and creating "environmental friendly" resources of energy, inspired me to participate more in the election process. Before I knew it, I was registering people to vote, contacting family/friends/colleagues via e-mails/phone calls, wearing Obama gear, and even giving a financial contribution to the campaign. I guess a "Community Organizer" is more powerful than some would think.

All of your commitments are very important to me, but the one that is paramount is your commitment to early childhood education. As the Preschool Special Education Coordinator for the state of Georgia (known nationally as 619 Coordinators), I experience first-hand the difficulties in educating preschool-aged (3 to 5 years) children with disabilities. There are several major problematic areas: inadequate funding, the lack of inclusive opportunities for preschool-aged children with disabilities in environments of typical developing peers, the absence of consistent training for regular early childhood teachers and childcare providers, and lack of special education allocations in all federally funded early childhood programs.

I know that you will not be able to right all of the wrongs of the previous administration, but it is my hope that you will invoke changes that will reflect positively for young children with disabilities. As I often state to educators, "If we believe in the philosophy that all children deserve the right to learn and to a free appropriate education, then it all begins in preschool."

Again, congratulations and best wishes. God bless you and your family. If I can be of service to you and your administration in improving early childhood education, please don't hesitate to contact me.

YES WE CAN!

Sincerely,

Jan E. Stevenson

Dear Mr. President,

Congratulations on your recent election, I expect great things from you. In particular, I am concerned about the current K–12 education system in America. As a trustee on the Lincoln Consolidated School's Board of Education in Ypsilanti Michigan, I have dealt with this issue for over a year. I commend the federal government for trying to improve the mediocre performance of schools through the No Child Left Behind Act; however, this act did not solve the biggest problems facing school districts today and it created several new problems. During your first term I believe you need to address the inequitable funding of schools nationwide, the lack of centralized curriculum and technology resources, the manipulating of performance data, and the inaccuracies of standardized tests.

As a member of the Board of Education, one of the biggest injustices we argue against is the wide range of per-pupil foundation allowances. We receive about $7,200 per student, but the Ann Arbor public schools receive almost $10,000 per student. How are we supposed to provide the same quality of education to our students if we do not have access to the same resources? I believe these taxes should be levied by the federal government and dispersed through the state's Department of Education to allow local oversight as well as equality of funding. This would give schools with large populations of low income families the ability to provide the same education to their students as schools with large populations of middle and upper income students.

One of the largest non–student related expenditures to local schools is technology and curriculum resources. Schools need these functions to maintain a modern and adequate learning environment but these costs could easily be shared at an Intermediate School District level. The federal government should provide incentive funds to school districts looking to be proactive and efficient. Again, these funds would go through the state's Department of Education to the ISD to help pay for the consolidation of services. This, as well as several services could be centralized county-wide for a more efficient delivery of services.

No Child Left Behind is a good start toward using data to make decisions, but there are too many incentives for districts to manipulate data to cheat the system. Just looking at data in my county, I see a school district with a 99% graduation rate compared to my district's 85% graduation rate. One may realize a 99% graduation rate is almost impossible to achieve, but once you break down the data it makes sense. Not only does this school have a very low retention rate (they pass students who probably shouldn't pass) but they also offer an alternative high school for failing students. The graduation rate of these failing students is reflected by this alternative school and not in the high schools statistics. The data collection needs to be streamlined and standardized to increase the accuracy of these numbers in order to properly assess the performance of school districts.

Finally, the federal government needs to develop alternatives to standardized tests to evaluate a school's performance. Schools need to teach their students many soft skills that cannot be tested in a standardized test, and depending on the demographics of the school district, these soft skills may be more valuable to the students than the education they receive. School spending should also be one of the factors the government looks at when evaluating the grade of a school. In particular, the percentage of a district's per pupil foundation allowance that goes toward administrative and overhead costs. The fiscal responsibility of a school district is also very important to insure districts are doing everything possible to spend the money directly on the students' education.

I know this is a large task but I have faith you will do better than the previous administration. We are at a time in this nation's history where we need a great leader with a vision. You are this leader. The education system is at the heart of our democracy and if these changes are not made soon, we will be in trouble. I provided the information needed to start the process of education reform but this is definitely only the start of the journey.

Respectfully,
Jeremy Keeney
Trustee, Chair of WASB Legislative Relations Committee
Lincoln Consolidated School's Board of Education

Dear President-elect Obama,

I would like to congratulate you on the landslide victory of your election as president of the United States. As an African-American woman, I did not think I would live to see the day a person of color gets elected to serve in the highest office of this country. I do not expect a great deal of changes, but the fact that somebody else has a chance, is enormous.

My wish is that something be done about the educational system in this country. It is deplorable! The children are not learning and they are being left behind. It would be nice if the people who are in charge of educating our children are held accountable, from the U.S. Department of Education to the teacher's aide. I know how important it is to have an education and I would like to see other with the same opportunities.

Once again, congratulations on your success!

Greta Blake

CHAPTER 25

Foreign Policy

In a global environment where this nation is actively involved in two wars, many writers, and particularly young people, took up their pens to express their opinions about war and peace to the new president. President Obama had in the pre-primary season declared himself to be against the war in Iraq, and he made a commitment to bring the troops home as soon as possible. Here, in these letters, comments and concerns are voiced about the nation's role and function in the international community.

Dear President Obama,

It's quite a challenge to write you a letter because your campaign revealed you to be a deeply thoughtful man, but everyone's experience is different, so I've decided to pass on a bit of what I've learned from living with my family in my community, and from my experience as an activist, a college professor, and a professional mediator.

Martin Luther King, Jr., once said that the arc of the universe bends towards justice. It's not a good thing to act in a way that is counter to the direction of the universe, but many people will urge you to do just that, in the name of expediency or to protect American interests. There will be so many temptations for you to abandon the moral core that brought you to the presidency. During the campaign, you were able to overcome these temptations. I remember, when so many people urged you to put out negative campaign ads in response to those of the McCain campaign, you refused and explained that it was a matter of what kind of campaign you wanted to run; you said that you would stick with decision to be truthful and respectful regardless of what the other side did. I campaigned for you in working class neighborhoods in Pennsylvania, and many people told me how much they respected that decision. Why did that particular comment strike so many people as a positive reason to vote for you?

Perhaps it is because people are starving for proof that community is possible, that all lives matter, and that the world has not been turned over to narrow interests, greed, tribalism, and expediency. The great force shaping the world right now, on one level, is globalization. Globalization has no moral core. It has no concern for justice. Every country in the world is experiencing, in one way or another, the destabilizing effects of globalization—the immense, practical changes taking place. But what is more destabilizing than the concrete manifestations of globalization is the awareness that considerations of justice are not made by the governments that negotiate the treaties and make the deals. Every country, including our own, feels threatened. Nations that feel threatened, like individuals who are threatened, react with anger and fear, rather than with reason and confidence.

There were other competent candidates for president, but I supported you because I believe you have a moral core. Your ability to articulate your core moral principles and to act from them is what can lead to greater stability in world affairs. Without the belief that justice is a consideration for powerful governments as well as less powerful ones, the world is always tense. Those around you will sometimes seek to persuade you to turn aside from considerations of justice. That concern has to be paramount, public, and visible for the tensions of people and nations to begin to ease, so that real problem solving can begin.

Your job and yours alone, will be to remember who you are, and what the founding principles of this nation are.

Most recently, I taught Plato to students at the Weill Cornell Medical College in Qatar. The students came from all the Arab countries, as well as Iran, India, and a few from Russia and the United States. Reading Plato's Dialogues with these very bright and engaged students was one of the great pleasures of my life. Often, they brought their families to meet me, and I asked them all the same question: "What shall I tell people when I go home about peace in the Middle East?" Always the answer was the same: "Tell them that when the conflict between Israel and the Palestinians is resolved justly, there will be peace." I hope that you will be able to move toward this goal.

The conflicts I have helped to resolve as a mediator range from disputes between two individuals to large environmental disputes involving multiple parties, government agencies, and organizations. But in all these mediations, there is one constant: People will not settle until they feel they and their perspective have been understood. Not accepted or agreed with, just understood. I have found that when one side can say to the other, "I see why you did what you did, given your perspective on the situation and your interests. I don't agree that was the best thing to do, but I understand it now," then, and only then, do real negotiations begin about how to solve the problem. It astonished me in the early years of my work to see how reluctant people are to simply say that they understand another perspective. I think people often equate understanding with agreement, but understanding is merely the necessary prelude to finding an agreement. Your willingness to speak to leaders without pre-conditions, that is, as equals in the effort to resolve conflicts, is very welcome. This signals that power will not be the only determinant of policy. Now, perhaps there is a chance for understanding and diplomacy.

I'm grateful for what you have already done for the U.S. and the world. Friends and family world-wide celebrated your election with us. Everyone knows that you will make mistakes and take wrong turns. It's inevitable, but we know you have our interests at heart and that you will work toward the common good that protects us all. My family and I will hold you in our hearts as you begin your work as president.

Sincerely yours,
Linda Shaw Finlay

President Obama,

My father is a strong conservative member of the Republican Party. Up until this election I shared my father's political views. Although I was on the fence concerning many key issues that the Republican Party had a clear view on, when the current economic crisis began to hit this past fall, I decided that many of the conservative ideas and opinions were not working, or were obviously taking too long to show an effect. As I took a closer look at your ideas on how to solve the current economic crisis I saw a few key items I agreed with. The idea of increasing tax breaks to middle and lower class Americans seems like a much better idea than giving the most tax breaks to the top five percent. The trickle down effect that has been a staple of Republican economic theory cannot save the American economy in its current state. Key changes must be made and I believe you have the capabilities to get these changes moving. I do realize that the economy is in such a poor state that it will not be fixed a few days or weeks, but most likely multiple months.

Your views on foreign policy are also more agreeable with me. I am currently a member of the United States Air Force. I would go and fight were I ordered by my superiors, but I would prefer it to be for a cause that is worthwhile. The conflict in Iraq is not a worthwhile venture because it is hurting our ability to combat the real center of terrorism in Afghanistan. I believe your plan to withdraw troops from Iraq and increase numbers in Afghanistan is the best plan to keep a lid on terrorism. I truly hope that Iraq does not fall back into the same situation it was in before we came once we start to withdraw. It would be a shame for that to happen when so many service men have given so much in the Iraq conflict.

I believe you have the strong will and knowledge to be a capable president and lead this country on a path to change for the better.

President Barack Obama,

Congratulations on your historic oath of office and beginning a new chapter in American politics and history. I watched the inauguration from my house at the University of Michigan in Ann Arbor and was amazed when the news channels showed aerial footage of the Mall—it was a quite a sight to behold as so many proud Americans witnessed you taking the oath of office and officially becoming the president of the United States of America. Where the last eight years have been marked by corruption, secret politics, and engaging in a series of events that ignored the civil liberties that are guaranteed to citizens by the Constitution and Bill of Rights, I have immense hope and confidence that your administration (and hopefully the next eight years) will be marked by a renewed responsibility and honestly with regard to the executive branch.

Throughout the primary season, I was an unwavering supporter of Senator Hillary Clinton and was turned off by the singular slogan of "hope" and building an entire campaign around it. When you clinched the nomination, I supported you as a loyal Democrat, as I knew that our values and positions lined up. Your inauguration speech marked a departure from this unrestrained hope and the acceptance of reality and what can be accomplished by your administration. Your words were reminiscent of Martin Luther King, Jr.'s, "I have a dream" speech, but one that was adopted to tackle and address our contemporary crisis and problems that our country faces now and in the years to come.

This country is currently experiencing the worst economic crisis since the Great Depression, but I believe that it is international affairs and foreign policy that will define your presidency. You have the unique opportunity to end an unjust war that was began under false pretenses and carried out in a corrupt manner, and give the Iraqi people the gift of complete self-determination and control of their own destiny. The current crisis in Gaza shows that it is indeed time for renewed talks of peace with the goal of a two-state solution. For too many decades have the Israelis and Palestinians been killing each other and getting nowhere except furthering hard feelings. Our country needs to repair its credibility in the international arena and once again become the moral authority in the world. I hope your administration, especially through our new Secretary of State Hillary Clinton, is able to promote effective peace talks.

Once again, congrats on taking the oath of office for the highest office in the land and good luck with all that your administration hopes and works toward accomplishing.

Dear Mr. President,

I wanted so badly to vote for you. The plan for America laid out during your campaign was nearly flawless in it's harmony with my ideals except for the one issue that I really care about: the War on Terror.

You didn't vote for the Iraq War, and you want to pull out our troops; I agree with all this. What I don't like about your stance, is the emphasis placed on finding Osama bin Laden. In September 2001, our collective moral stance was tested, and we failed. With the world on our side, we had a chance to really make an example of terrorists around the world, and turn the other cheek. We had a chance to be truly Christ-like and "forgive those that trespass against us." Politically speaking, going to war against Osama legitimized his movement as much as negotiating would have. Instead, the War on Terror has become about avenging the deaths of thousands of Americans and seems more and more like the actions of an irrational and grieving parent just separated from their child: too upset to think clearly, too jaded to come to terms with their morals, too enraged to forgive. Much like the many parents and soldiers that experience a loses, they cry for justice and claim we must press on. Should you find Osama, I wonder, what will you do with him? Send him to a secret prison? Am I to endure another show-trial? Must we see pictures of him hanged to feel better? If you catch and kill him, you will regret it as any humble man should.

I am an American, and I forgive Osama bin Laden. I forgive him not because he deserves it, not because his act of violence has been far surpassed by our own, not because there is evidence that he was not the only force involved in 9/11; but because forgiveness is the only way to stop the violence. It has been a standard of statesmanship to equate politics and war since the consolidation of Germany. Look where it has left us. Nearly a century of solid warfare, creating generation after generation of scarred young men. I tell you now, no empire was destroyed by actions of an outside aggressor without first having poisoned itself. The War on Terror, this conflict without end, is our poison. Economically, politically, ideologically, and morally, it will destroy us.

Cast aside the desire for satisfaction, tend to our wounds, and gear us for the future. Give us new sources of energy, and watch the terrorist motivation to kill and bomb dry up without American money. This is the only way to save America as we know it.

President Obama, you are all that is left between the American state and Jacobin chaos.

Hopefully,
David Lohnes

Dear Mr. Obama,

Congratulations on your election. You had my full support during the election process, and my undying support for the next four years. As part of the "young people" demographic, I must convey to you (as I am sure you have heard many times before) the extreme sense of urgency that I find myself and my generation. We want to create change in this world to make it a better place. We need YOUR HELP.

Please help us put out the fire in Africa. Northern Uganda, Darfur, Zimbabwe, the "Democratic" Republic of Congo; all of the citizens of these nations are suffering from disease, malnutrition, and violence. Please, let us spend more money on making the world a healthier, safer, cleaner place for all of Earth's children rather than on war, violence, and death.

Please lets continue to work on defending equal rights for every, single American. The bans on gay marriage are shameful, appalling, and backwards. Please lead our nation towards true equality, true liberty, and true happiness.

You will continue to have my support. I believe in you as a person, a president, and as a fellow American.

Thank you,
Rachel Lauderdale

President Obama,

I sincerely wish that U.S. troops will withdraw from Iraq as soon as possible.

Dear President Obama,

I would like to congratulate you firstly on your historic win in the most exciting election in recent history. I couldn't vote because I'm not a citizen, but I would have voted for you because your speeches held so much promise in truly changing America. However, the most important issue to deal with right now besides the economy is the Iraq War. I know you're a busy man, and there are a hundred issues on the table that needs to be prioritized, but war is pointless and comes at the expense of civilian and military lives. You said last week that if the Iraqi army improves and there are reductions in violence, we can "draw down." But what if the situation continues to deteriorate? Are troops going to remain indefinitely in Iraq? I recognize there are a multitude of factors to be taken into consideration such as possible collapse of Iraqi government, there are always two sides to every decision, but this has been such a protracted war. When I first came to the University of Michigan, I was surprised to see the flag flying at half-mast a few times a week. My roommate told me that someone, probably a soldier, was most likely killed in the war. This really startled me, especially from a non-American perspective. I can't imagine how terrible it is for a mother to receive news that her son has been killed. This war has definitely got to stop.

Sincerely,
Alissa

Dear President Obama,

First and foremost, congratulations. Your victory is historic. It has been a long time since the youth, and the rest of the public were so engaged in politics. Just remember that the next four years will be history too. I hope that you are able to accomplish the changes that you've promised us. America is counting on you. Personally, I hope that you improve the reputation of the United States abroad. People all over the world are saying that you will change America for the better. You are intelligent and charismatic. People, including me, believe in you. Now more than ever, we need the change that you stand for. I believe that you can do it.

I would like you to get our troops out of Iraq. I know that this is a very complicated issue, but the American people and the world want it. I believe in increasing the troops in Afghanistan. That is where the real terrorists are. The world supports us there, and I believe it would earn some respect for finishing what we started. We need to listen to our neighbors and learn to respect them. America is not alone and cannot accomplish its goals of peace and democracy by itself. We should strengthen our interests in the UN. We are a superpower and it's time we used that power for good. We should strengthen our commitment to human rights. The tragedy in Darfur has gone on for far too long as have other atrocities around the world. We do not necessarily need to invade these countries, but by providing humanitarian aid and peacemaking troops when needed. We need to improve our global warming policies. The world looks to us for guidance, but now they are looking down on us. We should finally support the Kyoto agreement. The rest of the world has and now it is our turn. These things won't be easy, but they are necessary. I fear that if we do not reverse course now, it will be too late. The United States needs to polish its reputation and reassert itself as a leader worthy of being followed.

All the best,
A Proud Citizen

President Obama,

I'm worried about your choices for several of your foreign policy advisers. Here is why. Please address this and what you will do for justice and accountability.

The first adviser I will mention is former Indiana congressman and Democrat, Tim Roemer. He was a member of the 9/11 Commission, and a representative of the war-profiteering weapons makers Boeing and Lockheed Martin, which also happen to be the world's largest defense contractors. While in office, Roemer voted for the Iraq War and said this: "The threat from Saddam is grave and growing and it's something we're going to have to address in the not-too-distant future." That statement mirrors the rhetoric of Bush and Cheney exactly. Why would a President Obama, who spoke out against the war in 2003, be interested in someone like Roemer's advice?

Also on board is Washington insider and notorious cover-up artist Lee Hamilton. It's interesting to note that Hamilton, a Democrat, has been called upon several times to bail Republicans out of huge scandals. Democrat Hamilton was co-chair of the 9/11 Commission and the White House actually preferred dealing with him over fellow co-chair and Republican, Thomas Kean. According to *New York Times* reporter, Phil Shenon, the White House's "best support on the Commission came from an unexpected corner, from Lee Hamilton." Maybe this is because Hamilton is old pals with Dick Cheney, Donald Rumsfeld, and David Addington.

During the 1980s, when Reagan and Bush, Sr., were in power, Hamilton was the Chairman of the House Intelligence Committee, and chaired an inquiry into the Iran-Contra scandal. Also on the committee was Congressman Dick Cheney. Hamilton certainly dropped the ball on this investigation: he was well aware of a press report indicating that the Reagan Administration was illegally funneling weapons and money to the anti-communist rebels in Nicaragua, yet when the White House denied it, Hamilton simply took their word for it.

Hamilton would later admit that when he looks into allegations, he dislikes "going for the jugular." Indeed, Senator Tom Daschle opposed Hamilton's co-chairing of the 9/11 Commission, stating that Hamilton doesn't have "a taste for partisan fights," and seems to "always assume the best about people, Republicans included." Hamilton would also tell *Frontline* that he didn't indict Reagan or Bush because he didn't think it would be "good for the country." He gave this same answer to 9/11 family member Bob McIlvaine, who lost his son on 9/11, when McIlvaine had requested declassification of some vital 9/11 evidence.

Hamilton remained good friends with Dick Cheney, don't you find this troubling that he would be looking into the White House and its response to the attacks? Seems like a conflict of interest.

Another cover up which Hamilton took part in was the 1980 "October Surprise" incident. In 1992, there was a task force, chaired by Hamilton, to look into allegations of a plot to delay the release of U.S. hostages in Iran until after the 1980 presidential election, thus depriving President Carter of any credit for their upcoming release. The key figures involved were former CIA Directors, George H.W. Bush, and William J. Casey. There were allegations that the two had met secretly in Europe to broker a deal with the Iranians. Both of their alibis were dubious at best, and Casey's even changed several times, but Hamilton still accepted it. Journalist Robert Parry who has extensively researched the case had this to say about the task force and its kid's-glove treatment: "The Bush administration flatly refused to give any more information to the House task force unless it agreed never to interview Mr. Bush's alibi witness, and never to release that person's name. Amazingly, the task force accepted those terms."

Hamilton also refused to extend the 1992 investigation when yet more incriminating evidence was made available, according to the task force's chief counsel, Larry Barcella. It's also known that Hamilton was aware of classified documents from a Russian national security report detailing what Russian Intelligence knew of the October Surprise. Apparently, Russian Intelligence uncovered documents showing that William Casey had indeed traveled to Europe in 1980 to meet with the Iranians to delay the hostage release. With full knowledge of this information, and other intelligence reports on the matter from other countries, Lee Hamilton publicly exonerated President George H.W. Bush. Lee Hamilton's judgment and loyalty to this country are questionable to say the least.

President Obama, this is a very important matter. Do you support investigations of any kind into the previous administration? This is an opportunity to regain credibility so needed in the executive branch and oversight in government we've been lacking. Thank you and good luck as our new commander in chief.

Sincerely,
Michael Jackman

Mr. President,

What if the "official" accounting of what happened on 9/11 is false? What if, in fact, it's a lie, and a big one at that, complete with corporate/media/propaganda cover-up, especially with corporate/media/propaganda? Without the backing from the media the story wouldn't fly. What would that make this "War on Terror"? A fraud? Since when do steel buildings free fall to the ground, like WTC 7? From fire? What about WTC 7 anyway? Since when? Never have before or since. When did jumbo jets start disappearing when they crash, like the Pentagon and Shanksville. There really was no wreckage to speak of. Where were the wings, the engines, the tails, the seats, bodies, and everything else you see when a 757 hits the ground, they don't evaporate. The Kean/Hamilton Commission did a terrible job at answering all the glaring problems. More like a white-wash. Now, in their new book, they say they think the Pentagon lied to them. Ya think? A great read on this is David Griffin's *The 9/11 Commission Report: Omissions and Distortions*. They can't explain NORAD changing their timeline a total of 7 times, WTC 7, not one word, Able Danger, and a host of other relevant facts.WTC 7 is proof the "official" story is wrong. Ever watched the video of it coming down? They didn't play it much on CNN or NBC, ever wonder why? Because it's the smoking gun of the whole thing? It's proof because it's an obvious controlled demolition, which we all know takes weeks of planning, maybe months, hence fore-knowledge of the attack, which means, inside job, and somebody way up the chain of command, and NOT the president. When people say the president knew, I think they're mistaken. He's too dumb to be in on such a plan. He looks like he doesn't have a clue what is going on, sitting there in Sarasota. He, along with the country was hijacked that day be a group way up. Somebody ABOVE him. Probably someone wearing a highly decorated military uniform. Now we have "Operation Northwood's" which is proof the government/military will kill it's own people and blame it on a country they want to invade, in Northwood's case it was Cuba. A "false-flag" operation. This is what 9/11 was. Dick Cheney was handling all the different war games that helped the total stand down by the military. It was really a modern day coup d'etat. Webster Tarpley's book spells this out well. The public has been deliberately deceived into war, by an entity within our own government. The future of this country is in serious jeopardy with these folks controlling our government. It's really too bad the media has also been hijacked along with this country. This may be proof of "Operation Mockingbird," the CIA take over of the media. I hope you'll fight to re-open a new, real investigation.

Thank you.
Chris Noth

CHAPTER 26

Israel, Palestine, and the Middle East

Shortly after the election of Obama—but before his inauguration—conflict broke out between Israel and a militant segment of Hamas in Palestine. This became another hot button issue and several of these letters speak to the new president on this matter, both in terms of offering advice and making critical observations.

President Obama,

Support Israel and maintain a strong national security position in the world.

Dear President Obama,

This morning I watched you take the oath of office and finally become the 44th president of the United States. I'm a junior in college now, and I remember when you first sent out an exploratory committee for your candidacy during my freshman year of college. I was excited, excited for the change that you wanted to bring and I was optimistic about our country's future because of what you stood for. That excitement and optimism has since changed over the past two years. You see, I'm a Palestinian-American, and I have very strong familial ties in Palestine right now and I understand that the United States and Israel have this incorrigible bond, but that bond has allowed the United States to turn a blind eye to human rights violations happening in both the Gaza Strip and the West Bank. I had hope that the change you talked about would also allow for Palestinians to feel like someone who was willing to help them finally had the power to do so. While I appreciate your domestic policy, I cannot simply ignore your foreign policy because it has proven to be the policy that many past presidents have failed miserably at, and also is the one that hits close to home. I did vote for you and that does speak for itself. I do believe you can do the right thing, the just thing. I believe in you as the president of the United States and I do believe that you can bring a change to this nation and to the world; you already have by simply being elected. If I'm right about you, then even the disappointment of one voter is something you wish to avoid. Please inspire all kinds of change, even the change that is most difficult to make.

Thank you,
Ryah Aqel

President Obama,

As one of your many supporters, I chose to vote for you because of what you represent to me and other Americans: a progressive leader who instills hope and passion among a depressed American society. In the months leading up to election day, you were able to gain immense support from the youngest voting age group and get them politically involved in a way which has rarely been seen. Since I myself am a member of this age group, and was swayed by your tactics just like my peers, I hope that you will address the issues most important to me during your presidency. As a Jewish American and Zionist, the issues concerning the Arab-Israeli conflict and anti-Semitic terrorism take a valuable place in my heart and political mind. I would like to know what actions you plan on taking to address this issue, which is a passionate topic for millions of Americans just like me.

It is impossible to deny an immanent threat from Arab terrorists groups against Jews and Israelis both in an out of Israel; just last week Rabbi Gavriel Holtzberg and his wife Rivky were murdered by terrorists who took control of the Chabad house in Mumbai, India, along with six other hostages who had been staying in the house. The Holtzbergs were Americans, who chose to move from New York to India to open the Chabad house there; I feel that it is your duty as the American president to ensure the safety of all Americans, especially since there are thousands of others joining the Israeli army and moving to foreign countries to develop Jewish communities, just like the Holtzbergs.

Dr. Martin Luther King, Jr., once said, "Injustice anywhere is a threat to justice everywhere." While America is an entire continent away from the injustice occurring in the Middle East and surrounding nations against Jews, it is still our responsibility to take action to protect those being wronged. We as a nation stand for justice, and therefore we have an obligation to insure justice globally. What will you do for the people of Israel being attacked on a regular basis? What will you do to assist your fellow Americans who are taking their lives into their own hands in order to help the Israeli government in a way that America is failing to do? I hope my questions are answered in the most positive way possible during your presidency.

Sincerely,
Julia Linsner

January 20, 2009

Dear President Obama,

I did not vote for you. Nevertheless, I am captivated by your speeches and your ability to unite Americans. I am captivated by your campaign of change and hope that your policies will form this country into a country of honest, hard-working citizens. This is what the United States of America was founded upon and I hope that we, as a country, can locate our roots.

Although I did not vote for you, I am hopeful that you will lead our country into a new era. Specifically, I hope that during your presidency the Middle East, specifically the conflicts between the Israelis and Palestinians, can find peace no matter how minimal it may be. Although President Clinton failed to find a conclusive peace between Ehud Barack and Yasser Arafat during Camp David II, I hope that during your presidency you may be able to find some sort of peace.

Hamas is a terrorist organization and its rule and influence over the Palestinian people must be put to a halt. I hope that during your presidency you may unite the Palestinian people under one conclusive and authoritative body. With a respected government in place peace talks can then resume between the Israelis and the Palestinians.

Thank you President Obama for your message of hope and change. I look forward to following your progress throughout your presidency. Good luck and may God guide you and bless you and America!

Respectfully,
Donovan Asmar
University of Michigan '10
College of LSA, Political Science

Dear President Obama,

I am writing to you to urge you to reduce the United States' long-time pro-Israel stance on Mid-East foreign policy. For decades, the United States has been the big brother of Israel, giving the country both diplomatic and military (in terms of equipment) support. Meanwhile, Israel still continues to create a facade (and a weak one at that) that they are affording the Palestinians full and equal rights on their lands.

In reality, the Israeli government continues to create Jewish settlements in Palestinian lands, occupying key territorial positions that allow for increased Israeli authority over the impoverished Palestinians. Moreover, the Palestinians continue to be separated by walls and fences from key access roads. Normally, the Palestinians would use these roads to travel to and from work and to get food and drink for their families. However, Israeli roadblocks, in conjunction with the closure of roads to non-Jews have made life unnecessarily difficult for many Palestinians. These actions have been attempted to be justified in the name of national defense, but the underlying racism is clear.

Mr. President, if you do not wish to change the United States' pro-Israeli stance due to humanitarian reasons, consider the national defense argument. In his testimony for his role in the September 11th attacks, Zacarias Moussaoui stated that, "for me, the Jewish state of Palestine is a missing star on the flag of America," he went on to say that "[the United States is] the head of the snake. . . If [he wants] to destroy the Jewish state of Palestine, [he has] to destroy [the United States]." This is but one example of how the United States' staunch support of Israel is giving cause for radicals to justify terrorist plots and actions against innocent Americans.

I realize that the realm of international affairs and foreign policy is complicated and convoluted, with many actors in many areas of the globe playing key roles in every minute decision. However, given the international gravity of the situation in the Middle East, especially over the past month or so, it is paramount that you at least consider support of the Palestinians. I realize that actual change in this department is unlikely for an array of reasons which need not be discussed here. However, I do expect consideration of the alternatives to be at least presented to the round-table.

Sincerely,
Cameron MacConomy

Mr. President,

As you know, the world is a mess. We are faced with a terrible financial crisis, the Middle East is a disaster, and dangerous countries are getting their hands on nuclear weapons. There is no doubt in my mind that you face an amalgam of difficult issues. I believe that one of the most important ones is to keep our current alliance strong with Israel. Hamas was the worst possible outcome of a free election that could have happened. This group hides behind its citizens (hence the number of civilian casualties on their side). Firing rockets from civilian homes is cowardly, and Israel has every right to fire right back. Israel is the one and only stable and trustworthy democracy in the Middle East. We need to keep it that way.

In addition to Israel, I am also concerned with Iran and its influence in Iraq. As you know, the free elections took place, and the United Iraqi Alliance won the majority of the vote. This group is made up of Iranian influenced factions, such as the Supreme Council of Islamic Revolution in Iraq. Iran is growing stronger, and the United States did it a favor by taking out its number one enemy, Saddam Hussein. Something must be done to hold them in check.

Lastly, I am concerned with the instability in Iraq. At this moment, I am certain that the Bush administration had absolutely no idea what they were getting themselves into when they declared war on Iraq. The Sunnis have no influence, while the Shiites have control of the government. This situation sounds awfully familiar to what it used to be (except it was the exact opposite).

I wish you luck in the next four years Mr. President and I hope you make the decisions that can lead this country out of this dark time.

Andrew S.

Our failure in the West to sufficiently discuss the history of the Radical Islamist Movement too often leads us astray in a myriad of dead end policy searches for a way to peace. In it's historically rather brief 200+ years of prominence, Radical Islam, as fostered and promoted by the Saudi-sponsored Wahhabi movement, has thrown the greater Islamic world in a downward spiraling plunge into social and economic darkness. Wahhabism asserts at the peril of death, that Islam, which has evolved and been interpreted over the millennium, must now revert to strict adherence of the original Sharia, tenants of Islam, as preached by Mohammed in the seventh century. The most strident tenant of this Radical Islamic movement is that every one on the planet must accept their teachings or be eliminated. There can be no compromise or negotiation with this ideology. It is their Jihad, a philosophical, theological and military war to the death, and they believe Allah will see them through to victory.

It is said that the victors of wars write history. If so, we might ask ourselves how we would have history eventually record the outcome of this war/jihad. Let me suggest that history should record that . . . there was an Islamic religious and cultural conflict beginning in the 17th century that ended when the West finally put down Radical Islam by force and enabled Moderate and Modern Islam to reclaim its evolved traditions of tolerance for other traditions and to rejoin the family of nations in furthering civilization and its development through trade in goods and ideas with the pursuit of human liberty and civil rights.

Since 9/11, our government has gotten it right in our present unforgiving pursuit of terrorism by Radical Islam; a pursuit that must be intensified toward the ultimate victory over its intransigent Jihad. Since it is the foremost responsibility of our government to protect us, its citizens, this responsibility should come before tax breaks for the rich.

Sadly, the Iraq war has deferred the priority and funding needed to affect these changes. Tragically, that war has unleashed a Radical Islamic civil war in Iraq, with our troops caught in the middle.

Pathetically, we cannot now cut and run, but must redouble our unprecedented effort to a showdown with the forces that would bring Iraq under the rule of the Radical Islamists, and instead, establish a civil society; a model for moderate and modern nations in the Islamic world. In this, we must unabashedly learn to treat those threatening our mission as the Israelis treat Hamas, Hezbollah and the terrorists they face. It is the same Jihad and we must all pursue the same victory.

We have the power and the principles; we need to maintain our courage and will to write the history.

Please end the unconditional support to the Israeli occupation of Palestinian lands, and its killing of innocent civilians.

Dear Obama,

Throughout your campaign you pledged to restart the Israeli-Palestinian peace process, and voiced you support of a two-state solution.

The majority of Israelis also hope to see a two-state solution, which will guarantee peace and security for both sides. To accomplish this, a leader who will work for such policies must be elected in the upcoming Israeli election. Tzipi Livni is that leader, and she needs your support to run a grass-roots campaign similar to your own.

I ask that you help her to inspire in the Israeli citizens the hope for change that you so successfully inspired in us.

After this past administration's nearly non-existent effort to further the Israeli-Palestinian peace process, it's necessary that America demonstrate its willingness to support efforts towards peace for our strongest ally in the Middle East. Please follow through with your promises and help with this important issue at such a crucial time.

Thank you,
Katja Edelman

Dear Mr. Obama,

Congratulations on winning the 2008 presidential election! Your message of change has instilled in Americans, and people all around the globe, the kind of hope that is needed to combat that challenges we, as citizens of the world, face today. We look forward to a presidency that is firm and fair, with its policies geared towards the kind of moral neutrality that our world needs in these uncertain times.

I would like to call your attention to the long-standing and ongoing Israeli-Palestinian conflict that has plagued the Middle East for more than 60 years. I commend you, Mr. President, on your efforts to bring both parties to the table so that a just and lasting resolution can be reached, and peace can return to the region. The whole world seems to be in agreement that the solution to this conflict is two independent states existing side by side. This, however, means a complete withdrawal of all Israeli forces, and settlements, from Palestinian lands, to the 1967 borders, and a contiguous viable state for the Palestinians, with East Jerusalem as their capital. Until Israel complies with these modest terms, it is unlikely that there will ever be peace in that part of the world.

Mr. President, it will take a firm stance from the United States towards its historical ally to bring about such a resolution. Personally, I find it hypocritical that the United States does not apply the same standards to Israel as it does other nations. There is a blatant disregard for international law and human rights in Israel, a nation that continues to defy United Nations resolutions that specifically target and condemn her expansionist policies. Why did the United States failed to condemn the complete destruction of Beirut, and the loss of innocent lives, in the 2006 war fought between Hezbollah of Lebanon and Israeli forces? Why does the United States not condemn the illegal collective punishment that Israel is currently inflicting on Palestinians in the Gaza Strip as Israel continues to prevent United Nations' aid from reaching the innocent in Gaza who live in darkness, not knowing whether or not there will be another meal?

I find it hypocritical, also, to dream of peace in Israel and Palestinian when the United States continues to provide military aid to Israel to suppress a people who can never hope to stand up to their oppressors. With the backing of the United States, an illegal fourteen-foot wall can be passed off as a fence, and innocent people can be forced to live in a restricted capacity, being able to move from one part of Palestine to another only if Israeli forces at border checkpoints let them.

This bias from the United States is what has bred so much hatred for this great nation in the Middle East. Only when we understand the causes of the conflict can we undo the injustices and move on towards lasting peace. Your administration will have to be impartial in its approach to the resolution of this conflict, and both Fatah and Hamas will need to be at the negotiations for there to be a viable solution.

I hope that, in the area of foreign policy, your administration will make this issue a priority. The world is counting on you to be a just president, and a fair-minded leader of the world. Let us also see a positive change in your foreign policy. Let this opportunity not pass us by.

Yours Sincerely,
Fahad M Sajid

President Obama,

Throughout the past eight years, a lot has changed in my life. When the last president was elected, I was barely in middle school. Today, on the eve of your inauguration, I am a junior at the University of Michigan studying political science and Near Eastern Studies. My experiences through this time have allowed my thoughts and opinions to evolve with my attainment of new knowledge. I have developed a deep criticism of President Bush, especially on his foreign policy, and I must admit, I have supported your candidacy prior to your announcement that you would run. The reason I became infatuated with the possibility of your candidacy derives from a sense of your open-mind. You have a logical way of addressing the problems this country faces, and with the flawed foreign policy of the Bush administration, I find it vital to address such situations in a different manner. Many of your opinions have differed from President Bush, specifically, your diplomatic approach on Middle East foreign affairs. Therefore, in this letter, I would like to bring to your attention some of the issues in that specific region that I feel to be most important, as it is a subject of which I pay close attention to on a daily basis.

The first issue I would like to address is Iran. Iran represents a country that has had tension with our nation since the Islamic Revolution of 1979. President Bush took an especially hawkish stance against the nation. Nonetheless, I have to agree with your approach to Iran: the diplomatic approach. While they do explore the use of nuclear energy, it is important to note that they have made clear that they have no intention of using such power for military use. Furthermore, it seems unfair to the region that Israel maintains the ability to possess nuclear weapons.

This brings me to the next area of interest in the area: Israel. The Israeli lobby, today, is stronger than ever. Since its birth, the Jewish nation has maintained a special relationship with the United States. This special relationship has allowed Israel to get away with many war crimes and apartheid. I believe that the United States stance on Israel needs to be altered. It is not in the best interest of the United States to have such a relationship with any nation. Especially in a region of tension and conflict it is important to maintain neutrality, especially in the Arab-Israeli conflict.

I hope you take these factors into consideration during your presidency. I believe neutrality in the Middle East is a very important task for the president of the United States to practice.

Thank you for your time Mr. President.

Sincerely,
Ali Ajrouch
University of Michigan

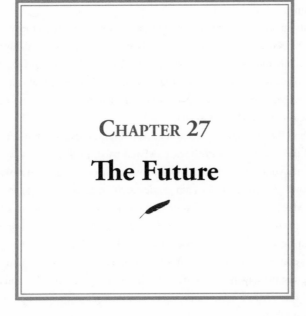

CHAPTER 27

The Future

Several of the letters in this volume of eyewitness accounts saw the historic election of Obama as a new start for the country, a chance for the renewal and revitalization of America. They spoke to President Obama about these perceived new opportunities. They address the desire for and the possibility of a better future under the Obama administration. These citizens write in order to illuminate the new president and others about their ability to see enormous potential for a bold new future; a new hope for all Americans and for the world.

President Obama,

Let me start by saying this letter has taken a while to find its form. My intent is to pass along words of encouragement if I can do so humbly. I believe every journey is composed of a series of parts, each part revealing its own piece of a story; some are notable by origin, others significant for their duration. Ultimately, all are defined by destination. By now the world understands what a historic event your election was, and its impact on the nation and the global community.

Your campaign has ignited the human spirit and given us the belief that we can do better and be better. Your words of hope and change evoke in all humans the possibility that changing the world is feasible. You have awaken the hope that lies deep within all people that the world can be a better place, and we all can come together and work to make that come to pass. I ask that as long as you govern this country, you never forget your message to us, the people, who have placed their hope and dreams in you.

I understand that the task you face will be daunting whenever the burdens of the people you serve and the unfair and, sometimes, cruel and harsh realities of our world make you weary. Recall what your faith tells you: "Come to me, all that are weary and are carrying heavy burdens and I will give you rest. For I am gentle and humble in heart, and you will find rest for your soul. Matthew 11:28-30. Use your abilities and talents that you have been given to continue to up lift society. I ask that you keep your heart clean and your mind pure so that you can help this country once again reach its potential and bring honor and glory to all of our citizens. In doing so, you will help this country impact the nations around us so that, yet again, we can point the way in the world and be the promise of a better life and a place where dreams do still come true. As you guide us back on the right path our hope and prayers are with you and your family.

Brandon Walton

Dear President Obama:

I write to you with little expectation that there is anything that you can do for me or the country. It's not that I don't think you'll try but I think that the belief that the president is all-powerful—like a king, a dictator, or semi-divine, is not realistic. The government is limited in what it can do for us or at least our government is limited in what it can do for us by the will of the people. The last administration has shown us that the will of the people is full of false hope and irrational faith.

The country is divided and some claim it is based on faith. I see the claims of "faith" as just rhetoric to justify a deliberate choice to ignore facts, science and truth. Those that think that because they are religious and that God is on their side find a reason to justify—the destruction of our environment, our public schools, our civil liberties, our soldiers and our government. They claim only for themselves the title of being patriotic because they can only see wars and destruction as a way to prove love of country. Their patriotism has sent thousands of soldiers to their death and bankrupted the country both morally and economically.

I heard your inauguration speech. You didn't promise us anything except that we would have hard choices and a lot of work. There was no talk of "shock and awe" and a war being won in a week. Tens of thousands of people wanted to hear that message and want to change. So maybe what you can do for us and the rest of the country is get us to do what we should have being doing all along. The idea that you don't need government and government is a hindrance on capitalism shows a failure to understand human history. We need government and we need a good one.

The day after the inauguration, the new secretary of agriculture was greeting employees at the door. I shook his hand as did one of my coworkers. My coworker told him that we would work hard for him as we walked away. He told us, "I'm going to work hard for you." It was the first time in eight years, I heard anyone in government believe they owed a responsibility to the American people.

I don't know that one man can change anything but one man can try and it looks like the people who you have appointed to help you run the government want to work hard for our country. So I don't think you can do anything for us unless we are willing to accept that hard choices have to be made and all the countries problems aren't going to be cured in a week, a month or even eight years. I think what you have done is resurrect the belief that we have our government functioning to help the American people and with the will of the American people working with you—I have no doubt that our country has a good future.

Yours truly,
Charlene

Dear President Obama:

I would like to thank you for all of the sacrifices you and your family have made in order for you to lead this nation. It is my sincere hope that the American people will all do their share to assist you in returning our great nation to its greatest nation status.

Although extremely exciting, your election represents more than African-American achievement. It represents hope for the world's future. People around the world cheered with Americans because a political leader was elected who truly has a progressive vision for the future: a vision where nations talk and at least attempt to find common ground. The energy behind your vision also is inspiring. Around the globe there is greater hope for tomorrow and renewed hope in ourselves. Together with positive thoughts and energy—yes, we can!!!

You and your family shall remain in my prayers.

My very best regards,
Allynne Tosca Owens

Dear President Obama,

I was extremely thrilled when you were elected to be our 44th president on November 4th. I feel your proposals for the economy, the War on Terror, and health care will make America the prominent nation it is supposed to be. Your call for change captivated Americans like no other candidate had in the history of the United States. I noticed family and friends who were much more involved in the political process than they ever were in past elections. Your rhetoric and calm demeanor throughout the economic crisis led many to believe that you were clearly ready to become president. On a personal level, I believe you bring a different perspective and set of ideals to Washington that can change the ways of the old guard. Good luck on being the leader of the free world.

Sincerely,
Josh Zeman

Dear President Obama,

I am excited about the future of the United States of America because of you, and I know that I am only one among many Americans that feel this way. I feel that now we finally have a bright future, and there is hope for us all. I have always felt proud to be an American, but today, as I watched you get sworn in, I can't ever remember feeling so proud. God bless you, your family, and the United States of America.

Mr. President, please let me add my congratulations to the many you have received. We, who lived through the civil rights movement, are thrilled to be alive to see you take the oath of office. You have given us a very important symbolic moment. We are of darker hue, African-Americans, Latinos, and South Asian Americans see ourselves in your face. You may go down in history as the Great Facilitator of the Post-Racial Society. Nonetheless, America is in serious economic trouble. Once in office, you will discover that it is worse than you thought. When they open the proverbial book of the presidency, you will discover that many things are worse than you thought. The pages will be sobering. I wish I could offer some advice in this letter but I do not have clue how to solve the economic crisis. My only advice is to beware of expert advice proffered.

First, the media will pretend it has the answers. Sometimes they confuse asking questions with knowing. Don't expect any ideas from reporters. They only look like they know what they are talking about. So far you have handled this group well. Nevertheless, reporters are waiting to prove that they can be objective about you. They love scoops and controversies. Remember they claim that they can also shape public opinion. They have the instant polls to prove it.

Secondly, there are the historians. They are poised to write the definitive biography of Barack Obama. For them, a book can be written for every day of your presidency. Some have already started organizing notes before you took office. Others will record every word that is written and said about you. Expect them to write positive reviews while you are in office. A few will write negative reviews. I trust that you have an in-house historian on staff. If not, you will be at the mercy of presidential papers readers.

Thirdly, there are political scientists. I am one of them. We make comprehensive evaluations of presidents and their policies. We have ready-made classification systems that we try to fit each president into. We make our living by comparing presidents over time and second guessing their responses to crises. Look for books about your staff and your campaign. Remember future students will read our assessments of your presidency.

You may be asking yourself if you read this letter, "What has this to do with governing?" Reporters, historians, and political scientists have nothing to do with governing; they are just your "attentive public" and they write books. We will not be there when the great decisions are made, but we will write about them. When you retire from the presidency, I hope that you will have time to read our ruminations, descriptions and comments. Have a sense of humor about it. Take care and good luck, Mr. President.

Dear President Obama,

Congratulations. I am proud to be part of a country that gives everyone, despite the odds against them, an opportunity to lead this nation. It is truly amazing to witness the journey that you've gone through, at least over the past two years. It is exciting to see all generations of people care about the future of this country; it seemed like people were energized about the outcome of the presidential election.

Now that you've won the election, I hope people will continue to express the same amount of emotion regarding the issues that face our country. The economy is down and no one seems to know remedy this problem, which affects millions of Americans every day. The situation in Iraq is not improving either; there is no easy way out, it seems. I know the American people have faith in your decision-making, so please live up to the promises you've made to the American people throughout the presidential race.

Good luck . . . it's not an easy job.
Katie Crumbaugh

Dear President Obama,

May God guide and protect you, as you begin to tackle the many problems currently plaguing our nation. From national health care, to climate change, to the War on Terror I, like many other Americans, am ready for a fresh start and new policies.

You currently have the hopes of many Americans on your shoulders. After the disastrous policies of the last eight years, I hope our nation can come together to make the hard choices necessary to create a better future for ourselves and our children.

May you govern from the middle and never forget that while citizens may disagree with your policies, or politics, they'll still be part of our great nation, and their points of view deserve consideration. As a moderate Democrat, I want solutions that work for the benefit of all citizens. I hope we can put aside the hyper-partisanship of the last eight years aw we make our nation a better place.

Your election has marked a milestone in American history. As our first biracial president, you have truly shown that Martin Luther King, Jr.'s, dream is possible. On election day, many Americans voted for you not on "the basis of the color of your skin" but instead "because of the content of your character." Because of this, you are a shining example of what is right with America. As the grandchild of immigrants myself, I am proud to call you my president. Your election has shown the world that anyone can do anything in America. It's not about who your parents are, but instead about what you do.

Good luck. May God bless you and the United States of America.

Sincerely,
Michael V. Radtke Jr.

President Obama,

Words cannot express how happy I am that you will be leading our country. I truly cannot think of a more qualified, intelligent, or rightful leader for our America. I am so thankful. Please know that you have inspired us—the youth—and that we stand behind you in your desire for change.

God Bless,
Ellen

President Obama,

You have made an entire generation become interested in politics for the first time. Keep up the good work and stay optimistic and confident.

God Bless,
JP Pitcher

Dear President Obama,

I appreciate the work you've done to include both parties in the government you are creating. I hope to see you restore good political standing with foreign governments and dignitaries. Also I hope you hold true to your word that you will reinvent systems that do not work such as helping retirees and homeless people.

Thank you.

Dear President Obama:

The honor is mine to write to you about how proud I am of your achievement on becoming elected president of the United States of America. I voted for you but I must admit that when you announced your candidacy I, like many at the time, doubted your ultimate success. That you are now president seems so surreal. We hope and pray that your continued success will include delivering us from the difficult challenges facing our country.

There are many letters here of congratulations and some of apprehension. Your journey has been riveting to us and of course we are increasingly more connected to the consequences for our own life chances. We are now witnesses to the drama of indecision and persuasion among your opponents and supporters as our fate seems to hang in the balance. We wonder, knowing our own previous doubt and the continued doubt of a well-meaning opposition, whether or not your proposals are the remedy for our problems. We wonder how decisive the election was for those who still oppose permitting you the chance to save us all as our elected president and leader. We wonder how decisive and resolute your leadership will be in the moments when some will still waiver.

You are our president now. Though we have never had a president like you, I hope that trust in your decisions builds and that convincing us to follow your lead becomes less entrenched. Our country is divided but for the sake of us all many who did not vote for you also want you to succeed, even some in spite of their opposition. I urge you to continue to believe in the best intentions among us in soliciting our support for your policies.

God bless you and God bless these United States.

With best wishes for you and your family,
Sherman C. Puckett